A LEGEND IN HER OWN TIME

"No other woman has had a greater impact on broadcast news than Barbara Walters. It was her tenacious pioneering, her infinite drive, her unbridled determination and unabashed ambition to succeed in the male-dominated world of television that opened the door for today's newswomen . . . It's doubtful that at any time in the foreseeable future will an interviewer-reporter come along who will reach the heights that Barbara Walters has attained. She has set a standard that few, if any, will ever match.

"Having worked in television as a news producer and writer, which were the first jobs Walters held, I was intrigued and perplexed as to how someone with her apparent handicaps—the speech impediment, the lack of journalistic credentials—was able to become so enormously successful . . .

"How did she surmount those obstacles? What was the secret to her success? Where did her die-hard persistence come from? What made her run so hard?

"It was for these reasons that I decided to examine Walters' life: to go back to the beginning; to sift fact from fiction; to dispel the myths—to set the record straight."

—JERRY OPPENHEIMER, from the Preface

Critical acclaim follows . . .

"FASCINATING . . . RIVETING DETAIL . . . INTRIGUING . . . Legwork and documentation are Oppenheimer's long suits."

—*Indianapolis News*

"The bio chronicles her hard work, persistence, and quest for perfection. But many tales might make the '20/20' co-anchor see red."

—*USA Today*

"INTERESTING AND REVEALING."

—*Library Journal*

"AN OBJECTIVE, WELL-ROUNDED BIOGRAPHY . . . A FASCINATING STORY WITH A HISTORICAL PERSPECTIVE."

—*Chattanooga Times*

"A feminine saga of ambition."

—*Mirabella*

"The author details Walters's steady rise on the *Today* show in the 1960s and her two failed marriages, and touches on her connection to the late Roy Cohn and on the background of her present husband, Mervyn Adelson, alleged to have dealings with mobsters."

—*Publishers Weekly*

BARBARA
WALTERS

AN UNAUTHORIZED BIOGRAPHY

JERRY OPPENHEIMER

SMP

ST. MARTIN'S PAPERBACKS

BARBARA WALTERS

Copyright © 1990 by Jerry Oppenheimer.

Library of Congress Catalog Card Number: 89-24132

ISBN: 0-312-92387-2

Printed in the United States of America

St. Martin's Press hardcover edition published 1990
St. Martin's Paperbacks edition/February 1991

10 9 8 7 6 5 4 3 2 1

For Jesse and Toby

ACKNOWLEDGMENTS

I am indebted to so many people who helped make this book possible. More than four hundred consented to be interviewed, ranging from Barbara's earliest playmates in Brookline, Massachusetts, to her friends and TV colleagues of the present in New York and Los Angeles. Fortunately, I was able to track down and interview friends and associates of Barbara's father, Lou Walters; their reminiscences of his colorful early days in the nightclub business in Boston, Miami, and New York added enormously to Barbara's story. I am especially thankful to Ed Risman, Ben Ford Abrams, Irving Zussman, Eddie Davis, George Gill, Eddie Jaffe, and Chickie James.

I am forever grateful for the guidance and cooperation I received from Shirley Budd, Barbara's closest friend, confidante, and first cousin, who helped me sort through the complex web of the genealogy of Barbara's fraternal and maternal family roots; that, along with Mrs. Budd's insight and perspective on Barbara, was of immense value. Because of the unauthorized nature of this book, I did not expect to get that sort of help.

I interviewed most of Barbara's classmates, from junior high school through college; luckily, she always attended schools with small student populations. In Miami, I thank Stu Jacobs, who tracked down out-of-town addresses and telephone numbers of classmates, all of whom had fascinating anecdotes and insightful recollections to share with me. Among those, I'd especially like to thank Greta Joseloff Steinberg, Stan Reich, Judy Nelson Drucker, and Annabelle Wald D'Augustine.

Barbara always seemed to be blessed with wonderful friends. I feel honored to say that I now count one of them, Joan Gilbert Peyser, among my own. Joan Peyser became Barbara's closest friend as a teenager. With an unswerving desire for truth, Joan

Peyser, a writer and biographer herself, was candid and honest about Barbara, but always compassionate and loyal. I don't think this book would have been the same without her perception, sensitivity, fairness, and analysis.

Sarah Lawrence College was a force for liberalism, free expression of ideas, and thought when Barbara entered as a freshman more than four decades ago. The women—and the few men—who were her classmates and teachers still held a strong commitment to those ideals when I approached them for this book and were therefore open to candidly share with me their thoughts and recollections of her. I thank all of them, particularly Theodore Joffe Edelman, Edith Revely Remoy, Anne Williams Ferguson, Shirley Plaven Klein, Jerry Weiss, Muriel Greenhill, John Blankenship, Bessie Schonberg, and Deby Kirschenbaum Salama.

Literally scores of people who have worked with Barbara in television—beginning with Sandy Becker, who was the host of a children's show that Barbara produced in 1953—spoke honestly and frankly about her. There were a few, though, who stand out for their extraordinary forthrightness, perceptiveness, and analysis of Barbara's character and personality as a TV newswoman, interviewer, friend, and co-worker. If awards could be given, they'd go to Jane Schulberg, John Lord, Anita Colby, Maureen O'Sullivan, Bob Cunniff, Chuck Horner, Doug Sinsel, Shad Northshield, Gail Rock, Pat Pepin, Anne Perkins, Mamye Smith, Steve Krantz, Alan Carter, JoAnn Goldberg, Julie Van Vliet Rubenstein, Bill Monroe, Marlene Sanders, Beryl Pfizer, Nancy Dickerson, David Adams, Frank Blair, Ray Scherer, Sander Vanocur, Don Meaney, Charlie Andrews, Jim Hartz, Stanhope Gould, Frederick Pierce, Walter Pfister, and William Sheehan.

Barbara has had an extraordinary, eventful public life, and a well-hidden private one. Many of those mentioned above, and others who appear in the narrative, were able to offer me a view inside of that world. But I have a very special thanks to Frank Ford, Judy Freed, William Safire, Mrs. George Sokolsky, Leonard Safir, Norman Roy Grutman, Mickey Kogas, Alexis Lichine, Jeremyn Davern, Edward W. Brooke, Ray Katz, Judith Crist, John Springer, Edna Shanis Tuttleman, Tex McCrary, Liz Smith, Joan Braden, Wendy Goldberg, and Joella Werlin for sharing their reminiscences and thoughts with me.

I'd like to offer my thanks to all those others who opened their hearts and minds to a stranger, taking time to answer my many questions: Salvatore Alfano, Alvin Alkon, Barbara Shiffman Altman, Madeline Amgott, Chris Anderson, Marcia Applebaum, Nick Archer, Steven M.L. Aronson, Harmon Ashley, Letitia Baldrige, Marty Baum, Joan Humphrey Barker, Keyes Beech, Shirley Rosenfeld Berman, Robert Blecker, Francis Aub Bloomfield, Joan Wedeen Blumenfeld, Lou Bradley, Gladys Chang Hardy-Brazil, Birdie Glanzer Brundage, Barney Calame, June Callwood, Anne Chamberlin, George Christy, Regina Cohen, Katherine Sloss Cohn, Jack Cole, Audrey Cooper, Ben Cossrow, Carolyn De-Harak, John Desmond, Katharine Kramer Douglas, Ross Drake, Judy Drucker, Rose Ebner, Arthur Edelman, Sarah Yates Exley, Marilyn Franklin Farber, Nancy Fields, Marie Finnigan, Craig Fisher, Jim Fleming, Evelyn Floret, Gloria Golub Frank, Rosalie Shearer Friedman, Barbara Gordon, Dr. Francis Kaplan Grossman, Barney Goodman, David Halberstam, Jean Harris, Judith Haskell, Judith Guzy Hanes, Alice Price Craig Hoffman, Joan Weinrib Hopner, Cy Howard, Ray Jacobson, Regina Landon Jick, Betty Powell Jones, Harriet Van Horne, David Kane, Lorraine Walters Katz, Anne Friess-Kirschner, Edward Klein, Pat Meyer Kovacs, Dick Krolik, Peter Kunhardt, Jonathan Kwitny, Joe Leff, Helen Mamber Levin, Barbara Lewis, Peter Levinson, Francis Lewine, Sonja Loew, Helen Udell Lowenstein, Josephine Lyons, William Scott Malone, Cathryn Mansell, Helen Marmor, James McCarthy, Cheryl McCall, Ken McCormick, Robert Metz, Hank Meyers, Nina Raginsky Mishkin, Al Morgan, Patricia Fry Morrissey, Susan Mulcahy, William Norwich, Mary Louise Oates, Colleen O'Connor, Marcia Mueller Pabst, Glora Palter, Harry Paul, Norman Pearlstine, Ruth Scheinfeld Pollak, Mary Lou Hollaman Randolph, Edith Kraeler Reiman, Marie Ridder, Marcia Elson Rodman, Mrs. Alexander Rosenberg, Martin Rubenstein, Susanne Hoeber Rudolph, Natalie Lazrus Roberts, Mrs. William Rosenblum, Patricia Leavitt Rosenthal, Dean Rusk, Patricia Ryan, Fred Schochet, Barbara Schulberg, David Schumacher, Suzanne Seitz, Ruth Leff Siegel, Dan Seletsky, Herman Seletsky, Mira Sheerin, Mike Sklar, Zelda Kaplan Silver, Arlene Milton Silverman, Irma Slater, Greta Andron Smolow, Jeri Rosenberger Soman, Richard Stolley, Margaret Straus, Marianne Strong, Nancy Sureck, Joan McLellan Tayler, Harold Taylor, Helen Thomas, John Throne, Anne Viccaro, Nicholas von Hoffman,

Cynthia White, Shirley Widerman, Jeannie Williams, Danny Wilson, Tom Wolf, David Yellin, Sarah Starr Wolff, Harriet Morse Zimmerman, Sidney Zion.

There are others who asked for anonymity for various reasons. I have respected your wishes, and I am grateful for your enormous assistance.

I'd like to point out that some dialogue has been reconstructed from interviews. In some instances, interview quotes have been modified without changing their meaning.

Among those friends I'd like to acknowledge who have given me support along the way are Dan Schwartz, Steve Coz, Steve Plamann, and David Perel. For listening, lodging, and laughing, I'd like to thank Gail Birnbaum. For loving me and living with me through the strain of this project, and putting up with the mounds of files, notes, clippings, transcripts, and computer cables that began to envelop our home, I thank my wife, Judy. For knowing the New York social scene and sharing it with me, I thank Richard Turley. Peggy Jackson was an excellent researcher, as was Jean DiSilva a transcriptionist.

And finally, I'm indebted to my editor, Toni Lopopolo, and St. Martin's Press, for having the class.

CONTENTS

PART III

PART IV

PREFACE

No other woman has had a greater impact on broadcast news than Barbara Walters. It was her tenacious pioneering, her infinite drive, her unbridled determination and unabashed ambition to succeed in the male-dominated world of television that opened the door for today's newswomen: Diane Sawyer, Connie Chung, Mary Alice Williams, among others. It's doubtful that at any time in the foreseeable future will an interviewer-reporter come along who will reach the heights that Barbara Walters has attained. She has set a standard that few, if any, will ever match.

As interrogator of the famous and infamous, she is nonpareil. As pursuer of the ultimate exclusive interview, she is unrivaled. An icon, Walters has reached that pinnacle of fame where her name has become indelibly etched alongside those of Jackie O., Monroe, Presley, Carson, Hope, Taylor, Hepburn. Like them, she is a legend in her own time.

Since her first appearance on the *Today* show in the early Sixties, Walters has fascinated television viewers from Tallahassee to Tel Aviv. I count myself as one of them.

Having worked in television as a news producer and writer, which were the first jobs Walters held, I was intrigued and perplexed as to how someone with her apparent handicaps—the speech impediment, the lack of journalistic credentials, the fact that she didn't have the prerequisite blond, blue-eyed all-American look—was able to become so enormously successful as an on-air news personality, particularly at a time when the few women in TV were considered window dressing.

How did she surmount those obstacles? What was the secret to her success? Where did her die-hard persistence come from? What made her run so hard? What was it about her that captivated the viewing public?

Those questions nagged at me and it was for that reason that I decided to examine Walters' life: to go back to the beginning; to trace her roots; to follow the path of her phenomenal rise to the top of the most visible and influential medium in the world. Along the way, I hoped to sift fact from fiction, to dispel the myths, to set the record straight.

All I really knew about Walters was what I'd read in the gossip and TV columns—items that were clearly spoon-fed by her or her representatives; of that much I was certain. There were also scores of unrevealing, pedestrian interviews and profiles, many by journalists Walters trusted who were writing for partisan publications. I'd also heard stories about her from TV and print colleagues, which I realized were rumors and apocryphal tales often tainted by jealousy, sparked by envy, and skewed by sexism. Somewhere between those two extremes, I believed, was the real story.

As I began my research in the fall of 1987, I quickly discovered that for someone so much in the public eye, someone who had built such an extraordinary career on probing the lives of others, Walters' own personal life was carefully guarded, sealed off from the world like a time capsule. Why such secrecy? What was there to hide, if anything? Another question had been added to the puzzle.

When I first proposed the idea of writing her biography, many in publishing were skeptical—even, it seemed, fearful—of taking on such a project. Their skepticism centered on the feeling, which proved completely unfounded, that no one would risk cooperating, and that few would be candid if they did. Their fear dealt with Walters' perceived powers—real and imagined—in the media centers of New York and Los Angeles where she reigned supreme; few wanted to chance alienating her, or receiving her wrath.

In fact, it wasn't long after I sent Walters the first of two letters informing her of my book—seeking any possible help from her, hoping to alleviate her anxieties about the project—that she was quoted by her friend, New York *Post* columnist Cindy Adams, as saying, "I'd appreciate it if no one cooperates." Walters asserted—some later said "projected"—that the book would be "that only-child, lonely-child . . . step-on-everybody-to-get-to-the-top, deep-psychological stuff." Some close friends of Walters felt she had erred in taking such a stance. Others couldn't help but wonder about her curious use of the term "only-child," since it was known that she had a sister who had an enormous influence on Walters' life and the direction it took.

Despite her efforts to keep people from cooperating, Walters was unsuccessful. But her actions shed additional light on what I soon came to realize was the extraordinarily complex persona of the subject I was pursuing.

In all, more than four hundred persons, including some of Walters' most intimate confidantes, her closest colleagues, generously agreed to be interviewed, many expressing sorrow and anguish over her public attempt to dissuade cooperation. Virtually everyone spoke for the record and on tape.

It was evident that they, too, were hoping to see all of the disparate pieces of the Barbara Walters mosaic put together for the first time.

Here, then, is her story.

Jerry Oppenheimer
January 1990

"*I don't think there is anything in my life that I would hide or that is so unbelievably painful that I wouldn't talk about it.*"

—Barbara Walters,
November 1988

PART I

"IT'S A SAD
FAMILY"

Barbara Walters was *not* born on September 25, 1931, as most reliable public references state unequivocally. She was actually delivered two years earlier, happy and healthy, by Dr. A. S. Troupin at New England Hospital in Boston on September 25, 1929—a month before Wall Street laid its famous egg, beginning the Great Depression.

For Louis Edward Walters, thirty-three, an intense, hard-working London-born vaudeville booking agent, and his wife, the former Dena Seletsky, a sweet, plain woman of thirty-one, who grew up in the crowded tenements of Boston's North End, the conception and birth of the baby they named Barbara Jill had been accomplished with great trepidation and a sense of foreboding. Tragedy had struck twice before in their attempts to start a family, so it had been a difficult decision for them to try a third time; they had already suffered so much sadness and pain.

Lou Walters was naturally proud of their firstborn—a son, whom they named Burton. It was an easy pregnancy for Dena, and the beautiful baby was delivered without a problem on October 17, 1921, by Dr. Samuel Breck at Summit Hospital in Brookline. Burton was born about a year and a half after Lou and Dena were married, which virtually coincided with the opening of Lou's first booking office.

To celebrate Burton's birth, Lou dispensed expensive cigars to his show-business cronies, boasting that one day he and his son would be partners in a major entertainment enterprise, and everybody had better stand clear!

In the not too distant future, in fact, Lou would become the creative genius behind a string of highly successful nightclubs—known as Lou Walters' Latin Quarter—in Boston, Miami, and New York City. He would have wanted his son Burton to be in business with him, the heir to the entertainment kingdom he was building.

But shortly before Christmas 1922, the child, then fourteen months old, became violently ill. Lou and Dena watched helplessly as Dr. Herman Green tried his best to stop the chills and high fever that ravaged Burton's little body. The baby's breathing was rapid; his cries pierced the endless nights, signaling intense pain; his tiny, racking cough seemed to reverberate through the couple's modest apartment at 52 Fowler Street, in Dorchester, a predominantly middle-class Jewish section of Boston.

The doctor did all he could for Burton. But, finally, almost mercifully, death came to the baby on December 18, 1922. The child had died of lobar pneumonia, then a killer of many young.

His small body was laid to rest at Shari Jerusalem Cemetery in nearby Woburn, next to where his maternal grandfather, Jacob Seletsky, had been buried only eleven months earlier after being stricken by a heart attack at age fifty-two.

The death of Burton all but paralyzed Dena. For months, she was dazed, attended by Lou and by members of both families. Lou, too, was devastated, but he hid his feelings as best he could, by submerging himself in his work.

It took Dena four years to recover from the shock. She finally came to the realization that she wanted nothing more than to have another child. The depression that followed the tragedy of Burton had faded, and she was now looking forward to starting a family again.

She had finally grasped the fact that Burton's death was a freak quirk of fate; that he had been a healthy baby struck down by an uncontrollable illness; that she was a warm and loving mother. The guilt she felt had finally evaporated. Dena became pregnant for the second time. Life seemed good again. Lou's booking agency was thriving beyond expectations, and with his growing success the couple had moved from the apartment in Dorchester to a big house in exclusive Newton.

On May 19, 1926, at New England Hospital, Dena gave birth to a delicate girl whom the Walters named Jacqueline. At first, the child seemed perfectly healthy. But it soon became apparent that something was terribly wrong. When it came time for her to say "ma-ma," and "da-da," she didn't. There were anxious, hope-filled visits to doctors; expensive tests and examinations. Whatever was available was tried. But the diagnosis was clear: Jacqueline was not like other children, she was retarded. While her appearance was normal, she would always have the mind of a child, and she would suffer from severe stuttering.

First Burton's death; now this.

A cloud of sadness descended over the Walters family that would never really lift. The blow to Dena and Lou was incalculable, altering their emotional lives forever.

By the time Barbara came into the world three and a half years later, Lou and Dena were still traumatized by the tragedies of Burton and Jackie, and would remain so. Dena had silently pledged to devote her life to her retarded daughter, and Lou, it was clear, had lost himself in his career.

The effect of Burton's death and Jackie's birth on Barbara was staggering and lifelong. Barbara would be saddled with the burden of Jackie's problems virtually from the time she was old enough to walk and talk. Despite the fact that she loved Jackie, she also felt anger and resentment, shame and embarrassment, toward her sister.

It would take Barbara years to deal openly with those feelings.

"It is only recently that I've been able to speak of my retarded sister," Barbara wrote in 1970. "For a long time I evaded the subject. If someone asked if I was an only child, I would answer that I had a sister, and if they wanted to know more about her I'd tell them that she lived with my parents, in such a tone of dismissal that the subject invariably was dropped."

Because of her problem, Jackie received much of the love and compassion that Lou and Dena could muster.

Although the Walters worshiped Barbara and pampered her with expensive toys and clothes, summer camps, trips to Europe, and the best schools, the sensitive child could not ignore the special treatment that she saw her parents bestow on Jackie, and it made her both sad and envious. She had difficulty comprehending why she—the perfect one—stood second to her sister, the imperfect one.

"Dena devoted her entire life to Jackie," said Shirley Budd, Barbara's first cousin, closest friend, and confidante. "Jackie was so sheltered."

Barbara sometimes felt like an outsider in her own family; a sense of loneliness and rejection haunted much of her childhood, along with a craving for attention, and an intense desire to prove herself worthy of it.

Her feelings and emotions were consistent with the findings of a pioneer study of the effect of retarded children on the lives of their siblings that was conducted by Dr. Frances Kaplan Grossman, a professor of psychology, at Boston University.

In her landmark book *Brothers and Sisters of Retarded*

Children, published by Syracuse University Press in 1972, Grossman found that normal siblings "seemed damaged" by the experience. According to Grossman, they "were bitterly resentful of the family's situation, guilty about their rage at their parents and at the retarded sibling, fearful that they themselves might be defective or tainted; sometimes truly deprived of the time and resources they needed to develop because every support the family had to give was used in the care of the handicapped child."

Grossman wrote that "the clinical material strongly suggests that the normal brother or sister in a two-child family feels a great deal of pressure to achieve or more generally to make up to the parents for their disappointment over the retarded child."

Expanding on her published research, Grossman observed that the death of one child and the birth of another who was retarded resulted in "a multiply traumatized family system. It almost certainly makes the husband and wife angrier at each other, more blaming of each other, and less close."

All of this, noted Grossman, would lead normal children to feel "incredible anxiety about their own adequacy and safety. It makes for someone who can't trust; who is not able to be close to people; and who has a very poor and problematic sense of self because [he or she sees] everything fraught with dangers and risks."

According to Shirley Budd, Barbara suffered more from Jackie's retardation than Jackie did.

"Barbara couldn't do ordinary things like other girls," her cousin said. "Barbara did not have a birthday party, or have girlfriends over, because Jackie didn't. When Barbara wanted to go out with friends Jackie would get excited and say, 'Me, too! Me, too.' So Barbara would stay home, or read a book. When she got older Barbara didn't learn to drive a car because Jackie wasn't capable of driving."

As a child, Barbara craved attention from her father, but he spent most of his time working, usually not returning home until early the next morning. For this perceived rejection as a youngster, Barbara held Lou in contempt for many years. "I don't know whether it was animosity," said Budd, "but I think it was a little bit of anger. Instead of being home when Barbara went to bed at nine o'clock, Lou was off to the club."

Other paternal problems would affect Barbara during childhood and beyond—such as her father's compulsive gambling and his risk-taking in business—all of which gave her rampant insecurities.

"He lost a bloody fortune gambling," said Shirley Budd sorrowfully. "It's a sad family, you know. They had everything, and yet because of the loss of the child, and because of Jackie, they had sadness in their life."

"VERY CLASSY PEOPLE"

If Barbara's paternal grandparents, Abraham and Lilly Walters, had decided differently, Barbara might have become the premier television interviewer and newswoman of South Africa.

Around the turn of the century, Abe Walters, who had a small but thriving custom tailoring shop in London, and his wife, whose family, the Swartzes, had a prosperous woolens business, had seriously considered emigrating to Johannesburg, in the Union of South Africa, then part of the British Empire.

Walters had an adventurous, pioneering spirit, and the panorama of South Africa appealed to him. He had a vision of greater opportunities there and foresaw a completely new way of life for his family—there would be seven children in all—away from the crowded environs of London, but among Englishmen like himself.

According to family lore, Abraham and Lilly were born in England, but their parents had originally come from

Eastern Europe, most likely Lithuania, where there was a large Jewish population with a rich culture. In fact, some members of the Walters side of the family described themselves as "Litvaks"—Yiddish for Lithuanians.

Vilna, the capital of Lithuania, was a cultural center of Jewish learning and was known as the "Jerusalem of Europe." The state university, founded in 1579, was one of the oldest in Europe. The city also had an academy of science, a teachers' college, a music conservatory, an art college, and a law school. As a result, many Litvaks considered themselves intellectually and culturally superior, even if they never had a single day of formal education. It would be like living in Boston and acting pompous because Harvard was nearby.

This high-minded view that the early generations of Walterses had of themselves was handed down to their children, and their children's children. "My father always said [the Walters family] were Litvaks," said Lorraine Katz, whose father, Harry Walters, was one of Lou's brothers. "Litvaks were supposed to be the scholars, the brighter, the cultured."

While many Litvaks had this haughty attitude, other Jews held them in contempt, denouncing them as sharpies—shrewd in business, cold-blooded, and unsympathetic. The stereotype still caused dissension in the Walters family in early 1989. When Shirley Budd heard Lorraine Katz's description of the family, she angrily declared, "They were not Litvaks! They hated the Litvaks! Believe me, that's not true. This will upset Barbara."

Abe and Lilly Walters were not religious, although they went to services on Yom Kippur and Rosh Hashanah with their children. Barbara would grow up in a similar environment, with religion playing little if any role in her life. Speaking of the family, Budd said, "We were conscious of the fact that we were Jewish; we never denied that we were Jewish, and we were proud to be Jewish. But we weren't the Friday night shul-goers."

Sometime before the decision was made to emigrate, Abe and Lilly decided to visit the United States. Walters, an avid reader, had learned much about a city on the West Coast called San Francisco, which seemed to have the same adventurous spirit he envisioned in Johannesburg, and he had a strong desire to see it. Such a trip in those days was enormously expensive and took vast amounts of time. But one summer, Abraham, Lilly, and their first child, Rose—Shirley Budd's mother—sailed to the United States. They saw San Francisco, New York, and Boston during their grand tour.

When the family returned to London from their American odyssey, the decision about emigrating to a new land was still pending. Despite the golden opportunities he saw in America, Abe still favored South Africa. But Lilly, a strong and determined woman, put her foot down. "My father told me my grandmother wanted to come here not there, so that was the choice," said Lorraine Katz.

Just before the family was about to move to America, a terrible tragedy befell young Lou. While playing, he fell on a broken milk bottle and a shard of glass pierced one of his eyes, which was lost. His parents took him to the best doctors and the missing eye was replaced with a glass one. The artificial eye was done so well that few ever knew that Lou was half blind, or could even identify which of his blue eyes was the real one. He had no problems as a child as a result of the accident. He loved to read and write and, according to family legend, even received an award from King Edward VII for an essay he'd written.

His eyesight handicap surfaced years later in the worst possible place—at the card table, where Lou spent half of his adult life playing high-stakes gin rummy and losing because, some say, he couldn't read the cards correctly.

Abe and Lilly Walters and their brood arrived in America around 1910, settling first in Boston and later moving to Newark, New Jersey, and then to the North Jersey seashore community of Asbury Park.

Everyone seemed happy about the move except Lou. "It made me the most desperately lonely kid in the world," he said years later. "I wanted to go back."

In America, Abe continued his trade as a tailor, and the family followed many of its old British traditions, such as observing tea time every day. In fact, the family's allegiance to England was so strong that in 1936, when King Edward VIII abdicated so that he could marry the American divorcée Wallis Simpson, Abe and Lilly went into virtual mourning. "They were absolutely grief-stricken. It was just as if a member of the family had died," said Shirley Budd. "Although they all became American citizens, they still had their love for England. I hate to use the word but my grandmother and grandfather were *snobs*. They were strictly English in every sense of the word."

At tea time, when he came home from his tailor shop, Abe put on a smoking jacket, and Lilly brought out her fine English china, silver, and linens. For formal dinner parties, she had beautiful "lapkins," which were larger than normal napkins. In the bedrooms, the pillow cases were edged in handmade lace. Abe and Lilly were voracious readers and their house was filled with books, an interest their son Lou would inherit.

Lilly, like the rest of the family, had an aristocratic manner and she treated herself in queenly fashion. Every afternoon, for instance, she would lie down for a beauty rest with Pond's cold cream on her face to keep her skin youthful, and a slice of cold cucumber over each eye to avoid puffiness. Long before health and diet regimens were in fashion, she had decided to refrain from eating meat and eggs, and she never smoked.

"It was a beautiful, elegant home," said Budd, who spent her early years living with her divorced mother in her grandparents' home. "They were very artistic, very aesthetic, almost intellectual. I hate to use the word, but they were very *classy* people."

Lou would become the most famous of Abe and Lilly's

children, being recognized internationally as the "modern day Ziegfeld" for the spectacular floor shows he produced, and the nightclub empire he helped build. Eventually, though, his life would fall apart.

The Walters children, all of whom developed cancer before they died, were an interesting, creative, and dynamic lot: Harry was a successful merchant in Asbury Park; Barney operated a small hotel in Atlantic City that went under just before the big gambling boom; Belle was an artist married to a prominent entertainment industry lawyer; Florence directed a prestigious New York art gallery; Rebecca was married to a violinist who worked with glamorous French-born opera singer Lily Pons. Rebecca's son, Allan, Barbara's first cousin, wrote an offbeat travel guide to Europe's sexual hot spots.

The Seletskys—Barbara's mother's family—were a more stable but less colorful clan, and were looked down on by the Walterses.

"We had nothing to do with her family whatsoever . . . ," said Shirley Budd. "[The Seletskys] just weren't intellectuals, and my grandfather was a very intelligent man. The [Seletskys] were regular middle class. It isn't very nice to say about my grandmother and grandfather, but they were bluenoses. Barbara's elegance comes from the Walters side; her artistic temperament comes from the Walterses. There's certainly nothing artistic about the Seletsky family. They were in the shoe business."

Barbara's maternal grandparents, Jacob Seletsky, born in 1870, and the former Celia Cohen, born in 1874, were part of the great wave of Jewish immigrants who arrived from Russia in the late 1800s. The Seletskys and Cohens settled in Boston's North End, a melting pot of immigrants living in crowded tenements on narrow streets where pushcart vendors hawked their wares. Seletsky worked as a shoe salesman. As with the Walterses, they had seven children; Barbara's mother, Dena, was the first, born on January 31, 1897. Two of her brothers, Eddie and Max, who changed their name to Selette, would work for Lou in the years to come.

"My mother and father struggled—you struggle with seven kids," said another brother, Herman Seletsky, who went into the shoe distribution business. "But they managed somehow or other. All I know is they brought us up right."

A BOY WONDER

J ust let me get my hands on enough velvet and chromium," Barbara Walters' father once said, "and I will build nightclubs like the world has never seen before, luxury like the Roman emperors never dreamed of. I will give them shows that will be lovely, but also breathtaking. I will have teams of apache dancers touring all over the world. And I will give all this, and an eight-course steak dinner, too, for a reasonable price."

Lou Walters' vision had its beginning shortly after the family arrived in Boston, when he answered an ad for a six-dollar-a-week job as a talent spotter for a booking agent named Johnny Quigley.

Lou was a skinny kid, weighing little more than a hundred pounds, and standing four inches over five feet. He had a hooked nose, high cheekbones, a mouth too wide for his face, close-to-kinky dark hair, and he wore owlish glasses to buttress his glass eye, tinted blue to match the color of his real one. He looked more rabbinical than show business. But there was something about the kid that struck Quigley's fancy: Lou had class, what with that fancy limey accent, and all that talk about seeing some of the great vaudevillians perform at the London Palladium. For a young punk, he had a quiet, gentlemanly way about him. He seemed bright and mature for his age, and he wore a suit and tie, so Quigley hired him.

Quigley's agency, which had offices in the Little Building and ran on a shoestring, was booking vaudeville acts into small theaters throughout New England and the Canadian provinces, so he needed lots of bodies—dancers, jugglers, singers, magicians. Most of the major acts were then under long-term exclusive contracts with the powerful United Booking Office—and any entertainer who tried to get work through an independent like Quigley chanced being black-listed.

Lou's initial job was to comb theaters, taverns, and street corners in and around Boston looking for up-and-coming talent that needed representation. He'd bring the appropriate acts to Quigley the next day, and usually they were signed up. Lou, Quigley soon discovered, had a knack for finding and grading bookable talent. And that meant money in Quigley's pocket; he took a handsome commission out of every act's pay envelope.

Lou was a natural. Not only did he exhibit an expertise for finding talent, to Quigley's delight, he had the knack for getting acts booked, too. Lou could schmooze with the best of them, and he had an air of sincerity and credibility, despite his age, all of which combined to make him a great salesman. He had no trouble convincing theater managers to hire Quigley's talent.

By seventeen, Lou was a full-time booker. Show business had become his life. The enthusiastic young Walters pursued his job with evangelical fervor, going far beyond the mandate that Quigley had set for him. On his own, Lou traveled to distant cities and towns to visit vaudeville theaters, viewing talent he had heard about, making notes on their bookability, and memorizing the routines of those who caught his fancy.

At various amateur shows, he made some extraordinary discoveries: a young juggler named Fred Allen; a songwriter named Jimmy McHugh; and a comedian named Jack Haley, among others.

Lou's travels gave him numerous contacts in the business. In short order, he had developed an enviable network of theater owners, agents, bookers, managers, and talent, all of whom liked and respected the kid who seemed far older and wiser than his years.

By the time he was twenty, Walters was signing several hundred acts a week and earning close to two thousand dollars a year. Driven, obsessed with his career, determined to be a success—that's the way his friends remembered him.

In 1919, a year after the Great War ended, Lou met Dena Seletsky and fell in love. She was a tiny girl with dark hair and eyes and a quiet, shy demeanor, but equipped with a pretty figure and great legs.

The Seletskys welcomed Lou with open arms.

A few months before Lou married Dena—he was then twenty-five and had already been in the business a decade—he asked his boss for a twenty-dollar-a-week raise. "He put an extra five in my envelope," Lou said years later. "I returned it, and quit. With my last seventy-five dollars I began my own booking office. It was just enough to pay the rent, and turn on the lights and phone."

Ben (Ford) Abrams, an old friend and colleague of Lou's in the early days, remembered the story a bit differently. "Louie stayed with Quigley for some time, and then on a certain Monday he opened up his own office and took away most of the accounts from Quigley. It was a highly competitive business."

The Lou Walters Booking Agency was established on the second floor, above Macy's Drugstore, at the corner of Tremont and Stewart Streets, in Boston's lively theater district.

Whether the clients were Quigley's or Lou's own finds, the agency opened for business with a lucrative stable of variety acts, ranging from accordionists to zitherists, and Lou was an overnight success, booking his first act into the St. James Theater.

While Lou was making good money as a booker, his ace card was his personal flair for production. The average vaudeville show in those days consisted of five or six acts, one of which was called a flash act; a dance number with a few pretty girls; a tumbler or two; and some scenery. Lou's shows were more polished, featuring what would become the Lou Walters trademark—a line of beautiful girls.

With his own business, he was working around the clock, sometimes generating as much as a thousand dollars a week in income, he claimed. And Lou spent it as fast as it came in. He began wearing expensive suits, which he'd buy by the dozen when they were on sale—reduced from fifty dollars to eleven dollars—in Filene's basement. He bought imported white shirts with French cuffs, and had lots of fancy cuff links, which he'd show off by sitting around his office in his shirtsleeves.

He treated Dena like a princess, slipping an expensive diamond engagement ring on her finger, and a beautiful mink stole over her shoulders. The wedding of Lou Walters and Dena Seletsky took place on May 30, 1920, in a rented banquet hall in Boston, the ceremony performed by Rabbi Abraham Rosen, of Malden.

Lou gave Dena the fur stole on their wedding night, one of the few evenings in their more than fifty years of marriage that he wasn't out working—or playing cards. He loved gin rummy, but he'd bet on anything.

In the little waiting room outside his office, where some of the acts would sit around hoping for a booking, Lou kept his own personal numbers writer. "They used to call them 'nigger pools,'" said Abrams, who was one of Lou's entertainers before becoming an agent and a producer. "This man would sit there pretty near all day and anytime anyone would mention a number—a hunch number— Louie would put a quarter or a dollar on it. Other numbers guys would have to go from one place to another to take bets, but this fellow was making all of his money from Lou."

In those early days, with the money rolling in and the world his oyster, Lou was thought of as a warmhearted, generous young man; a soft touch for friends and relatives. "He was a hell of a guy," said Herman Seletsky. "If I wanted anything, I could get it from Lou—money or anything else."

Though things at home were unhappy and stressful because of the death of his baby son, Burton, in 1922, and the birth of his retarded daughter, Jackie, in 1926, Lou had become a boy wonder in the talent-booking business in Boston and environs. It was the era of the flapper—the "Roaring Twenties"—and people were out to have a good time. Prohibition was in force, and Boston had its share of wild speakeasies owned by racketeers who turned to Lou for entertainers, willing to pay handsomely for his services. With vaudeville at its peak, Lou's booking agency was doing enormous business, and he was earning an estimated $65,000 to $75,000 a year.

"He lived up to the dollar. He wasn't one to sit back," said Ed Risman, a long-time business associate of Lou's. "He wanted a fine place to live. He gave the family everything that they wanted or needed. He wasn't one to say, 'Let's hold back and put it in the bank.' If he had the money he spent it, or he gambled it."

Lou bestowed lavish gifts of furs and jewelry on Dena. Some believe he gave her the presents as reparations in lieu of his companionship because he was never home; others feel they were his way of assuaging Dena's deep sadness over Jackie's problems. The Walterses' magnificent eighteen-room house in Newton was filled with expensive furnishings, art, sculpture, and a library of first editions. Lou was driving expensive Packards, Lincolns, and La Salles, spending every dollar he made.

But by the time Barbara was born in September 1929, Lou Walters' champagne bubble was starting to burst. Like millions of other bullish speculators, he had purchased stocks and bonds on margin. When the market crashed on "Black Thursday"—twenty-nine days after Barbara's birth—her father took a heavy hit. Along with his gambling debts and a continuing slowdown in his business, the family was forced to vacate the big house and return to a modest apartment in Dorchester.

Like two locomotives racing toward one another on the same track, converging events were about to spell catastrophe for Lou Walters. One, of course, was the Depression. The other was the fact that a show business era was ending: the curtain was dropping on vaudeville, Lou's bread and butter.

The writing was on the marquee, and it said *The Jazz Singer*. The first talkie, starring Al Jolson, a vaudevillian himself, had opened to capacity audiences in November 1927. Motion pictures had caught the fancy of the American public; across the country owners of vaudeville houses began converting their properties to movie theaters.

By 1933 Lou Walters was flat broke; his office was closed, the fancy cars gone. He was forced to borrow from friends—even employees—and to sell Dena's furs and jewelry and much of their furnishings in order to pay the rent and buy food for Dena and the kids—Jackie, seven, and Barbara, four.

Lou started hustling small jobs, booking banquets of local jewelers and shoe manufacturers, holding out hope that vaudeville would make a return engagement.

"For a fast two years or so," Lou would say later, "I was strictly a bum."

His low point was when an ex-gangster operating a hole-in-the wall saloon jabbed a finger in his chest and snarled, "You're a has-been, Lou. You're washed up. All you know is from acrobats. I wouldn't have you booking my shows if you was the last booker in the world."

THE LATIN QUARTER

To the children in the fifth grade at the Lawrence School on Francis Street in Brookline, Barbara was a strange and mysterious little girl. After school they went home to milk and cookies, but Barbara—skinny, with inquisitive green eyes and long, dark wavy hair—had a different sort of life. Most days she took the MTA trolley downtown to an exotic place called the Latin Quarter.

There, in the shadowy nightclub, the air filled with the smell of stale cigarette smoke and the sweet scent of showgirls' perfume, she'd find Lou. Barbara would give him a kiss and then seek out a quiet place backstage where she would curl up and conscientiously do her homework.

Going to the club after school, instead of playing with her friends at home, was the only way Barbara got a chance to see her father.

"The club was Lou's life," said Ed Risman, who was Lou's general manager for many years. "In those days we closed at two o'clock in the morning. By the time you went out and had coffee and bullshitted about the day, maybe you'd get into bed around five or six. It was a full day, and he'd be back in early the next afternoon."

The year was 1939. In New York, an event took place that went unnoticed by the Walters family, one that would have a profound impact on Barbara's life. The World's Fair had opened with "The World of Tomorrow" as its theme. With the throw of a switch, President Franklin D. Roosevelt brought a new technology to life—a big box with a little screen flickered in the RCA Pavilion and fair-goers saw commercial television for the first time. "Now at last we add sight to sound," proclaimed David Sarnoff, the head of the Radio Corporation of America. "It is an art that is bound to affect all society."

Across the Atlantic—and soon on this side—the novelty of radio with pictures was of no consequence. In Europe the flames of war were being fanned: the Nazis had invaded Poland, and Britain and France had declared war on Germany. Back home in Brookline, at the movie house, Barbara and her friends, unaware of those ominous clouds, watched with delight as Judy Garland sailed over the rainbow as Dorothy in *The Wizard of Oz*.

Barbara was a shy, quiet, sensitive and intensely private ten-year-old who was ashamed of her father's business. So she didn't tell her friends that the man on the screen who was playing the understuffed scarecrow, Ray Bolger, from Dorchester, and the Tin Man, Jack Haley, from Boston, were friends of Lou's; that they had worked for him, and that she'd even met them at his nightclub. She was that embarrassed about what he did for a living.

"Barbara was introspective. She wasn't like one of the regular kids," recalled a woman who had gone to grammar school with her. "She was different, weird, odd. Not one of the bunch. The kids would talk about what was going on in her life because of the nightclub her father owned. Kids didn't know what nightclubs were, or about that kind of life. It was mysterious and fascinating and stimulating to us. It was like some great big secret she had."

Brookline was a quiet, conservative Boston suburb with an upwardly mobile, Jewish middle-class population. Most families, like the Walterses, lived in pleasant four- and six-family brick apartment buildings on tree-lined streets in walking distance of the school. But that's where the similarity ended.

The fathers of Barbara's friends were young doctors, lawyers, engineers, and schoolteachers who had dinner at home every night with their families. Lou was the only one in show business, so his lifestyle was the source of much speculation and gossip, which Barbara's well-tuned antennae had picked up. She was mortified every time the other children bragged about what their fathers did, expecting she'd be asked to talk about hers.

The other embarrassment she faced was her sister, Jackie. By going to the Latin Quarter after school, she didn't have to be her sister's sole playmate, or hear the taunts and invective hurled at her by some of the other children. Barbara was very protective of Jackie and often was forced to defend her, sometimes getting into fights with kids who made fun of Jackie. It hurt Barbara so much to see her sister treated like that, but she knew there was nothing she could do.

Most days Lou or Dena would bring Jackie, then thirteen, to the club, too. She'd sit in her father's office, or wander happily backstage among the show people, who accepted her warmly.

In a sense, both children felt protected at the club. For Barbara and Jackie, the frenetic world of the Latin Quarter was as safe and sane a harbor as the traditional homes to which the other children went after school.

The Walterses were living in a second-floor apartment off Harvard Street, a short walk from the school. Many of the mothers in the neighborhood had help—a cleaning woman who came in once or twice a week, a "schwartze" who cooked dinner every so often. But Lou and Dena had a seamstress who spent long days at the apartment because Barbara and Jackie loved her; she was a woman who became a virtual surrogate mother for the children during those early years.

"We were all fairly comfortable—not rich, not poor. I would say upper middle class at that time," said Joan Weinrib Hopner, a fifth-grade classmate of Barbara's. "We had a maid living at our house. But the maid wasn't a seamstress. That was kind of fancy in those days."

When Barbara was a senior in high school, the seamstress died, inspiring Barbara to write a moving reminiscence about her for the school literary magazine.

The woman's name was Elizabeth Dorethews, Barbara wrote, but her nickname was "Dodey," which was the title of the story. Barbara described Dodey as a lonely, eccentric, elderly woman who lived in a boardinghouse. Besides dressmaking for the Walters family, Dodey baby-sat for the girls when Lou and Dena were at the club. The woman became an integral and much loved member of the household. Barbara felt she had been a positive influence on her life, making her happy and secure when she felt sad and lonely.

"It was Dodey who taught us to pray each night and the first Bible stories I ever heard were those she told me," Barbara wrote. "Today I realize that a good part of my philosophy was hers, for she would often give us bits of 'universal wisdom' in easy-to-swallow, candy-coated doses."

Neither the Depression nor the death of vaudeville was able to keep Lou Walters down for long.

Even at his lowest ebb, he devised a financial arrangement that would allow him to reopen his business. He put together a small group of agents and bookers and moved them into offices in a building near the old Statler Hotel. Lou paid the rent and the agents paid him a percentage of their bookings, all under the umbrella of the Lou Walters Booking Agency.

A friend of Lou's, a Boston nightclub owner named Jack Levaggi, gave him a chance to book acts for his place. But Levaggi ignored all of Lou's suggestions. On his own, Levaggi hired big bands during the course of which he discovered Ella Fitzgerald. But working for Levaggi was a good experience for Lou; he learned the mechanics of the nightclub business.

Walters and Levaggi fought constantly. "He didn't try to build up a unique atmosphere. He didn't hire unusual acts," Lou complained. "If a Boston columnist came in to review a new show, Levaggi would [charge him for his meal.] I used to beg him to splurge on big ads every weekend, but he used to laugh and say the only time you should advertise is when you advertise it for sale. I used to sit around the club all the time feeling sad and complaining. Finally, he said if I was so smart why didn't I open my own nightclub."

So Lou made a deal with another friend, Ralph Snyder, who owned the Bradford Hotel. Lou rented the fifteenth-floor penthouse Cascades Roof cabaret, which had always been a failure. Lou booked the acts and the music and gave Snyder the admission charge and Lou got a percentage of the profits. As part of the deal, Lou was also given free office space in the hotel for his booking agency. The Cascades venture was a huge success.

Encouraged by his achievement, Lou felt he had enough experience to open his own club. In late 1937, he leased a dilapidated former Greek Orthodox church at 46 Winchester Street in a poor, semi-industrial area of Boston near Park Square. Lou chose the building because it had high ceilings from which he envisioned trapeze artists swinging over the heads of his customers, and it had old stone walls that gave it a European flair.

Lou was in the process of getting the building cleaned

up when, in 1938, he saw a Rudy Vallee movie called *Gold Diggers in Paris*. There was a reference to a place called the Latin Quarter, which had an exotic sound to it; Lou instantly decided that was the name he'd give his new club.

A friend had promised to put up the initial financing, but backed out at the last minute. "I was stuck with the lease," Walters recalled, "so I decided what the hell, I'll go ahead and open it anyway." Lou needed $2,500 but there wasn't anyone willing to invest in such a speculative venture, especially with someone who was a known gambler and as financially unstable as he was.

"His father, my grandfather, Abraham, would have assisted him with the money," said Shirley Budd. "But Lou wanted to do it on his own." Rejecting aid from his father, Lou borrowed instead from loan sharks, one of whom charged him two thousand dollars in interest on twelve hundred dollars for six months. "He paid through the nose," said Ed Risman. "We were fortunate. The Latin Quarter made money. If it didn't he would have been in the soup."

Lou managed to decorate the place for pennies. He found a young artist, who had studied in Montmartre in Paris, who painted murals of apache dancers on the walls. At junk shops, Lou bought inexpensive Toulouse-Lautrec posters, and old chairs and tables, which he covered with red and white checked tablecloths. The room was romantic and exotic, dimly lighted with candles.

More important, Lou was the first Boston nightclub owner to emphasize a slickly produced floor show; he had found his niche, and the Latin Quarter was an overnight success.

Eddie Davis, a friend and competitor who owned the Fox and Hounds Club, said, "The Latin Quarter caught on a week after Lou opened because he had a line of beautiful girls. Lou brought Parisian-style entertainment to Boston."

Lou could not have done it without the help of Ed Risman, who had been running a club called the Casa Mañana. Risman's expertise was food and beverage, the management of which could make or break a nightclub. Lou heard of Risman's reputation and a few months after the Latin Quarter opened he offered him a job.

"I decided to make the switch," said Risman years later. "I decided to take a chance on him."

It was a decision he wouldn't regret. For the next twenty years, Lou and Risman would make a successful team, opening and operating two other highly successful Latin Quarters in Miami and New York, but by then a tough money man from Boston by the name of Elias Moses Loew would be in the picture.

Before long, Lou jubilantly saw the need to expand. He built a new club adjacent to the old building at a cost of $180,000.

With his overwhelming success, Barbara was seeing even less of her father—and her mother. The opening of the Latin Quarter virtually coincided with Lou and Dena's nineteenth wedding anniversary. Dena had changed quite a bit from the shy and retiring girl Lou had married. She was more confident and sophisticated; she wore makeup and fancy clothes and had put on weight. "She'd become a very zaftig, satisifying-looking gal," said Risman.

Dena also was keeping closer tabs on Lou by spending time at the club. Intimately aware of his proclivity for gambling both at the card table and in business, Dena decided to keep Lou on a short leash. She didn't want him doing something foolish that would jeopardize what clearly was a financial triumph.

Lou's gambling wasn't Dena's only concern. She also was alert to his womanizing, a peccadillo that was well known among his colleagues. Lou was in a business where he was surrounded night and day by the kind of women other men could only fantasize about—exotic, statuesque lovelies, some of whom were willing to do almost anything to become a Latin Quarter showgirl. It was a glamorous job that sometimes led to movie and stage careers, but more often to a life of leisure as the pampered pet of a wealthy sugar daddy.

As the proprietor, Lou felt he had the right to handle the merchandise, and he did. As one colleague observed, "It takes a very strong individual to run away from it, and Lou wasn't that strong."

"Lou would say to a new girl he favored, 'Honey, take your clothes off and walk around. I got to see your figure,' " recalled a crony. "Then he'd shut the door to his private office. Afterward he'd give her thirty or forty bucks for the cab ride home. He used to brag about it."

Of all the girls who passed through the club—and Lou's private office—over the years, he was said to have been truly smitten by one in particular: a tall, alluring, educated brunette with a beautiful face, long legs, and an interest in literature, which she shared with Lou.

As a family friend noted: "If Dena knew the details, she would never let on. Dena was that clever and smart. Why would she confront him and chance losing everything? She knew what his life was like; she just wanted to make sure she was up-to-date on who the latest one was. Dena had a way of making certain Lou *knew* that she knew—without her having to say anything. He'd feel guilty and drop the girl until the next one he fancied came along. Dena knew it was never love. It was usually just a one-night stand. Still, it hurt."

Dena had a spy in Lou's inner circle—her brother Eddie Selette who, along with Max, was working for Lou at the time. Max was close-mouthed but Eddie was a talker, and though he was loyal to Lou, Dena was able to weasel information out of him about what Lou was up to.

"Dena became very visible at the club," said Risman. "She was a very determined woman—very aggressive, outspoken, and inquisitive. She'd sit in on discussions, and she wasn't afraid to tell Lou what she felt or how she felt. If she had an opinion, she voiced it and she was usually right—and I always admired Dena for that. She had her own mind. She wasn't a little Jewish mother. She was a ballsy woman."

Lou himself admitted, "She's turned out to be my severest critic, and in this business you need one."

Lou wasn't letting an opportunity pass him by. With the club closed for the summer months, he began putting on spectacular Sunday afternoon and evening Latin Quarter–style shows in a hotel ballroom in Falmouth on Cape Cod. As part of the deal, the owner gave Lou the use of a cottage, which the Walterses shared with Risman and Max Selette. While the men worked, Dena watched over Barbara and Jackie, who spent a wonderful summer playing on the beach.

Some of Barbara's happiest times in those days were spent at Camp Ferosdel in the Berkshire Hills of western Massachusetts where she forged a lifelong friendship with another girl who had a handicapped sister. Throughout her life, in fact, some of Barbara's strongest friendships were based on mutual adversity of one form or another.

Camp Ferosdel was a quiet, noncompetitive, creative, and comfortable environment located on a vegetable farm owned by an eccentric doctor from New York. The campers, mostly Jewish boys and girls from New York, were proud in a reverse-snobbery sense about the fact that the place had only cold water and no electricity. Ferosdel was a wonderland for the city children. During the days there were crafts and games; at night they'd sit around a campfire in front of the head camper's cabin listening to music on a Victrola.

Barbara Shiffman Altman's parents sent her to Ferosdel because her sister, who had cerebral palsy, had spent several enjoyable summers there. They saw it as a safe haven for their handicapped child because the physician-owner was in attendance at all times.

As with Barbara, Altman felt a strong responsibility toward her older sister along with the related burdens and stresses. So Barbara, who shared the cabin with Altman's handicapped sister, caught Altman's eye immediately as someone special. "I was very touched," she said years later, "by how straight and caring she was without pitying."

Altman learned why on the first parents' visiting day when Lou and Dena arrived with Jackie in tow. At that point, Barbara had not revealed her own sister's problem. When she saw Jackie, though, Altman knew instantly the reason for her young friend's compassion and sensitivity. "I was very tuned in to that kind of thing," she said. "If I saw someone who was less than normal, or different from normal, I knew it."

After that, the two girls became inseparable. "I don't think we ever discussed our sisters at any great length," Altman said. "We had an understanding of what it was like. It was a given. It was rarely something you needed to talk about because there it was."

After several seasons of being together at camp, the two girls lost track of each other. Their friendship, though, would resume a half-dozen years later when, by coincidence, they would be assigned neighboring rooms at college.

At home in Boston, Barbara entered a shaky adolescence, with few friends and only her schoolwork, to which she was devoted. She tried as best she could to block out the problems with Jackie and her parents.

Typical of an adolescent's desire to experiment with things adult, Barbara started smoking on the sly. Her partner in crime was a creative, artistic youngster, Judy Haskell. The two went to different schools in Brookline, but had met and become fast friends. As Haskell recalled, "We were in her apartment one day, in the narrow kitchen, and we secretly smoked these Egyptian cigarettes that had cotton in both ends. The cotton was probably there to protect them in shipment and we didn't realize that we should have taken the cotton out. We had to suck very hard to get any smoke. I remember both of us wondering why they were so hard to smoke and finding it a big adventure. When we were together it was just the two of us and I remember thinking, 'How nice she is.' "

Those innocent hijinks, the serenity of Camp Ferosdel, and the small-town familiarity of Brookline were about to give way to one of the most tumultuous and unhappy periods in Barbara's young life, one that would have a lifelong impact on her.

"POOR LITTLE
RICH GIRL"

In 1940, Lou unexpectedly uprooted the family when he opened his second successful nightclub, the Miami Latin Quarter. Barbara, then eleven, was forced to leave behind her few friends for a lonely, unhappy existence in a strange, rambling house on sparsely populated Palm Island where Chicago mobster Al "Scarface" Capone had his winter home.

There were no other children on the island except for Jackie. The house, located next to the Latin Quarter, was enormous and intimidating—an elegant palace built for Prohibition rumrunners in the Twenties, with a huge living room and numerous bedrooms, one of which was turned over to a dressmaker who maintained the club's showgirl costumes.

Dena enrolled Barbara in an expensive private school across Biscayne Bay in Miami Beach. Each school day she was driven there by a chauffeur. The school catered to the offspring of other affluent, itinerant Northerners who operated businesses in Miami during the winter season.

Barbara became increasingly shy and withdrawn, finding it difficult to make new friends at school among the other children who came and went frequently. Lou, busy with the new Latin Quarter and another acquisition, the Casanova Club, was rarely at home. Dena had her hands full taking care of Jackie and keeping tabs on Lou. As a result, Barbara was left to fend for herself.

"She was a serious little girl—very quiet, very lonely," said Marilyn Franklin Farber, who befriended Barbara during visits to the island. "She spent a lot of time with her sister. She was very protective of her."

Mostly, Barbara stayed close to the house, playing with her dog, sitting by the water, waving at passing sightseeing boats.

"I felt like the poor little rich girl," Barbara said years later. "The great big house. The chauffeur to drive me to school. I was very lonely. I had a very dreary adolescence. I read a lot. I dreamed a lot."

Palm Island was a strange environment for a child. In the early Twenties and into the Thirties, the tiny slice of land was home to the Palm Island Casino, a swank gambling den catering to high-rollers of the sports and society set. Later, the club was run by famed showman Earl Carroll, who produced his leggy "Vanities" revues there.

In Boston, Lou was looking to broaden his horizons. When he heard that the old club had fallen on hard times and was available, he got an investor to put up some money and the two of them, along with Ed Risman, refurbished the place. Like the Boston club, it was an overnight sensation. For a six-dollar minimum, customers got dinner or drinks and the dazzling floor show and beautiful girls that were becoming synonymous with the Lou Walters name. But there was no gambling. "It just didn't fit into my scheme of things," said Lou, a notorious gambler. "I wasn't a member of the clique."

Despite Lou's proclaimed lack of membership, J. Edgar Hoover's FBI kept close tabs on him over the years, beginning when he opened in Florida. An FBI intelligence report of the time noted: "This place puts on perhaps the most elaborate show in the Miami area. . . . Due to this fact, it attracts . . . the hoodlum and gangster element."

In late 1941, Lou's successes had come to the attention of Elias Moses Loew, a tough, fast-living Bostonian who came to America from Austria as a poor Jewish immigrant in 1916 and amassed a fortune in movie theaters, hotels, and prime real estate.

Loew had decided to open a nightclub in New York for the oddest reason—to "get even" with the city. Loew's wife at the time, Sonja, a raven-haired Czech beauty, had discovered a small, tastefully furnished restaurant, the Café Old Europe, near Seventy-third Street and Broadway, which was owned by a group of German Jewish refugees who were on the verge of bankruptcy. The owners sought a loan from Sonja, who called Loew immediately; he had a soft spot for refugees since he had been one himself. "Why don't we buy the joint?" Loew responded, and he did, for sixty thousand dollars. But the day he took possession, all of the French furnishings, the crystal chandeliers, and the kitchen equipment had been repossessed.

"Mr. Loew was furious," said Sonja Loew. "He said, 'New York owes me thousands of dollars. New York is going to give it back to me now a hundred times.' He was so angry because he was suckered." Loew telephoned Lou in Miami and gave him the following order: "Go to New York and look for a place. I hate New York and I want to get my money back."

Lou Walters was elated. New York had always been his goal; he considered Boston and Miami small-time.

Not long after he arrived in the city, he found a vacant, triangular-shaped building on Broadway and Forty-eighth Street that once housed the old Cotton Club, George White's Gay White Way, and the Palais Royal, all of which had flopped. The site seemed jinxed, but Lou reported to Loew confidently that he could turn the white elephant into pure gold. "Go to the Lido in Paris and bring over a show," Loew instructed. "I want to open with something very big. Money is no object."

Loew gave Lou full creative control, some equity, a good salary, and his name on the marquee; the latter, according to Sonja Loew, was done "to boost Lou's ego and make him work harder."

In New York, Lou had to do business with the mob, at least indirectly. One day three men sporting black fedoras and cashmere coats paid him a visit. They told him that, in order to get the proper certificates and licenses that would allow the club to open, he'd have to buy his liquor and other supplies from certain gangland-approved vendors. At first Lou laughed off the extortion attempt. But after a city inspector showed up with five single-spaced pages of building code and electrical violations, he realized he faced big trouble.

"I went in and said, 'Mr. Walters, I hate to tell you this, but I think you better make a deal with these people,' " said George Gill, a veteran Broadway maintenance electrician who was installing lighting at the club and knew the fix Lou was in because he'd seen it happen before.

"Lou and I had several conversations about this," said Gill. "He wanted to know about the background of these people. Lou had some pretty good political contacts from Boston who he hoped could help him. Lou had a lot to offer these politicians. First, he had chorus girls—and that was a good solution for a lot of problems."

But none of Lou's powerful friends could help. "Lou did business with the people they told him to," said Gill. "I never wanted to know how it worked because I never wanted to become a witness."

On April 22, 1942, on schedule, Lou Walters' Latin Quarter opened to a full house. The premiere show was called "Folies des Femmes," and Broadway columnist Richard Manson declared the club a success: "For a two-dollar minimum, children, you can get Paris, Loew's State and a steak sandwich—a formula that's founded nightclub dynasties."

With the New York Latin Quarter an instant hit, once again Lou moved Dena, Barbara, and Jackie, this time from Palm Island to New York City, and installed them in a beautiful apartment overlooking Central Park, in the middle of bustling, wartime Manhattan.

For Barbara, who was almost thirteen, New York would be a brief respite from the loneliness and alienation she felt in Florida. For the first time, she would find herself accepted, becoming part of a crowd. She entered eighth grade at the exclusive Fieldston School with other children much like herself—precocious, well-to-do, and Jewish.

Fieldston was an outgrowth of the Ethical Culture Society, a humanistic organization that emphasized the ethics of Judaism without the dogma. But few parents, if any, actually were members of the society. Most sent their children there because of the school's academic reputation, or for the prestige. The classes were small and the students received personalized attention. The campus was in the Riverdale section of the Bronx; every day Barbara was picked up and delivered outside her apartment by a Fieldston School bus.

The student body was very cliquish, and Barbara joyfully found herself being welcomed into one of the groups: a coterie of rich, bright, glib, and sophisticated New York girls who years later would be referred to somewhat disparagingly as "Jewish American Princesses."

Their preoccupation seemed to be boys—talking about them and ogling them, nothing more—shopping, makeup, and clothes. Most of her friends lived in fancy apartment buildings on Fifth and Park Avenues. Like them, Barbara started wearing lipstick and jewelry, and went shopping for clothes at Saks Fifth Avenue and Lord & Taylor. She was stylish, wearing expensive cashmere sweaters, pleated skirts, bobby socks, and penny loafers. Boys found her attractive, but standoffish; she was pretty with a sultry gypsy-child look, shiny dark hair, green eyes, olive complexion. Barbara delighted for the first time in an active social life during this period.

"She didn't appear to be an exceptional student," said Jean Claster Milling, a Fieldston classmate. "She was just average. She was interested in clothes and appearance and social life. She wasn't interested in sports. She was one of the ladies who appeared not to want to break their nails." Barbara flunked gym and home economics.

During her time at Fieldston, Barbara had decided, in the unequivocal way that only a teenager can, that she had found her calling in life.

"She was determined at that time to get into 'show business'—and she talked about it a lot," recalled a Fieldston friend, Enid Kraeler Reiman. "But she wasn't involved in school plays and I was wondering how she was going to do it. She was a very attractive young girl, quite confident, very bright, and maybe a little more worldly or sophisticated because of her exposure to her father's world."

The two became friends for a time after Reiman had spent a summer working as a gofer at the Greenwich Playhouse in Connecticut, fetching coffee for Tallulah Bankhead and Bert Lahr. After she mentioned her experience to Barbara, the two "spent our days talking show biz at school."

But even to Reiman, her show biz confidante, Barbara rarely talked about Lou or the Latin Quarter, which had become the hottest club in town. She was still ashamed of what he did. He was not a doctor, lawyer, banker, or stockbroker like other Fieldston parents. "Barbara never bragged about her dad or his contacts," Reiman said. "As a matter of fact, she was pretty closed about it."

The sophistication and worldliness that Barbara's friends saw in her at school also was apparent at home where Lou and Dena began treating her differently, friends observed.

"I always got the feeling that Barbara was treated as the man of the family because the other sister had the problem," said Myra Polsky Martin, a chum of Barbara's at Fieldston, who often spent time at the Walterses' apartment. "Barbara's father gave her a lot of responsibility. I remember her feeling that she was a responsible person; that her dad relied a great deal on her. I was extremely protected as a child, but she seemed to be very open with her parents. She was treated like an adult."

Perhaps because of the deference accorded Barbara by her parents, her respect for them diminished, and she was often nasty and rude to them in the presence of others. Friends remember Barbara making snide remarks to her mother; Lou was rarely around so Dena took the brunt of Barbara's ire.

With her talk about a show business career, and her budding Manhattan sophistication, Barbara was spending a considerable amount of time at the Latin Quarter. The Walters sisters were often in the club at the same time, but while Jackie was in the dressing rooms, fascinated with the showgirls and stars, Barbara was interested in the technical aspects of the business. Backstage, she befriended George Gill, who had become the club's chief electrician.

Barbara would come to me and say, "Mr. Gill"—it was always *Mister* Gill—"I want to look at the show from the spotlight booth. May I?" I'd say, "Barbara, this is your father's nightclub. You can go anyplace you want." She'd say thank you and go up and watch the show from the spotlight room.

She was a terrific kid and very, very smart. One of the things that intrigued her was my stage electrician's road box. I kept books and tools in it. She was fascinated by the test lamp; I would show her how it lit when certain wires were connected to it. She was always asking me questions—"What is this used for? Why do you do this?" Always talkative, inquisitive.

Barbara loved Fieldston and her set of friends. She was happy in New York, and had even come to enjoy spending time in her father's nightclub. She and her friends would ride the subways and buses; bike in Central Park; go to movies and museums. She was happier than she'd ever been.

But before she had a chance to finish ninth grade at Fieldston, Lou decided once again to return to Florida—the place Barbara despised—to expand his nightclub operations. For a third time, Barbara was uprooted, forced to say goodbye to her friends—to leave behind a safe and relatively happy haven.

SORORITY GIRL'S
FIRST KISS

Barbara returned to a Miami that had become a virtual armed camp because of the war. Some one hundred thousand troops were stationed there—the hotels had become billets; the restaurants, mess halls; the parks and beaches, physical training facilities; and nightclubs were used as classrooms.

Like the young soldiers displaced from their homes and loved ones around the country, Barbara, too, would feel isolation and loneliness during her second stay in Miami. The joy she felt in New York would fade under the bright Florida sun.

Because the army had taken the Latin Quarter and the adjacent mansion over for the duration, the Walterses moved into a smaller two-story white stucco house with a small front lawn on Sheridan Avenue in a quiet residential section of Miami Beach. Barbara thought she'd be happier there; she had felt so detached and confined on Palm Island. Otherwise, life at home hadn't changed much. Rarely were Lou or Dena there for Barbara; a housekeeper was present much of the time.

Lou Walters' arrival in Florida again sparked the interest of the FBI, which was keeping a tight surveillance on the nightclub business as it related to mobsters and violations of wartime manpower and pricing regulations. An informational report from the Special Agent in Charge of the Miami Field Office to J. Edgar Hoover noted that Lou and a partner had purchased the Colonial Inn in Hallandale, just north of Miami, on March 29, 1944, for $110,000, and that Lou's and Dena's names were on the deed. The report said that Walters and his partner "expect to open the Colonial Inn during the coming winter season as an exclusive gambling casino."

Another FBI memorandum noted that Lou and his partner also purchased a club called the Dunes in Palm Beach County—Dena's name was again on the deed—and that they "were making a gamble that the office of Sheriff of Palm Beach County would change hands in the May 1944 election," which could bring about legalized gambling there.

Barbara was well aware of her father's problems; when Lou was home, which was rarely, he and Dena talked openly in front of her about his financial ups and downs, treating her as an equal in their contretemps. Barbara was riddled with anxieties because of Lou's continuing troubles; she began living with a fear that the sheriff would come beating down the door, putting the family out into the street like paupers. Elias Loew once recalled hearing Barbara ask her father, "Daddy, what is going to become of us if you lose all our money?"

Not long after the Walterses moved to Miami Beach, Barbara discovered a run-down house on an overgrown lot a few blocks away where an old hermit lived, and he became her first friend in the neighborhood. Most of the other children were scared of the place and gave it a wide berth. Lonely, curious, and empathetic, Barbara met and befriended the man. Every so often she'd walk over to his place and spend time talking to him. As with the eccentric Dodey in Boston, Barbara felt compassion, affection, and fascination for the loner.

Barbara enrolled at Miami Beach Junior High, which was part of a complex that included Miami Beach Senior High. The schools, with a predominantly middle-class Jewish student body, had high academic standards and sent a majority of its graduates to college. Most of the students were born and raised in Miami Beach and had gone through school together. Some were the sons and daughters of hotel and restaurant owners, wealthy, pampered children; others had parents who worked in those establishments. It was a closed, cliquish crowd that considered people like Barbara "snow birds"—interlopers who came for the winter season and then left. As a result, Barbara would experience great difficulty being accepted, and sometimes outright rejection.

The sophistication and maturity that Barbara felt with her friends in New York seemed to have evaporated on her return to Florida. "She didn't wear makeup and she didn't dress fancy," said Greta Joseloff Steinberg, the daughter of a Miami Beach hotel owner, who befriended Barbara in school. "She was not a glamorous young lady; she was anything but. She was very plain and unassuming. Barbara did not have many friends, through no fault of Barbara's. She was very quiet and you really had to seek her out and be with her because she was very shy. We didn't talk about the usual things that most girls that age talk about—like boys and clothes."

After school Greta often spent afternoons at Barbara's house. During one visit, Barbara revealed that she still had a favorite doll, a "Debutante Doll," with which she played make-believe games, especially when she felt lonely. Expecting Greta to laugh at her, Barbara was overjoyed to learn that Greta had a similar doll and sometimes played with it when no one was around.

"We swore each other to secrecy—she said she'd never tell anyone and I said I wouldn't," Steinberg disclosed. "Here we were thirteen or fourteen years old still playing with dolls. If anybody found out, we'd be a laughingstock. I didn't even want my sisters to know. I think it was an unusual thing to do at our age."

At one point early in their friendship, Barbara and Greta were discussing siblings and they discovered they both had brothers who had died before they were born. The girls felt this bonded them in a mysterious sort of way.

In a similar vein, Barbara became friends at school with Judy Nelson Drucker, who had a retarded younger brother. Their friendship was forged for much the same reason as Barbara's was with fellow camper Barbara Shiffman Altman: the mutual misfortune of having handicapped siblings.

Barbara rarely mentioned Jackie to her new classmates, so they were taken by surprise if they came upon her at the house.

"I don't think that many people knew there was a Jackie," said Gloria Palter, one of the few girls in whom Barbara confided her secret early on. "I felt very good when she brought me to their home and introduced me to her sister. I felt privileged because I had to be someone whom Barbara trusted. Barbara kept Jackie very hush-hush. I remember when I was invited over she said, 'I bet you didn't know I have a sister, but I do and she's retarded.' I was very surprised. I remember she showed a great deal of love for her. Barbara was very affectionate to Jackie."

Judy Drucker was an aspiring singer who, because of her voice studies, had little time for socializing or school activities. "Barbara was sort of out of it also," said Drucker. "She didn't hang around with a lot of kids. She was quiet, a loner, and I was, too. So the two of us found each other." For company, Barbara often tagged along when Drucker went to her singing lesson.

Barbara entered tenth grade—class 10A-6—at Beach

High in September 1944, determined at fifteen to become more popular and optimistic that she would be invited to join the best sorority in school, Kappa Pi. "It was the crème de la crème," said Greta Steinberg, a member, whose sister had been in it before her. "The girls in Kappa Pi were very sophisticated—the popularity gals of the school, the beauty queens; you might say they were snobs."

Steinberg and another friend, Jackie Knapper, whose family owned the Lord Tarleton Hotel, a favorite of entertainers working in Miami and the hotel where the Walters had a cabana, proposed Barbara for membership in Kappa at a meeting held at Steinberg's house.

In hopes of becoming a pledge, Barbara began socializing more, entertaining friends at pool parties at the Palm Island house, to which the family had returned. She also started arranging with Lou to allow her to have functions at his clubs. All of this, she hoped, would impress her classmates and influence her acceptance into the sorority.

But the Kappa leaders, meeting in secret, turned Barbara down.

She was devastated. One friend remembered seeing her burst into tears, sobbing and almost hysterical. But as quickly as the flood of emotion came, it ended, the friend recalled. "It was like Dr. Jekyll and Mr. Hyde. She went from being very vulnerable to an iceberg in two minutes. Barbara was never one to show her emotions. She was very private."

As the sister of a handicapped child, as the daughter of troubled parents, Barbara had learned self-control; to keep her feelings inside; not to wear her heart on her sleeve.

"I never found out why she wasn't accepted in Kappa," said Steinberg, still saddened years later by Barbara's rejection. "They never gave a reason. Perhaps she wasn't flashy enough. She certainly wasn't the kind of individual that you would associate with the kind of life that her parents lived. She was just the antithesis—very sweet, and very introverted."

After Barbara was turned down by Kappa, she and Steinberg drifted apart.

Beach High's student population was small and close-knit enough for Barbara's rejection by Kappa to become the subject of gossip and speculation. Many felt she was turned down because of a promise she made but couldn't keep. Barbara had invited many of the school's most popular students and some of the Kappa sorority sisters to a party at Palm Island. Teen idol Frank Sinatra was singing in town and Barbara gave the impression that he might make an appearance at her party. "He never showed and she lost face and didn't get in the sorority," said a fellow student, John Throne, who had been invited to the party.

Stuart Jacobs, who was in Barbara's class, heard the Sinatra story, too. He felt the show-business environment in which Barbara lived made her adolescence more difficult. "She was overwhelmed by what used to take place in her house with all those big names that came through there. It wasn't a very pleasant thing in her life."

Barbara's friend Judy Drucker hated the sororities because of the snobbishness and elitism they spawned. "They were so cliquish. It was a snotty [school] community in those days." To make a statement against the sorority system Drucker and a few friends formed a tongue-in-cheek group called Emanon, which was No Name spelled backward. The group had no activities whatsoever and anyone could join.

The rejection by the Kappa girls didn't dampen Barbara's determination to join a sorority. She was finally invited to pledge for Lambda Pi by the sorority's president, Annabelle Wald D'Augustine, who sat next to Barbara in homeroom. "She was not particularly outgoing," said D'Augustine. "She didn't take a leadership role, and there were lots of opportunities for people to get involved. In class, she didn't offer the answer all the time or try to get attention. I knew everybody and I tried to introduce her to people and involve her."

One of Barbara's friends in Lambda Pi, Shirley Rosenfeld Berman, was a popular, active girl, whom Barbara seemed to idolize. Barbara, who sat behind Berman in class, was effusive in her compliments. "You have a gorgeous profile," she'd whisper to Berman. "I wish I looked like you."

During pledge week, Barbara was required to carry her future sorority sisters' schoolbooks, wear her clothes backward, and, in general, make a fool of herself, all the while expressing undying devotion to the group.

On Christmas Eve of 1944, Barbara and two other girls, Zelda Kaplan Silver and Harriet Schwartzman, were inducted into Lambda Pi at ceremonies held at Lou's Colonial Inn. It was a big event and all of Barbara's sorority sisters invited dates. Lou supplied food and soft drinks and the kids danced and watched the show, which featured the Duncan Sisters.

A couple of years later school authorities banned sororities and fraternities at Beach High; parents complained about the discrimination that existed, and the hurt it caused.

Around the time Barbara joined Lambda Pi she got her first big crush on a boy, Stan Reich, also fifteen, who played baseball for Beach High and was a member of the school's elite fraternity, Keystone. Barbara had invited everyone in her homeroom, including Reich, to a pool party on Palm Island.

A poor boy whose father was a grocer and whose mother worked in a dress shop to help make ends meet, Reich had never encountered such affluence as at Barbara's—the big house, the pool, the marble fountain, the huge closet the size of a vault where the Walterses stocked their groceries. It was like a scene out of *Goodbye Columbus*, Reich observed years later. The poor Jewish boy meeting the Jewish princess, except that Barbara appeared embarrassed by her family's apparent riches, according to friends.

After the party, she and Stan began dating. Reich faced

a typical teenage dilemma; he didn't have a car. To get to Palm Island from his parents' small apartment on Fourteenth Street in South Miami Beach, he had to take a series of buses, and if he stayed after midnight, when the last bus left, he'd have a long walk home. But he found Barbara worth the effort.

"She was really a wonderful girl," Reich said. "She was very pretty and slender. I really liked her hair and her eyes. She wasn't overly developed, but she had a nice figure and she had class. She was a refined young lady."

To Reich Barbara seemed to have everything, or almost everything. "I never saw her parents once," he observed. "Nobody was ever at the house. When I asked her why, she told me that her mother and father owned some nightclubs and were busy running them. I remember seeing her father's and sister's pictures on a table in the living room and asked about her sister, but Barbara really didn't want to talk about her. She did not want to talk about her father's businesses. She never, never wanted to talk about anything personal."

Most of the time Barbara and Stan would take romantic moonlit walks around the island. One night, after their second or third date, as they strolled hand in hand in front of Al Capone's mansion, Barbara allowed Reich to kiss her.

"It was kind of an awkward kiss," he remembered. "We bumped noses. I tried to show affection and she tried to show affection, but we really didn't know how to do it yet. There was certainly no passion involved. It was just kind of, 'Gee, I really like you' and 'Yeah, I really like you, too.' "

Barbara also became pals with Stan Reich's best friend, Ray Jacobson, who felt that Barbara had problems making friends because the other kids were wary of her as an outsider, and jealous of her father's affluence and prominence. He saw Barbara as "guarded about the kids taking advantage of her father's connections. The problems related to her sister also affected her outlook of the world. She was always concerned about her sister and that affected her relationships with other people."

The romance between Barbara and Stan eventually fizzled and she started dating a boy in her French class, Edward Klein, who was the president of Beach High's French club, which Barbara had joined. In 1941, the Kleins moved from Brooklyn to Florida for the warm weather which the boy required for his health. Like Stan Reich, Klein, the son of a traveling salesman, came from the poor South Beach area and didn't have a car, so he and Barbara often rode buses when they went out.

"She wasn't the most outgoing person in the world," Klein recalled. "She didn't have a bubbling personality. She was introverted and wasn't happy to be living in Florida. She wanted to be back in New York. But she was attractive and very bright. She wasn't flighty. She seemed to have her two feet on the ground. In the time I went out with her, I don't think we kissed once. We were very friendly without a good deal of romance."

Barbara seemed to be emerging somewhat from her shell, becoming more active in school life. On April 11, 1945, Beach High had its annual Student Day and Barbara taught a fourth-period English class. She also participated in the school's annual minstrel show, as a member of the chorus. It was a full-blown, Southern-style pageant, with some students in blackface.

In June the school term ended, and Lou decided to move the family back to New York to devote full time to the Latin Quarter there.

Most of his ventures in Florida had failed. Financially strapped, he was forced to give up much of his interest in the Miami Latin Quarter to Elias Loew.

While the family was in Florida, Lou made several unsuccessful attempts at producing vaudeville-style shows for the legitimate Broadway stage, losing money for himself, Loew, and other investors. His first spectacular, a musical revue called *Artists and Models*—a name he purchased from the Shuberts—bombed, despite headliners such as Jane Froman, Frances Faye, and the young Jackie Gleason. One critic called the show a "museum piece." Another Broadway effort, a variety show called *Take a Bow*, starring Chico Marx, was also panned.

Even worse, Lou's pride and joy—the Boston Latin Quarter—was gone.

"He actually lost the club in a gin rummy game," said Ben Abrams.

Lou had gotten into one of his all-night sessions at the Friars Club in New York. As usual, he was on a losing streak, a major one, but he refused to leave the game. Desperate for quick cash, Lou urgently called a business acquaintance in Boston and convinced him to back him. Over the phone he gave Lou a line of credit, with the Latin Quarter as collateral. Lou continued playing and losing. At dawn he was broke and the club was gone.

It was neither the first nor the last time Lou would risk the family farm at the card table.

Barbara felt relieved when she heard the family was returning to New York. Later, when she became famous, she would paint a dismal picture of that period of her life. Barbara's friend at Beach High, Shirley Berman, remembered being shocked when she read an article in which Barbara asserted that she didn't have one friend when she went to school there.

"I thought by being in the sorority she was accepted," said Berman. "I don't know whether she had this feeling that she was only being accepted because she was Lou Walters' daughter or that we really didn't like her. I liked her and I always thought that we were very good friends until I read that article."

John Throne, who became a psychologist, said, "Barbara wasn't happy in Miami. Maybe she just blocked the whole thing."

"THE VALUE OF SECRECY"

The family returned to New York, moving into a small, dark Victorian-style apartment in the Buckingham, a residential hotel at Fifty-seventh Street and Sixth Avenue, a noisy, bustling intersection in the heart of midtown Manhattan. Lou was financially strapped again and the Walterses were living like transients for the time being. Over the next few years, as Lou's fortunes rose and fell, the family would bounce from drab flats to luxurious penthouses overlooking Central Park or Park Avenue.

At sixteen, Barbara had ridden on the Walters roller coaster long enough. She had become a cynical, suspicious, and embittered young lady. While she craved Lou's attention and affection, she distrusted him and seethed with anger at his irresponsibility and financial recklessness. Not surprisingly this love-hate relationship would profoundly influence her feelings toward men and her relationships with them. As it turned out, Barbara would find herself immensely attracted to men of dark and powerful mien, much like her father's; like him, two of her three husbands would be show-business entrepreneurs. And it is an anomaly of Barbara's professional life that she would follow in the footsteps of the man whom she held in such contempt as a young woman, and of whose business she felt so ashamed.

Dena infuriated Barbara with her failure to face up to the severity of Lou's foolhardiness, and she resented her mother's preoccupation with Jackie, still missing the maternal attention that was focused on her retarded sister. Dena, Barbara felt, had lost touch with the reality of the family's situation. As Jackie got older, Dena began denying the extent of her retardation, viewing it merely as a speech defect. Barbara was the only one who faced the reality of how serious the situation was.

As for her own feelings toward Jackie, Barbara was riddled with guilt: Why, she would ask over and over, was she born such an achiever while Jackie was so deprived? Haunted by her sister's affliction, Barbara knew she would have to justify her own superior intelligence; she would, she realized, have to rise above the crowd. She dreamed of a life of success, stability, and financial security. She already was convinced that one day she would be responsible for her parents and sister.

"Barbara had a kind of strength and bitterness that we didn't have," said a close friend.

> She told me, "You can afford to be idealistic, but I have to do something in the real world." I remember very clearly her saying she had to have a career, that she really felt burdened by her retarded sister and her mother and father. She felt strongly she'd have to support them.
> Her attitude was tough, disciplined. She was rather grim and determined and more serious than most of the kids. I always had comfort. All my life my father earned a good, steady living. Barbara's family went from rags to riches a number of times. She knew she couldn't depend on her

father, and that her mother and retarded sister couldn't
depend on him for their old age. Barbara was a very intelligent girl, always. She was serious about responsibility.

In September 1945, Barbara unhappily entered her junior
year in high school. She hoped to return to Fieldston,
where she had friends, but the administration denied her
application because of her previous sudden departure to
Florida. Disappointed, she was forced to look elsewhere.

After taking an admissions test, Barbara was accepted
at Birch Wathen, an expensive private institution that one
graduate, Marcia Elson Rodman, a classmate of Barbara's,
described years later as "a small, gentile-run, Jewish
school."

Miss Louise Birch and Mrs. Edith Wathen, who had
come from Columbia Teachers College, founded the
school as a kindergarten in 1921. Birch had taught Theodore Roosevelt's children in the White House one summer
and had tutored Nelson Rockefeller when he was a child.

By the time Barbara arrived there, the school was considered progressive, but it really wasn't. "It was a reactionary,
closed environment," said another classmate, Helen Udell
Lowenstein. "We went down to a settlement house at
Thanksgiving time with the canned goods which it was cus-
tomary to collect, and the old lady who owned the school
cautioned us about taking a cab with a black driver."

What Birch Wathen offered its students was a firm
grounding in the basics, virtually guaranteeing admission
to an Ivy League or Seven Sisters college. The school was
then located in two townhouses at 149 West Ninety-third
Street, a block and a half from Broadway where the kids
grabbed a hamburger, a Coke, and a smoke at their favorite hangout, a place called Cord's. The students went to
the Henry Hudson Hotel for indoor athletics, and the girls
played field hockey in the Sheep Meadow in Central Park.

Birch Wathen reeked of Old World charm—the fireplace blazed in winter, copper pots were filled with flowers

in springtime, the rooms had wood paneling and wainscoting. Birch Wathen had much the same cachet as Fieldston. Academic standards were high, classes were small—there were only thirty-four in Barbara's entire 1947 graduating class. The students came from affluent and predominantly Jewish families. There were a few boys, mostly girls, many as cliquish and snobbish as those Barbara had encountered at Fieldston and Beach High.

Two groups predominated: the East Siders, some of whom came to school in chauffeured limousines or taxis, and the West Siders, who walked to school, some escorted by live-in servants, or doting parents, many of whom were German Jewish professionals, wealthy businessmen, intellectuals, or old money. Barbara was probably the only student in the history of the school at that point who lived south of Fifty-Ninth Street, let alone in a hotel.

"Birch Wathen was really snotty," said a classmate of Barbara's, Jeri Rosenberger Soman, the daughter of a prominent jeweler, who started at Birch Wathen in nursery school and lived on Park Avenue. "Barbara wasn't in either group. She would have liked to have been. I befriended her because nobody seemed to like her or wanted to talk to her. I felt sorry for this gal who had a speech impediment. She didn't have much of a sense of humor. She was sad, a real loner. It was hard for her, her father being what he was. In those days, being the owner of a nightclub didn't sound so classy. Barbara was sort of living down her parents' reputation."

Helen Udell Lowenstein also saw Barbara in a similar light. "She was a kid who had no home life. That's sad. I heard her talking about her parents being out until—I don't know if she said one o'clock. She saw them early in the morning and that was about it. That was a time when I was going home to active political arguments at dinner time and she didn't have that kind of dinner."

A fellow Birch Wathen student, David Kane, was once invited by Barbara to go to the Latin Quarter with her.

"After we found out that her father ran the club we used to kid her a lot about it."

It was hard for Barbara to escape Lou's notoriety. Every day the entertainment pages of the New York newspapers trumpeted advertisements for the Latin Quarter. The gossip columns, thanks to the club's press agent, Irving Zussman, always had a steady flow of items about the impresario, and the Broadway columnists reviewed the Latin Quarter shows.

When the Walterses moved into a beautiful apartment in the ritzy building at 998 Fifth Avenue, "people gossiped, saying, 'Oh, her father owns that *nightclub.*' It apparently was not the 'in' thing to be in that business at that time," said Natalie Lazrus Roberts, who was at Birch Wathen with Barbara. "That was a building that had the Delacortes of Delacorte Publishing; there was a former Secretary of the Navy living there."

At one point, Barbara's connection to the Latin Quarter became the object of lighthearted teasing in *Birch Peel,* a student parody of the regular school newspaper, *Birch Bark.* The story, dealing with the lives of Birch Wathen students, described Barbara as "the present owner of that successful club, 'The Arabian One Third.'"

Though done in jest, the mock newspaper article stung Barbara. She had become hypersensitive to criticism of any sort. Years later as a television star, she would be even more thin-skinned, sometimes overreacting to negative comments or stories about her in newspapers and magazines.

Besides Lou and Barbara, there also were whispers among the students about Dena. One close friend of Barbara's at Birch Wathen said a story had circulated that Barbara's mother had been a "bubble dancer" as a young girl and that's how Lou had met her.

Barbara's feelings regarding her perceived treatment at Birch Wathen stayed with her. She rarely acknowledged her connection to the school, and ignored reunions and requests to participate in alumni activities. "We have never been able to get her to step in here for two seconds," said an alumnus. "She simply won't reply to any of our letters."

Marcia Elson Rodman said Barbara was a difficult person to get to know. "As far as I was concerned, she was cold and distant. We eventually lived in the same building at 91 Central Park West where her parents had the penthouse and I used to meet her in the hallway and she'd walk right by me. She'd be in the elevator and not know who I was. That's difficult because we had such a small class at Birch Wathen. She was an entity who we knew was there. But we never broke her shell. We never got close to her."

Years later Rodman was involved in a business venture with political writer Theodore H. White, and learned from him that Barbara hadn't changed much from the way she remembered her. When Rodman told White that she'd gone to school with Barbara he winced. He told Rodman that he had once met Barbara at a party and found her "acerbic, difficult, and pushy." Barbara wasn't famous at the time, but she told him, "You may not know me now, but you *will* know me."

Pat Meyer Kovacs, a Park Avenue girl, said that if she had to vote for the Most Likely to Succeed in the class of 1947, "I would never have chosen Barbara. She was extremely bright but very introverted. She made no effort to be friendly. Granted it was very tough coming in when she did because most of us had been there a minimum of four years. But she was not the kind of person to make friends. [When she became famous] I couldn't believe she was the same Barbara Walters whom I knew in high school. I never thought she would end up in a profession where she would have to relate to other human beings."

Barbara tried to fit in as best she could at Birth Wathen, at least in terms of fashion. She wore the white wool socks, penny loafers, and sweaters that were popular with the girls. Barbara had a very small waist and she'd cinch her full, pleated skirts with wide leather belts, and wear simple but elegant jewelry, a gold or pearl necklace.

But even that effort on her part to become part of the crowd sparked criticism. One classmate said years later, "Although Barbara dressed like everybody, she didn't look comfortable in her bobby socks. It was appropriate attire and she looked like everybody else but she didn't seem comfortable in those clothes. She was just not a comfortable girl."

Despite her conservative outfits, Barbara had one outstanding feature that caught the attention of her classmates: her hands. She had long tapering fingers and her nails were carefully manicured and painted bright red, more like those of a Latin Quarter showgirl, or an East Side matron, than a high school junior.

Barbara's first and best friend at Birch Wathen was Joan Gilbert Peyser, a gifted pianist, who had entered with her in eleventh grade as a transfer student from the High School of Music and Art. Peyser's previous year had been much more traumatic than Barbara's: her mother had died suddenly of cancer; her grandfather had died from the shock of the tragedy, and her brother had been shipped to the Pacific in the last bloody months of the war in 1945. As the two new girls in the eleventh grade, both having gone through emotionally difficult times, they instantly bonded. Once again, mutual adversity had forged a friendship for Barbara, one that would last a lifetime.

"We were very different, disparate personalities when we were kids, but we meshed," said Peyser. "Barbara wasn't an outgoing person. She wasn't a gregarious girl at Birch Wathen, not very cheerful. She didn't have many friends. She was certainly very, very smart and a hard worker, but basically reclusive, rather isolated, not open, very private."

Because of a flair for writing, Barbara became one of

English teacher Margaret Elizabeth Stanton's pets. Two of Stanton's other favorites actually did become writers— Peyser, whose work included a best-selling biography of Leonard Bernstein, and Judith Tarcher, who became novelist Judith Krantz.

Because of Stanton's interest in her, Barbara became active in *Birch Leaves*, the school's literary magazine, eventually becoming the publication's "head reader" in her senior year under editor Pat Fry Morrissey. "It was quite a horrid little magazine," recalled Morrissey. "But I always admired Barbara. She was a very strong and intelligent person who had a rather rough family life. I always thought of Barbara as having a very glamorous life because of what her father did. I had never been in a nightclub."

One of the fictional short stories Barbara wrote for *Birch Leaves* was entitled "Beyond," a fantasy about loneliness, isolation, and death. Barbara wrote of finding herself in a place devoid of all people and animals, a place where everything was "silver or blue. . . . There was no warmth," she wrote. ". . . I looked for shelter, but there was none, just a vast emptiness. I huddled against a tree for warmth, but a silver twig pricked me and a silver branch pushed me away. How strange I thought, a tree pushing me away." Barbara described meeting an "exquisite" woman who welcomed her. "Her touch was like ice. . . . She came towards me, encircling me with her arms of ice. . . ." She concluded by writing, "There is a world of blue and silver and someday, sometime, I shall find it again."

Stanton once assigned the class to write an autobiographical story. Peyser took the assignment quite seriously. She wrote about the hellish year she had just experienced, and candidly dealt with the awakening of her sexuality. After Stanton graded the paper, Peyser showed it to Barbara.

"Barbara looked at it incredulously," recalled Peyser years later.

She said, "Oh, my God, no one expects you to tell the *truth* in an assignment like this!" She was shocked that I would have come forth with anything this revelatory. I took her reaction very seriously and I thought, How could I have so foolishly exposed myself? I didn't think, Oh, look at this tough girl!

In looking back on that incident what's important to me is that Barbara, even at the young age of sixteen, saw the value of secrecy. She was astute enough to know that indiscriminate self-revelation is not a skillful way to go through life. It was not that she advocated lying. She simply understood precisely *what to leave out.*

Barbara appeared to have had deep insecurities. I don't remember her as ever being free enough to open herself to anyone and my guess is she isn't very different today. If she were to write an autobiography, as I understand she says she will do, it will probably be a series of anecdotes devoid of any effort to use personal material to interpret her very complicated life.

Barbara's insecurities often surfaced in her relationships with young men. Sometimes after a date with a boy who liked her, she'd tell a friend: "I can't be sure he really likes me; maybe he's just interested in me because of my father." On the one hand, Barbara was embarrassed about Lou's life, but on the other she was quite aware of the notoriety, glamour, and fame that were attached to his name, and how seductive these were to some people.

Joan Peyser recalled meeting Barbara for lunch at NBC when she was on the *Today* show. Resembling a glamorous movie star that day, Barbara was wrapped in black mink down to her ankles and she wore sunglasses. As the elevator stopped at various floors, men greeted her warmly. When the car stopped on the ground floor of the RCA Building, Barbara pulled Peyser aside and demanded, "Tell me the truth, what do you think each of those men think of me?" Dumbfounded, Peyser could only respond that the men seemed friendly and courteous.

"I was overwhelmed," said Peyser,

> that at that stage of her life she would still be that insecure.
> The English subtitle of what she was asking was—"Does
> this one hate me? Does that one hate me? Does the other
> one hate me?" When we were in high school, Barbara
> asked, "Does he like me because of *me,* or because of who
> my father is?" She always thought it was something exter-
> nal—the money, the fame, not the fact that she was and
> is an interesting woman, or a good-looking woman.

The problem would plague Barbara's relationships with
men for years to come. And one day her daughter would
face a similar quandary—agonizing over whether people
liked her for herself or because she was Barbara Walters'
daughter.

Barbara dated fairly often while she was at Birch Wathen
but friends noted that she didn't appear to be passionate
or sexual. "I feel," said a friend, "that it was this dark business about her sister that was somewhere in her head. She
was trying to figure it all out."

Dr. Grossman, who wrote the book on retarded children and their normal siblings, said that relationships with
men and sexuality could be a problem for the healthy
daughter.

The normal child has come out of a family, she observed,
where "the marriage has been in difficulty all of her life
by virtue of the retarded child and that makes it hard to
trust that one could have a good relationship with a man.
When the normal sibling sees that the product of the parents' relationship has been death or damage, it also makes
it harder to trust, which means [she's] not going to be open
to establish genuine intimacy. [She's] going to be burdened
with old issues and old games that [she's] going to continue
to play out, rather than being free to meet as an adult and
build something new. Good sex requires trust. The normal

sibling would not have grown up trusting, so sex would be difficult. It would be complex and problematic."

Jackie was a constant in Barbara's life. At Dena's behest Barbara was placed in the position of bringing her sister into her social world, which was difficult because Barbara still withheld the fact of Jackie's existence from almost everyone.

"I never knew about her sister," said Jeri Soman, who had befriended Barbara when she first came to Birch Wathen. "Nobody knew in those days. She kept it to herself." Another classmate, Patricia Leavitt Rosenthal, recalled, "We all went to each other's houses. I got the impression Barbara was shy about having people know she had a retarded sister." Marcia Elson Rodman said, "I used to feel very sorry for Barbara. It was always drummed into my head that when you had a retarded sibling getting married and all those things were very difficult."

Barbara admitted only a few select friends to that very private part of her world that involved Jackie, who turned twenty while Barbara was at Birch Wathen. Under pressure from Dena, Barbara was forced to arrange dates for her sister. Jackie was not unattractive and there was no physical evidence that she was retarded, until she spoke. Like Barbara, she was a petite brunette. Overcompensating for Jackie's condition, Dena dressed her inappropriately in fashions more befitting a matron than a young woman, giving her an odd appearance. A typical outfit would include a pillbox hat, dress, high heels, and a fur piece around her neck. However, when she spoke, once she could get past the stuttering, she sounded like a child.

When Barbara went on a double date, she would sometimes ask the boy to bring a friend for Jackie. However, she would not tell him that her sister was retarded. It wasn't until the young man arrived at the apartment and was introduced to Jackie that he learned of her handicap, which made for embarrassing and awkward moments.

A close friend of Barbara's from Birch Wathen, remembering that time, said, "Can you imagine how she felt as a young girl bringing a guy into the house and introducing him to a sister who was retarded and whose speech was impaired? It was clearly embarrassing for Barbara socially. She resented Jackie during this time. But she never once showed her resentment or embarrassment. She hid it as best she could. Dena forced Jackie and Barbara into those social situations. It was the mother's way of being a decent human being to the retarded child. But it was very hard for Barbara."

When Joan Peyser married a psychiatrist, she got a call one day from Dena Walters asking if there was some way Joan's husband could direct her to a good speech therapist because she felt that Jackie's sole problem was her speech. "My husband and I looked at each other and said, 'Speech defect?' He certainly knew from my description that the problem was far greater than a speech defect. That was an incredible denial on the part of Mrs. Walters. It suggests that the Walterses never really confronted the fact of Jackie's retardation. But Barbara certainly did."

Dena's reaction to Jackie's situation was not unusual. Dr. Grossman pointed out that "When there were no obvious physical stigmata it was harder for the family to come to terms with the acceptance of the child as being damaged in some way. These families never gave up the feeling of 'Well, if this kid really tried, they could do it.'"

As recently as early 1989, several years after Jackie's death, the extent of her retardation was still the subject of dispute within the family. "Jackie was not *really, really, really* retarded," said Shirley Budd. "Unfortunately the minute she'd say hello to a doctor, she was immediately stamped retarded because it would take her ten minutes to say hello or how are you."

The spring of 1947 was a joyous time for the Birch Wathen senior class; graduation was near.

With college looming, Barbara took the entrance examination at Sarah Lawrence, a small, progressive school for women in the New York suburb of Bronxville, a thirty-minute train ride from Grand Central Station. She was accepted for admission because of her essaylike responses to pages of questions of a personal, philosophical, and literary nature. The school had a fine faculty and high academic standards. But Barbara's criteria for choosing Sarah Lawrence were location and social life: it was close to home and several of her friends from Fieldston were going there.

As was traditional at Birch Wathen as graduation neared, the seniors devoted an assembly to the reading of poetry, with the selections ranging from the works of W. S. Gilbert to those of Robert Lowell. Margaret Stanton directed the event, and Helen Udell Lowenstein acted as the master of ceremonies. *Birch Bark*, which ran a story about the ceremony, noted that "Barbara Walters read [W. W.] Gibson's somber poem, 'The Stone.' The rather depressing atmosphere created by this poem was immediately dispelled when Dave Klotz read Ogden Nash's amusing verse, 'The Banquet.' "

The class yearbook was distributed to the students. It showed a girl in bobby socks and saddle shoes holding a 1947 pennant. In Peyser's, Barbara wrote an intense, emotional, and loving entry, noting how wonderful Peyser had been to her, and how her sense of humor and understanding had helped Barbara get through a difficult time in her life. Barbara said she wanted and needed Peyser's friendship forever.

Barbara posed for her yearbook picture, looking forlorn, unsmiling. The quotation under her name, from Francis Quarles, a seventeenth-century English poet, read: "The glory of a firm, capacious mind."

COLLEGE, COHN, AND THE COLD WAR

Can a school without classrooms, without bells to summon laggards to work, whose avowed ideal is few or no rules, and whose student government can defy faculty suggestion . . . survive?"

That was the question the New York *World* posed to readers in an article about Sarah Lawrence College nine months after the institution opened in October 1928.

The school was the brainchild of educator Sarah Bates Lawrence, who envisioned an experimental curriculum in the liberal arts for women. When she died in 1926, her husband, William Van Duzer Lawrence, established the thirty-one-acre campus on the grounds of his country home, in Bronxville. It was an odd location for such an avowed avant-garde teaching institution; Bronxville was an uppercrust, ultraconservative enclave where few, if any, minorities could buy homes.

Sarah Lawrence sparked controversy from its inception, rewriting the old rules of college education. Required courses were eliminated in favor of a curriculum planned individually for each student; conventional examinations and a normal grading system were replaced by faculty reports, and the lecture system was abandoned for small classes and discussion groups. The only other school with a similar bent was Bennington College in Vermont.

By the time Barbara Walters arrived to start her first semester in September 1947, as a member of the class of 1951, Sarah Lawrence had become a chic and expensive place to receive an education. (Biographical sources state that Barbara was in the class of 1953, which, like her date of birth in those references, is inaccurate.)

Sarah Lawrence attracted a mix of Wasp party-girl debutantes who craved New York nightlife; self-styled bohemians in shirttails and dungarees who were drawn by the drama, dance, and art courses offered as part of the curriculum; brilliant academic achievers who felt more comfortable in an environment less structured than Barnard or Radcliffe; and a contingent of more conventional, well-heeled, predominantly Jewish girls from New York City—Barbara's crowd.

Barbara arrived on campus with a wardrobe that cost a fortune. Before school started, she and Dena went on a shopping spree in the exclusive fifth-floor Country Clothes department at Lord & Taylor, where Barbara chose expensive plaid skirts, silk blouses, and cashmere sweaters.

"This was the first time I had ever been exposed to this kind of Jewish American princess consumerism," said Theodore Joffe Edelman, a campus activist involved in European relief work and civil rights, who was president of the Student Council in 1950. "Every day I saw her wear something different. Barbara was not considered to be in the top group because she was very much a Jewish princess and in those days there was a very intellectual, politically oriented, sharp, with-it kind of group at Sarah Lawrence, and she was the ultimate consumer type."

When Barbara moved her things into a suite on the third floor of a Tudor-style dormitory named after a charter trustee of the college, Julia Titsworth—the residents called the place " 'Sworth" because of the anatomical image the name evoked—Barbara was thinking vaguely of studying acting or writing, or of taking courses that would lead to a teaching career.

The next four years—Barbara's college years—were a turbulent time in America.

With the end of World War II, unprecedented prosperity was sweeping the land. Postwar industrial strikes had ended with large salary increases for labor, and the United States was quickly returning to a consumer economy. President Harry Truman lifted wage, price, and salary controls. Americans were on a spending spree. Reunited with their families, veterans took advantage of the GI Bill to buy homes in the new suburban developments that were rising across the land; shiny cars and spiffy labor-saving appliances were on their shopping lists, too. Of the two and a half million students matriculating that fall of 1947, more than half were war veterans; for the first time in its history Sarah Lawrence admitted about fifty men, to the delight of some of the girls and teachers.

In the late 1940s, most Americans still got their news from radio and newspapers and their entertainment at the movies. But those who could afford them were starting to buy television sets. Several months before Barbara started college, *Kraft Television Theater*, the first regularly scheduled dramatic series, went on the air. Between Barbara's freshman and sophomore years, the number of television sets in American homes jumped from 15,000 to 190,000. Soon names like Milton Berle, Howdy Doody, Ed Sullivan, Arthur Godfrey, Kukla, Fran, and Ollie, and Dave Garroway would become household words. Studies started to show that children in homes with TVs were spending as much time in front of the sets as attending school.

In 1948, the political conventions in Philadelphia became the first major news and public affairs event to be televised nationally, with John Cameron Swayze, a former Kansas City *Journal Post* reporter, as the anchorman. Swayze soon was hired at $110,000 annually to anchor the nightly *Camel News Caravan*, which ran film clips of world events, used crude graphics, and had reporters in the field. Every show ended with a shot of a smoldering Camel cigarette in an ashtray; the sponsor was Reynolds Tobacco. Stations were being added every month to the networks of NBC and DuMont, with ABC and CBS on their heels. That year the Radio Corporation of America demonstrated color television for the first time.

Despite the postwar recovery, events here and abroad were taking an ominous turn and television news, still in its infancy, would mature quickly in documenting them.

Our ally in the war, the Soviet Union, had become our arch-enemy. As statesman Bernard Baruch warned a Senate committee, "We are in the midst of a cold war which is getting warmer."

The Cold War.

Suddenly "Commies" were behind every bush; the "Red Scare" was abroad in the land. The House un-American Activities Committee (HUAC) targeted Hollywood, probing subversives in the film industry; soon present and former federal officials became subjects of committee scrutiny, followed by academics, intellectuals, artists, and writers.

"I have here in my hand a list of two hundred and five . . . members of the Communist Party . . . still working and shaping policy in the State Department," declared Joseph McCarthy, an obscure Senator from Wisconsin, in a speech before a Republican women's club in Wheeling, West Virginia, in February 1950.

The tactics of the Senator and his soon-to-be sidekick—a young federal prosecutor from New York named Roy

Marcus Cohn—would destroy many lives and spread fear, hysteria, and hatred. Cohn's reputation grew from his participation in the still-controversial atom bomb spy-ring prosecution and execution of Julius and Ethel Rosenberg. Cohn was a junior assistant to Irving Saypol, then U.S. Attorney for the Southern District of New York, who oversaw the case, which began with the Rosenbergs' arrest in the summer of 1950.

Some of the nation's universities and colleges, especially bastions of liberalism like Sarah Lawrence, became targets of HUAC and McCarthyism. At Sarah Lawrence, President Harold Taylor objected to the committee tactics and refused to cooperate by forcing faculty members to sign loyalty oaths. As a result, the school was on the committee's hit list. Concerned students and teachers rose to the defense of friends and colleagues accused, usually without basis, of un-American activities.

Among those campus activists, Barbara Walters was nowhere to be found. Instead, the woman whose friends and news sources one day would run the political spectrum from President Richard M. Nixon to Cuban leader Fidel Castro, from Egypt's President Anwar el-Sadat to Israeli Prime Minister Menachem Begin, spent her college years either oblivious to, or consciously ignoring, the political and social turmoil swirling around her on and off campus.

"Barbara wasn't very interested in political issues. She wasn't active in college. She was not prominent in any way," said Cathryn Mansell, who taught literature and drama at Sarah Lawrence and had Barbara as a student.

One of the burning campus political issues at the time involved a member of the Student Council who was denied entry into the United States from her native Canada after a Christmas break because a photograph of her marching in a May Day parade had appeared earlier in a New York tabloid. Suspected of being a Communist, the incident ended her career at Sarah Lawrence despite vocal protests by faculty and students.

"The school was very politically active at that time. It was considered to be quite 'Red' by the academic community as a whole, but it was also considered to be quite dilettante. People called us smoked-salmon socialists," said Edith Reveley Remoy, who served as editor-in-chief of Sarah Lawrence's weekly newspaper, *The Campus*, belonged to the Student Council, and lived in Barbara's dorm.

Regarding the case of the ousted student, Remoy said, "There were people on campus who not only stood up but who screamed at that time. It was a very controversial issue. There were some really outspoken people in the student body. Barbara was not one of the strident ones. The one word that comes zooming in at me about her is chic, always well turned out, really elegant."

Naturally, classmates of Barbara's were very much surprised years later when she surfaced as a high-powered television newswoman and interviewer.

When Barbara was a sophomore, Harold Taylor had a vacancy in the English Department and invited the writer Mary McCarthy to be an instructor for a year.

After her term ended, McCarthy castigated the college in a caustic satire called *The Groves of Academe*, excerpted in *The New Yorker* in 1951, and published in full a year later to rave reviews.

The novel dealt with Jocelyn College, a progressive school for women. The plot focused on a popular, outspoken, but lazy literature instructor, Henry Mulcahy, who got his walking papers from college president Maynard Hoar, a liberal who had fought against the Communist witch hunts of the time. Mulcahy decided shrewdly that the only way he could save his job was to pretend that he was a Communist; Hoar would never fire him because it would smack of precisely the kind of right-wing tactics he despised. In the end, Hoar resigned and Mulcahy remained.

McCarthy wrote thus of Jocelyn, its students, and their parents:

. . . the stiff-spined, angry only children with inhibitions
about the opposite sex, being entrained here remedially by
their parents, as they had been routed to the dentist for
braces, the wild-haired progressive-school rejects, offspring
of broken homes, the sexually adventurous youths looking
to meet their opposite numbers . . . the cold peroxided
beauties who had once done modeling for Powers and were
here while waiting for a screen-test, the girls . . . who could
"sit on" their hair and wore it down their backs, Godiva-
style, and were named Rina and Blanca . . . the conventional Allysons and Pattys whose favorite book was *Winnie-
the-Pooh* . . .

The McCarthy story caused anger and concern among a
number of students, but again Barbara's voice was silent.
"She didn't call attention to herself in any way," recalled
Harold Taylor. "I don't think Barbara was interested in
any of it," added Bessie Schonberg, who directed theater
and dance at Sarah Lawrence.

It certainly was a college where you could easily be involved. We were very active, very outspoken, very political—but not Barbara. She lived a fairly happy life as an
undergraduate doing courses that she enjoyed with profes-
sors whom she admired. But she did not stand out as a
particular personality. It's fascinating that an intelligent
young person like herself could be oblivious, or apparently
oblivious, to all those commotions that were going on. She
was in a very expensive college having a very expensive education and probably enjoying it most of the time in a social way.

Appropriately, a cartoon next to Barbara's photo in the
1951 class yearbook depicted her as an ostrich with its
head in the sand.

While others railed against the questionable motives and
tactics of HUAC and Joe McCarthy, Barbara had become
friends with, and was actually starting to date, McCarthy's

sidekick, the secretly homosexual Roy Cohn, beginning an intimate, lifelong friendship.

Cohn, whom many considered physically unattractive, was introduced to Barbara for the first time in Miami by her father—at Barbara's request. According to Cohn, Lou said, "My daughter wanted to meet you. She's a great admirer of yours." Barbara shook hands with Roy, saying, "I wanted to meet you. Period."

Barbara would always be attracted to powerful men like Lou; Roy Cohn was the first to fit the mold.

Both Barbara and Roy had gone to Fieldston, but only for a short time and not together, although they had mutual friends. At Columbia University Law School, Cohn got his law degree at age twenty, and was working as an Assistant U.S. Attorney at twenty-two, when Barbara was a junior at Sarah Lawrence.

Years later, after she became famous, one of the cherished mementos in Barbara's office was a copy of Roy Cohn's book, *A Fool for a Client,* which was inscribed: "For Chickie—who I always knew would accomplish Joe McCarthy's dream of restoring me to daytime television." (The reference was to Cohn's controversial role in the televised Army-McCarthy hearings.)

Anne Williams Ferguson, who met Barbara at Sarah Lawrence and became a longtime friend, remembered that Barbara and Cohn were dating "seriously" while she was at college. "I was appalled," declared Ferguson, noting that she and another close friend of Barbara's at Sarah Lawrence and later, Dorothy Morrow Sheckman, couldn't "talk her out of it." On one occasion, she remembered, Cohn picked Barbara up on campus in a limousine. "I saw her getting into the car. Roy Cohn was very recognizable."

Irving Zussman, the Latin Quarter's press agent, recalled seeing Barbara and Roy spend evenings together at the club during the time Barbara was at Sarah Lawrence. "I was there when they came in. They had a preferred table on the balcony near her father's table where Lou could look over the whole room," said Zussman.

"Barbara didn't often get passionate about people," Joan Peyser observed.

> [But] the first person she became extremely passionate about, and that only in the head, was Roy Cohn. I recall her talking about him after meeting him and the intensity of her attachment to him. [But] I never heard Barbara use the word "love." Even when we were adolescents who were vulnerable and capable of having crushes, I don't think I ever heard Barbara use the word "love." *Ever.* About anyone.
>
> I know she wanted to marry Cohn. At least, I remember her telling me she did.

Looking back, Peyser felt Barbara was unaware of Cohn's homosexuality, which he kept well hidden, denying it to the day he died of AIDS in 1986. "Barbara felt the only problem with Roy was that he was very tied to his mother. She didn't understand. None of us did. We knew virtually nothing about homosexuality then," Peyser said.

Anne Williams Ferguson agreed with Peyser's assessment of the Walters-Cohn relationship. "I think it was love on Barbara's part. I don't think she had any idea [Cohn was gay.] I don't think *he* cared. Barbara was the one who had the crush or whatever you want to call it."

Barbara's cousin, Shirley Budd, acknowledged that Barbara had told her that Roy once asked for her hand in marriage. Cohn himself said that the proposal was made in the early 1960s.

"Roy meant it," said Budd. "He would have married Barbara in a minute if she would have just played his hostess. His true love I think was his mother. She was always the hostess for him. When she died he would have loved to have someone like Barbara. Roy was a homosexual, but he adored Barbara."

Once asked about his relationship with Barbara vis-à-vis his mother, Cohn said, "She and my mother never got along. They were both strong women. My mother always wanted me to get married as long as I didn't get married to *anybody*." Roy had lived with his mother, Dora, until she died—when he was forty-two.

Despite Cohn's desire to marry Barbara, Budd asserted that Barbara and Roy's relationship was platonic. "Everything Barbara gained from Roy was intellectual, or newsworthy, or gossipy," Budd said. "Everything that Roy did for Barbara was done intellectually—not physically or sexually or sensuously."

Their lifelong relationship, whether romantic or platonic, mystified and horrified Barbara's friends, family, and broadcasting colleagues. None could fathom the association between Barbara and Cohn, who went from being the despised Red-baiter to mob mouthpiece, Manhattan disco maven, and connoisseur of rough trade.

John Lord, who would become a close friend and associate of Barbara's when they joined the *Today* show, said, "Roy was a bastard. One could say that to Barbara and she would still say, 'Well, on the other hand he's very kind and he takes care of me.' "

Anne Williams Ferguson recalled once having lunch with Barbara and expressing concern about her relationship with Cohn. "I said, 'Barbara, are you out of your tree? This guy is a crook. He can only damage your reputation.' She acted defensively." Bessie Schonberg observed, "I think she's probably been very innocent in some ways—not that you could possibly really be good friends with Roy Cohn and be innocent."

"Barbara didn't associate Roy Cohn with anything unpleasant," according to Shirley Budd. "She has the ability to turn things like that off if she wants. With Roy Cohn—who was hated by ninety percent of the people for half of his life—Barbara absolutely blotted all of that out of her mind. She was able to do that because it wasn't pleasant and she doesn't like to think about unpleasant things."

Barbara developed her form of mind control during her childhood and adolescence, blocking out to some degree the problems of her family, Budd said. "Otherwise she wouldn't have risen to the heights she did under those circumstances."

In 1968, Cohn, by then the ultimate New York power broker, would perform a service of enormous magnitude for Barbara, a favor for which she would be forever grateful and in his debt, one that would bond her to him long after he was dead and buried.

When she first went to college, Barbara had dreams of becoming an actress and took courses in that direction. She admired and felt she resembled the actress Katharine Cornell. Barbara was lucky in that she arrived at Sarah Lawrence at a time when the performing arts were being taken more seriously and making great strides. The college had gathered an exceptional array of talented instructors. One of those with whom Barbara studied was Madalyn O'Shea Gray, head of the acting program. In the mid-1930s, Gray had been associated with Hallie Flanagan of the Federal Theater Project. Barbara also worked closely with John Blankenship, a brilliant set designer, who directed some of the department's productions. Among others with whom Barbara had contact were the choreographer José Limon and the composer Norman Dello Joio, whose opera *The Triumph of Saint Joan* had its world premiere at the college.

One of Barbara's chums and, for a time, her roommate, was Marcia Barnet, a wealthy girl from Woodmere, Long Island, who also had a vague interest in becoming an actress. Barnet was a chic, sophisticated, tough-talking, hard-drinking young woman who went under the unusual nickname of "Mike." She was dark-haired like Barbara, but more striking, outgoing, flamboyant, and rebellious. Barbara was always controlled and sober, not one to break the rules. They made a curious pair.

When the weather got warm on the mostly female campus, the shapely Barnet would show off her sensational legs and body in the tightest and shortest shorts imaginable in those days. "Very sporty," was the way one classmate saw her. An expert horsewoman and aficionada of German shepherds, Barnet was caricatured in her yearbook as a sexy fish with long eyelashes drinking out of a bottle. "That wench is stark mad, or wonderful froward," said a quotation from *The Taming of the Shrew.*

In the period when they were bosom buddies, Barbara and Marcia would often go up to the roof of Titsworth on warm, sunny days to work on their tans. Barbara was usually anxious and obsessive about everything she did, so she planned her tanning regimen carefully: she would tie her big toes together with a piece of cord to keep her legs from turning outward, thus assuring an even tan. Even with something so mundane, Barbara was a perfectionist, a trait that would come to the fore in coming years.

Barbara and Marcia "were inseparable," recalled Shirley Plavin Klein, who was two years behind Barbara's and Marcia's class, but lived in Titsworth and eventually inherited Barbara's room, the biggest in the dorm. "Barbara and Marcia were always on campus together and there were many, many weekends when they went into the city together. Marcia was a party girl, a fun girl."

When Barbara and Marcia first reported to Madalyn O'Shea Gray's theater class, their attitude was "What's this all about?" recalled a classmate. "They came across as rich, spoiled, and tough."

In her sophomore year, Barbara tried out for and was cast in the December 1949 production of Irish playwright Sean O'Casey's *Juno and the Paycock,* in which she played Mary Boyle, the daughter of a ne'er-do-well Irishman, Jack Boyle. With her Boston–New York accent and slight speech impediment, Barbara did not come across like Ethel Barrymore.

"I have the memory of her not being very good," said Jerry Weiss, who played the role of Joxer Daly. "She seemed a little stiff." One of the war veterans at Sarah Lawrence, Weiss graduated in Barbara's class and later went on to become a professor of drama at Utica College.

One of the actresses in *Juno*, Shirley Plavin Klein, recalled that Barbara worked extraordinarily hard on her part, but bombed on stage.

"Her interest in theater was more than her ability, which wasn't outstanding," said Klein. "I remember them rehearsing her and rehearsing her. She wanted very much to get every last bit of whatever help she could. She wanted it to be a very good performance. She tried very hard. There was nothing to work with."

John Blankenship, who taught Barbara in the theater department, put it more bluntly:

> Barbara wasn't a very good actress. She wasn't one of the outstanding talents. She never had a very important part, but she was diligent and determined, bright and dependable. But she wasn't an outstanding student. She probably wanted to be an actress, and of course her father owned the Latin Quarter. [But] she didn't play off the contacts of her father. If anything she played them down.
>
> There were people who were talented at Sarah Lawrence. Unfortunately, a lot of the people who are the most gifted actors and actresses don't go into it because they can't take the rejection. [But] I don't think rejection particularly bothered Barbara.

Wearing a leotard with a cutout of a musical instrument on it, Barbara also appeared in the production of *Tubby the Tuba,* a delightful operetta performed by the players for children at local hospitals. Once or twice a week, as part of a community project, she tutored poor children in dramatics at a settlement house in nearby Yonkers.

Bessie Schonberg recalled having conversations with Esther Raushenbush about Barbara's plan of study and career goals. At various times Raushenbush was dean of the school and its president. But she also acted as a student adviser, or don, as it was called at Sarah Lawrence. Barbara had gone to Raushenbush because she couldn't make up her mind whether she wanted to study theater and acting or to pursue literature and writing.

"I think Raushenbush warned Barbara in a way against going into theater, that she thought that Barbara's gift was stronger in the literary field and I think Barbara listened," said Schonberg, who agreed with Raushenbush's assessment of Barbara's theatrical talent, or lack thereof.

"I had all the pull to be an actress but no push," Barbara confessed much later in her life. "My father certainly introduced me to all the right people, but I was really too shy. If I were told I was not right for a part, I would have taken it personally."

In good spirit, Barbara helped Schonberg and five other female teachers with a dance routine for the faculty's annual show. On the evening of the performance, each of the teachers—all well over the age of consent—pranced on stage wearing genuine Latin Quarter showgirl costumes, skimpy, befeathered, and besequined. Looking them over backstage with a cool eye, Barbara said, "Go ahead, girls, have a fine time!"

Barbara took Raushenbush's advice seriously, because she started writing about acting rather than doing it, becoming the dramatics editor and theater and movie critic for *The Campus.* Barbara had two columns—"Reviewer's Corner" and "Aisle Seat."

Barbara showed a talent for the simple, uncomplicated style of the broadcast news writer that would help her advance in television some years later.

No extraordinary journalistic talent was necessary to get on the *Campus* editorial staff, nor was a burning desire essential to be a fledgling Margaret Mitchell or Anne O'Hare McCormick. All a girl had to do was show her face in the office on the first floor of Dudley Lawrence and a job would be found for her.

At the time Barbara made her appearance, there was a stack of gratis tickets sitting on feature editor Deby Kirschenbaum Salama's desk, with no one apparently willing or able to take the time to go into the city to see the plays and movies the publicists were promoting.

The paper needed a "critic," and show business was the only subject about which Barbara seemed to have a serious interest, so her name was added to the masthead, and her byline began appearing regularly, mostly covering artsy off-Broadway productions, along with campus theater. The job gave Barbara a sense of importance, and a legitimate excuse to go into the city on week nights when she did much of her reviewing.

One of the plays that most fascinated Barbara was *The Father*, by August Strindberg, which she saw at the Provincetown Playhouse on MacDougal Street in Greenwich Village. In her October 12, 1949, review Barbara wrote: " 'The Father' tells the story of a husband and wife who continually quarrel with each other in their efforts to gain supremacy in the home. However, in a larger sense, it is the story of 'the strife between the sexes,' man's conflict with woman, and their inability to really understand each other. . . . In [Strindberg's] eyes, woman is man's enemy and ultimate destroyer. . . ."

The editors thought of Barbara as a hard worker who never missed a deadline, but whose writing left something to be desired. They ran her heavily edited pieces to encourage more students to work for the paper. The hope was that others would say, "Well, if Barbara Walters can do it . . ."

College life didn't appear to raise Barbara's political or social consciousness. But being at Sarah Lawrence did have one positive effect. For the first time since her brief stay at Fieldston, Barbara found herself an integral part of a tight-knit circle of friends: bright, affluent, smug young women who never had to deal with the kind of rampant insecurities that fed on Barbara like tapeworms.

Being part of the group gave Barbara a patina of their steadiness and self-assurance, concealing the fragility that made her so shy and withdrawn. There was a harder edge about her, a more polished veneer. On the surface now, she appeared to be confident and secure.

Moreover, membership in the group helped erase some of the hurt Barbara still carried as a result of her high school sorority rejection. She now had her own informal sorority; the girls even rendezvoused in Europe during the summer between their junior and senior years. Members of the group felt like sisters to Barbara; her real one was mostly a burden. These girls would remain loyal to one another for a lifetime. They'd be honored guests or bridesmaids at each other's weddings, offer solace when a divorce occurred, have a shower for the birth of a baby, and mourn at the funeral when one died at an early age.

"Barbara enjoyed being part of the group. It was important to her," said a woman who was a member.

> All of the girls were quite affectionate toward one another—warm, loving, and dear. They were exchanging views for corroboration. They could talk to each other without meeting up with too much criticism. Most of us were virgins. Barbara was most definitely a virgin. She was afraid of being hurt. She was frightened, skittish. Most of our discussions were really over "Do I do it, or don't I do it?" with a man. The consensus was, "If I sleep with him, I'll have to know him over a period of time or marry him."

As an individual, though, Barbara was still emotionally troubled and would remain so for many years to come.

Barbara always wore expensive, fashionable clothes but in college she became one of the best dressed, which added to the image of her as a happy and popular girl. Everyone admired her chicness and style, which were partly due to advice from one of the girls in the group who later became a fashion magazine editor.

"Barbara looked marvelous," said a friend and classmate, Muriel Greenhill.

> She was a model's size and always had new clothes. I was always struggling to lose the extra ten pounds and was really very envious of what seemed to me her ability to wear anything and everything. She was much more confident about clothes and looks and makeup. She had always been with women who dressed well, show business and theater people. She picked it up.
>
> One day we were shopping at Saks Fifth Avenue and she said, "I'm going to show you that I am not a perfect person who can put on anything and look marvelous. I'm human just like you are." And she chose something that was not particularly becoming and tried it on to show me. That was a rather generous thing to do. I had no sense of confidence. It was not a strange thing to do. She was trying to show me that I looked good in some things and not in others and she looked good in some things and not in others. She was showing me there wasn't any magic about it.

In hopes of expanding her popularity, Barbara opened her parents' apartment in New York for social gatherings.

The Walterses had moved into a duplex and on Friday nights some of the girls would take the train into the city from Bronxville and meet their dates at the apartment before going to a Broadway show or nightclub.

The guests entered on the lower level and came up the staircase where Dena, acting as hostess, greeted them with Jackie at her side. "You had to talk to Jackie," said a classmate of Barbara's who was a frequent visitor. "Dena was pretty gutsy to set up shop there in order to give this daughter an opportunity to talk to people. It was embarrassing for all concerned, but there was no way to get by her." For most of Barbara's friends at Sarah Lawrence, the initial visit to the apartment was the first time they learned that Barbara had a sister, let alone a retarded one.

Despite her love for Jackie, Barbara still found it trying having her around, especially when young men came to call. One of Barbara's dates at the time, Joe Leff, the brother of campus friend Ruth Leff Siegel, said, "Barbara was troubled about Jackie. Jackie used to embarrass her a little. I was always a great favorite of Jackie's. When I came to the house Jackie would be waiting for me while Barbara was finishing getting dressed. Barbara would always be a little put off that Jackie was involving me in conversation. Barbara let [her feelings] be known."

Despite how dedicated Dena was to Jackie, many of Barbara's college friends, even members of the group, had difficulty warming up to her. They found Dena "terribly consumed with looking good" . . . "very affected" . . . "the most appalling sort of social climber" . . . "no culture" . . . "no depth." But Barbara seemed to have become closer to her mother during her college years.

In her junior year, with the support of the group, Barbara was elected president of Titsworth, which gave her a seat on the Student Council. She'd hold court on the third floor in her large corner room, the most comfortable in Titsworth, airy and light with a big bay window.

Barbara was responsible for making certain that the forty or so girls in the dorm abided by the school's loose-knit rules about signing out, not having boys in their rooms, and not drinking. Barbara and other dorm presidents were on a student discipline committee that dealt with serious breaches of regulations, and she was thought of as being "reasonable, ameliorative, equitable—not going to either extreme" in meting out punishment, recalled Edith Remoy.

Often girls came to her with personal problems, which she took to heart, offering guidance and advice; or she acted on her own when a crisis developed. Because she had grown up with a handicapped sister, Barbara had a maturity and sensitivity toward the problems of women that others seemed to lack.

When a nasty dispute arose in another dorm between a popular Jewish art student from New York and a bright black premed student—an incident in which charges of racism and anti-Semitism were starting to be hurled—Barbara and members of her group stepped in to ease the tension by inviting the Jewish girl to move into Titsworth with them.

While sororities were not permitted at Sarah Lawrence, strong cliques developed within the dorms based on ethnic, religious, and regional similarities. Cliques even formed on different floors of the dorms. In Titsworth, during Barbara's tenure, the gentile girls on the first floor had little interaction with the third-floor Jewish crowd, and Barbara made no attempt to change things.

"Barbara never came into our rooms and we never went into her rooms," said Joan McLellan Tayler, who came from San Francisco. "There was just a separation which you get with groups of people. I never saw any communication between her and the California girls, for instance. I didn't consider her to be friendly. I don't remember her being a person who smiled. Barbara was somebody in the dormitory who we weren't particularly fond of. There was an attitude that she felt she was better than we were."

Barbara's crowd speculated that anti-Semitism existed at the college because they had all been assigned to Titsworth, many of them on the third floor. "It was such a subtle thing. We all showed up at school and we were all in the same little house," said Muriel Greenhill, a Jewish New Yorker. "We all cared about the college, and felt we were lucky to be there and we were not particularly inclined to question that sort of thing at that point in history."

Margaret Straus, a New Yorker, who lived down the hall from Barbara for two years, remembered Barbara's group as "sort of a private club . . . a pack. They were a little defensive. They seemed to have barriers. They seemed to accept certain people more as friends than others. It had to do with their New York Jewish backgrounds. It was more of an inclination on their part, but I don't think they verbalized it."

Straus recalled a day when several Titsworth girls knocked on her door "and asked me point-blank whether I was Jewish. They couldn't decide, and I refused to tell them."

As part of her confident new image at Sarah Lawrence, Barbara dated often, with Roy Cohn and others. By the time she was a senior, Barbara was thought of as a social butterfly by some of her classmates.

The only telephones in Titsworth were three pay phones on the first floor and they always seemed to be ringing with calls for Barbara from her suitors. The freshmen, whose rooms were near the phones, became her unofficial receptionists, yelling up the stairs, "Bobbie Walters, phone!" Most of Barbara's dates were with young men like Cohn who were pursuing careers in the professions.

Ruth Leff Siegel introduced Barbara to her brother, Joe, and they dated on and off until well after Barbara left college. A Columbia graduate, Joe was tall, blond, athletic. Five years Barbara's senior and working in the family's yarn-spinning business, he found Barbara attractive, interesting, charming, and articulate.

"We were always very good friends, but we *never* . . . That may sound peculiar but that's the way it was," Leff recalled. "I'm of a generation—and a lot of guys were of a generation—that felt a woman who is that bright and alert and aware tended to put guys off who just wanted to get in a girl's pants. Barbara was most attractive and had a lovely figure. [But] I don't recall her being one of the girls I made a move on."

Barbara was a good pal who would go out of her way to do a male friend a favor. "One time I was down in Florida with some fellows and we had nothing to do," Leff said. "I wasn't seeing Barbara at that time but I knew she'd be down there. I called her and said, 'Barbara, I'm here with so and so—how about if we come down to the Latin Quarter and you fix us up with some dates for after the show?' She arranged for us to go out with some of the showgirls."

Another man who went out with Barbara while she was in college—he later became a doctor with a lucrative practice in New York—had a different view of Barbara. "Let's put it this way, she hasn't changed very much. I dated a lot with her. This woman was exactly the same then as she is now—a cold bitch. She was and is a very cold, tough, hard-driving, self-involved, egotistical woman. She had a lot of problems. Her home was not a warm, loving place. There's no question about that, and that had a lot of effect on how she was with men."

Barbara also faced a problem common to many Sarah Lawrence women: men assumed that since they went to such a progressive school, they were sexually liberated. But her attitude in college was "If you want me, marry me," which understandably left a lot of her dates angry and frustrated. She was quite conventional and, at that time, the conventional thing was to be a virgin.

Relationships with men would always be difficult for Barbara. Dealing with the opposite sex was one of the few areas in her life in which she did not toe the middle line; she either appeared cold and distant or acted like a lovestruck teenager.

Returning to campus one Sunday from New York, Shirley Plavin Klein ran into Barbara at Grand Central and found the president of Titsworth, whom she always thought so confident and self-assured, obsessing over whether the man she dated that weekend really liked her.

"She just kept retracing the whole thing," said Klein, "asking me whether she should have said this or that to him. She was not sure where she stood when the date was over and she was agonizing about whether or not she would see him again.

"She was this very sophisticated, kind of impersonal girl. She was always busy with her social life, which was well established, and I was kind of in awe of her. But that day I saw a very deep hurt somewhere in her. There was a sadness about her. I could sense it. I saw it in her eyes."

While Barbara had lots of dates, she "wasn't self-confident with men," said Barbara's friend, Marcia Applebaum Chamovitz. "I got the impression she was afraid boys wouldn't want to marry her because of Jackie. She was worried about whether she would ever have a child like that."

Like many young women, Barbara had a romantic view of love during her college days. She once read Mika Waltari's *The Egyptian*, the cover of which carried a drawing of a man's profile. Barbara fell in love with the image, swooning over it—wondering aloud who had modeled for the cover, and expressing how wonderful it would be to have such a man.

Barbara's dream was that a knight on a white horse, preferably a Jewish knight with a Harvard or Yale medical or law degree, would sweep her off her feet. Before she found him, her scenario went, she would do something with the education she had received at Sarah Lawrence—exactly what, she was still uncertain, but it would be somewhat akin to what she knew best, show business. But in the end, she prophesied, she would get married and have a family.

That's the direction Barbara was certain she was headed when she said goodbye to Sarah Lawrence for the last time in the spring of 1951, graduating in the top quarter of her class.

9

"GET YOUR FOOT
IN THE DOOR AND
WORK YOUR WAY UP"

Ted Cott was, as a friend said years later, "besotted with Barbara—and he was in a position to help her career; that was chiefly it."

Twelve years Barbara's senior, Theodore B. Cott was vice president and general manager of NBC's owned and operated television station, WNBT, in New York, when Lou Walters called and asked him as a friend whether he could find a job for his daughter, who'd recently graduated from Sarah Lawrence.

That summer, Barbara took a secretarial course, learning speedwriting and typing. She also got a part-time job with an advertising agency, where she did some copywriting. But she saw the glamour attached to the growing medium of television and asked her father to see if he could find her a spot doing anything at one of the local stations.

The moment Barbara arrived for her initial interview with Ted Cott, he was smitten with her. At the time, Cott, divorced and the father of two little boys, was dating a beautiful actress on a TV soap opera. A short, physically unattractive man, he had the ability to attract good-looking women because of his position.

"Ted was very dynamic, clever, forceful—a kind of wunderkind," said Steve Krantz, a Hollywood producer, who had been program director at WNBT. "But Ted was a very self-defeating man. He had as many enemies as he had friends." Barbara was attracted to Cott, Krantz said, because "he was very entertaining and, in the context [of WNBT], powerful. He wasn't Robert Redford, but he did have charm."

Disliked by many of his employees, Cott was Napoleonic in stature and demeanor, and some thought he resembled Roy Cohn. Cott was RCA chief David Sarnoff's fair-haired boy at the time; his power attracted and intrigued Barbara.

Cott sent Barbara to the station's publicity, promotion, and advertising department where, in early 1952, she was given a job writing press releases for various programs. She also got an opportunity to demonstrate an ability to get a news scoop. Around the time she arrived, there was a newspaper and cab strike in the city, and the publicity department was helping to gather news. Barbara was able to secure an exclusive interview with a taxi association official and to find a photo of him, which impressed the station's powers.

Before long, Barbara and Ted were an item.

They were seen together in public—at the theater, in restaurants, at Frank Sinatra's big comeback engagement at the Meadowbrook in New Jersey, and at Cott's penthouse apartment on University Place in the Village, where Barbara was often the hostess for cocktail parties he gave. Through Ted, Barbara began meeting New York's media crowd—Tex McCrary, Jinx Falkenburg, and Eloise McElhone, for whom she would later work, among others. A pal of Cott's, Len Safir, who was advertising and promotion manager at the station, would one day recommend Barbara for a job with his brother, Bill Safire (who had added an *e* to his name), in McCrary's public relations agency. On a vacation in Miami, Cott and Krantz spent time with Barbara and Dena, socializing and having dinners together. And there would be one memorable weekend Krantz would spend with Barbara, Cott, and the woman who would become Krantz's wife, Judith Tarcher, Barbara's friend from Birch Wathen.

Despite Ted and Barbara's seemingly close relationship, they were not intimate, although it was said she wanted to marry him. "Barbara got involved with him and was crazy about him because he was a power figure in her life," said a friend.

Alan Carter, a staff producer, took Barbara out a few times until it became clear that her only interest was their boss. Carter saw a coldness in Barbara, and felt that sex and romance were not important to her. "One didn't think about her in sensual, sexual terms although she was an attractive lady," he said. "It would be hard for me to put the label of 'sex goddess' on her. For me there was some kind of barrier there. I felt a distance in her.

"She was somebody who was career-bound, which doesn't obscure the woman, but it certainly puts a different gloss on her. You didn't have to be around Barbara long, or in any particular capacity, to know there were some real insecurities there."

In early 1953, less than a year after Barbara was hired, Ted Cott arranged for his girlfriend, who had little if any experience, to become "producer" of a daily fifteen-minute, live children's program called *Ask the Camera*.

(Years later, Barbara gave the following advice to young women wanting to break into television: "Get to your local station, get your foot in the door, do anything, just get in there any way you know, [and] work your way up.") In Barbara's case, she was fortunate to have a little help from the boss.

Having come from the station's publicity department, having learned the value of PR at the feet of a master self-promoter—Lou Walters—and being the boss's girl, Barbara advanced to what was basically a glorified gofer's job and turned it into quite an advertisement for herself—in *TV Guide*, no less. It was the first of what would be thousands of newspaper and magazine stories about her during her career.

Under the headline YOUNG PRODUCER, the May 15, 1953, issue of America's best-selling weekly television program guide lauded Barbara—with three flattering pictures (one of them showing her holding hands with Lou at the Latin Quarter) and fawning copy—as being one of the "bright, young people in responsible jobs" in television, noting that "she may be the youngest [producer] in the field."

Ask the Camera, which lasted about a year, was conceived when Cott noticed that the station had a library of stock film that wasn't being put to much use.

"Barbara's job really wasn't complicated," said the show's host, Sandy Becker.

> The job of producer at that time was an umbrella for many different duties because this obviously was a very low-budget operation. We were deluged every week with letters containing questions from kids—How are bowling balls made? Barbara and a helper culled the letters and narrowed them down to the ones for which we had film. She turned the stuff over to me and I would make the comment in between, and read the letters, and do the commercials. While I was on the air, Barbara sat in the control room with a stopwatch and would pop in with a last-minute change or whatever. Script material and rehearsals were unheard of for this kind of show. We used to just wing it.

Coifed and dressed to kill, Barbara seemed to float on a cloud of self-assurance. Inquisitive, energetic, seemingly mature beyond her years, she appeared unintimidated by her new surroundings; was, in fact, quite at home. Despite having Cott as her "rabbi," Barbara felt she had to prove herself and she did; everyone found her extremely capable and professional for someone recently out of college with no experience.

"Barbara was very industrious, aggressive in the pursuit of work," said Steve Krantz, who as program director was Barbara's immediate supervisor.

"There was an assertiveness," added Becker. "She knew what she wanted. This was her coming-out party. She was very serious about what she was doing."

While she was producing *Ask the Camera*, Barbara was responsible for bringing her Birch Wathen friend Judith Tarcher together with Steve Krantz. (Tarcher had been seeing Barbara's first cousin, Selig Alkon, who also worked as a producer at WNBT, but they were not dating steadily.) Barbara decided to play Cupid, inviting Krantz, Tarcher, Cott, and Alkon for the July Fourth 1953 holiday at Montauk Manor, a resort hotel on the tip of Long Island. Everyone met for breakfast at the Walterses' penthouse before leaving for the weekend.

"Barbara introduced me to my wife," said Krantz. "It was essentially a blind date. It was a dressy place and none of us were prepared for it except Barbara. She brought some dressy clothes and Judy had to borrow a dress from her for the dance that night. We had a wonderful time, and I called Judy the Monday morning after we got back to town and asked her out. We got married six months later."

When *Ask the Camera* was canceled, Barbara and Ted had a parting of the ways. Any hopes Barbara had—and some friends said she did—of a possible marriage to Cott were dashed. At first Barbara was hurt, the friends said. But others felt that Barbara never thought of marrying Cott. "She would never have considered that," said Krantz. "Ted was lacking in a fair amount of social graces and I think those are important considerations for Barbara."

Barbara's next short-lived job was doing some production work for Eloise McElhone, an effervescent, blue-eyed, dark-haired, plump television and radio personality, who was best known as the star of a fluffy network panel show called *Leave It to the Girls*. McElhone also wrote a ditsy column for the New York *Journal-American* offering advice to women and their boyfriends, such as "How to Be a Dream Girl's Dreamboat."

Fueled by her relationship with Ted Cott, Barbara's television career appeared to be skyrocketing. But by mid-1954, it had fizzled like the romance. Barbara was among the unemployed and unattached, but "true love" was waiting right around the corner.

PART II

10

MEET MRS. KATZ

One of the best-kept secrets in Barbara's life involved her first marriage to a New York businessman, Robert Henry Katz.

The public record—numerous stories and profiles about Barbara over the years—described it as a marriage lasting less than a year and ending in an annulment. For example, in a syndicated January 30, 1972, profile on Barbara, *Washington Post* Style section writer Sally Quinn wrote: "[Barbara] was married once before in a 'very short, very sad' marriage which was annulled."

Some sources ignored the marriage altogether. A *Ladies' Home Journal* cover story in March 1988 stated flatly that Barbara had been married only twice, not three times as was fact.

In the late Eighties, some of Barbara's friends and relatives were still under the impression, or were perpetuating the myth, that Barbara's marriage to Katz was quickly annulled. Shirley Budd said, "Her first marriage was an annulment. It was just wrong to begin with. It was nothing."

In fact, Barbara's marriage lasted much longer and ended far differently than has been portrayed over the years.

In early February 1955, Miami had become Mecca for thousands of New Yorkers escaping one of the bitterest winters in memory.

Rooms at the grandiose hotels on Miami Beach were booked solid. Restaurants were jammed. The exclusive shops on Collins Avenue were mobbed and the nightclubs were doing a record business. Joe E. Lewis was headlining at Lou's Latin Quarter; Jimmy Durante, along with the Will Mastin Trio, featuring Sammy Davis, Jr., was at Copa City; Xavier Cugat and Abbe Lane were at the Saxony, and there was a mambo festival at the Isle de Capri.

In the mid-Fifties, Miami was still *the* winter vacation capital for northerners, a flashy and expensive resort for an affluent, predominantly Jewish crowd. Two decades later the city would be transformed into a poor and violent melting pot rivaling any banana republic—a murder and drug capital glorified on television by two vice cops named Crockett and Tubbs. In the national consciousness, Uzis and cocaine would replace cabanas and oranges as the city's symbols.

But on a glorious day in early February 1955, with New York frozen solid, Miami was a paradise. One of the vacationers wending his way through the airport was a handsome young man, Bob Katz. The main purpose of his visit was to see his father, Ira, who was recovering from a heart attack. The elder Katz, owner of a successful baby bonnet manufacturing business in Manhattan, was recuperating as an outpatient at the Miami Heart Institute. The Katzes were Rumanian Jews. Bob's grandfather had come to the United States in 1882, and Ira was born in 1890. Bob's mother died when he was an infant. Ira Katz remarried and had three children—twin girls and a son, Conrad. After his second wife died, Ira remarried twice more. Bob thought he'd combine the visit with his dad with a week of relaxation under the sun.

The trip, however, turned out to be much more than that.

At thirty-four, Bob was good-looking, with fine features, black hair, and blue eyes. Standing five nine and weighing about 160, he was fit and trim from playing tennis and golf. He traveled often for pleasure and enjoyed the theater. Besides his small apartment on Horatio Street in Greenwich Village, there was also a pleasant family getaway home in Westhampton. He enjoyed popular music and played the piano. His love of pop music had been a source of irritation in the Katz family. His father and mother fought with him to study classical piano but he refused. Otherwise, he was a good Jewish boy who was sent to the proper schools and summer camps and generally had the best of everything.

Bob had a keen mind, graduating from the Wharton School of Finance at the University of Pennsylvania. During World War II he served as a lieutenant in the Navy and had several friends who were killed in combat. Back in civilian life, Bob proved to be a savvy, low-key businessman who eventually took over his father's company. A conservative Republican, Bob was a history buff who enjoyed reading historical biographies.

Women found Bob attractive and, his friends say, he was often the target of marriage-minded girls from good families. A happy-go-lucky bachelor, he was a real catch for the right woman.

She was about to come along.

"Bob? Bob Katz? Is that you?" The voice sounded familiar. Bob was waiting for a cab outside the airport terminal building when he heard his name called. He turned to see Barbara, slim and tanned, smiling and waving at him. Bob had first met her six months earlier at a party at Ted Cott's apartment. They had run into each other at other parties on a few subsequent occasions and found each other attractive and interesting, though they'd never dated. So Bob was pleasantly surprised to see her again at the airport.

Barbara was idling away the winter in Miami with Lou, Dena, and Jackie. At twenty-five, she wasn't working and had no apparent goals or aspirations. The job she had at WNBT with Ted Cott had not convinced her that she wanted to spend the rest of her life working in television, or working at all for that matter; it had been an interesting adventure. Lou was supporting her and she seemed content with that situation, spending her days lying on the beach or lolling at poolside.

There was no one special in her life at the time, so Barbara was happy to run into Bob. They chatted for a few moments before Bob jumped into a cab and headed for his father's hotel, leaving Barbara at the curb. No plans were made to get together.

The next day Bob and his father were relaxing in their cabana when he heard the same familiar voice. Peering around the corner he discovered Barbara in the next cabana. They spent the afternoon together by the pool and Barbara accepted Bob's invitation to join him and his father for dinner that night. It was a wonderful evening, and Bob felt an immediate rapport with her. Barbara had a certain undefinable style that intrigued him: witty, chic, bright, and even his father Ira nodded his head in approval of the new girl. Barbara was excited about the prospects of seeing Bob again. She found him good-looking and fun. He was sophisticated but not serious; bright and witty, but not a stuffy intellectual. He was "with it" and she liked that.

They agreed to meet the next day at poolside, had dinner together again that night, and for the rest of the week spent most of their time in each other's company.

One night toward the end of the week, Barbara invited Bob to meet her at the Latin Quarter. Lou and Dena were having a party at the house later that evening and Barbara wanted to introduce him to them. Normally reticent about family matters, Barbara opened up to Bob, telling him about her insecurities concerning Lou and forewarning him that her sister was retarded. That night at the house, for the first time since Bob had met her, she seemed uncomfortable—especially when they were around Jackie. She was moody and tense. That aside, their chance encounter was turning into a sudden romance. The next day Barbara appeared to be her same vivacious self.

At the end of the week, they returned to New York. Barbara moved back into the Walters apartment and Bob returned to his place in the Village. He was now Barbara's steady beau and she immediately and proudly introduced him to her friends. They were thrilled for her; she seemed happier than they ever remembered.

"He was a rich young man in New York. He was attractive. She was attractive. I didn't find it a surprise. I thought they were quite delightful. He loved her. She seemed to love him. They both wanted to please each other," said a college friend and confidante of Barbara's.

Because this friend had been married for several years at the time—Barbara had been a bridesmaid at her wedding—Barbara took her into her confidence, seeking answers to often naive questions about marriage. Barbara was both excited by and scared of the prospect of matrimony, which she felt was very possible with Bob. Always sensitive, she had watched her parents' marriage at close range with misgivings. Barbara had seen and felt the emotional waves on which her mother rode. She thought of her sister—and her dead brother—and knew and feared the dangers of childbirth. Barbara also felt peer pressure. She was one of the last of her friends who was still single—this in an era when all nice girls were finding husbands and starting families. Yet somewhere in the far recesses of her mind was the thought of independence—of not falling into the marriage trap at all, of pursuing some other goal. Barbara needed the kind of answers that no one could give her.

"We were really the first of the women who had the idea we were supposed to have a life of our own, but there was no one there to show us the way," said Barbara's friend.

Bob was so taken with Barbara that he stopped seeing his closest friends as often as before, so that he could focus almost all of his attention on her. There was no doubt in anyone's mind that he had fallen for Barbara and she for him. There was a constant round of dinners, parties, evenings at the theater. On Friday nights, Barbara and Bob began joining Lou, Dena, and Jackie for dinner at the Latin Quarter in New York. Lou and Dena approved of Bob. They saw him as the perfect young man for Barbara. She had only one goal in life at that point—snaring Bob. She thought for sure she wanted to be a wife, nothing more.

Barbara was "very much involved with the ritual of dating, the ritual of engagement, the ritual of marriage—dealing from the mythology of novels, of romantic literature," remarked her friend.

In April 1955, just two months after their chance meeting at the airport in Miami, Bob Katz asked for Barbara Walters' hand in marriage and she readily said yes. Bob placed a handsome diamond engagement ring on her finger, and Barbara immediately broke the good news to Lou and Dena and all her friends. Like her married friends, she wanted a traditional June wedding. Of course, Lou would produce the affair. He booked the ballroom of New York's Plaza Hotel and started laying plans for the most spectacular wedding a father could give his daughter. The impresario would make it the best ever—even if it took his last cent. It would be a wedding produced by a showman.

But as plans progressed for the wedding, there were changes in Barbara that concerned Bob: she frequently seemed moody, depressed, unhappy. Reality had begun intruding on their storybook romance, as it does with so many intense relationships. For the first time they began having tiffs, with Barbara snapping at Bob, finding things to criticize. Bob started seeing a coldness surface in Barbara that he had not perceived during their Florida courtship and after they returned to New York. He was looking at her in a new light, and she at him. Barbara began questioning their relationship, their engagement.

Suddenly, inexplicably, in mid-April there was a change in Barbara's attitude. The engagement was over; Barbara gave the ring back to Bob. Afterward, there were tears and guilt; she had sunk into a depression, ashamed that her wedding plans had fallen apart. In Barbara's circle—a milieu of well-to-do, proud, and egotistical young women— a broken engagement was tantamount to a scandal. Barbara felt anger, embarrassment, despair.

For a week, maybe two, they did not speak. Bob believed the relationship was over and he felt a sense of relief. He'd only known Barbara a few months and everything had moved so fast, had been so incredibly intense. Bob, too, had become concerned about Barbara's moods, what he perceived as an underlying unhappiness. There was an emotional incompatibility that had begun to manifest itself, and it concerned him.

Suddenly, out of the blue, Barbara telephoned Bob to say she was sorry; she wanted a reconciliation; she wanted to move forward with the wedding plans. But Bob had qualms. After all, Barbara's decision to call off the engagement raised serious questions about her love and sincerity. For a time, Bob was intransigent. Unlike Barbara, he was not embarrassed by the broken engagement; it was not as if he had left her waiting under the chuppa.

A few days later a distraught Barbara appeared on the doorstep of Ira Katz's apartment on lower Park Avenue at seven in the morning, pleading with him to convince his son to come back to her. Ira Katz called Bob and told him about Barbara's visit, recommending that his son talk to the seemingly frantic young woman as soon as possible. A few hours later Bob received a call from Lou Walters, presumably at Barbara's behest, who wanted to see him at the club as soon as possible.

Lou, in a warm, fatherly way, told Bob that he and Barbara were two nice kids who were great together and that they shouldn't let a little spat ruin their chances of a future together. He advised Bob to meet with his daughter and talk things out.

Bob met with Barbara and she convinced him that they should go back together. He gave her the ring again and they kissed and made up. Bob was still strongly attracted to Barbara and that overcame his growing concern over her changeable moods and behavior. Plans for a June wedding were back on track, with Dena and Barbara helping with the preparations.

On May 1, Bob and Barbara's engagement notice, a short paragraph, appeared in the *New York Times.*

Less than five months after they met, Bob and Barbara were married on the evening of June 21, 1955, in the Terrace Room of the Plaza Hotel on Fifth Avenue. Lou gave Barbara away, and Jackie was her maid of honor. Ira Katz was best man for his son. There were more than a hundred guests at the black-tie affair. Lou had arranged for the best food, the finest French champagne, and a big band. It was a truly elegant affair. Lou thrilled the gathering with big-name celebrities. One of the performers was Johnnie Ray, the hard-of-hearing singer whose offbeat single "Cry" made him an overnight sensation. Another guest was "Mr. Television" himself—Milton Berle, a close friend and card-playing crony of Lou's.

"It was a gorgeous wedding," recalled one of Barbara's aunts. "It was a very plush affair—just like in the movies. And Bob was a very handsome guy."

"This was all from the era of large, lavish weddings. It was genuinely impressive," said a college classmate of Barbara's. "Those of us in that crowd who had gotten married all had impressive weddings. We either married at the Pierre, the Plaza, or the Sherry-Netherland. But Barbara's wedding was something special. A great deal of attention was paid to the food, the wine. Barbara was very much involved in planning this."

Lou spent a bundle on the wedding, an estimated twenty thousand dollars, which was a tidy sum in 1955. According to friends of Barbara, it was money he didn't have. He had to borrow to pay for the affair, they claimed.

After the party, Bob and Barbara—still a virgin, according to her friends—crossed Fifth Avenue to the Hotel Pierre where they spent their wedding night.

The next day they flew to Europe for a three-week honeymoon: Paris, Florence, Venice. They explored the museums and ate in the best restaurants. On the way home, the Katzes made a stop in Switzerland where Bob had some business.

The happy couple returned to New York in mid-July to set up housekeeping in Bob's small, one-bedroom apartment on Horatio Street near Twelfth Street. Bob loved the apartment, but Barbara expressed her displeasure about living in the Village. She wanted to be uptown, closer to her family and friends. Barbara was never part of a Village crowd—the word "bohemian" was not in her lexicon. She wanted to be on the familiar territory of the Upper East Side.

Barbara did not settle into the traditional role of a Fifties housewife, and Bob didn't expect her to. No apron and dustcloth for her. A cleaning woman came in a day or two a week, and the Katzes mostly ate out. Barbara hated cooking, doing it only when she gave small dinner parties for her girlfriends and their husbands or dates, all of whom found Bob to be a very pleasant and sociable fellow. Barbara's former college crowd dominated their social calendar, and Barbara was usually the arbiter of where she and her husband went and what they did. Barbara and Bob often double-dated with Eloise McElhone and her husband, Bill, an advertising executive, who were part of the chic Stork Club set. Bob's friends, however, were not part of their circle. They just didn't seem to fit in with Barbara's crowd, so he would meet his chums for lunch. Barbara and Bob mutually agreed not to start a family right away; there was still lots of time, they thought. For the time being the Katzes felt that an unencumbered city life would be more to their liking.

Barbara's days were devoid of any substantive activity; she spent them mostly gossiping with friends on the phone or lunching with them uptown—taking a cab, shunning the subway. Often, when her friends were busy, she'd while away a day with Dena and Jackie. At nights, the Katzes rarely stayed in, Barbara preferring a movie or the theater to a quiet time at home. There was a tenseness about her that precluded the kind of comfortable warmth and intimacy that young marrieds often develop. She seemed to have little interest in social issues, politics, or current events; instead, she liked to read the society and fashion pages and the gossip columns, where she followed the comings and goings of her show-business, media, and society acquaintances. She envied that sort of notoriety and, years later, her name, too, would appear in boldface on a regular basis in the columns.

As the weeks went by, an unhappiness descended on Barbara. The moodiness that had erupted during the courtship began to surface again. Bob was not the type of person who pried and Barbara rarely spoke about her problems, protecting her privacy even in marriage. She was constantly agonizing over Jackie and the situation at home with Lou. She was also concerned about her marriage and whether she would or could succeed as a wife, intensifying her already deep-rooted insecurities. Bob presumed Barbara was having normal marital adjustment problems, but she'd already begun building a wall between them.

Finally, after a month or two, Bob suggested that Barbara's unhappiness stemmed from the fact that she had nothing to occupy her time; why not think about getting a job? After all, Barbara was a bright, educated, talented woman.

Those were attributes that attracted Bob in the first place; so why should she waste her days doing nothing? There was a big, wide world out there. Somewhere in New York she could find a job that interested her. After all, the Walters name was well known in the city; she was not just someone off the street. Bob's suggestion was like a bolt of lightning to Barbara.

The idea of working buoyed Barbara's mood as had meeting Bob months earlier. She was excited about the prospect and immediately plunged into the hunt with vigor.

11

BARBARA
THE BOOKER

In the mid-1950s, at the time Barbara began her job search, CBS was in the process of launching a new early-morning show to compete with NBC's juggernaut, the *Today* show.

With its debut at 7:00 A.M. on Monday, January 14, 1952, NBC had proven with *Today* that early-morning television could be successful. While the show faced the wrath of critics, the public seemed to love it, and so did the advertisers. *Today* fast became the electronic equivalent of the first cup of coffee of the day for millions of Americans. The show was conceived by a brilliant broadcasting pioneer, Sylvester (Pat) Weaver.

Weaver noticed that television's early-morning hours were devoid of any quality programming. He was confident he could make them golden. People turned on the radio and got their news and weather as they dressed and had breakfast. They would never think of watching television at that hour. It seemed almost immoral. Weaver had a vision that he could change those habits with the right mix—a radio-style show on television offering an easygoing blend of information, weather, news, and entertainment.

Weaver had a high-minded blueprint for *Today*. "We want America to shave, to eat, to dress, to get to work on time. But we also want America to be well informed, to be amused, to be lightened in spirit and in heart, and to be reinforced in inner resolution through knowledge." He saw the show as "a bird's-eye view of the world and its happenings."

As *Today*'s anchor, Weaver selected gangly, eccentric Dave Garroway, a graduate of NBC's announcer school, who ranked near the bottom of his class. Garroway had worked as a newsman and disk jockey and had caught the attention of executives with his offbeat style. In 1948, he was offered his first program, *Garroway at Large*, which became the model for Ernie Kovacs, Steve Allen, and David Letterman—lots of sophomoric humor, camera tricks, and backstage antics. Along with Garroway, Weaver hired Jim Fleming as the newscaster for the *Today* show and toothy Jack Lescoulie to do sports and clown with the other talent. Later a chimpanzee, J. Fred Muggs, became a regular, appalling critics and some staffers.

By the mid-Fifties *Today* was seen in virtually every major and medium market and local affiliates were being added weekly. The program could make or break a guest or a product because of its national influence. A writer appearing on the show to promote a new book was virtually assured of having a bestseller. Saran Wrap became a major product after Garroway held the transparent wrapping over the camera lens to show viewers how clear it was. *Today* was becoming a monster success and had gone into the black. It was America's alarm clock. There was no competition. *Today* was the *New York Times, Life* magazine, the *National Enquirer,* and the Ringling Brothers, Barnum and Bailey Circus all rolled into one. It combined hype and depth in a brew that was unbeatable.

When Bob Katz suggested to Barbara that she get a job the first place she thought to go was the offices of *Today*. She met with one of the writer-producers but was told there were no openings. Apparently upset at not being welcomed aboard with open arms, Barbara warned the executive that "one day everybody is going to know about me at NBC and I hope you're going to be around to remember this visit."

Barbara job-hunted for about a month. Her last stop was at CBS where a strong effort was underway to compete with *Today*. CBS had first mounted its attack in 1954, with the *Morning Show*, a news and special events program hosted by newscasters Walter Cronkite and Charles Collingwood. Carol Reed did the weather and Jim McKay handled sports. One of the main amusements of the show were the Bil and Cora Baird puppets, which pantomimed current hit songs. Not surprisingly, despite Cronkite's and Collingwood's already established prestige, the program bombed.

A subsequent, lighter format of the *Morning Show* starred Jack Paar—"the perennial summer replacement," as *TV Guide* dubbed him at the time. Paar's players included Betty Clooney, the singer; José Melis, the pianist; and Cuban bandleader Pupi Campo. The puppets remained on the show. Charles Collingwood and Winston Burdett shared the newsreading duties.

Later, the two-hour time slot CBS had allocated for the venture was cut in half—with the eight-to-nine o'clock segment given over to what would quickly become a very successful children's program, *Captain Kangaroo*.

But CBS still wanted to capture some of *Today*'s audience in the seven-to-eight time slot.

"I hired Barbara mostly because she had a darling ass, which I never got near," said Charlie Andrews, a longtime Garroway associate, who was producing yet another version of the *Morning Show* in late 1955 starring a young co-

median, Dick Van Dyke, and cohost Cronkite. Van Dyke
was soon replaced by Will Rogers, Jr., son of the famous
humorist. Andrews was directed to wage war against *Today*
with a small budget and a few staffers.

"I was looking for a guest-getter," he said. "Barbara
came up for an interview and she was obviously a sharp,
aggressive, ambitious girl—and really stunning in those
days. She was one of the best-looking kids on the block.
Some people walk into a room and you know their wheels
are spinning. Barbara was one of those people. She just
created one great impression."

Luckily, there was an opening for her.

A young aspiring actress, Estelle Parsons, had just quit
the *Morning Show* to return to *Today* where she had for-
merly worked as a production assistant and later a weather
girl—the first of what would be a long line of so-called
Today Girls, of whom Barbara would eventually be the
last.

Once hired, Barbara shared an office with another
woman, Madeline Amgott, a feature coordinator on the
show. Amgott had previously worked as a Washington reporter for the San Diego *Journal* and the *Greek National
Herald*. Her broadcasting experience was on a radio program called "Halls of Congress," for which she produced
dramatizations of congressional debates. Barbara and Amgott forged a close friendship. Almost two decades later,
Amgott would be hired to produce a daily program for Barbara.

But for now Barbara was nothing more than a pretty,
glorified gofer.

"I just knew Barbara would be good at what I wanted,
which was someone to get on the phone and dig up some
guests and to be there to do all that shit those people have
to do," said Andrews. "We were on early in the morning.
No rehearsal. No money. No writing. No costumes. None
of that crap."

During the tenure of Dick Van Dyke, Andrews—with

the help of Barbara and Amgott—essentially brought a bit of burlesque to television. The *Today* show needn't have worried. The *Morning Show* was laughable.

Typical was the way the staff produced weather reports. According to Andrews:

A guy that I had known somehow or another was the public relations guy for Wickeewashee Springs, a tourist attraction in Florida. They had a bunch of girls breathing through hoses swimming with fishes in a deep, beautiful spring. So this guy came to me and said, "You've gotta help me get some press or I'm going to lose my job. I haven't had any luck." I told him I couldn't do anything for him but I asked him what he could do for me. He said, "I can bring a tank in here and bring a girl who can eat bananas under water so you'll have some sex."

As I say, I had no budget so I told him that he would pay for the tank and the water and the installation and he agreed. So he brought a big tank into the studio and I had a map of the United States painted on the outside of the tank and I gave the girl swimming in the tank a grease pencil. And Dick Van Dyke would say, "There's a low over Texas," and the girl, breathing through a tube, squirming under water, would draw a circle over Texas. And then Dick would say, "There's a high over the Rocky Mountains," so she'd put a line over the Rocky Mountains. It was funny and absolutely useless as far as weather was concerned, but we had to do national weather. That was the mandate. We did this for a week and we got some attention, some phone calls and a couple of postcards, which was the first notice the show ever had.

The submerged weather girl, a cutie in a bathing suit named Ginger Stanley, did four dips a day in the water, which was heated to 94 degrees. The wacky underwater bit generated enough interest to catch the attention of *TV Guide*, which devoted a page to the stunt in the February 4, 1956 issue, under the appropriate headline "Fair and

Wet, 'Morning Show' Dunks Its Weather Girl and Gets Some Publicity."

Barbara seemed to have a flair for this sort of drivel. Like her father when he was starting out, Barbara had a booker's eye for talent. After the underwater tank was removed from the studio, she excitedly brought to Andrews' attention a girl who had just won an amateur archery contest. "So, I'm off and running," remembered Andrews.

I had a big target made of straw in the shape of the United States. I put the girl at one end of the studio and Dick Van Dyke would say there's a low in Texas and—*twang!*—the arrow would fly across the studio and hit Texas. And there's a high in Michigan and we'd get a shot of the girl pulling this big bow back to her nose and—*flip!*—the arrow would go into the Rocky Mountains. Well, it was funny. Dick Van Dyke could take advantage of it.

Next we got a logger who could throw a double-bladed ax for fifteen feet and hit stuff. So we had him hit Texas and hit the Rocky Mountains. And then we got a carnival guy who threw knives around his wife. She'd stand in front of the map of the U.S. and he'd throw a knife along her hip into Texas.

We finally ended up with a marvelous old magician, Kudabux, who could shoot a twenty-two blindfolded. We'd put bread dough in his eyes and he could hit Michigan that way. And it was funny. What we were really saying was: Isn't all this national weather silly?

Barbara and Madeline's job was to find people who could throw things, and line up other guests. They would deal with the publicists and the booking agents and all that stuff. Barbara would generate story ideas. For half an hour in the morning the girls would say, "There's a new book written by so and so about how you can't screw your dog" and then we'd decide whether that was a good thing for the show or not.

While Bob Katz felt Barbara had no interest in a career—and had to be prodded into getting a job—her co-workers felt differently. They saw a hard-working, driven, ambitious young woman. "If you put twenty girls in a room, Barbara would be one of the two smartest girls there," said Andrews. "She could think things out. She was street-smart certainly, logical, not afraid to work. Look at all the idiots in this business. Sooner or later, Barbara would float to the top. She was going to be big in television—one way or the other. She was ambitious, determined. You could see it in her eyes."

Barbara had found a home in television. For the first time, she was in an environment where she felt completely confident, secure, at ease with herself. She loved the excitement, the immediacy, the freneticism, the deadlines. It suited her personality. Barbara thrived on the backroom intrigues, the politics—all of which she would one day become expert in. She relished being an insider—enjoying the gossip, the dishing, the cynicism and black humor of her broadcasting colleagues, and she basked in their adoration. Interesting, powerful men—the type to whom she always was drawn—were paying attention to her. It was like joining a family where she felt loved and wanted.

Like the nightclub arena where her father thrived, Barbara discovered that she flourished best in the electrified world of the television studio. In many ways they were similar places, but television was exclusively hers, not Lou's.

"Barbara had a unique vision," observed Amgott, who worked with Walters on the *Morning Show* for six months before it was canceled. "She always knew what she wanted to do. She made opportunities for herself all through her life, as far back as then. She always knew she wanted to be in front of the camera."

Barbara had an interest in fashion, so she proposed to the producers that they start airing fashion segments on the show. In those days, fashion shows translated into sexy, inexpensive television and women viewers loved it. Barbara produced the whole package, sometimes doing the commentary. The powers that be held their noses when they heard her voice and slight speech impediment but Barbara came cheap.

The first time a model didn't show up, Barbara told the director, Av Westin, "I'm a size eight. I could do it." And she was given the go-ahead for her first-ever on-air appearance. On several subsequent occasions Barbara would don the outfits and unabashedly strut before the cameras.

"She openly expressed her desire to get on camera and kept looking for ways to do it," said Amgott. "Her voice was unpleasant. She had speech problems, and she didn't care. She went ahead."

Whatever shyness and insecurity Barbara felt off camera disappeared when the red light went on, signifying she was on the air. She was absolutely at ease in front of the camera. Sometimes she would pull Amgott into the act to fill in for a model who didn't show. Those fashion pieces represented Barbara's first on-air work. Half a dozen years later, when she was hired as a writer on *Today*, Barbara would use the fashion gambit again, arranging for herself to cover the Paris shows. "She always knew that was her way in," observed Amgott.

When the *Morning Show* with Dick Van Dyke ended in early 1956, production started on a new program renamed the *Good Morning* show with Will Rogers, Jr. The show was a creation of both the news and entertainment divisions. Because there was no videotape technology, the program was done live twice each morning, for the East Coast and the Midwest. The West Coast and mountain states were served by a similar program called *Panorama Pacific*.

Rogers, in his midforties, was an actor, entertainer, and former congressman, who played the role of his father in a 1951 film, *The Story of Will Rogers*. He was chosen to host the show because of his folksy image and famous name, but he turned out to be difficult to work with and the early-morning audience found him bland.

"Everyone on the Dick Van Dyke show knew in advance they were going to be closed down. Everyone knew that a new show was going to take its place. So they came over to talk to me and I would hire those people whom I thought I could use," said the new executive producer, Mike Sklar. Barbara and Madeline Amgott flipped a coin to see who would be interviewed first by Sklar, and Barbara won the toss—and the job. "She was very crisp, very businesslike. She didn't fool around. She was very straightforward. She impressed me as smart," recalled Sklar. He hired her to do the same work, booking guests and generating story ideas.

There was other good news for Barbara. Bob's lease on the Village apartment had expired. The couple went apartment hunting uptown where Barbara happily chose a place and a location more to her liking—Madison Avenue in the low Eighties, about six blocks from her parents' Park Avenue apartment. The couple went on a furniture shopping spree to appoint their new digs. Barbara engaged an up-and-coming interior decorator, Richard Hare, to modestly do the place. They seemed, for the time being, to be settling in. With her job and new apartment, Barbara appeared happy.

Barbara thrived on her job, seemingly becoming increasingly blind to everything else. Work, she found, was like a drug—an aphrodisiac, a form of escapism, a crutch. With it, she was able to overlook her sporadic depressions; forget her insecurities about Lou and the guilt and the burden she bore about Jackie. The television studio had become a haven. Because of her early-morning shift, Barbara was going to sleep at nine or ten every night and getting up at four A.M. to get to the studio. Bob and Barbara were like two ships passing in the night, their lives no longer in sync. Barbara had allowed her job to take precedence over everything else. Without realizing it at the time, she was establishing a pattern that would prevail throughout her life, helping to destroy two marriages and sound the death knell to other relationships with men.

Barbara also began telling friends that she wasn't happy in marriage.

"We spent a lot of time talking about it because I enjoyed being married and she was not enjoying it," said a woman confidante. "It didn't seem to be a good marriage, and she was also very concerned about failing in it. On one hand, she wanted to continue. On the other hand, it seemed untenable." Bob was also unhappy, but neither of them made a move.

Barbara had a strangely intoxicating effect on her new bosses at the Good Morning show. She did not possess classic good looks or charm school poise, nor was she particularly brilliant. Yet, the men who worked with her were captivated. For many, it was the first time they had come in contact with a chic, glib New York woman, and they were intrigued. A number of men in the business at the time were midwesterners, gentiles, who had little if any contact with Jews, especially Jewish women in broadcasting, before migrating to the television capital in New York. Their ideal, for better or worse, was Waspy blondes. With her chutzpah and street smarts, Barbara was an exotic to them.

"She was gorgeous. She really was beautiful. And she was the best-dressed woman I had ever seen," recalled Robert (Shad) Northshield, a former Chicago newspaperman who was one of the two producers on the new morning show. "Later we came to know that such people were Jewish American princesses. But if so, if she was the first one, she was one of the nicest ones."

Other than Madeline Amgott, who had met Bob, few if any of Barbara's colleagues knew she was married. Barbara never introduced Bob to her growing circle of male associates at work. She kept that part of her life separate. Barbara was expert at compartmentalizing, and she went overboard regarding secrecy about her personal life.

The old-boy network was just then forming in the still-embryonic world of television. The Northshields and Andrewses and Westins and other directors and producers with whom Barbara worked would rise to major network executive positions in the years to come. Through her determination and hard work, Barbara ingratiated herself, becoming—as much as a woman could in those days—part of their circle. Certainly she would struggle. It would be an uphill battle for her. But the relationships she was now forging would help later on. Barbara was there with these men in the trenches when it all began, and they would always remember her when it counted.

Luck was with Barbara. She had broken into television at the right time and the right place. For example, five years after the *Good Morning* show folded, Northshield and Barbara would be thrown together again when she was hired at the *Today* show as a writer by another CBS alumnus, Fred Freed. As *Today*'s producer, Northshield assigned Barbara to her first big story because he knew her from "the old days" at CBS. Barbara was one of the few female members of the old-boy network, and it would help her along the way.

Mike Sklar had been commissioned to produce a homey, eclectic program for an hour a day, five days a week. One of his objectives was to have his staff originate feature ideas and news; to go beyond what *Life* magazine was doing weekly and the *New York Times* daily. But the staff was constantly frustrated, failing to come up with innovative material, so Barbara proposed her old standby.

"All you would say was, 'Barbara, have you got any ideas?' and she'd say, 'Well, I'd like to do a fashion show,' " said Sklar. "And she'd go out and organize the whole thing. She'd bring in a package. She did that sort of thing quite often. She was a very hard worker."

The new *Good Morning* show was, in Northshield's words,

going to revolutionize CBS and the world. The show had probably the greatest concentration of talent since July 1776 in Philadelphia. Av Westin was one of the directors. Andy Rooney was one of the writers. It was that kind of staff. [But] the show was, in most ways, an abject failure because we were up against *Today*.

Barbara was one of the writers or perhaps at that point she wasn't called a writer, maybe a researcher or talent co-ordinator. She knew people in show business. I and most of the people were journalists rather than entertainment people. So we were either put off by the show biz bullshit or enchanted by it—and refused to admit that—or maybe a combination of both.

But Barbara was from show business. She would drop a name, a Milton Berle, and she was talking about someone who had called her to ask how her father was.

That aspect of Barbara's life titillated Northshield and the others. "When a newcomer came aboard, people would nod discreetly at her and whisper, 'That's Barbara Walters. You know who Lou Walters is?' And they'd say, 'Yeah, I think I do, somebody like Ziegfeld.' And you'd say, 'Well, that's his daughter,'" recalled Northshield.

The *Good Morning* show's executives saw Barbara's show-business connections as a valuable resource whether they tapped into them or not, and Barbara was quite aware of their worth, and therefore hers in the eyes of the brass. Through her dad, she knew the leading agents and managers, and the stars themselves. Being able to call an agent or a manager and say you were Lou Walters' daughter and you worked for CBS television pulled a lot of weight around town. And in a pinch, Barbara could always get Lou to make a call for her. For the first time in her life, Barbara saw that being the daughter of a famous nightclub owner could be an asset, not a liability. It gave her a gloss of power, prestige, and panache, at least in the world of television.

Barbara worked hard, did her homework, did the scut

work. She'd labor around the clock without complaint if asked to.

Looking back years later, Sklar saw Barbara's intense need to prove herself as part of a deep-seated hunger for recognition—a craving that would last throughout her career.

"She'd had difficulties because the Walters family had another daughter who was retarded," said Sklar. "And a great deal of attention was spent on that child and Barbara suffered. She wasn't given the attention that she wanted. She always sought very hard—by being a good worker, a good person—to get attention and approval. I heard this and it certainly tallied with the way she worked. She was a very hard worker. She was very faithful. She was very reliable. She was utterly responsible. She went out of her way to help."

While Barbara proved herself a success, the show died. The major problem involved the host, Will Rogers, Jr. During one show Rogers intently questioned an attractive female guest about politics. She tried hard to answer his questions but seemed mystified as to why he would be probing her on such a subject. It turned out that Rogers thought his guest—screenwriter, playwright, and novelist Anita Loos—was Clare Boothe Luce.

"We were always under the sword," said Sklar. "They would give you six months to get the show on and to get a rating, but the show was one long failure. They tried everything but they never gave anything a chance to develop."

Sklar was axed and reassigned to start a new CBS science series. Barbara got some of the staff together and gave him an expensive Mark Cross attaché case as a going-away gift. Over the years Barbara would become famous in the industry for those sorts of gestures—giving gifts, arranging parties, writing thank-you notes; it was good politics.

On July 26, 1956, shortly after eleven P.M., two ocean liners—the Swedish *Stockholm* and the Italian *Andrea*

Doria—collided in the fog off Nantucket, leaving more than fifty people dead or missing. Jim Fleming, Sklar's successor, immediately dispatched Barbara and a producer, Dick Siemenowski, to the scene.

"The studio was full of survivors the next day," boasted Fleming years later.

> We scooped everybody. It was just the kind of thing Barbara was so marvelous at. I've never run into anybody who was such a marvelous go-getter. She was so dependable. Everyone was very impressed with her.
>
> Barbara was sort of a spark plug in that whole staff. The rest of them were kind of old pros and they had been bored by what went on before. But she was on the go. Anything you gave her to do she delivered. You could say get Herbert Hoover and she would. I thought she was the most professional youngster I ever ran into. She was young but she was mature.

As with other executives on the staff, Fleming found Barbara incredibly focused, determined, and ambitious.

For Barbara the *Morning Show* was a fantastic career opportunity. For years afterward, network biographies and press releases about her glossed over the fact that she was little more than a guest-getter, exaggerating her role in a way that gave her past more prestige by tying it to a respected television journalist. For instance, a 1977 ABC press release said Barbara "was a writer for CBS Television Network morning broadcasts anchored by such newscasters as Walter Cronkite." Those releases were used by newspapers as factual material to place in stories about her. As recently as 1988, veteran broadcasting executives, when asked about Barbara's early years, still thought she had started out as a newswriter for Cronkite at CBS.

In 1957, Will Rogers, Jr., and his lariat were put out to pasture. Other staffers on the canceled show looked forward to new projects. But there was nothing on Barbara's horizon—except returning to deadly dull days in that apartment on Madison Avenue and her marriage, which was clearly on the rocks.

The year 1957 would be one of Barbara's worst.

She had become increasingly alienated from Bob, and he from her. Barbara's career—now seemingly over—and her growing independence were in part responsible. So were her mood swings and depressions, which added to the emotional distance between her and Bob. Barbara also had come to the realization that marriage was too confining for her; she felt constricted by it, whereas a career gave her limitless horizons, an incredible sense of freedom without dependence or commitment. Barbara and Bob now seemed to have little in common. Both were unhappy. Now that she was out of work, away from the fix of the television studio, the dark moods returned.

Entering its third year, the Katz marriage began to crumble.

Sometimes when she was depressed, Barbara would leave Bob for a day or two to stay at her parents' apartment. But the gloomy situation in the Walters household made her more melancholy, and it became even more intolerable in that summer of 1957.

For Lou had made a decision that would change the family's and Barbara's life forever.

After years of personality clashes, business and philosophical differences with his financial backer, Elias Loew, Lou Walters decided to cash in his Latin Quarter chips and strike out on his own, at a time when the club was riding high. Lou was taking the biggest gamble of his life, against the advice of his family and his closest friends.

What's more, he'd chosen the worst possible time to go independent. The country's economy was failing, and a recession—a time when fewer people would be going to nightclubs—was just over the horizon. Why spend money to see Milton Berle when you could watch him at home

on television? Scantily clad showgirls? You could see it all
in *Playboy* for a buck. The type of variety acts Lou featured
were found every Sunday night, courtesy of Ed Sullivan.
Pocketbooks were closing, tastes were changing. And one
fact was indisputable: television had become the supreme
entertainer; the *real* modern-day Ziegfeld, serving every cultural taste. Lou was fast becoming an endangered species,
but he was blind to it all. He was living in the past; his
daughter Barbara had seen the future.

Lou's trouble began during the winter of 1956 when he
suddenly and inexplicably withdrew his remaining stake
in the Miami Latin Quarter to build a new cabaret on the
site of the old Copa City. Loew was shocked and insulted.
After all, he had done so much for Walters over the years,
and now Lou was tossing him aside to become a competitor. Despite his defection from the Miami operation, Lou
agreed to continue running the New York Latin Quarter.
Loew was furious at Walters, but he kept his anger to himself. A shrewd businessman, he knew he needed Lou's
show-business expertise to keep the flagship New York
club on top.

In June 1957, Lou went to Europe to scout novelty acts
for his soon-to-be-opened Miami club, the Café de Paris.
When he returned, Lou had an even bigger surprise for
Loew. The impresario had decided to completely sever his
ties so he could open a competing club in Manhattan, too.

It was as if Lou had declared war on Loew.

There was a round of hectic meetings between the two
men. Loew hoped to convince Lou to change his mind.
Big money was involved. The New York club alone was
grossing five million dollars annually at the time.

Dena and Barbara also tried desperately to change Lou's
mind because money was at stake with them, too. Even
though they despised Loew, his presence in Lou's life represented some semblance of financial security for the family. As long as Lou was affiliated with Loew, Dena, Barbara,
and Jackie knew there would be filet mignon on the table,

Miami Beach in the winter, European vacations, and a Park Avenue address. But no one—not even Lou's respected confidant and longtime associate, Ed Risman, whom Lou spent more time with than Dena—could reverse Lou's decision about striking out on his own.

Lou was adamant. He felt that his new clubs would be successful because of his name and reputation. Risman disagreed and tried unsuccessfully to convince Lou otherwise. "Unfortunately," said Risman, "he thought his name was bigger than the Latin Quarter. I cautioned him at the time. I said, 'You know the Latin Quarter is above everybody.'"

Loew immediately took over the management of the Miami and New York clubs, and placed Ed Risman at the helm.

Lou leaked the split to the Broadway columnists. The New York *Mirror*'s Lee Mortimer wrote, "Another Broadway epoch comes to an end July 22 when Lou Walters, world famed as the 'Modern Ziegfeld,' severs his connection with the fabulous Latin Quarter, on Broadway." Lou Sobol saluted Lou in his *Journal-American* column, writing, "Broadway will miss Lou Walters. . . . Walters operated in the old-time tradition—plenty of show, beautiful showgirls, pert, lively chorus girls, a variety of acts with the entire bill usually headed by a star."

Lou's decision became one of the biggest show-business stories of the year. Almost two decades later a career move by Barbara would have similar reverberations.

Lou's last hurrah opened on July 22. It was entitled "The Latin Quarter Follies"—ten acts, twelve scenes, including the Frindts' Morlidor Trio, a unique novelty act discovered by Lou in which two shapely women propelled a swivel-hipped man through acrobatic contortions. The *Mirror*'s Frank Quinn called the whole show "a gorgeous display marking Walters' exit. Broadway will miss him and the Latin Quarter will have a high quality revue to console it after he leaves."

That night, after the second show, the club's entire

working corps and top bananas from all of Broadway gathered to wish him well. The next day Lou left for Miami to put the finishing touches on his new club, and make plans for his New York spot. If his apprehensive family and friends had to give this venture a name, they would have dubbed it "Lou Walters' Follies."

Lou poured every cent he had into the new clubs—all $424,000 he'd gotten from Loew the previous January in exchange for his share in the Latin Quarter.

Barbara was devastated by her father's decision. She knew that unless he was successful he would lose everything he had worked for over the years. The family would be ruined. If that happened, Barbara was certain that she alone would be responsible for the support of her parents and sister. An enormous burden would be on her shoulders. It was a nightmarish vision she'd had since adolescence when she first realized how precarious the family's existence was with a compulsive gambler as the breadwinner. What more could go wrong in her life? she wondered. At twenty-eight, her marriage was hanging by a thread; her blossoming career had been broadsided; and now her father had put everything they had on the come line.

Barbara's spirits were lifted somewhat when Jim Fleming, who had gone into independent production, telephoned to ask if she'd be interested in working as a researcher on a pilot he was developing for CBS. Fleming was impressed with Barbara's work and knew she would be an asset to his latest project. Naturally, Barbara jumped at the opportunity. She desired nothing more than to drown her troubles in work, something she would do throughout her life.

The network hoped to make a series out of journalist Jim Bishop's concept of re-creating major historical and news events. The program was to be called *The Day That . . .* The pilot episode on which Barbara worked dealt with the day that a B-29 bomber crashed into the Empire State Building. Barbara worked for about two months, writing and researching, alongside Fleming; Hubbell Robinson, a CBS executive; and Gerald Green, a colleague from the *Morning Show.* "There again she was marvelous, she had a terrific capacity for doing it. She was savvy about everything," said Fleming.

But the program was not put into production, and Barbara was out of work again.

Barbara spent Christmas 1957 in Miami with her family while Bob stayed in New York. Lou's new club had opened and everything had been going well until the holidays. Business was business and Risman had booked two killer acts into the Miami Latin Quarter—Lou's old friends Milton Berle and Sophie Tucker. It was stiff competition for Lou's new Café de Paris.

Barbara spent New Year's with her parents in Florida. On her return to New York, she and Bob agreed that the marriage was over.

They agreed to get a divorce and each hired an attorney. Barbara had talked about her marital problems with Lou and Dena and with her friends, and sought their counsel. "I just didn't see why she should stay if it wasn't good, even if the reasons weren't brilliant or marvelous," said a friend. "I said, 'What's the loss? So it was an expensive wedding ceremony, so big deal.' "

Instead of separating, Bob and Barbara stayed together in the Madison Avenue apartment until the final decree, still months away. Bob's attorney recommended that he remain on the premises so that he wouldn't be accused of abandonment. Barbara's lawyer was pushing for a favorable settlement, which resulted in the proceedings dragging on for almost six months.

With both of them continuing to live together during the negotiation stage, there was a lot of tension in the apartment. It was an embarrassing time for Barbara. She felt like a failure for not being able to make a go of it, blaming herself for the marriage's collapse. The impending di-

vorce from Bob was a blow to her pride and ego. It was
a horrendous time for her.

During those terrible months, Barbara felt isolated and
alone. It was all the more difficult because she wasn't working and had nothing to occupy her time except contemplating her impending divorce and worrying about how
her father's new club was faring in Miami. And the reports
from Dena were not encouraging. Barbara turned for support to one of her high school friends, Marilyn Landsber-
ger, who visited Barbara often, the only break in the icy
silence and palpable anxiety that permeated the apartment. Marilyn was supportive, attempting to help Barbara
emotionally during that period.

In late March, Barbara got the bad news that her father's
new Miami venture was on the verge of bankruptcy, ending its first season, never to reopen. Hard luck hit Lou
when Miami suffered its most disastrous season in history
along with the business recession. Lou left Miami a failure,
but he still felt he could take New York by storm with his
new club, which he also called the Café de Paris.

Barbara chose the easiest, fastest, and least expensive
place to get a divorce in those days, the state of Alabama.
New York at the time had very restrictive grounds for divorce, requiring proof of adultery. Reno divorces were in
vogue but there was a six-week residency requirement.

But the "Heart of Dixie" state required no minimum
time for residency.

All that Barbara was required to do to get her divorce
was to satisfy the court that she was a bona fide resident
of the state, which could simply be accomplished by filing
an affidavit.

During the third week of May 1958 Barbara flew to Alabama. Her case was presented in the obscure, northwest-
ern Alabama town of Hamilton, the seat of Marion
County.

In an affidavit, Barbara said of the marriage, "I could

stand it no longer." She asked to "resume my maiden name of Barbara Walters."

Barbara swore that she had not used Bob's "credit for any purchases or incurred any debts or obligations of any kind for which [Bob] may be liable except as listed."

They included: "Louis M. Segall, D.D.S., $40; S. B. Gusberg, M.D., $20; Mrs. Rosa Preston, dressmaker, $85; Saks Fifth Avenue, $350.95; Bloomingdale's, $68.22; and Travelands, Inc., $96.80. Total, $660.97."

In the separation agreement, Bob agreed to pay Barbara "the sum of One Hundred Fifteen Dollars weekly for her support" until she remarried. In addition, he promised to pay Barbara "on May 31st, 1958 a single lump sum of Sixteen Hundred Dollars."

On May 21, 1958, Circuit Judge Bob Moore, Jr., signed the divorce decree. Bob and Barbara had been man and wife exactly one month short of three years.

In the many years following the divorce, Bob Katz has maintained and continues to maintain a gentlemanly silence about his ill-fated marriage to Barbara Walters. About five months after their divorce, he met a beautiful younger woman, Rita Krupsik, who was an artist and photographer. In July 1989, Bob and Rita Katz happily celebrated their twenty-ninth wedding anniversary; during those years, Barbara Walters had two more marriages.

THE FAMILY BREADWINNER

In May 22, 1958, the day after Barbara's divorce, Lou Walters' new Café de Paris opened on Broadway near Fifty-third Street—five blocks north of the Latin Quarter. Seating twelve hundred, the shocking-pink and golden white club—the former Arcadia Ballroom—became Manhattan's largest and most glittery, featuring such marvels as a swimming pool shaped like a giant champagne glass, into which stripteaser Sherry Britton dived; a skating rink that showcased the Czech ice queen Mira Slava, who had escaped from behind the Iron Curtain, and six stages to spotlight the other variety acts and the girls. A trick publicity photo showed Lou holding a shapely showgirl in the palm of his hand: a lively portrait of the confident, enthusiastic, energized showman.

"I'm really going to bring back Broadway!" Lou declared. "This will make the Latin Quarter look old-fashioned. Wait until you see those girls. They're all beautiful, all thirty of them. I'm still young enough to open a place that Broadway really deserves. . . . We'll take the audience on a tour of Paris . . . the Moulin Rouge . . . cancan girls . . . the whole works." Lou made it sound like he had it in the bag.

Anticipating stiff competition from the master showman, rivals Elias Loew and Ed Risman oversaw a $150,000 renovation of the Latin Quarter that included such marvels as a rain curtain permitting tropical water effects and electrically operated bird cages in which the showgirls could swing over the heads of the audience.

Lou was paying the highest café rental in New York, $125,000 annually on a guarantee and percentage basis, and he'd spent $70,000 to remodel—retaining Rube Bodenhorn, who designed the decor of the Latin Quarter, to supply the motif. There was a small army of waiters, busboys, cigarette girls. The list of personnel—lighting and sound people, costumers, makeup artists, musicians—went on and on.

As the payroll mounted, so did other problems. Just days before the opening, Loew went to New York State Supreme Court, getting a temporary injunction restraining Lou from using the name "Lou Walters" in connection with the club. Lou intended to put his name up in lights, confident it could draw crowds on its own. But Loew's attorneys asserted Lou had agreed not to use his name in connection with a New York nightclub for three years when he and Loew severed their partnership months before.

Lou also alienated his other Broadway confreres, who claimed he was starting a talent war by opening a new club. All the big spots—Loew's Latin Quarter, Jules Podell's Copacabana, Jack Silverman's Old Romanian, and Ben Maksik's Town and Country in Brooklyn—featured big-name entertainers and elaborate floor shows. As the owners saw it, Lou was adding to the competition for talent, which meant paying higher salaries. It got so intense that Ed Risman unsuccessfully dangled an astronomical fifty thousand dollars a week in hopes of teaming Mae West with Rock Hudson, to go up against Lou's opening night headliner, Betty Hutton.

Lou's reasoned response to his competitors' complaints was "Anything that takes people away from TV is good for everyone."

Sadly, the old impresario would soon have to eat those words. The Café de Paris was a disaster from the beginning.

"All kinds of things happened that shouldn't have happened," said showgirl Chickie James, a Brooklyn-born platinum blonde who was one of Lou's most loyal and dependable girls from the Latin Quarter. "There was a huge swimming tank on the stage that exploded one night and water went all over the stage, the tables. It was a mess. One thing seemed to go significantly wrong after the next. I suspected there was a crew in there sabotaging him."

There were other problems, too. One of Lou's attorneys, Salvatore Alfano, recalled that he wasn't able to secure the cabaret license from the police department until the very afternoon of opening night. Loew also put heat on Lou's vendors.

"He was the meanest bastard that ever lived," asserted press agent Irving Zussman. "He gave out orders to his liquor, food, and linen suppliers—'If you deal with Lou Walters, you can't deal with me.' I imagine most of them followed what he said because the Latin Quarter was solid as a rock and the Café de Paris was a new venture."

One night, during the first week, Chickie James came to work, looked up at the marquee, and squealed with delight: CHICKIE JAMES PRESENTS CAFÉ DE PARIS. Lou devised a brilliant maneuver around the court injunction. As Chickie James observed, "My name was synonymous with the Latin Quarter. So having my name up there was almost like saying 'Lou Walters' Latin Quarter."

Loew was furious when he strolled by the club that night and saw Lou's strategy.

There was more trouble nine days after the club opened when Lou's headliner—singer, actress, comedienne Betty Hutton—announced she wouldn't remain for another two weeks as Lou had hoped. Hutton, a Paramount Pictures star known as "the Blonde Bombshell," was making her first nightclub appearance in New York since World War II when she worked with Danny Kaye.

"I'm really in a fix," Lou complained. "Who do I get of her stature? There's no one available at a minute's notice."

Desperately seeking a replacement for Betty Hutton, in a virtual state of panic, Lou made his most inappropriate booking ever: a wild rock and roll singer from Memphis who had recently made national headlines for marrying his thirteen-year-old first cousin. Lou's decision to hire Jerry Lee Lewis for his Broadway debut underscored the irrational state of mind the showman was in at the time. The Café de Paris had just hit an iceberg and Lou was going down with the ship as Lewis nearly destroyed a piano, singing "Great Balls of Fire" and "A Whole Lotta Shakin' Goin' On" to a virtually empty house.

Lou Walters had reached the end of his rope.

When even Lewis didn't show up the next night, the depressed and exhausted impresario returned early to the Hotel Navarro where he and Dena had rented a small apartment. The Miami and New York Café de Paris investments had eaten up most of his money, so the Walterses were forced to give up their Park Avenue place. A few hours later, Lou was rushed to Mount Sinai Hospital, unconscious and near death, victim of a heart attack, a nervous breakdown, and some suspected an attempted suicide.

It had been only twenty days since his Café de Paris dream turned into a nightmare.

On June 20, just two days short of a month since the club opened, Lou's Café de Paris filed voluntarily for bankruptcy, listing liabilities of $500,000.

After the forced closing of the club, Lou began a slow

recovery. Released from the hospital, he and Dena went to Miami where the doctors ordered the still-despondent impresario to rest.

Barbara inherited many of her father's traits: his devotion to work to the virtual exclusion of all other concerns, his preternatural show-business instincts, his penchant for secrecy, his propensity for privacy, and his susceptibility to mood swings and depression.

But Barbara was not the dreamer her father was. A pragmatist, she quickly sized up the situation: the Walters family was in dire financial straits; something needed to be done, quickly. Creditors would soon come banging on the Café de Paris's doors; medical bills were mounting; the family had to eat and needed a roof over its head; and Barbara shuddered at the thought of any gambling debts Lou might have outstanding.

According to a colleague of Lou's, Barbara got up her courage and asked for an emergency loan from one of Lou's pals, a flamboyant bear of a man and a habitué of the Latin Quarter, Louis Arthur Chesler.

A power broker of the first order, Chesler's friends and acquaintances ranged from powerful politicians to mobsters. A Canadian-born promoter with a Midas touch, he'd made millions in Florida land development, was chairman of Seven Arts Productions Ltd., a major film production and distribution company, and had helped establish casino gambling in the Bahamas—a venture that came under law enforcement scrutiny because of its alleged ties to organized crime. Chesler was a great crap shooter and card player who often sat in on Lou's gin rummy marathons.

As Lou Walters' daughter, Barbara grew up with dynamic, tough businessmen like Chesler in the background. She was fascinated with, and attracted to, their brand of wheeling and dealing, their power and machismo. So it would not be surprising that Barbara would seek financial help from Chesler, a generous man with a heart of gold when it came to friends down on their luck.

Chesler took a liking to, and became friendly with, Lou's colleague Irving Zussman. During one of their get-togethers, Chesler confided that he'd loaned Barbara fifteen thousand dollars to help her father through his financial difficulties, and that she had paid him back in a timely fashion. "This girl can have anything she wants from me," Chesler told Zussman. "Bit by bit every week she made payments until she cleaned up the debt."

Now Barbara began job hunting with the knowledge that the support of Lou, Dena, and Jackie was squarely on her shoulders; at twenty-nine she had to become the family's breadwinner.

The Café de Paris tragedy "was a real education," she said some years later. "We were suddenly bereft. I probably would have stayed married if I had anticipated that. I would have been too scared to call it off."

In New York, Barbara pounded the pavements looking for another job in television, using her old contacts, chasing down leads, to no avail. The recession that leveled the nightclub business and financially destroyed her father was also affecting the television industry. Jobs were nonexistent. The networks and local stations were cutting back. And, if by some chance a writing or production job opened, it certainly wouldn't go to a woman.

Barbara finally got a sixty-dollar-a-week job, heading up and being the sole employee of the newly created radio and television department at Tex McCrary, Inc., a well-connected New York public relations firm.

John Reagan (Tex) McCrary gave Barbara a chance because he was an old friend of her father's. "Lou had a wonderful reputation at a time when various Mafia people ran nightclubs in this town," said McCrary. "The showgirls that worked for him were looked after as though he were their uncle."

Convinced she would make a good employee, McCrary sent Barbara to his top executive, William Safire, with the instruction to "take this girl under your wing."

Barbara was officially hired by Safire, an innovative Mc-Crary PR man and one-time producer of the radio program that Tex did with his wife, Jinx Falkenburg. He'd started out with the company doing research for Tex and Jinx's syndicated newspaper column. Safire had been with the McCrary organization since 1949, following in the footsteps of his brother, Len Safir. Later, Bill Safire started his own public relations firm, before rising to national prominence as a speechwriter for President Nixon, an author, and a conservative columnist for the *New York Times*. But in those days, Safire was making one hundred dollars a week as a McCrary vice president, overseeing public relations for corporate accounts ranging from Levitt to Zeckendorf, along with the new TV and radio department in which Barbara worked.

Safire and Barbara didn't know each other when she came aboard but they had mutual friends, including Roy Cohn and Ted Cott. Safire also knew that his brother was a friend of Barbara's, and called him to ask about her. "I gave Bill the highest possible recommendation," said Len Safir. "Barbara was very lovely, sweet, and very attractive and I enjoyed her company and we were good friends."

Bill Safire was also impressed.

"I didn't have the foggiest notion about her father's problems," he said years later. "She didn't make a point of it. I hired her strictly on merit. It struck me she would be a perfect woman to pitch guests to radio and television producers. She wasn't making much more than a secretary. But people would kill for those jobs. They were glamorous jobs, and frankly fast-track jobs."

Barbara's work entailed sifting through press releases and letters extolling the virtues of McCrary's corporate clients. She'd zero in on the most interesting personalities, find some newsworthy angle, and then try to interest local

TV and radio producers in an interview. She also had the job of writing personality and corporate profiles of clients. Barbara was now on the other side of the street from where she had been in television as a booker; she was learning the art of flackery in the shop of a master. The experience would serve her well when she returned to television.

Though Barbara's assignment was rather mundane, the McCrary organization was a fascinating environment in which to work, and was a well-known training ground for others, such as Mike Wallace, who would rise to national prominence.

It was also a colorful place because over the years McCrary had assembled a stable of prestigious, sometimes controversial individual and corporate clients, some of whom needed their images polished. Around the time Barbara joined the firm, McCrary briefly handled PR for New England textile magnate Bernard Goldfine, a central figure in a Washington influence-peddling scandal involving Sherman Adams, an aide to President Eisenhower. When Lou Chesler came under attack at a Seven Arts stockholders meeting regarding his Bahamian gambling venture, it was McCrary who defended him, serving as Seven Arts' vice president of corporate affairs.

Barbara didn't dress or act like someone forced to bring home the bacon. While she was earning a modest $3,100 a year, she still had her weekly alimony, which was more than twice her salary. Combined, it made for a relatively comfortable income in those days. The first day she came to work the sun hit the diamond on the gold chain around her neck and the reflected rays caught the eyes of the other women in the office. "Oh, my! That's not for real, is it?" they asked incredulously, gathering around, admiring the rock. "The girls were a bit jealous," remembered McCrary's longtime assistant, Carolyn DeHarak. "It was a rather large diamond."

Barbara smiled, enjoying the attention. "This is my engagement ring," she boasted, holding it up like a trophy for their inspection, explaining that she had detached the three-carat stone from the setting and put it on the chain immediately after her divorce from Bob Katz. The other girls nodded, returning to their typewriters, looking dejectedly at their own costume jewelry. "That was a time when women were wearing a single diamond on a chain," said DeHarak. "Barbara was very fashionable."

But not very friendly. Her female co-workers found Barbara to be private, cold, aloof. She didn't socialize with the other women, all of whom had lesser jobs than Barbara's. "I think she enjoyed being around men, and felt more comfortable around men than women," observed DeHarak. "She was always friendly with Safire."

Safire and Barbara would occasionally go to a client dinner together but they never dated. "We became buddies or pals," he said. Safire found Barbara to be "crisp and businesslike. She didn't wear her heart on her sleeve. She wasn't gushy."

So Safire thought he'd make a point about her femininity at an office Christmas party where everyone was exchanging gifts. Safire's present was conservatively wrapped in a slim box. Barbara opened the package and held up its contents proudly: it was a sexy black negligee. Everyone gasped, knowing Barbara's conservative bent. But Barbara ran over to Safire and gave him a big hug. "Everyone got the point that I thought Barbara was a girl," said Safire.

Some two decades later, when Safire was "a media biggie or a White House aide," as he put it, Barbara was a guest at a somewhat formal party honoring him. With lots of other famous people gathered around, Barbara gave Safire a present. The gift turned out to be a sexy pair of black silk pajamas. Barbara gave Safire a sly look. He knew right away why she had chosen such a gift for him. Barbara hadn't forgotten the way Safire had made her feel more human in the eyes of her co-workers years earlier.

Barbara worked hard at McCrary's, quickly learning the ropes of the public relations game. She had an instinctive touch, a showman's feel for knowing precisely which program would be best for a particular client. She did her homework, getting to know the right bookers and producers. She made impressive presentations, demonstrating to a producer what made for a good show. Barbara took on every assignment with the same focused determination; nothing fazed her. And she felt no qualms about huckstering, even when she took on the assignment of hawking a one-armed golfer to show producers.

"She was quick-witted," said Safire. "She would go right for the news or where the human interest was. Of course that same talent applied later."

One day Barbara marched into Safire's office and demanded a ten dollar a week raise. She felt she deserved some financial recognition for her hard work, and she did.

As she sat before her boss, tensely awaiting his decision, Safire, "from the pinnacle of my economic profundity," gave the anxious young woman a lecture on a law of economics that she'd never forget.

"Barbara," he said firmly, "there are a great many young women in this big city who would give their eye teeth for this kind of job and that's why, because there's an enormous supply of labor for this job, we are able to get somebody for this low. So supply exceeds demand, which is why the salary is so low, and that's why you're not getting a raise.

"Barbara swallowed hard and took it. I mean, she wasn't about to quit. She was doing a fine job, and God knows she deserved a raise. But I gave her the supply and demand bit, because we were pretty cheap there. Nobody got any money. Everybody got huge opportunity, huge responsibility, and went on to do good things from there. But money? No."

Many years later, when Barbara became a television news star and had just accepted an unprecedented salary of one million dollars a year, one of the persons she immediately called was Bill Safire. "Hey," she yelled triumphantly over the phone, "remember that lesson you taught me years ago? Supply and demand? It works!"

"I've always thought of that call as a kind of nice recognition that she remembered her roots, that she wasn't going high hat," said Safire.

Barbara learned an even greater lesson while working for McCrary, one that would help her reach that seven-figure pinnacle. She learned how to ask the questions no one else did. Over the years, when she spoke profoundly of her talent as an interviewer, she never once gave credit to a slim, mimeographed tract for her enormous success.

"I gave to Barbara and all my kids a sort of textbook that we called 'Couch Questions,' " said McCrary. "The concept was you start out easy and you wind up tough." "Couch Questions" was developed by Len Safir for the inexperienced young reporters and researchers who were hired by McCrary to preinterview subjects for the "Tex and Jinx" programs and newspaper column. Tex wanted lively, revealing anecdotes about his guests. Barbara used the style manual when she interviewed corporate clients for press releases and TV and radio appearances.

The questions, written in the early 1950s, echo like veritable sound bites from the popular *Barbara Walters Special* programs of the mid-1970s and 1980s—the kinds of questions that became Barbara's trademark as an interviewer, such as "If you could be any character in history, who would you choose to be?"

"Those were questions that would trigger some revealing story," said Safire. The couch-questions concept stayed with Barbara and she turned it to her own use when she became a TV interviewer. "Great minds think alike," quipped Safire.

Barbara left the McCrary organization in 1960, remaining friends with Safire and Tex over the years. But after she became a TV star she described that period of her life as her "dark ages" years, telling one interviewer, "I had to plant news items and be aggressive. I hated it, but I was very good at it."

Somehow Lou had pulled himself out of his depression and recovered sufficiently from his heart attack to start producing shows again—in Miami and Las Vegas. But between the time Barbara left the McCrary organization and joined the *Today* show in early 1961, she went through another difficult period with her father, one of the most humiliating yet.

In the aftermath of the Café de Paris fiasco, an investigation disclosed that Lou had failed to report and pay $16,164 in city cabaret and gross business taxes.

While the amount might seem inconsequential today, the fact that the evasion was linked to one of the biggest names in the nightclub business sparked headlines in newspapers from New York to Miami, along with running stories in *Variety*. All of Barbara's friends and colleagues were aware of the scandal; her father had embarrassed her once again.

In February 1960, Lou was released on one thousand dollars bail and ordered to appear in Municipal Court on November 15, 1960, but he failed to show. "Seek Lou Walters on Tax Charge," headlined the *Journal-American*. "Night-Club Man Sought, Lou Walters Fails to Show Up Here for Tax Case," said the *New York Times*. "Lou Walters Faces Arrest On N.Y. Claim," wrote *Variety*. With Lou's failure to appear for his court appearance, Magistrate Edward J. Chapman revoked his bail and issued a bench warrant for Lou's arrest charging him with defrauding the city of tax money.

On November 23, 1960, Lou returned to New York and surrendered, telling Magistrate Chapman that he had been out of the city on the day of the hearing and could not afford the cost of transportation to New York. He was released for another hearing. A month later, the back taxes were paid and Magistrate Morton R. Tolleris levied an additional three-hundred-dollar fine against Lou.

Another sad and embarrassing chapter in the flamboyant career of Lou Walters had come to an end. In Barbara's life a new, momentous chapter was about to open.

THE *TODAY* SHOW

Though highly successful and generating huge profits, the *Today* show was in a state of near anarchy when Barbara Walters telephoned producer Fred Freed in the spring of 1961 to inquire about a writing job. Freed, who had left CBS with hopes of producing documentaries at NBC, loathed the program, which had taken its toll on a number of producers before him.

Freed's immediate predecessor, Shad Northshield, was inexplicably given the boot by erratic *Today* host Dave Garroway on the day after Christmas 1960. Actually, Garroway had his lawyer do the dirty deed, hoping to sweeten the blow over an expensive lunch. "We didn't want to ruin your Christmas and Dave didn't want to be here to tell you," the lawyer told Northshield, whose immediate response was, "What a prick!" Northshield was moved over to the news division, but would soon return to *Today*.

The sudden firing of Northshield was just one of many incidents suggesting strongly that Garroway was going off the deep end after a decade on the show, and Freed feared he would be pulled down with him, going the way of Northshield and the others. At the time, the program had been renamed *The Dave Garroway Today Show.* Privately, *Today* staffers had dubbed the $350,000-a-year Garroway "Big Spooky" because of his increasing weirdness.

Garroway was calling Freed at home at all hours with real and imagined problems, sometimes actually crying, forcing Freed to coddle and soothe his star like a baby— or a mental case. If that wasn't enough, Garroway had wrested control of the show from Freed, who had been at *Today* only a short time. Freed took pride in his organizational abilities, while Garroway liked to wing it, often dumping a show's lineup at the last minute, causing pandemonium in the studio. As producer, Freed had ultimate responsibility for what was broadcast, and with Garroway a loose cannon, Freed's career could have gone up in smoke had a disaster occurred on the air.

"The problem for me, really, was to hold the show together, not make it better, just keep it going from day to day," Freed recalled. "[Garroway] was then under a lot of physical and mental pressure. . . . During the time I was there he had become very unsure of himself; the pressure was endless. *Today* was just like mercury, you put it on in the morning and it's gone. . . . *Today* was Garroway's show, not mine, and that's not the way I like to function."

The problems were there for anyone to see on the set— a minefield where bizarreness and paranoia reigned, and a cutthroat atmosphere prevailed. Beryl Pfizer, the Today Girl at the time, kept a log of Garroway's odd behavior. Once, during a station break, he suddenly turned to her, confiding that a half dozen of his teeth had fallen out on the way to work and that he had glued them back in, displaying a bottle of "teeth glue" in his desk drawer to "prove" it.

Despite his queer manner, "Getting in good with Garroway was a good part of anyone's success there," Pfizer noted. "There was a highly competitive atmosphere on the show, and everybody was suspicious of everybody else." *Today* writer Charles (Chuck) Horner agreed: "It was a knife-in-the back kind of situation." Freed's lieutenant, associate producer Craig Fisher, said the *Today* show staff was large enough "so it could be factionalized and always was. Everybody bitched about somebody else once or twice a week."

Freed was hoping to survive this snake pit long enough to join his friend, Irving Gitlin, a colleague of Edward R. Murrow's and a respected documentary producer. In 1960, Gitlin was made executive producer of creative projects for NBC News and Public Affairs after losing to Fred Friendly for the prestigious job of executive producer of *CBS Reports.*

A CBS alumnus, Freed joined the *Today* show in early 1961 on the advice of his agent, J. G. (Jap) Gude. Their strategy was to prove to Gitlin, with whom Freed had worked in the past as a writer, that Freed had what it took to be a producer of a major network program. Then, they hoped, Gitlin would hire Freed to produce documentaries. "Fred never wanted to do the *Today* show," said Judy Freed, his wife at the time. "No way did he give a damn about that kind of thing. All he wanted to do was documentaries with Irv Gitlin. The *Today* show was not his idea of heaven."

So when Barbara called Freed seeking an audience to discuss job possibilities, she was talking to a distracted and discontented man who was biding his time on a show that was governed by chaos. But that situation, combined with the people she knew, helped Barbara to get hired.

Aspiring television writers were constantly calling *Today* seeking jobs and most, if not all, were given the typical brush-off: mail us your résumé. Barbara got through because she was not an unknown quantity—and because she used every contact and connection she had to snag the job. For one thing, she was a friend of a *Today* writer-

producer, Lester Cooper, who was a longtime pal of
Freed's; they had worked together at CBS. Barbara had
asked Cooper to put in a good word for her with Freed.
Cooper later told his wife, Audrey, that he had arranged
for Barbara's initial interview with Freed and felt, in a
sense, that he was responsible for her getting hired. Years
later he expressed irritation that Barbara had never given
him proper credit for his help. There's no doubt that Cooper had been helpful to Barbara and would continue to
be so sporadically in the future.

Besides Lester Cooper, Barbara had another friend at
Today, reporter Paul Cunningham. They'd met by chance
waiting for a flight to New York from Miami while she was
still working for Tex McCrary. She'd charmed Cunningham and he'd taken up her cause with Freed, letting it be
known that Barbara was a pretty and talented young
woman who had early-morning TV writing and booking
experience.

Barbara's connection with Tex McCrary, however,
probably helped the most.

While at CBS, Freed had been pushing to produce a
magazine program called *Celebrity*, the pilot of which pro-
filed an important McCrary corporate client, New York
real-estate czar William Zeckendorf, Sr.—the Donald
Trump of his day. Zeckendorf's real estate company, Webb
& Knapp, came under Bill Safire's jurisdiction at McCrary,
and Barbara once hosted a party for Bill Zeckendorf, Jr.,
as part of her duties for McCrary and Safire. It was then
that Freed would have first met Barbara and been impressed with her. That impression, along with Lester Cooper's and Paul Cunningham's recommendations, certainly
helped Freed decide to hire her—along with input from
his wife.

"I had good judgment and he trusted me," said Judy
Freed. "He gave me a rundown about Barbara. She obviously had the credentials and the background. Fred didn't
feel *Today* was a serious journalistic show, so she seemed

right for that sort of thing; and I was always eager for him to hire women. I said she sounds great, terrific. As long as Barbara didn't make life ridiculous for him, I just don't think he cared that much. It was hard to get him to even watch the show in the morning."

As a final step before hiring her, Freed assigned Craig Fisher to take Barbara to lunch. Freed wanted to be certain Barbara wasn't going to be a difficult employee. The prevailing feeling among men in the business at the time was that the few women in television were "bitches" who were impossible to work with.

One story that circulated in the fraternity of network television news and public affairs writers, directors, and producers in New York in those days, a tale that prompted gales of macho laughter, and one that underscored the determined chauvinism that existed, involved famed anthropologist Margaret Mead. Because of a foul-up involving the scheduling of a guest for a highbrow Sunday afternoon program on CBS, Mead was proposed as a fill-in guest. A film editor who had worked with her before thought she was a terrible prima donna. When her name was suggested, the show's director said, "Oh, Christ, that bitch!" And Shad Northshield, who was the producer, said, "It's a live show and it's got to get done. Yeah, maybe she's a bitch, but let's not forget she's *our* bitch. We use her."

Over lunch, Fisher was impressed with the attractive, well-dressed, and poised woman who sat across the table from him. "Barbara was obviously very verbal—and very intense. No matter what we talked about she had an intelligent opinion. I had the idea that she would be a terrific asset to the writing staff." Fisher reported his "gut feeling" to Freed that Barbara "appeared to be a bright lady . . . a really swift individual."

Freed hired Barbara as a writer on a thirteen-week freelance basis at the Writer's Guild minimum scale plus a negotiated fee, about three hundred dollars a week. Her first assignment on the show was to do writing and research for "The Face."

The beautiful Anita Colby had earned the sobriquet in the mid-1930s when, as a model, she was sitting with her father, New York *World* sportswriter and Pulitzer Prize–winning cartoonist Bud Counihan, and his pals Ernest Hemingway and Quentin Reynolds. The men were discussing the war in Spain when Anita—who was considered the Paulina of her day—started chattering away about something other than the serious, manly subject at hand. Reynolds turned to her and said affectionately, "The Face speaks." The men laughed, Anita blushed, and the term stuck.

Colby became the most famous model to bear the stamp of John Roberts Powers; she was a five-foot-seven, chestnut-haired, green-eyed beauty whose face appeared on thirty-two magazine covers in one month. She'd also appeared in a few films and was an assistant to David O. Selznick.

In the spring of 1961, the S&H Green Stamp Company decided to retain Colby, then forty-seven, as its national spokeswoman. The campaign included a segment to be hosted by her on the *Today* show. A highly successful promotional gimmick, Green Stamps were given away to customers as an incentive to shop at certain supermarkets and service stations. Housewives would save the stamps in small books and then redeem them for gifts.

Colby agreed to do *Today* as long as the S&H segments were presented as legitimate news features, rather than as a hard commercial pitch. "I didn't want to sound like a huckster," she said. Colby, a classy woman with an upper-class Boston accent, would often joke good-naturedly on the air about the sponsor, telling viewers, "I just *stah-ted* a new *stah-mp* book. Can you *im-ah-gine* how *fah* I have to go to get that limousine in the catalog?"

Freed introduced Barbara to Colby who liked her immediately. "She had to impress *me* to get this job." While

Colby didn't remember her, Barbara pointed out that they had met at Tex McCrary's office once or twice. And Barbara flattered Colby by recounting all of the nice things she'd heard about her from various guests on Tex and Jinx's show. Barbara struck Colby as a serious young woman with a sense of humor. After Barbara made "some cute remarks," and asked a few pointed questions, Freed ushered the two women into Garroway's office for his approval, which he nodded. As Colby left his office she thought to herself, "That man is iffy. He's on something."

Before joining the *Today* show, Colby had owned and operated the Women's News Service, which supplied features to some two hundred newspapers around the country. She had a backlog of stories from which to draw and numerous well-known friends and sources who could appear as guests on the show. As a result, she told Barbara, "Don't worry, don't knock yourself out."

At the time Colby joined the show, *Today* was being taped for next-day airing, with Frank Blair's news reports inserted live. On the day her segment was scheduled to premiere, April 12, 1961, Colby tuned in from the fashionable East Side apartment she shared with her father and mother and saw Garroway on live, interviewing a Yale professor. That morning the Russians had won the "space race," at least temporarily, by launching a cosmonaut, Major Yuri Gagarin, into orbit in a five-ton sputnik.

Henceforth, Garroway intoned to the viewers, the whole show would be done live. "Good reporting," said Colby's father to the set. "I said, 'God, that means I'm going to have to get up in the morning. This is not in my contract.'" The daily grind of the show eventually became so exhausting for her that she fainted in the studio once during a rehearsal.

For Barbara, being assigned to Colby was perfect. Anita represented the kind of women to whom the upwardly mobile, status-conscious Barbara would always be drawn— well-bred, urbane, cultured, and socially well-connected ladies who lunched; women whose names appeared in boldface in the society and gossip columns; chic women who offered Barbara entree into circles that could help her professionally and socially.

Barbara and Colby had mutual interests such as fashion. She would have Barbara arrange for people like Eugenia Sheppard, the fashion editor, to appear with an exclusive report on the Paris fashions. Colby had Barbara set up interesting demonstrations, such as having fashion designer Pauline Trigère cut an original piece on camera. "We did a good job together," said Colby, "and got a lot of firsts."

Colby, who initially thought Barbara's goal was to be a television writer, soon realized that her true ambition was to be sitting in front of the camera, not behind a typewriter. It was as if Barbara was playing Eve Harrington to Anita Colby's Margo Channing. Barbara certainly wasn't conniving and vicious like Ann Baxter's vixen in *All About Eve*, but she unquestionably displayed the same determination, ambition, and drive—and would be equally as successful.

"Had I been the same age as Barbara, I'm not sure I would have been too happy about her because I think she would have killed me," Colby recalled, laughing at the memory of their association. "She had a bit of pushiness and aggressiveness. I was not as forward as she. I said to myself, 'Thank God I'm not her age, she'd clobber me.'"

Colby observed that Barbara "longed to be on television.

> She didn't make any bones about it. She told me, "I'd love to do this someday." I could see, when I was on the air, the way she'd stand off to the side and mouth the words she'd written for me. She was pining to be in my spot.
>
> One day she said, "I think of you when I see myself." I know she admired me for what I had done, the fame I had received. She was always polite and respectful to me.
>
> I said, "Look Barbara, I've had it. I've had all the fame.

I'm really not interested in this. I want to know how much you want it. I think you could take over at the desk. It could be more than doing the S&H Green Stamp thing. I'll put in a word for you. I'll take you to my diction teacher." And she said, "Oh, yes. Oh, God. I want it so badly. I do. I do!"

Colby took Barbara to her voice coach, a man who had a number of television celebrity clients, and an interesting technique. In order to demonstrate the distractions of doing live television, he'd ask his students to start talking while watching themselves in mirrors that lined his Manhattan studio. As they talked, he'd have them cut out paper dolls while trying to confuse them with hand signals. Barbara told Colby she found the man's technique "interesting" but she never returned to his class.

Barbara was a pragmatist; she wanted practice, not theory. So Colby began giving her protégée opportunities to get on camera.

One of Barbara's first location assignments for Colby was to cover fashion week, when all the fashion editors in the country descended on New York to cover the designer shows. *Today* had a camera at the scene with Barbara, while Colby did narration at the studio. It was Barbara's first appearance, albeit a minor one, on the *Today* show. Viewers saw the models on the runway, and the fashion reporters running to the phones to call their publications. The show was not in color in those days, but you couldn't miss Barbara in the crowd. She was smart enough to wear a white skirt and blouse so she would stand out from all the others.

"Oh, she was shrewd," said Colby. "I used to marvel at her. She did everything meticulously, to have it all completely right."

Barbara started finding stories that she could do on camera, generating more exposure for herself.

Revlon had just opened a glamorous salon in midtown

Manhattan. At Barbara's suggestion, Colby arranged for her to be there with a camera to illustrate how the other half lived to a legion of frumpy housewives across America who were getting their dour husbands and bratty kids off for the day. Viewers saw Barbara's head swathed in a big towel, her face covered with cosmetic gook, her body wrapped in a sheet, and her feet dangling in a little pond while she was having a pedicure and toenail polish applied. It was a funny scene and Barbara played it to the hilt.

"Barbara was very clever," said Colby. "Not only had she written those segments, but she acted them out."

Colby also was awe-struck watching Barbara ground herself in the dynamics of the *Today* show. Barbara knew she wouldn't be working for Colby forever, and since the S&H segment was essentially an insert, and therefore somewhat separate from the rest of the program, she felt it would be to her advantage to move into *Today*'s mainstream.

Virtually overnight, Barbara got to know everyone on the staff—the directors, the assistant directors, the editors, camera operators, floor managers, the other writers—who they were, what they did, and where they stood in the chain of command. "If she couldn't get in through the door," observed Colby, "she'd come through the window. She was all over the lot. I never saw anybody who covered so much territory. She was very ambitious."

Today writer Charles Horner was sitting in his tiny office one morning working the phones when a well-dressed, striking brunette appeared in the doorway. "Hello, I'm Barbara Walters, the new writer," she said. "Hi, I'm Chuck Horner. Welcome aboard and good luck." Barbara stepped closer and sat on the edge of Horner's desk. "Well, frankly, Chuck," she said, "how the hell do you write this fucking show?" Horner laughed. "Have you got an hour?" he asked.

Horner, eleven years Barbara's senior, married and a former head writer for radio and TV kibitzer Arthur Godfrey, was instantly captivated by her, and they became fast friends. Not only had she charmed him with her choice of adjectives, but she mesmerized him with her look, literally and figuratively. "She was a very sexy girl. I'm a man and she was a great addition to the staff even though she hadn't done very much. I felt immediately attracted to her."

Horner, who had joined the show a year earlier, explained to Barbara that the job was demanding and tough; that you were lucky if you could go home at a decent hour; that you practically lived at the damned studio. He gave her a verbal map of the pitfalls and a roster "of some of the people to watch out for who would sandbag you."

"I noticed her eyes," Horner recalled. "I was impressed by the way she looked at you; her eyes were very inquiring. When she talked she looked straight into your eyes. When there was a pause you could see that the machinery in her head had been set in motion by what you told her. She was already organizing things, getting things done, moving forward."

Anita Colby agreed: "Barbara had enormous powers of concentration, *enormous*."

As Barbara began to learn the ropes, Garroway was acting more bizarre.

His paranoia and crazy gestures were rampant. He shocked Beryl Pfizer by telling her that he had installed microphones in the gargoyles in front of his East Side townhouse so that he could listen to people plotting to break in. Another time she saw him drink a cup of tea after dipping a hairbrush in it and running the brush through his hair.

In his private life, the marriage of Garroway and his second wife, Pamela Wilde de Coninck, an actress, ballet dancer, and movie and TV producer, was on the rocks. Garroway was taking drugs that kept him awake, so he would spend his nights tweaking the engines on his classic cars. Meanwhile Pamela, the mother of three-year-old Dave Garroway, Jr., was being treated with medication for a nervous disorder. On April 28, 1961—shortly after Barbara joined the show—Garroway's wife took an overdose of barbiturates, and was found dead in her bedroom.

Pfizer never forgot that day—not only because of the terrible tragedy but because that was her last day as Garroway's female cohost. She had taped the show on the 28th and it was aired on the 29th, along with a live news cut-in reporting that Mrs. Garroway was dead.

Pfizer was the latest casualty in a long line of so-called Today Girls—some famous, some not—whose job it was to do weather, make pleasant chitchat, and act cute and pert; they were TV's equivalent of the geisha. The roster included a one-time Miss America, Lee Ann Meriwether; a former Miss Rheingold, Robbin Bain; actresses like Betsy Palmer; and singers like Helen O'Connell.

Years later, when Barbara became famous, it was reported that she was the first woman writer on the Today show to become "talent," a myth that became fact in future stories about her. For example, a June 1967 Boston newspaper profile by a television columnist stated unequivocally: "Of the many ladies who have been featured regularly at one time or another, at the 'Today Show' desk, only one was never a model or an actress. That would be Brookline-bred Barbara Walters, who has worked with [Today] for more than a half-dozen years, first as a writer, and more recently, as on-camera reporter-interviewer."

But Pfizer was neither a model nor an actress and was, in fact, the first writer to make the Cinderella-like transition in 1960, almost four years before Barbara put on the glass slipper. "It is true that I was the first Today writer to get on air," said Pfizer. "I've never understood why the record has been so fuzzy."

Barbara Walters and Anita Colby joined the Today "family" during the period leading up to Pfizer's last day on the show. At the time, Barbara, Anita, and Beryl were the only women regulars on Today's talent and production roster. There were a few lowly female gofers; the rest were secretaries. So when Barbara and Colby came aboard, Pfizer watched them with interest—but she had little contact, since Anita and Barbara, for the most part, put together their S&H package independently. Pfizer was aware of Colby's well-publicized background, and had heard a bit of scuttlebutt about Barbara.

"I was aware of her because Lou Walters' Latin Quarter was a big thing when I was growing up out in New Jersey. I was quite aware that she was the daughter of an impresario and that she had a show-business background, and I think that stood her in good stead. My God, that made her a lot more savvy about how to do things on the air than the rest of them. Her public relations know-how helped, too. She knew how to get in touch with people. She knew how to pick up a phone and get to them."

A competitive spirit and a jealous mood prevailed in the studio. Pfizer, who was a few years older than Barbara, had everything Barbara desired: the on-air job; the blond, June Allyson, girl-next-door look; even recognition in print—these were credentials Barbara wanted and would one day possess.

"We [women] were tougher on each other than men were on women in those days because there were so few jobs," Pfizer said. "The one writing job on the Today show and the one on-air job on the Today show had everybody in town fighting. We didn't know that was discrimination back then. I always thought I had the best of everything. It was a plum job at that point."

A few weeks after Beryl Pfizer left the show she made an appointment to meet with Bill McAndrew, who headed the news division at NBC. Pfizer, who was known and respected for her work on Today, was hoping for a job as a reporter. "He just looked at me and said, 'We already have a woman reporter.' And that was that. The thing that made me so furious looking back on it is not what he said, but that I accepted it and didn't pick up the desk and slam it down and say, 'Yeah, but you got a man—does that mean you have only one man!' It was a long time before we got with it and realized that things didn't have to be that way just because that's the way we grew up."

Besides the permanent Today Girl slot, there was another entity known as the Girl of the Week. These were moderately successful, attractive young women—models, actresses—who wanted to be on the show for a quick fix of national exposure. "Sometimes they couldn't even read. They were extraordinary," recalled John Lord, an Englishman who joined the show as a writer in mid-1961 and became a close friend and officemate of Barbara's. "The 'Girl of the Week' was literally someone who came into the studio and stood there and read copy. I remember writing a line for one of them to read introducing a woman singer. It said, 'Now, here's a girl who's really going places.' Clearly, Barbara didn't like the idea. I don't think any of us really liked the idea. It was silly."

But agents were constantly pitching women to the show and Garroway was intrigued with the idea of discovering new talent, as he did with Pfizer, so the concept stayed, at least for a while.

"Barbara knew about all those beauty queens who had worked on the show and she didn't think she could make it as a beauty queen," Pfizer observed. "She saw me and she said, 'Okay, a writer can make it.' And so she decided that she was going to lay heavy on being a writer and make it on the show that way."

Barbara could not have been working for the show at a better time. Garroway's increasingly outlandish and erratic behavior was signaling the end of his long reign, and that boded well for her. Under his regime, writers and producers were axed routinely if they didn't mesh with his quirky personality. Garroway would have found Barbara too controlled, too rigid, not creatively offbeat enough in her thinking to interact with his warped view of things. He cherished writers who had a preoccupation like his for the odd and unexpected. "Nobody ever could have made it the way Barbara Walters made it on the show if Garroway had remained in charge," Pfizer contended. "He wouldn't let anyone move in on his turf, which was being in charge of the interviewing and everything else."

Garroway was never the same after the death of his wife. He had been negotiating for a new contract at the time but the powers at NBC knew he was unstable and volatile and they had second thoughts about meeting his demands. Just before air time one morning in June 1961, Garroway stretched out on the studio floor and refused to get up. When word of his tantrum reached the executive suite it was quietly decided not to renew him. Garroway went upstairs and resigned. Subsequently he would make a few vain attempts to return to broadcasting, but his time had long passed. In July 1982, Dave Garroway, then sixty-nine, died of an apparent self-inflicted gunshot wound in his suburban Philadelphia home.

With Garroway gone, a new era was beginning at *Today*, and Barbara was in on the ground floor.

NBC president Robert Kintner, a one-time print journalist and strong advocate of news and public affairs programming—when he was at ABC he preempted the soap operas for the Army-McCarthy hearings—turned *Today* over to the news division, which had always been envious of the show's position, panache, and independence. Fred Freed was given the task of pink-slipping some of Garroway's cohorts. Freed knew that with Garroway gone, he would soon follow, and he was gleefully counting down the days. His brief tenure during Garroway's last months had proven to Irving Gitlin that he had the makings of a network producer, and he would finally be given the opportunity to produce documentaries. His agent's scheme had worked.

Kintner decided to pit several of NBC's top correspondents against one another for Garroway's job, each getting a two-week tryout. The contenders were John Chancellor, just returned from covering the Kremlin; Edwin Newman, back from Europe; and veteran Washington correspondents Ray Scherer and Sander Vanocur. All four newsmen did their tryouts but Chancellor immediately caught Kintner's eye and he got the job. Newman was assigned to replace Frank Blair in the delivery of hard news, with Blair taking over sports, weather, and feature material.

Kintner's plan looked good on paper. But in the end the only one who would truly benefit from the new format was Barbara Walters.

Chancellor's first request when he came aboard was that Shad Northshield return as producer. They were buddies who had worked together years before at the Chicago *Sun-Times*. When Barbara heard the news about Northshield, she was ecstatic; they'd hit it off so well on the old CBS morning show.

"By this time at *Today* we were all more experienced and more sophisticated," said Northshield. "We were once again trying to invent something. It would be the first time in history that anyone tried to put on an entertaining news program, and we would try very seriously."

For a time, Barbara continued writing the S&H segment for Anita Colby. But with Northshield running the show she became a full-time staff writer.

Barbara was now sharing a small office with John Lord, a handsome, bright, and witty writer who was hired by Freed two weeks before Garroway left the show. Lord had started in American television in 1960, working on an ABC documentary series, *Winston Churchill: The Valiant Years*.

Lord and Barbara's office became the focal point for boisterous behavior and camaraderie. The third member of the group was Northshield. "John loved her and she him and they were a great brother-sister-like team. They used to share this little office, so I'd hang out there because the three of us would laugh a lot," said Northshield.

"It all jelled because Chancellor was ready for a giggle

and so were we," added Lord. "Barbara was funny. She was hip. She had this ironic edge, and she'd clown around, but it wasn't to get anybody's favor. It was just the way she was. What I liked most about her were her intelligence and her extraordinary sense of humor. You'd make jokes and she'd react very quickly. People thought she was sharp and critical, but I never found that."

Others on the staff saw Barbara in a different light—a tough, street-smart aggressive woman determined to get all she could for herself.

"She cultivated that," Lord observed, "but underneath she was very far from that." Lord saw a bravado in Barbara that hid what he perceived to be shyness, insecurity, and a lack of sophistication.

One of Barbara's first features that Northshield approved was about bicycling in Central Park. Barbara was never athletically inclined, but bicycling was something she had enjoyed since she was a child. She proposed that the piece would show an interesting slice of New York urban life to viewers around the country. Northshield readily agreed. Barbara wrote and edited the film story, which was aired "on a day like the Fourth of July when nobody was watching," Northshield recalled. "She kept asking to do it, and we did, and it was good."

Northshield was always looking for ideas and Barbara pitched her old standby: coverage of a fashion show. Except this one was neither to be in the studio, nor filmed in the garment district. Barbara proposed, and Shad approved, of her going to Paris for three weeks to cover the Dior and Maxime fall shows. Paris! Three weeks! The other more senior members of *Today*'s otherwise all-male writing team reacted not unexpectedly: they were furious. While it was a "womansy" story, the trip and the kind of perks that went with it naturally made her colleagues jealous, and that envy quickly turned to a resentment that manifested itself in overt sexism toward Barbara among some of her male colleagues.

Beryl Pfizer's replacement as the Today Girl, Robbin Bain, normally would have narrated the piece. But on her return from Paris, Barbara had another suggestion for Northshield: Why should someone else read the script that she had written, for film that she had edited? Wouldn't it be more authoritative for her to do the voice-over since she had been on the scene? Northshield agreed.

Thus, on August 29, 1961—with an introduction by Frank Blair—Barbara Walters made her first official on-air appearance on the Today show. Blair watched Barbara closely and saw not a scintilla of nervousness; her voice and hands were steady, her manner confident. Northshield was extremely pleased—the assignment was a success and Barbara seemed able to handle herself well on camera. It looked like he had made a good discovery. And no one seemed too bothered by the fact that she had pronunciation problems.

Barbara's appearance also impressed other NBC News reporters who weren't even aware of her existence up to that point. "I watched the show that day and thought, 'This girl is pretty good,'" said Ray Scherer. "I wrote her a note about it and I got back a very effusive thank-you. Barbara was delighted that somebody had noticed her." Barbara did such a good job that she would be sent again the following year to cover the Paris couture openings.

Barbara's on-air appearances, at that point, were sporadic. Her main duties included writing copy for the talent, setting up interviews, generating story ideas, and preinterviewing guests for the show. The latter was one of the more interesting facets of the job because most of the guests were famous and fascinating people.

One day Barbara was sent out to preinterview the director Otto Preminger, who was going to appear the next day. Barbara got all dressed up for the assignment, but when she arrived at the office her colleagues began teasing her about her fancy outfit. Barbara ignored the ribbing, boasting that Preminger was a friend of her family and that she wanted to look particularly nice for him. End of discussion.

A few hours later, Barbara returned to the office and told Northshield that a terribly embarrassing incident had occurred. She explained that, while she was talking to Preminger, one of her stockings had gotten loose and started to slide down her leg, the one she curled under her as she sat on his sofa. Her garter, it seemed, had snapped. She tried to deal with the runaway hose as best she could under the critical gaze of the famous director. It was, she said, a very daunting experience.

Moments after she finished telling the story to her amused producer, a messenger arrived with a dozen long-stemmed American Beauty roses for Barbara. In an envelope attached to the flowers was the errant garter, which Preminger had found between the cushions. "She died," remembered Northshield, still chuckling years later, "but she took it well."

PHILIPPE OF
THE WALDORF

Around the time Barbara joined the *Today* show, she was in the midst of a quiet romance with a suave, thrice-married roué eighteen years her senior, a man who was a convicted white-collar criminal. He was Claudius Charles Philippe—known internationally as "Philippe of the Waldorf."

At the time Barbara started seeing Philippe—which was not long after he figured in a federal grand jury tax evasion and kickback probe—he had just joined the Zeckendorf Hotels Corporation, following almost three decades as the Waldorf-Astoria's vice president in charge of catering, head of its banquet department and kitchens, and director of sales. With Philippe as the Waldorf's guiding genius, the hotel did a bigger banquet and catering business than any other in the world.

Philippe was a dapper figure in his custom-made conservative English suits by Wimbledon, ties from Sulka, and white poplin shirts from Paris with French cuffs and gold button cuff links. During his heyday, the slickly dark-haired, blue gray–eyed Philippe commanded with an iron hand an army of Waldorf head waiters, assistant head waiters, waiters, cooks, stewards, page girls, file girls, and stenographers. He even had personal French- and English-speaking secretaries available around the clock.

With so many activities in the hotel to oversee, Philippe often didn't see daylight for days—living in a fifth-floor apartment at the hotel, Suite 5-E, that was filled with books, china, and personal memorabilia. Though loving his work, Philippe lived for the weekends when he would be driven in his white Cadillac to his elegant country house, Watch Hill Farm, in Peekskill, New York, where Barbara became his constant companion in the early Sixties.

Philippe was a highly visible and engaging figure in New York society. He all but single-handedly established a Manhattan society tradition, a charity affair known as the April in Paris ball. One day he got on the phone and called his friend, the famous party giver, Elsa Maxwell. "Elsa, we ought to give a party for the two thousandth anniversary of the founding of Paris—something fancy." She agreed, and the event has been held every October since the first one in 1951, the year Barbara graduated from Sarah Lawrence.

He also organized two great wine and gourmet societies—Les Amis d'Escoffier, which consisted of some two hundred chefs and related purveyors of food who held two dinners a year at various New York hotels; and the Lucullus Circle, a group of wealthy and powerful men such as David Rockefeller, Bernard Gimbel, Duncan Hines, Alfred Knopf, and Alexis Lichine, who gathered five times a year for dinner and wine selected by Philippe.

Barbara met Philippe through the other impresario in her life, her father. Claude Philippe and Lou Walters mixed in some of the same circles, had mutual friends in the entertainment and restaurant fields, dealt with some of the same vendors, and their business endeavors sometimes converged. When they began seeing each other, Barbara and Philippe also had mutual friends such as Roy Cohn, Bill Safire, Tex McCrary, and Jinx Falkenburg, among others.

The Lou Walters–Claude Philippe connection was fascinating in that, in so many ways, Philippe could have been Lou's clone, which was an attraction for Barbara. They were both born in London and learned their respective trades as teenagers, becoming enormously successful. Both were small, intense, and agile men—charming and creative, extremely private and domineering. Walters and Philippe shared a love for the finer things—vintage wines, expensive clothing and jewelry; literature, ballet, and theater. They both smoked cigars, wore black horn-rimmed glasses, and dressed conservatively. While neither was handsome, they had a charisma that worked its magic on women and men alike.

Like Lou with Barbara, Philippe had a beautiful, bright, healthy daughter named Claudia, who was a student at Wellesley. Although twelve years younger, she and Barbara got along exceptionally well, almost like sisters, during the time Barbara was involved with Philippe. Weekends at Watch Hill Farm, Barbara fit in like a member of the family in Claudia's eyes. In New York, Claudia accompanied her father and Barbara to the theater. Claudia liked Barbara—finding her warm, amusing, funny, and intelligent—and saw an enormous amount of closeness, affection, and respect between her father and Barbara.

Lou Walters and Claude Philippe had other similar attributes. Both were workaholics, perfectionists, and tough taskmasters, traits Barbara also shared. Furthermore, Lou and Philippe were self-destructive men who lived on the edge—Lou as a compulsive gambler, Philippe as a man who played by his own rules. They were men who got into serious legal and financial entanglements—Lou with his nightclub failures, bankruptcies, gambling and business debts;

Philippe with his sexual overindulgence and criminal activity that could have resulted in his going to prison.

On October 2, 1958, Philippe's society friends were shocked when the headlines screamed that the famed Philippe of the Waldorf had been indicted by a federal grand jury on four counts of income tax evasion totaling $88,706 for the years 1952 through 1955. Additionally, he was indicted for concealing the receipt of "cash, currency, or kickbacks" from caterers supplying the Waldorf-Astoria at a time when he controlled purchases of $2,500,000 worth of food and $1,000,000 worth of beverages annually.

The criminal case against Philippe came less than four years after he was the subject of a highly complimentary twenty-two-page profile in *The New Yorker*, which was written as if about a reigning monarch. He was that famous, that renowned, that held in awe, that worthy of such a treatment. In an eerie foreshadowing, a *New Yorker* cartoon, unrelated to the Philippe piece, but appearing on one of the pages of the profile, showed two convicts in a prison chapel, one saying to the other, "Which commandment are *you* in for?"

At his hearing, Philippe pleaded not guilty to the charges. He faced five years imprisonment and a fine of ten thousand dollars on each of the counts if found guilty.

The case destroyed his esteemed career at the Waldorf, but his wealthy and influential friends rallied around. Eight months after the indictment, he resigned from the Waldorf to join the Zeckendorf organization as a consultant in the planning, development, and operation of a new midtown hotel. Meanwhile, the case dragged on for two years. Finally, in September 1960, while he was involved with Barbara, Philippe dropped his cries of innocence and pleaded guilty in U.S. District Court to evading $25,471.43 in income taxes and was fined ten thousand dollars.

Several months after the conviction, Zeckendorf and Philippe parted company more than a year before his contract was to expire. He then joined Loew's Hotels, Inc., as general manager of the Summit and Americana Hotels in New York.

Normally intensely private about his personal life, Philippe was extra discreet about his relationship with Barbara. Jeremyn Davern, who worked for Philippe for four years beginning in about 1959, remembered that when Philippe had a date with Barbara he would note it in his appointment book in code.

"To hide the fact that he was seeing Barbara Walters," Davern said, "he would write 'seven o'clock LQ.' And LQ stood for Latin Quarter, which I thought was really kind of marvelous and intriguing."

Davern recalled that Barbara occasionally visited Philippe at his office, and she was interested in meeting her because of the Walters name. "Barbara was a young, attractive woman around New York trying to get ahead. She liked Claude Philippe a lot. He was a real charmer. One became accustomed to having women fluttering around him. I didn't really get the impression that he was in love with her. I think he liked her. She was pretty smart and he liked smart women."

Philippe didn't have to pursue women; they came after him in droves, according to a number of women who knew him. Mira Sheerin, one of his assistants, recalled being handed letters by Philippe from women desiring to see him. "Because I knew French he would give me all of his personal mail to answer," said Sheerin, who worked for Philippe from 1963 to 1968. "I would be flabbergasted by what the women were writing to him. I would see these letters and blush. These were women with whom he had a personal relationship. Sometimes there were names I could recognize."

To many women Philippe was a Svengali. "He had something very sexual in him," said Sheerin. "While he could be very gallant, at the same time he would not stick by all the rules that American women expected, at least the rules of the women in the Sixties. But then there would come this magnificent bouquet of roses. He would sweep them off their feet, *literally*. He would make women feel very feminine and desirable even if this was not the case, even if he did not feel that way. He was so different from the American male."

Philippe was aloof with women, thus making himself more desirable. As a result women would pursue and seduce him. "Why they would do it is probably because one of their friends would tell them Claude was really terrific [in bed]. You know how that goes with many ladies," said Sheerin.

For Barbara, a relationship with a man such as Philippe was extraordinary to those who knew her—completely out of character, unthinkable. Men with whom she had been involved up to this point in her life saw her as cool and controlled, not warm or passionate. She was also a woman who was always conscious of her image and reputation, which could have been threatened because of Philippe's excesses and legal problems. But Philippe's charm, his alchemy, whatever powers he had over women, apparently had a strong effect on Barbara, greater than any other man before him. She seemed less inhibited and circumspect with him, more open to the joys of love and romance.

Despite her show-business upbringing, her Sarah Lawrence pedigree, and the chic and confident mask she wore, Barbara was, in some respects, rather provincial and inexperienced. Therefore, Philippe's sophistication, his worldliness, attracted and entranced her. From Philippe, Barbara got a sense of European style, a cosmopolitan gloss. In a way, Claude Philippe was her Henry Higgins.

While Philippe was discreet about Barbara around his office, there was no attempt by either of them to hide their affection on weekends at the farm in Peekskill. Barbara even began inviting *Today* friends such as Shad Northshield and his wife, and John Lord and a date, for lunches and dinners that she cohosted with Philippe. "They were very close and we had a wonderful time with them," said

Northshield. "I remember a perfectly wonderful lunch up at his place. He was a terrific guy, a very interesting man, and they were very fond of each other. It was lovely to be with them. He was quite a bit older and Barbara was pretty young." But their relationship was "absolutely a romance," concluded Northshield.

Barbara's infatuation with Philippe, or his with her, eventually cooled; no one is really sure which came first. "She just sort of faded out," said Jimmy McCarthy, a friend and employee of Philippe's at the farm. Around that time, too, Barbara became involved with theatrical producer Lee Guber.

In the mid-Seventies, Barbara heard disquieting reports that Philippe was contemplating writing his memoirs.

"When Barbara heard that Claude was thinking about writing a book, she said to me, 'Oh, God! I hope he is not going to mention me!'" said Alexis Lichine, a wealthy wine merchant, who was dating Barbara at the time. "I don't think she was very proud of the image that Claude had. She was apprehensive about how she'd fare if he wrote the book. This was in the days when she was very wary about how she'd be regarded by the outer world."

In October 1978, three days before the April in Paris ball, Claude Philippe suffered chest pains and went to see his doctor, who immediately ordered him hospitalized. A day or two after the ball, Philippe underwent heart surgery, but he fell into a coma and died on Christmas morning of 1978.

Barbara mourned Philippe's passing, but felt relief that he never had an opportunity to put pen to paper.

PASSAGE TO INDIA

In March 1962, Barbara Walters celebrated her first anniversary as a writer for the *Today* show with an unexpected gift that would give her career its biggest boost yet—a story assignment that any aspiring journalist, broadcast or print, would covet, and one that again sparked envy among her male colleagues on the writing staff.

Shad Northshield assigned Barbara to accompany First Lady Jacqueline Kennedy on a twenty-seven-day "semi-official" goodwill visit to India and Pakistan; an international story of glamour and pageantry that would have Barbara rubbing shoulders with the best and the brightest of the world's press corps; an assignment that would open doors for her in Washington, and enable her to forge friendships that would serve her career well for years to come.

The genesis of Mrs. Kennedy's trip was a U.S. visit the previous fall by Prime Minister Jawaharlal Nehru, who reciprocated by inviting her to see his country, an invitation she quickly accepted. The U.S. Ambassador to India, John Kenneth Galbraith, a close friend of the Kennedys, thought such a trip by the First Lady would make for marvelous public relations.

"Ken first talked to Jack about it, and when we talked about it at the Cape, Jack said I could bring Lee [her sister, Princess Radziwill] along, and it all sounded informal and fun," Jackie Kennedy said.

At first, the visit was to be "private"—with minimal press coverage. But media from Washington to Warsaw were hungry for stories about Jackie, the beautiful, stylish, trend-setting First Lady of Camelot. What was first planned as an intimate ten-day visit escalated into an almost month-long traveling circus—a menagerie of camels, elephants, and horses included. At the peak of the coverage, some one hundred press, television, and radio representatives were tailing the First Lady—from her initial stop in Rome, where she saw the Pope—to India and Pakistan.

In early 1962, as the date for the trip neared and publicity started to build, Northshield, who loved big, sumptuous events, decided it would be a great story for the *Today* show to cover. He was a producer with extravagant, sometimes wild ideas; he once considered sending writer Chuck Horner in pursuit of the Loch Ness monster—long before that kind of story was being done on television, let alone in the supermarket tabloids. Moreover, he didn't want to leave coverage of the trip to the regular NBC News people because the *Today* show would, as he put it, "suck hind tit" to the *Huntley-Brinkley Report.*

Northshield knew that two veteran reporters were going to be on the scene for NBC News—White House correspondent Sander Vanocur and Welles Hangen, who was based in New Delhi. But Vanocur would be busy pulling together material for a one-hour special that was scheduled to air about a week after the First Lady's return, and Hangen would be busy filing for the evening news.

Northshield decided to go for it.

For Barbara, the gift unexpectedly arrived during one of those many bull sessions she and Northshield had in the office she shared with John Lord. Northshield, who still hadn't decided whom he was going to send, mentioned the story and the fact that it would be a great coup for the *Today* show. "It's a terrific story!" he enthused. "Can you imagine Jackie climbing up on an elephant!" Barbara immediately had a suggestion: a story like this needed a woman's touch. Viewers, Barbara observed, would want to know what Jackie was wearing, how her hair looked—the kind of dishy coverage that a man couldn't get his teeth into, the sort of gossipy minutiae Barbara herself savored.

What's more, she informed Northshield, she might even have the inside track on Jackie. Barbara slightly knew Lee Radziwill from Sarah Lawrence, and she also had a passing acquaintance with Letitia Baldrige, the First Lady's social secretary; the two had crossed paths when both did public relations work. In fact, Barbara reminded Northshield, Lester Cooper's wife, Audrey, had gone to Vassar with Tish Baldrige. Barbara was still a good friend of Cooper's, despite the fact that Northshield had fired him. Barbara felt the Coopers would be able to help ease the way for her.

"I know I can swing this," Barbara told Northshield confidently. "I think Jackie would welcome me along." Northshield didn't need any more convincing. Barbara had the assignment.

While the *Today* show was now under the aegis of the news division, there still was a healthy competition between the *Today* staff and the NBC News people. "Barbara and I were linked in a kind of 'We're going to outwit NBC News together' attitude," Northshield said.

The fact that Barbara had never covered a news story of this magnitude didn't seem to phase her. She'd been running on chutzpah from the very beginning anyway. "Barbara just went off and did it," noted Northshield. "It was like the star being unavailable and all of a sudden the seamstress takes over and we call it *Forty-Second Street*. In those days in television that could happen."

Chuck Horner had come to work on the *Today* show, too, without a scrapbook of clips with his byline on them. "That's the way television was then," he said. "I talked my way into writing for [Arthur] Godfrey. I'd never written for anybody. Barbara was now keeping all the balls in the air. In other words, you talk a good game until you learn how to play."

At the next production meeting, Northshield announced that the show was going to cover Jackie's trip, and everyone present expressed enthusiasm for the story—until he revealed that the person going on the assignment would be Barbara.

"It came as a surprise to me," said Horner. "This was a matter of mixed emotion. You'd think, well, God, that would be a great thing to do for me or any writer-producer in that meeting. My thought at the time was, 'She's moving very fast.' "

Horner naturally was envious—as were the other writers—but he quickly came to the realization that the assignment was perfect for Barbara, despite her lack of experience. "We talked quite a bit. She told me about her family. I knew about Lou Walters. She told me as a little girl how those big-name celebrities came to her house. So when the time came for her to go with Jackie Kennedy I realized she was better prepared than any of us because Jackie Kennedy was just another celebrity to her, and she had been there with people like that. She had a feeling for celebrities. She was the perfect person to do it. Shad was right. You just snapped your fingers and said, 'Yeah, she's a natural.' "

John Lord recalled that Barbara was terribly excited about the trip but kept quiet about the assignment around the office. "That was part of her professionalism," he said. "She was personally thrilled to death by the idea because it was going to be Jackie Kennedy. But she didn't jump around. She was aware that people were jealous."

By mid-February, Barbara had talked to Lester Cooper, then producing a Mike Wallace interview show for Westinghouse Broadcasting. Cooper got in touch with Letitia Baldrige, informing her that his friend Barbara would be on the press plane with Mrs. Kennedy and that any favored treatment would be much appreciated. "I will keep an eye out for Barbara," Baldrige responded.

Barbara was right on the mark when she told Northshield that interest in things feminine would be the major news of the trip. The *Washington Post* published a titillating story by society reporter Winzola McLendon speculating on whether Mrs. Kennedy would wear a wig to maintain her appearance in places along the way where hairdressers might not be available. And women in Mrs. Kennedy's party were instructed to bring voltage adapters for their portable hair dryers and insect repellent for their beds, reported a breathless *Newsweek* story about the trip, headlined FIRST LADY: A PASSAGE TO INDIA.

Barbara also was eager to generate news about the trip and her role in it—helping the NBC publicity department draft a press release on her forthcoming coverage of the event. "One of the first things Miss Walters did when she heard she would go on the trip was to buy a wig," said the release that went out to the newspapers. "On a trip like this," Barbara explained, "it will be very hard to take care of your hair. By having a brunette wig identical to my natural hair, I'm prepared to look my best for the fanciest occasion at a moment's notice. Even Mrs. Kennedy is taking a wig."

Along with the wig, Barbara planned to pack tea bags and toilet paper, John Lord said, laughing about it years later. He finally convinced her that such supplies were available in abundance in the places where the press would be staying. "She didn't realize they had tea in India," Lord said with wonderment. "She was really a small-town girl.

Barbara had not been around too much at that point. She was from Brookline and New York. She seemed suave, but she hadn't traveled an awful lot."

On March 1, Jackie and her sister, Lee, two maids, and two Secret Service agents, along with an assistant White House press secretary, boarded Pan American Flight 114 at New York's Idlewild Airport for a flight to Rome, where Jackie would spend four days before going on to India. Also on board the plane were fourteen reporters and photographers. One of them was Barbara Walters.

The bravado and confidence that Barbara radiated about the assignment before leaving New York all but vanished in a pool of insecurity and apprehension once the plane became airborne. The reality of it all suddenly came into sharp focus; here was her biggest opportunity yet to prove herself and she knew that, if she failed, any chance of a career as a television journalist could be lost.

Barbara was an unknown quantity to most of the other reporters on the trip. None of them had ever heard of her and, if they had seen her sporadic reports on the *Today* show, she had not registered with them. During the trip, several of the women reporters roomed with Barbara. They remembered her as being tense, uneasy, and depressed.

"She didn't have a great deal of self-confidence," recalled Marie Ridder, who was covering Jackie's trip for Ridder newspapers and was being syndicated by the North American Newspaper Alliance. Ridder, who roomed with Barbara for several nights, said, "She seemed somewhat nervous about doing a good job. She was nervous about the assignment in general, nervous about doing interviews. She cared about how she looked. She worried about whether she was doing well. She talked about it [her concerns] all the time."

Ridder, who knew quite a bit about Indian history, coached Barbara on the subject during the trip, which helped Barbara with her reports and in asking intelligent questions.

Fran Lewine, covering Jackie's trip for the Associated Press, remembered that Barbara "was asking other reporters about how we did our jobs. I'm sure she watched us."

Barbara was apparently having problems getting her reports on the air. Ann Chamberlin, who was a staff correspondent for *Time* magazine, heard Barbara grumbling that the *Today* show wasn't doing anything with the material she was sending back. "I had the impression she was miffed. She was complaining about it. She struck me as somewhat depressed," said Chamberlin, who roomed with Barbara one night. "She just said, 'I've been on this trip and never got anything on the air.' She said she was very frustrated in her efforts to get her copy on."

It's apparent that Barbara went on the trip with unrealistic expectations of getting an interview with Jackie Kennedy, expectations that certainly rubbed off on Northshield. But the First Lady would only give one such exclusive on the trip—to her close friend Joan Braden, who was writing for the *Saturday Evening Post.* Mrs. Kennedy was adamant about not speaking to the press during the trip. Quotes were short and not very colorful—"What fun!" was a typical First Lady gem that reporters dutifully filed after one staged event.

Most of Jackie's words were filtered through Galbraith, Braden, or Baldrige. The story was nothing more than a spectacular photo opportunity: Jackie visiting hospital patients in New Delhi; Jackie on horseback; Jackie in front of the Taj Mahal; Jackie and her sister on the back of a camel; Jackie on a rouged and golden-tusked elephant named Biblia. Barbara's colleague from NBC, Welles Hangen, tried as best he could for an exclusive, but he was forbidden from renting an elephant himself to cover Jackie's ride aboard a pachyderm. The First Lady broke a one-day photographic record that former President Eisenhower had previously set.

All of this added to Barbara's anxiety about failing at her assignment. Hangen was trying to get scoops by renting

elephants. Photographers were deluging their desks with
pictures. And all Barbara seemed to be doing was agonizing
about not getting anything on the air. She finally became
so desperate that she started literally begging Tish Baldrige
for help, pulling out all the stops.

"Barbara hounded—she hounded to get access to Jackie," Baldrige remembered. "But Jackie didn't want to
cope with the American press. Mrs. Kennedy said 'absolutely not' to any interviews with any of the media, any
of the television people—absolutely not. She had people
to see, things to do and learn. At a certain point Barbara
said, 'This is my big chance to break through. It's my whole
career. I'm going home in total shame.' She even told me
the cost of bringing the NBC crew over. It was ridiculously
low. But she said, 'This is going to be the end of the network. I'm going to be fired. I'm going to be ruined.' "

Baldrige was a pro. She'd heard every journalistic ploy
in the book. But Barbara's act—if it was one—was convincing.

Baldrige felt sorry for Barbara and went to Mrs. Kennedy, telling her, "You've got to give this girl a chance,
otherwise she's going to go home in disgrace. She's going
to be fired. She's going to go home with nothing—no special footage of you.

"Barbara was very bright and good, so Mrs. Kennedy
said okay, and she did it. Barbara asked her some questions. They exchanged a few words. Jackie wasn't doing it
with anybody. It was such a victory for Barbara. She really
came home a success. She wouldn't have gotten anywhere
if I hadn't gone to bat for her. I talked Jackie into it."

Some journalists threaten, cajole, or bribe with drinks
and dinner to get a story. Barbara found that begging,
whining, and stamping her feet could do the trick—the
poor little rich girl playing poor little rich girl. She didn't
care about pride. If getting down on her hands and knees
got her what she needed, she'd do it. Years later, even after
she'd become a celebrity and her journalistic skills were

finely honed, she'd still resort to her old act in order to get an exclusive, or to match a competitor's story.

Barbara's drive and enthusiasm impressed a young NBC producer, Walter Pfister, who had gone to India to produce some background segments on Jackie's journey for a program called *Chet Huntley Reporting.* Pfister had run into Barbara at a White House briefing prior to departure and he left thinking, "She's a pretty damned good reporter; really worked hard; wanted to succeed, did her homework." He liked her "attitude and excitement about the trip."

Fourteen years later, when Barbara Walters was being lured to ABC for a million dollars a year, Walter Pfister was one of the network's news department vice presidents who would play a role in the decision to hire her. And it was his memories of her in India as "an aggressive, active, interested reporter" that helped him make up his mind that she would be more than just another pretty face.

Next to Lee Radziwill and Tish Baldrige, the woman who was closest to Mrs. Kennedy on the trip was Joan Braden, the wife of Tom Braden, publisher of the Oceanside *Blade-Tribune* in California, and mother of seven children. Barbara befriended her, forging a relationship that would open doors for her in Washington. Joan Braden had worked diligently for Robert F. Kennedy during John Kennedy's 1960 presidential campaign, and Jackie and Joan became close friends.

Like Barbara, Joan was a journalistic neophyte. She had managed to wangle an assignment from the *Saturday Evening Post* to cover the trip because she had total access to Mrs. Kennedy. On the flight over, Barbara and the other reporters and photographers had seats in the tourist section, but Braden was up front with Jackie. In Rome, she accompanied Jackie to a private audience with the Pope, while the other reporters milled around outside. Naturally, the rest of the press were resentful and envious.

Barbara and Joan Braden had only a nodding acquaintance on the trip until Jackie's visit to the palace of the Maharajah and Maharani of Jaipur. While waiting to interview the Maharani, Barbara and Braden struck up a friendship. Because of Braden's close ties to Jackie, Barbara saw a story—and an opportunity. She invited Braden to be her guest on the *Today* show to talk about the trip and Jackie. Barbara's invitation flattered and delighted Braden, who readily agreed. Even nicer, Barbara said Braden could stay at her apartment with her in New York. Barbara also loaned Braden a small sum of money to buy some bracelets to bring home, another reporter on the trip recalled.

Barbara returned from the assignment exhausted but triumphant. "I found out what it was like to be really tired," she said. "I thought I'd never recover." Her fear of failure was groundless, but that anxiety would stay with her throughout her career. During and after virtually every assignment, she'd obsess over whether she'd done a good job or not.

"It was my first experience on such an assignment, and I was pretty green," she admitted after returning from India. But Barbara had gotten special footage of Jackie, with a bit of help from Tish Baldrige, who didn't get any credit. "Nobody gets close to the First Lady," Barbara boasted, suggesting that she had the ability to do just that. Barbara found Jackie to be cool and remote, a description that would be pinned on Barbara herself when she became famous a few years hence. During the trip Barbara also got a better look at Lee Radziwill, which she parlayed into her first byline in a national magazine—a profile called "Jackie Kennedy's Perplexing Sister," which ran in *Good Housekeeping.* The article added to Barbara's exposure, prestige, and credibility.

Shad Northshield was thrilled and delighted with Barbara's coverage, and her job was intact, her career on track. "Barbara did a beautiful job," Northshield recalled. "She was so grateful for the assignment and generous in her gratitude. It was a very important milestone in her career."

John Lord also saw the trip as "Barbara's big breakthrough, a perfect story for her. It was a combination of the things she was good at—mingling with the rich and famous, and reporting. It gave her tremendous exposure."

Within days after Barbara returned to New York, she followed through on her promise to have her new friend, Joan Braden, as a guest on the show. Braden had interviewed Jackie extensively on the flight back to the United States and the story appeared in the *Saturday Evening Post* under a headline that read: AN EXCLUSIVE CHAT WITH JACKIE KENNEDY—"She tells a close friend about her life as America's First Lady and reveals behind-the-scenes details of her recent good-will tour."

Now Barbara would have an exclusive chat herself before a national television audience with Jackie's close friend. The evening before her appearance on *Today*, Braden arrived in New York to spend the night with Barbara and was somewhat surprised to find the meager circumstances in which she was living. Instead of the glamorous Manhattan apartment Braden expected of a television network newswoman like Barbara, she found her living in a spartan one-bedroom place on East Seventy-ninth Street. The twin beds in her small bedroom made it difficult to move without stubbing a toe; the bathroom was the size of a telephone booth, and the living room was virtually devoid of furnishings.

That night the two women sat around talking about their lives. Braden expressed admiration and a bit of envy for the interesting career Barbara was pursuing. And Barbara said, "I think it's wonderful that you have seven children and that you adore your husband."

"She told me about having been poor and about her father and her sister whom she took care of," Braden recalled. "I remember being interested in not only how generous but how gracious she was in describing this to me. She wasn't complaining or saying, 'This is why I'm doing what I'm doing.' There was none of that. She was just sort of matter-of-fact about it.

"At four o'clock in the morning we got up and she put rollers in her hair and we went downstairs and caught a cab to NBC. *Four A.M.!*" Braden appeared on the show, despite the pain of an impacted wisdom tooth, and gave Barbara a juicy interview about Jackie—the capper of Barbara's coverage of the India trip.

After the program, Braden flew back to her family in California, arriving there almost simultaneously with a gracious note from Barbara thanking her for being on the show and doing such a marvelous job.

Over the next few years, Braden made occasional trips back East and Barbara made sure they got together. In 1968, the Bradens—now the parents of eight; they were the family on which the TV series *Eight Is Enough* was based—moved to Washington. Tom Braden became a well-known political columnist and commentator, and Joan was one of the belles of the town, eventually holding a prestigious post in the State Department.

Through Joan Braden and her elite circle, which included such notables of the time as party-giver and Johnson Administration insider Barbara Howar, Barbara was able to extend her growing network of prestigious government sources in the nation's capital. Henry Kissinger was one of those who would top the list.

Barbara's befriending of Braden in India would begin to pay off, and Jackie's trip would turn out to be a far greater success for Barbara than she could ever have imagined at the time.

ANOTHER
SHOWMAN IN
HER LIFE

With her career on track, Barbara's personal life took a turn for the better, too. By 1962, she had set her sights on Lee Guber, a producer and partner in a chain of successful summer tent theaters—an impresario like Lou.

Barbara met Guber, nine years her senior, at a party shortly after he established the New York office for the Music Fair theaters that he and two friends, Shelly Gross, a high school chum, and Frank Ford, an advertising executive and radio talk show personality, started in the mid-Fifties.

Guber was considered a fantastic catch, and women were constantly chasing him. He was successful, charming, craggily handsome, dapper, and athletic. "He was a simpatico guy," said a woman who knew Guber. "He was a guy who could talk to girls without being macho; a guy who could just be a warm friend to a woman." An aficionado of jazz and theater, and a gourmet cook, Guber had a beautifully furnished and decorated bachelor's co-op apartment near the Museum of Modern Art.

Lee had quite a few good-looking women on the line, but there was something special about Barbara. He was particularly attracted to strong, talented, intelligent women, and Barbara fit the profile.

Leon Guber, born November 20, 1920, was a nice Jewish boy from Philadelphia whose parents, Jack and Elizabeth Guber, owned a succession of small Center City hotels that catered to show people. The Gubers sometimes lived in the hotels when finances were tight, which was frequently, and Lee picked up spare change lugging the well-worn valises of vaudevillians and burlesque players, which gave him a taste for show business.

Lee fought on the boxing team at Temple University where he earned a business degree. He married a pretty Philadelphia girl, Edna Shanis, who had their first child, a son, Zev, while Lee served with an Army artillery unit during World War II. A daughter, Carol, was born about a year later.

After the war, Guber bought the old Senator Hotel at Ninth and Walnut Streets in Center City, which had a drab club on the ground floor.

In those early days, besides catering to transients, Guber used the hotel as a gun drop—but for a worthy cause. He was clandestinely collecting weapons for the Israeli freedom fighters who would win independence in 1948. Every night, Jewish veterans arrived at the hotel with their German Lugers and Italian Berettas, which were shipped to Palestine weekly.

Guber's primary interest in the Senator was the hotel's club, called the Rendezvous. He turned it into *the* late-night spot, headlining jazz stars such as Louis Armstrong, Billie Holiday, Charlie Parker, and Ella Fitzgerald. The club, which became Guber's life for a time, attracted a hip crowd and interesting women, for whom Guber always had an eye.

One of them was a blonde who had the looks, demeanor, and body of a showgirl, but who actually worked as a medical technician at a local hospital. She was crazy about Lee, cooking dinner for him and delivering it to the club late at night. She once accompanied Guber to the golf course wearing a tight short-sleeved sweater, short shorts, and high heels, ruining more rounds of golf that day than a sudden thunderstorm.

"That's what got Lee in trouble with Edna," said Frank Ford years later. "The fact that she knew he was running around. That nailed the coffin down [on his marriage]."

In the mid-Fifties, Edna and Lee were divorced and she quickly remarried. Years later Edna Tuttleman acknowledged that she was aware of Lee's extramarital affairs "and that was one reason why we eventually separated."

After the split, Lee returned to college and earned a master's degree in sociology, and he and Ford began producing music concerts, presenting such diverse talents as Renata Tebaldi, Andrés Segovia, Dave Brubeck, and the Count Basie orchestra. Lee also got an offer on the Senator from the Philadelphia Electric Company that he couldn't refuse, and for the first time in his life, he was financially well off.

Shelly Gross conceived of a way to part Guber from some of his new money. He proposed that the two of them open a tent theater. "Shelly," Guber said, "get the fuck out of here or I'll throw you out." But Guber, Gross, and Ford each anted up five thousand dollars, raising close to one hundred thousand dollars from forty-four friends in business and the professions, who formed a limited partnership.

In June 1955, the same month Barbara Walters married Bob Katz, the Valley Forge Music Fair—a blue-and-white-striped tent with a seating capacity for seventeen hundred—opened near the Philadelphia suburb of Devon with a production of *Guys and Dolls*; in the cast was a local announcer named Ed McMahon. Their next show was *South*

Pacific. By season's end, the partners had turned a fifty-thousand-dollar profit, and they were on their way.

When Barbara met Guber, he was in charge of production for the organization, which had expanded to include the Westbury Theater in Long Island, and tents in Camden County, New Jersey, Painter's Mill in Baltimore, and Shady Grove, near Washington.

The partners had chosen a perfect time to start the business—musical comedy was at its peak on Broadway and they had an array of shows from which to choose—*Can-Can, Pal Joey, Kiss Me Kate*—and audiences clamoring to buy tickets. Gross, who managed the operation, used to jokingly complain to Ford, who oversaw advertising and publicity, that "Guber's got the broads, you've got some interesting people to talk to, and I'm stuck with the toilets."

Guber liked to call the Music Fair presentations "paperback musicals," because they were produced for mass audiences who would never have seen them on Broadway.

Barbara and Lee, who had been dating on and off, became serious in 1962 around the time his company, Music Fair Enterprises, made a public offering of one hundred thousand shares at five dollars a share.

Because the business was booming, Frank Ford decided to drop his popular 11 P.M.–2 A.M. radio talk show in Philadelphia that he performed in front of a live audience noshing on corned beef sandwiches and desserts. On the night of his last program, Guber introduced Barbara to Ford for the first time.

"Lee had never raved to me about her before," Ford said. "He just told me he was dating this girl who was a writer on the *Today* show."

In their initial meeting, Ford found Barbara bright, attractive, and inquisitive. Over coffee, Barbara was stymied that Ford was giving up his successful show. Barbara had difficulty understanding why anyone would give up success. "This is tough, isn't it, Frank?" she asked. Ford had to explain to her that he, Lee, and Shelly now had a responsibility to their stockholders and therefore had to devote full time to the business.

"I thought she was a driving woman who was very ambitious and I don't mean that in a pejorative sense," Ford observed.

> I got that impression because she asked very incisive questions about our business. She wanted to know who drew audiences and who didn't; she wanted to know about the personalities of celebrities with whom we dealt—what so-and-so was really like off-stage.
>
> Lee had no trouble finding beautiful women who were crazy about him. Having been in the nightclub business, he was around a lot of them. He was no star-struck stud. But Barbara was in a different league from the other women. We knew a lot of actresses. They talked about themselves. Barbara didn't. She asked about other people. She was looking for information. She listened.

During a subsequent trip to Orange County, California, to look at some real estate, Ford saw how much Barbara wanted to nab Guber, and how ambivalent Lee was about the situation.

"She would call him every night at our hotel," Ford said. "After Lee got off the phone he'd say to me, 'Jeez, I don't know what to do. She's really after me. She wants to get married and I've had one bad marriage and I don't know whether I should marry her or not. I don't know if I'm ready for that or not.' I remember saying to him, 'Boy, if you don't know, don't do it. You've got to be awfully sure.' He would just listen. She persisted. She chased him. She was the main pursuer."

Never leaving his Philadelphia roots, Guber kept an apartment in Center City where he often spent weekends visiting his children, family, and friends. Despite his qualms about marrying Barbara, she became his constant companion and often accompanied him on his visits home.

On one occasion, he arrived with Barbara at his ex-wife's house in the Philadelphia suburb of Bala Cynwyd to visit Zev and Carol.

"He only brought her once," said Edna Tuttleman. "I never could figure out why. It was very awkward, yet we all got along. It was a surprise visit. I guess he wanted to show her where he came from. She was shy, very quiet. I didn't think it bothered her [being in my presence]."

At another gathering in Philadelphia, Barbara appeared cold and aloof. The wife of one of Guber's pals decided to have a dinner party in Barbara's honor to introduce her to some of Lee's Philadelphia friends. To everyone's chagrin, Barbara spent most of the evening sitting in a corner, leafing through magazines.

"She was very standoffish, very cool to everybody, and didn't go out of her way to be friendly," recalled Frank Ford, one of the guests. "[The woman who gave the party] was highly insulted and very hurt. She had gone to all the trouble to have a nice dinner party and Barbara seemed bored to death by the whole thing, and wasn't at all impressed with Lee's Philadelphia friends. [The hostess] said, 'I'll never invite her again!' I felt that Barbara was a snob. She was not impressed with 'little people,' or unimportant people. She wasn't about to extend herself to be nice to anybody."

LEARNING HER CRAFT

A couple of months after Barbara returned from her successful Jackie Kennedy assignment, yet another management and talent shakeup hit the *Today* show.

Barbara's friend and mentor, Shad Northshield, and *Today* host John Chancellor, were fired. Bob Kintner's experiment to turn *Today* into a serious, news-oriented program had been a disaster—the ratings had plummeted and the sponsors were fuming.

The show was on location at the Beverly Hills Hotel about to go on live at four A.M. (seven A.M. Eastern time) when several executives arrived at poolside and handed Northshield and Chancellor their walking papers.

"We lasted about a year," said Northshield, a veteran of network programs and pogroms. "To this day [Chancellor] will say he quit. The fact is we were both fired. The year Chancellor and I did *Today* was experimental and it was a very, very good show. It also was—and I believe this is an historical fact—the only year in *Today*'s very long history that it lost money—so it was a failure."

It was even worse than Northshield imagined at the time.

"The show had gone so far downhill," said Frank Blair, "that the NBC board of directors met to decide whether it should be taken off the air. We survived, but by only one vote. However, the pressure was on us for drastic change."

Barbara and the other *Today* staffers would now have to reinvent themselves for the new producer, Al Morgan, and the new anchorman, Hugh Downs.

Beefy, crewcutted, and egomaniacal, Morgan, then forty-three, looked—and sometimes acted—more like a Marine drill sergeant than the extremely talented and successful novelist, playwright, and scriptwriter that he was, according to colleagues. Unlike Northshield, his orientation was show business rather than news, which was a plus for Barbara.

When an NBC vice president first tried to hire him to replace Northshield, Morgan said, "Are you nuts?" Morgan had never even watched *Today*, except in hotel rooms while eating breakfast. "Who the hell watches television at that hour?" he thought. But when the executive called again asking what he could do to change his mind, Morgan reeled off a list of outrageous demands, starting with a whopping salary. The executive said okay, and Morgan became the *Today* producer, which he later described as "a dream job . . . it's like being the last absolute monarch."

Despite the fact that Morgan and Downs had previously worked together, the chemistry between them was nonexistent and they would battle one another virtually from the first day of Morgan's six-year reign. But it would be on Morgan's watch—and thanks to Downs's prodding—that Barbara got the opportunity to move from writer to on-air talent with her first network contract.

Morgan made some major changes. Under him, pretaping of the program was ended and it returned to a live status. He moved the show out of the confines of a closed studio and back into the fishbowl environment in which it had started. The program now emanated from NBC's windowed ground-floor studio on Forty-ninth Street in Rockefeller Center. Between seven and nine A.M. when *Today* was on the air, Morgan watched the program in his pajamas at home in bed eating breakfast and chain-smoking, handling decisions and problems by phone. He felt he got a better sense of the program that way, and he didn't mind delegating authority. After the show ended, Morgan drove to the studio.

Describing his production technique to *TV Guide*'s Neil Hickey shortly after taking over *Today*, Morgan said,

> You have to cast the principal roles of this show for balance and viewer identification, almost as if it were a soap opera. [Jack] Lescoulie, for example, is the extrovert, the eternal juvenile type who maybe sometimes goes to parties, gets a little soused and puts a lampshade on his head. Hugh Downs is everybody's son-in-law—the man every mother wants her daughter to marry; he's knowledgeable, aware of everything that's going on, a skillful performer. [The Today Girl] is the female interest: quick, bright, good-looking. We try to build up an on-screen relationship between them to give the viewer the impression they're really involved with each other and that after the show they all go off and have breakfast together.

Of course, it was all illusion.

Hugh Downs had all the qualities the NBC powers wanted when they signed him to replace Chancellor: he was amiable, easygoing, with a boy-next-door quality.

Downs began his career in 1930 at the age of nineteen as an announcer in Lima, Ohio. Eventually he was discovered by the same NBC executive who found Garroway and Chancellor. After serving in the Army, Downs joined the network in 1943. His first shot at the big time was in 1954 when he was cast opposite Arlene Francis on the *Home* show.

At the time he was recruited to host *Today*, Downs was Jack Paar's announcer-sidekick on the *Tonight* show, and the host of a popular morning quiz show, *Concentration*, which he would continue doing.

Downs was required to do commercials on *Today*. To the show's primary viewer—Mrs. Middle America— Downs as pitchman was as trustworthy as an Eagle scout, which made the boys in NBC sales orgasmic with delight.

Barbara heard that as part of Morgan's sweeping changes, he planned to replace the holdover Today Girl, actress Louise King, with a new woman. She approached Morgan and suggested herself, but he rejected her out of hand. While he had seen and been impressed with Barbara's coverage of Mrs. Kennedy's trip, he felt the Today Girl should be more glamorous, mature, and experienced.

Morgan's choice for the female spot on the show was an attractive weather girl from St. Louis, Pat Fontaine. Downs had never met her, so Morgan arranged for the three of them to get together for lunch. At the restaurant, Downs was shocked to learn that Morgan had already hired her without consulting him. The first volley in the war between the producer and the host had been fired. To make matters worse, Morgan made no secret of his lack of respect for Downs.

Meanwhile, Barbara was plodding along, performing the daily round of scut work that the program required—writing introductions and closings to film pieces, preinterviewing guests, reading books, and developing questions for Hugh and Fontaine to ask the authors. Every week or so she'd come up with an idea for a light, "womansy" feature. Barbara would grab a cameraman and produce, write, and edit the story, usually on her own time. She would continue in this vein for another two years.

Each writer had full responsibility for overseeing a show a week—and Barbara always made certain that her program had one or two of her special film features in it—giving the show her imprimatur and, more importantly, getting her name and face on the air as much as possible.

Typically, Hugh would say, "We have a special report from Barbara Walters," and Barbara would introduce the story and do the voice-over. When the film ended, Hugh and Barbara would have a brief discussion about the story, and then the camera would return to the host.

Jane Murphy, a production assistant, who would marry Morgan's successor as producer, Stuart Schulberg, observed that Barbara

> was essentially the same creature then as she is now. She liked famous people and powerful men. . . . She had a very high-profile kind of life; she wasn't overly friendly, and she was very chic. Barbara had a very real agenda and knew very clearly what she wanted. She was not interested in poverty. She was not interested in the social good. She was interested in power and money. She's never been hypocritical about that. She's never pretended otherwise. There were very few women who had the combination of stamina and drive that Barbara had. She worked all the time.

Morgan saw Barbara's ambition and talent, and began using her increasingly to do features.

"She really learned her trade," he said. "She wasn't a great writer, [but] she had a feeling for the form of the medium. She had a feeling for how to tell a story. She was bright enough and smart enough to go to the technical people at NBC and learn how to cut film. She got along beautifully with film crews. We could send her out on an assignment and know that she'd come back with an eight- or nine-minute feature."

Barbara worked harder than the other writers, some of whom were just collecting their salaries and joking about it. All of the scripts came across the desk of production assistant Gail Rock, a University of Nebraska broadcast

major, who read them carefully and was often appalled at
what she saw. (She felt she could do better and eventually
became a successful playwright and television comedy
writer.) Rock could tell who was doing their homework
and who wasn't; who read the books written by upcoming
guest authors and who didn't; who was goldbricking. "Barbara," said Rock, "was thorough, worked longer hours
than anybody, really did her homework. She was taking
that job very seriously, really going at it. She was smart and
ambitious because she wanted them to put her on the air."

Barbara went about her work with grim determination
and had gotten a reputation as a tough taskmaster.

"I was scared of her," said Rock. "She was very tough
and if you screwed up, you didn't want to be on the wrong
side of her temper. You just knew that if you were going
to work with Barbara you'd better work hard and do it
right because she wouldn't tolerate sloppiness. She was
highly professional and she expected that same behavior
from other people. If you were lazy or sloppy she would
really not appreciate it and she would tell you."

Anne Perkins, another production assistant, an aspiring
writer, said, "Barbara was a perfectionist. She knew everything she had to know—and then some, so that nobody
could hit her over the head. She worked hard on what she
looked like so she looked good on camera. She worked
hard on her speech. She knew what *they* wanted—'they'
being management—and she tried to give it to them so
that she could get on the air."

With her New York sophistication and polish, Barbara
intimidated some of the younger women on the staff. Summoned to do a report on the air one morning, Barbara realized the dress she was wearing required a slip. With only
moments before air time, Barbara raced down the hall,
grabbed Gail Rock out of her chair, demanding to know
whether she was wearing a slip. When Rock answered in
the affirmative, Barbara shoved her into a closet. "Take
it off! I'll give it back later." Dumbfounded, Rock slid out

of the undergarment and gave it to Barbara, who put it on and sprinted back to the set with seconds to spare. "If she wanted something," said Rock, "she said so and that was it."

Barbara's fear of competition from the younger women—dubbed the "kindergarten" by Morgan—was evident. All of them were bright, good-looking in a more acceptable Wasp way for television than Barbara, and eager to succeed in broadcasting. But they were a notch below Barbara—and that was fine with her, at least until she got what she wanted.

When she was first beginning to get on the air regularly with her film pieces, Barbara sometimes ambled down to where the production assistants worked. They were surprised when she graced their presence because most of the other writers—not to mention the regular on-air talent—rarely paid attention to them, viewing them as peons.

Barbara felt that spending time now and then with the P.A.'s was good politics. Barbara learned early that having the support of underlings in television was important. If they didn't like you, they could easily sabotage you on the air. In the early years Barbara always made an effort to appear friendly to cameramen, lighting and sound people, floor managers, and film editors. Another reason for spending a bit of time with the P.A.'s was to get the latest gossip—who was being hired or fired; who was sleeping with whom; Barbara liked to keep up on such intelligence.

During one visit, Barbara made what amounted to an informal survey, asking each of the younger women whether they were interested in doing on-air work.

"I remember saying with big wide eyes, 'Well, I really don't want to be on air, Barbara,' and she said, 'Well, uh-huh, all right,' and she toddled off, sort of disbelieving," said one of the "kindergarten" graduates years later. "It was very much a survey by her and we were amused by it. It had to be difficult for her to make the rounds and be discreet and mask her true intentions, but we could see what she was up to. It was pretty savvy of her to get reaction as to who might be her competition."

Barbara had a special fondness for Gail Rock.

When the show went on location to Puerto Rico, Rock became sick during a bus ride along the winding, bumpy roads that snaked through the rain forest above San Juan. Downs and Lescoulie and the other men on the bus didn't know what to do. Barbara ordered the driver to stop at a small town, marched Rock off the vehicle and helped her to the local *farmacía*. Speaking no Spanish, she managed to somehow pantomime the fact to the druggist that the young woman next to her was violently carsick and was about to faint. Barbara sat Rock down on the ground and gave her whiffs of ammonia to revive her. "She did her paramedic bit," said Rock. "She was amazing. She just took charge and handled it—no language barrier got in her way. Everybody else kind of stood around looking like, 'Gee, what do we do?' Barbara's the person to have with you in a crisis."

Barbara also took a personal interest in Rock's choice of clothing and had discussions with her about the benefits of cosmetic surgery.

Once, when the show was on location in Hollywood, and the staff was staying at the Continental Hotel on Sunset, Barbara spotted Rock wearing a sexy dress with her hair done in a new style. Barbara ran over to tell her how marvelous she looked. "Have you ever thought about having your nose done?" Barbara suddenly asked. Surprised by the question, Rock, in fact, acknowledged that she had, but wasn't certain whether she could go through with it. With that, Barbara gave her the name and number of a plastic surgeon, encouraging her to have the surgery.

"Barbara certainly did take a look at me personally," said Rock, who was ten years Barbara's junior. "I finally did do something about my nose. Barbara was very observant. I think she knew I was toying with the idea of doing myself over."

Over the years there would be much speculation that Barbara herself had undergone cosmetic surgery, sparked by the indisputable fact that as she got older, she got better looking, which naturally set tongues wagging. The names of various plastic surgeons were bandied about. Steven M. L. Aronson, author of *Hype*, a 1983 gossipy book about celebrities, wrote that Barbara got an eye-lift and face-lift in March 1981, from Dr. Thomas Rees of New York. Barbara denied Aronson's claim, asserting, "If I push the bangs off my face, you can see quite a few gray hairs but no scars." She has credited makeup and lighting people for enhancing her looks. "People are always writing her, 'Tell me the name of your doctor, tell me the name of your doctor,' " said Shirley Budd. "She's had no plastic surgery. It's a lie!"

As Barbara's success grew, colleagues in the business— even in those early years—could not contain their envy. Many suggested that she had slept her way to the top. Rumors abounded as late as the summer of 1989 that Barbara had reached the top of her profession by sleeping with anyone who could advance her career.

But there is no truth to the stories.

Barbara was aware of the rumors, and scoffed at them. Interviewer David Frost once asked her on the air about the secret of her success. "I worked very hard for twelve years," Barbara responded dryly, "and then I slept with the producer." Frost drew in his breath and Barbara smiled. "David," she added, "do you really think if I'd slept with the producer it would have taken me twelve years?"

Barbara had a single-mindedness about having a successful career, possessing power, and making money, but sex played no part in helping her reach her goals. Aside from her own unbounded ambition, dedication, and drive, Barbara always had savvy personal managers and agents advising her and doing her bidding. At the same time, she herself was a brilliant corporate politician and gameswoman, with a talent for cultivating the right people.

In the early days, women in television, particularly in news and public affairs, felt they had to show they were tougher than any man in order to succeed—their ideal being the grizzled city editor turned TV executive that was personified by Ed Asner's character, Lou Grant. Barbara had a different view. She had no desire to cover riots or go to Vietnam and slog around in fatigues and combat boots as a few women reporters did. Barbara realized that she could get further having the proper social contacts and graces, being impeccably put together, being a female.

While most NBC executives found Barbara attractive, many didn't find her sexual or sensual and, as a result, did not pursue her, nor did she pursue them.

"I never did think of her like that," said a former NBC executive who was in a position to help Barbara's career. "I never felt that kind of chemical reaction to her that one does with other women. Certainly I think if the circumstances were right I would have thought of her in those terms as a lover, but she would never allow it. And I was in circumstances with her where it could have happened."

Chuck Horner, who worked beside Barbara as a writer during the Northshield and part of the Morgan regimes, maintained that Barbara was successful because of her talents.

"When I met her, and as we worked together, and the others worked with her, we all found her very attractive. Every guy saw that, but did nothing. The possibility of her making her way up in the show by sleeping around would have been easy. But there was a feeling of respect for her as a person and for her ability. I can't imagine in a thousand years Barbara doing that to get somewhere. She certainly made no overt moves. She was a real professional, a hard-working lady, intelligent, with goals, and that's how she made it."

Barbara's *Today* pal, John Lord, who rose from writer
to producer at NBC and remained friends with Barbara
for years, recalled traveling with her and being in what
could have become compromising situations. During one
trip with the show, Lord said,

> I'd drop by her bedroom in the morning and chat and so
> on, but I never had any thought of sensuality there. Sex
> wasn't the first thing that came to mind with Barbara.
>
> She is probably the most controlled individual anyone
> will ever meet. I really never knew that she had a vice. I
> would have been astonished if she had one. I've known
> her for years and I never even once heard her tell a really
> dirty joke.
>
> One of the attractive things about Barbara was that she
> didn't mess around. You never felt she was coming on. She
> was very feminine and had a feminine approach. She was
> someone of the opposite sex with whom you could have
> a very full relationship without wanting to screw her. It
> could be that the thought passed through one's mind, but
> sex wasn't the prime thing with her.

Jane Murphy Schulberg, who worked on *Today* with Barbara from the Sixties and into the mid-Seventies, said,
"Sex is not what drove her, but she certainly used sex appeal."

"We knew everything that was going on at *Today*," said
Gail Rock. "It was a hotbed of intrigue there; an unbelievable Peyton Place. But Barbara never participated in any
of the shenanigans. She was very hip about office politics.
She absolutely kept her nose clean. She didn't sleep with
anybody. She just did her work."

"GOT HIM!"

Shortly after noon on Friday, November 22, 1963, the world came to a screeching stop.

In Dallas, Texas, an ex-Marine named Lee Harvey Oswald shot and killed the nation's thirty-fifth President, John Fitzgerald Kennedy. NBC, like the other networks, began around-the-clock coverage of the story. The *Today* show's reportage was extensive, on the air for more than thirty consecutive hours. The bulk of the story came from Washington, where Barbara was assigned for the duration to cover Kennedy's funeral and related events.

Al Morgan viewed the assassination story as Barbara's "big break" on the show. "I found myself using her more and more. Pat [Fontaine, the Today Girl] didn't have the background for it."

For the second time in less than two years, a story involving the Kennedys was putting Barbara on the map, tragedy notwithstanding.

Barbara was on the air constantly during the coverage,

ad-libbing on the unfolding events and reporting the obvious feature stories. She was one of the few women on television involved in covering the story, mostly handling the
human interest angle—and she did it with the proper
aplomb, showing emotion when necessary, but without
falling apart, or shedding a tear.

"We had all been impressed by her professionalism,"
said Hugh Downs, who had anchored the program from
the NBC studios in Washington.

Barbara was assigned to the Capitol's East Rotunda
where Jacqueline Kennedy and the slain President's brothers, Robert and Edward Kennedy, knelt before the coffin
and prayed. "For a long time, as we waited for the White
House entourage to appear, Barbara kept the story from
sagging under its own tragic weight while fully projecting
the sadness of the occasion," said Downs.

"Barbara was gangbusters, absolutely marvelous," asserted Morgan. "At the Capitol we stayed on the air for
five hours and Barbara and Downs were coequals doing
the coverage. What she did was come of age and into her
own that day."

Still, when Pat Fontaine left several months after the assassination, Morgan again denied Barbara's request for the
spot, choosing yet another actress.

The tragic events in Dallas—not the most romantic impe-
tus for matrimony—brought about Barbara's marriage to
Lee Guber.

"It was a month after the Kennedy assassination, which
affected us greatly. We wanted to cling together stormily,"
Barbara said, sounding like she was back in the Drama Department at Sarah Lawrence.

Barbara and Lee had planned several times to get married, but at the last moment she had second thoughts, despite the fact that it was she who was pursuing him. It's
possible her indecision was based on rumors that Lee was
seeing other women. Barbara had even consulted old col-

lege friends to get their advice about whether she should tie the knot with Lee.

"She's had so many unfortunate relationships with men that I think she's very self-protective," said Anne Williams Ferguson. "I was visiting New York when Barbara invited me for lunch to talk about Lee. She said, 'Well, what do you think? Should I, or shouldn't I?' How can you answer a question like that? I didn't know Lee very well. We were dinner partners a couple of times and I found him to be a very dull man. I said, 'Barbara, this is a decision you have got to make yourself. I can't do it.' Barbara is not decisive when it comes to her personal life. She questions all of her motives; all of the other guy's motives. She's not secure."

Barbara had introduced Lee to her friends at the *Today* show and most of them felt he was a "mensch." But her pal John Lord felt otherwise. He'd heard stories about Guber's womanizing, but decided to say nothing to her.

"Guber was having it off with an awful lot of women while he and Barbara were sort of engaged and having a relationship," said Lord. "I remember being upset because he was philandering. This was just before they got married. I really didn't trust him too much."

Ben Cossrow, Guber's brother-in-law, acknowledged that prior to the wedding Barbara and Lee, who had "been together on and off—mostly on—took a trial separation. But they found out it was no good and they had to have one another."

Barbara had gone through the same kind of ambivalence eight years earlier, before she married Bob Katz. And she would go through a similar situation again years later prior to marrying her third husband.

"Pretty, perky, popular Barbara Walters called off the calling-off of her marriage to tent show tycoon Lee Gruber [sic]. The judge who'll marry them next Sunday is Marryin' Sam Di Falco," reported Hearst columnist Jack O'Brian, who was to Barbara in the Sixties and early Seventies what

New York *Daily News* gossip columnist Liz Smith became to her in the 1980s, a virtual personal publicist.

Despite the fact that she was still relatively unknown as a TV personality, Barbara's impending nuptial was the lead item in O'Brian's "On the Air" column in the New York *Journal-American* of December 3, 1963.

O'Brian's mention of Barbara was one of many he'd write in the early years of her career. These spoon-fed tidbits impressed the powers at NBC who always seemed amazed and delighted at the ink she could generate for herself and the *Today* show. O'Brian's items, therefore, were an enormous boost to her career.

Barbara didn't seem bothered by the fact that O'Brian, a supporter of Joe McCarthy, was detested in many liberal journalistic circles because of his right-wing views. Friends of Barbara's were as much aghast about her friendship with him as they were about her relationship with Roy Cohn, also a close pal of O'Brian's.

Judith Crist of the New York *Herald Tribune*, whom Al Morgan had hired early on as the *Today* show's movie and theater critic, said she was "ready to throw up" when she learned about Barbara's relationship with Cohn, and was equally upset that Barbara and O'Brian "were great chums" because O'Brian "was despised" by her liberal colleagues.

One of the reasons for the resentment was O'Brian's venomous comments in his column about CBS television news commentator Don Hollenbeck—a colleague of Edward R. Murrow. Hollenbeck committed suicide at forty-nine by sticking his head in the oven in the kitchen of his New York hotel-apartment on June 22, 1954.

The day after the tragedy, O'Brian wrote: "Suicide does not remove from the record the peculiar history of leftist slanting of news indulged consistently by CBS. Hollenbeck was typical of CBS newsmen. He hewed to its incipient pink line without deviation." Murrow's eulogy was somewhat different; he described Hollenbeck as "a friend of truth, an enemy of injustice and intolerance . . ." O'Brian had dubbed Murrow "Egghead R. Murrow."

Judith Crist recalled that she and her husband and Barbara and Guber had once gone to the theater where they ran into O'Brian, and Barbara gave him a warm greeting.

> Because we were obliged to talk to him, I asked Barbara, "How do you know [him]?" Barbara said, "Oh, it's his wife," [who] was apparently a great intimate friend of Barbara. And I remember Lee saying, "I just manage not to talk to Jack much," because I said to Lee, "How can you tolerate this?" [But] those [O'Brian items about Barbara] helped [her] a great deal.
>
> When I was a reporter I had covered Roy Cohn when he was an assistant U.S. Attorney and one could have nothing but contempt for him and despise him and consider him a villain. Any person of decent orientation would feel that way. Barbara was very naive [about Cohn] sexually and politically. I think Barbara at that time thought of herself as a very decent liberal person, and we talked as peers of liberalism. We were all of that orientation and I could not imagine her past "romance" with Roy Cohn. I thought it was almost schoolgirlish. She didn't know what a villain was.

Guber intensely disliked Cohn and O'Brian, and Barbara's friendship with them caused angry words between Lee and Barbara more than once. Guber considered Joe McCarthy "a fascist" and Cohn "scum," according to friends. One of Guber's pals was the comedian Ronnie Graham, who often speared the McCarthys of the world with his hard-edged political humor. "Lee was in the best sense of the word a liberal, partial to fighting against people like McCarthy," said Frank Ford. "It's interesting that Barbara would be friendly with a guy like Cohn. Of course, again, he was a powerful guy and had a lot of connections."

Concerning her friendship with O'Brian, Barbara was her usual pragmatic self. It served her best interests to be his friend and benefit from all the free publicity he gave her. After all, she was trying to build a career, not save the world.

The night before Barbara married Guber, Roy Cohn, who was still seeing her frequently, telephoned and pleaded with her to reconsider his proposal. "There I was at Chez Vito's," Cohn said, "talking to her on the phone for an hour. I told her I'd marry her. She said she couldn't marry me because she and Guber had already given a present to the judge."

In the wake of Cohn's death, Barbara adamantly denied that she and Cohn were ever engaged. But Dorothy Sokolsky, the widow of the conservative Hearst writer George Sokolsky, of whom Cohn was a protégé, asserted that Cohn and Barbara were in love and that Roy had given Barbara an engagement ring at least eighteen months before she married Guber.

> We were out together and Barbara showed me the engagement ring, [Mrs. Sokolsky claimed]. I said, "Oh, you're engaged?" and she said yes. Roy was sitting right there. We all congratulated her. Barbara was at my daughter's wedding with Roy in June 1962 at the Waldorf-Astoria, but she couldn't wear the engagement ring on her finger because Roy's mother was there, too. She had to take the ring off her hand and wear it on a chain around her neck. Barbara told me [it was Roy's ring] and I knew about it. She told me she couldn't wear it when Roy's mother was in a group with them.

Cohn's mother, Dora, disliked Barbara intensely and referred to her as "That girl!" Dora thought of Roy as her little Jewish prince and disliked and resented Barbara, whom she sneered at as "the daughter of a man who owns a nightclub"—certainly not the appropriate Jewish princess for her son.

"Her attitude was that if Roy was out in the evenings and he didn't come home for dinner that night she'd immediately call me to find out if he was out with 'that girl,'" Dorothy Sokolsky said. "His mother wouldn't have anything to do with Barbara. If he got married to her it would have been a difficult situation."

At the time Barbara and Roy contemplated marriage, Sokolsky believed Cohn was not involved in homosexual activities, and that his sexual preference was not an issue with Barbara.

John Lord, who described Barbara's relationship with Cohn as "powerful," thought that she "suspected" Cohn was a homosexual, "but I don't think she dwelled on it. Those were the days when one really didn't think too much about homosexuality. I doubt whether Barbara knew what homosexuals did [with each other], for instance."

Doris Lilly, a former New York *Post* columnist, recalled being in a nightclub in the Sixties with Roy, Barbara, and a "nice-looking" young man whom Roy had apparently picked up after he had fixed Cohn's TV set. Lilly quoted Barbara as saying, "I don't care what anyone does and I'm not prejudiced, but I wonder why he always has to bring these guys along."

Cohn had great respect for Barbara's opinions, according to New York Law School professor Robert Blecker, a close friend of Cohn's. For example, before Cohn purchased his townhouse on East Sixty-eighth Street, he asked Barbara to look the place over. She inspected the building from top to bottom. Cohn, who prided himself on his real-estate savvy, agreed to buy the property only after Barbara nodded her approval.

Rejecting Cohn's last-ditch effort at matrimony, Barbara became Mrs. Lee Guber on Sunday, December 8, 1963, in the East Side apartment of a high school friend, Marilyn Herskovitz. Unlike the production number at the Plaza that marked the occasion of her first marriage, only a few close friends of Barbara's and Lee's were present to witness her take the vows and watch Lou give her away for a second time.

When Marryin' Sam Di Falco declared, "I now pronounce you man and wife," Barbara looked more triumphant than happy. She said two words—"Got him!"

WAITING IN
THE WINGS

In early 1964, *Today* show executives concluded that Pat Fontaine—whom Al Morgan described as the "quintessential out-of-town personality"—would have to be replaced. When Barbara heard that the Today Girl job was up for grabs she immediately went to Morgan and asked for it, but once again he turned her down.

"Barbara was nagging to be on the air," recalled Jane Schulberg. "She was just badgering everyone half to death."

Despite being impressed with her work during the Kennedy assassination coverage a few months earlier, Morgan had strong reservations as to whether Barbara had the magic ingredients required to successfully cohost the show with Downs.

One of the reasons Morgan resisted promoting Barbara to the Today Girl slot was because he "worried" about her "lateral lisp"—her trouble pronouncing *r*'s and *l*'s.

Morgan sent her to a speech therapist who "I think had

been a speech therapist for Boris Karloff, who also had a lateral lisp," he said. "There wasn't much he could do for her. We also fiddled with her hair, with her clothes, and with her diction."

While the grooming process was underway, though, Morgan had his sights on a blue-eyed, brown-haired, middle-aged Broadway actress for the Today Girl job: a woman who had become famous running around half-naked in the late Thirties and early Forties playing the sexy jungle girl, Jane, in several of the Johnny Weissmuller Tarzan films.

Attractive, talented Maureen O'Sullivan, the mother of actress Mia Farrow and six other children, was fifty-three, and had the lead role in the Broadway production of *Never Too Late*, opposite Paul Ford, when she made a guest appearance on *Today* and impressed Morgan with her wit, charm, and style.

However, when he offered her the Today Girl job through her agent, O'Sullivan was wary. "I said, 'Oh, I can't do that, it's not my kind of thing,'" she recalled. "So Al Morgan said, 'Oh, come on.' He said, 'Try.' He finally convinced me to do it much against my will—so we had kind of a trial thing."

But, once again Morgan did not reveal his plan to Hugh Downs. It was a repeat of what occurred a year earlier when he hired Fontaine without consulting Downs. Before leaving on vacation, Downs specifically asked Morgan not to bring in a replacement without his approval, and left thinking they had an agreement. But when he returned, O'Sullivan had been signed to a contract. "Downs was outraged," said writer Bob Cunniff.

But no one was more furious over the hiring of Maureen O'Sullivan than Barbara Walters, who coveted the job but had to take a back seat once again to someone who wasn't trained or qualified for it.

"She was there every morning," said O'Sullivan. "The people in the makeup department and the hairdressers used to say, 'Uh-oh, Barbara's hovering around just hoping you won't go on.' Well, maybe she *was* hoping I wouldn't go on. She was an ambitious, talented woman."

Jane Schulberg, who watched the proceedings with a young but jaundiced eye, noted that, "Barbara made absolutely no secret at all that she wanted to go on the air and I'm sure Maureen knew that. Barbara was certainly that upfront about it."

Years later Barbara noted that when Morgan first saw O'Sullivan he "thought she was wonderful and made the mistake a lot of people make. They see someone do a wonderful interview and think they can come on and do interviews. So with a lot of publicity he hired Maureen, and it was a disaster."

Barbara wrote most of the copy O'Sullivan read on the air, and did the research and wrote the questions for her guest interviews.

One of O'Sullivan's first interviews bombed and set the pattern for what was to come. While interviewing Mr. Kenneth, a well-known hairdresser, O'Sullivan, working from Barbara's prepared list of questions, asked, "Do you like women?"

"Well, the question came out wrong for me," O'Sullivan allowed. "What I should have said was, 'Do you enjoy working with women?' The question offended him. He was angry about it. He saw it as a very rude question."

But O'Sullivan didn't feel she was the target of any sabotage. "No. I don't think so," she said, mulling over the possibility. "I think Barbara always knew she was right for the job. She wrote some very good interviews and then I did some very bad interviews. So Morgan put her on some of the interviews that she'd written for me and she was very good, too."

In many ways, the gracious O'Sullivan said she found Barbara being nice to her. "I got very bad mail on that show and Barbara was always the first to say, 'Oh, cheer up.' And when I would do a bad interview, she said, 'I just forget it and go on to the next.' "

Bob Cunniff, who shared a small office with Barbara, remembered her saying, " 'Why can't I be doing this?' She was quite upset that Maureen O'Sullivan was screwing up all over the place and she was just sitting there. I don't recall her ever saying to me, 'I'm waiting for her to fail'—but I think that's exactly what she was doing."

Judith Crist didn't see O'Sullivan as any real competition for Barbara. "Barbara was bright and ambitious and could deliver the goods," she said.

> She was in her early thirties then. Maureen was an older woman in my eyes. She did not have the kind of intellectual, New York smarts that Barbara had. I call them New York City Jewish-girl smarts—well educated, up on current affairs, sophisticated. My husband had been an administrator at Sarah Lawrence so I knew the Sarah Lawrence girl extremely well. There were two kinds—the artsy, smartsy, ditsy ones, or the smart ones—and Barbara was one of the smart ones.
>
> I thought Maureen was most charming. I thought that it was a brilliant idea to put her on the show because [her age group] was the audience that was watching. Barbara and I used to kid around that we really ought to appear in housecoats and hair curlers in order to relate to our audience instead of with those goddamned false eyelashes— which I dropped before she did.

The chemistry between Hugh and Maureen was highly volatile. One report had Hugh developing a bad back and Maureen shingles from having to work together. While he felt Pat Fontaine had a "rough competency" on the air, Downs saw O'Sullivan as someone who "couldn't develop a definite notion of how broadcasting worked . . . a lovely lady but a lame broadcaster."

Frank Blair, who read the news on *Today*, felt Maureen

was "miscast" for the show. "She was a sweet lady out of her element," he said.

Meanwhile, poor Maureen O'Sullivan was hurting.

"She was suddenly regarding the whole thing as a terrible chore," said Crist.

In makeup one day, Crist recalled, O'Sullivan "sort of broke down," expressing deep frustration and concern over how the viewers perceived her. "If I don't say anything, I get letters saying, 'Why do you sit there like a lump,'" she complained to Crist. "If I do say something people write in and say, 'Why don't you ever shut up?' I just can't do anything right. If people didn't like you in the movies, or in a play, you felt it was the character they didn't like. But on television it's you they don't like."

Worse than bad fan mail, and unbeknownst to the rest of the cast, was the fact that O'Sullivan was unknowingly abusing legal prescription drugs. "My husband had just died," she explained. "It was a very bad moment in my life. I had to support the children. The doctor had given me tranquilizers."

Some years later Downs said, "I never had any idea that the vague quality I took as a personality trait had been chemically induced."

Morgan saw that problems existed and assigned Cunniff to what was unofficially called "the O'Sullivan project," which involved trying to shape the stage and screen actress into a television type before the sponsors started raising hell.

The first year of Barbara's marriage to Lee Guber was not an auspicious one. In fact, their relationship was quite curious, to say the least.

Friends at the Today show saw the Walters-Guber union as picture perfect and—aside from Barbara's clear frustration about not being the Today Girl—thought she appeared happier than ever. Lee accompanied Barbara to the office Christmas party a few weeks after the wedding and everyone thought, "Oh, gosh, isn't he handsome, isn't it romantic," recalled a *Today* staffer.

But that just wasn't the case.

For the first six months, Barbara and Lee kept their individual apartments because she felt that living together made marriage so definite. As for their finances, each had separate savings and checking accounts. What's more, neither of them really wanted to get married, Barbara would admit some years later, to the surprise of friends.

One of the points of contention between Barbara and Lee early on was the fact that she wanted to have a baby. "It was a great hunger in her," observed Judith Crist. On the other hand, Lee had mixed feelings about the prospect of becoming a father again. After all, he had two children from his first marriage, which had ended because he was seeking more freedom. Another concern of Guber's was the indisputable fact that Barbara was determined to continue her career in television and he questioned whether she could have both.

Barbara apparently won out because early in her first year of marriage she conceived, but had a miscarriage—one of several she would suffer before deciding to adopt. According to one account, Barbara lost one of the babies after riding on a roller coaster at Disneyland while on assignment in Los Angeles. "She felt guilty thinking she should have known better than to go on that ride," said a former *Today* staffer. In another instance, she miscarried after a story assignment that, along with the travel, might have been too stressful for her.

Always extremely private, Barbara would never discuss such problems openly, or allow her inner feelings to show. "Often you'd hear something like 'I lost the baby,' but nothing more," said a former colleague. But she was hurting so much after the first miscarriage that one day when Al Morgan asked her in passing how she was doing, her anguish came pouring out.

"Barbara burst into tears," said Gail Rock, who was sitting a few feet away. "She was just trying to hold it together and all he had to say was something sweet and she just exploded. Al gave her a hug. He was very fond of Barbara, sort of a daddy figure to her. He was very comforting to her.

"It was clear that having a baby was the most important thing in her life at that point," said Rock. "She was really upset over whether it was or wasn't going to happen. Everybody was very sympathetic, really feeling for her."

Barbara sometimes vented her frustration about being childless. Over drinks one evening in the Gubers' living room, Barbara's friend Joan Peyser, who was unaware of Barbara's feelings, was proudly telling how her little boy had been selected to appear in a television commercial. Barbara startled Peyser when she suddenly snapped, "Joan, put the kid away!" Several years later, after she adopted a daughter, Barbara herself played the proud and doting mother role to the hilt—despite the fact that she was rarely home—boasting about the child and extolling the virtues of motherhood.

Another problem in the marriage at the outset was Lee's desire to succeed as an independent producer. Like Lou Walters, Lee Guber wasn't content doing what he did best. As with Lou, Lee was brash and foolhardy enough to think he could succeed on Broadway. His initial ill-fated attempts added to the stresses of the marriage, according to friends. Lee was fond of saying "being a producer is like being a gambler"—a comment that evoked memories of her father's early days and made Barbara cringe.

John Lord recalled being invited by Barbara and Lee to the opening of one of his disastrous Broadway productions and feeling terrible for her. "Barbara had a lot of faith in him," Lord said. "She had pinned a lot of hope on the show succeeding for his sake because he'd been a straw-hat-theater guy from Philadelphia."

Guber's first stab at Broadway was a musical adaptation of the Greek comedy *Lysistrata*. Set to the music of French composer Jacques Offenbach, it was a story about the mythical leader of the Athenian women who convinces her followers to stop having sex with their men. One associate said he knew that the show was in trouble when he saw that the chorus girls were clothed and the chorus boys were half naked. The show bombed.

Two other Guber-inspired productions in the 1960s also flopped—*Catch Me If You Can,* which closed after 103 performances, and *Sherry!,* after 71 performances. "They were terrible and Shelly and I both felt he didn't know what the hell he was doing," Ford said. "Lee simply did not have the ability, the know-how, the imagination, whatever it was to be a Broadway producer—or the luck for that matter. But he kept trying and he kept giving people work."

As late as August 1986, some eighteen months before his death and years after his divorce from Barbara, Guber was still flopping big. His last Broadway show, a more than five-million-dollar venture called *Rags,* closed after four performances.

"Barbara does something a little interesting with men," observed Joan Peyser. "She chooses men who appear powerful but finally are not. I am not speaking of their sexuality; I have no way of knowing anything about that. But I think each may have some kind of losing streak. I don't believe Barbara could be drawn to somebody who would really be omniscient in his financial acumen—or tough enough to control her."

PART III

THE BIG PAYOFF

The O'Sullivan project was a dismal failure. As a result, Al Morgan decided that Maureen O'Sullivan would have to go.

Her dismissal occurred in late August 1964 while the *Today* show was on location in Atlantic City covering the Democratic National Convention. It was handled rather tactlessly and it got O'Sullivan's Irish up.

According to one account, O'Sullivan was having what she thought was a friendly dinner with an NBC executive who, while she was discussing potential guests for the show, told her she was out. Another scenario had Hugh Downs claiming credit for firing her. "I told her first. She was not pleased by the way it was done, and years later she told me she had always thought I hated her."

O'Sullivan claimed she couldn't remember any of the specifics except that she was pleased to leave the show and that the decision to part was mutual.

Whichever way it happened, O'Sullivan was said to be

particularly incensed with Morgan, who convinced her in the first place to take the job against her better judgment, but wasn't anywhere to be found when she got the news that she would be off the show.

Morgan got wind that Maureen was understandably furious and feared that she would leak what happened to the press, generating bad publicity for the show. A couple of staffers, according to one account, visited O'Sullivan in her hotel suite with hopes of calming her with room service and pleasant conversation about her days in Hollywood, but the ploy failed.

Somewhere along the line O'Sullivan wisely got on the telephone.

The next day's headlines in the New York gossip and TV columns told her side of the story: " 'Today' Girl to NBC: No Tomorrow," declared one; "Maureen Smiles Way Out of Today Show," read another; "Maureen O'Sullivan Quitting Today Show," stated a third.

O'Sullivan charged that her role on the show was "asinine—it's not enough to sit there and smile every day with nothing to do." She said she felt "like an intruder" interrupting conversation between Downs and Jack Lescoulie. Asserting that the Today show was "simply no place for a woman," Maureen maintained that "they haven't created a place for a woman on it. I agreed to join 'Today' with the understanding that I would have something to do. I would never have left [Broadway] in a thousand years if I thought I would be sitting between two men on TV every day just smiling."

Morgan was quoted as saying, "If there's any failure it's mine for not finding her a suitable role after I persuaded her to come to the show. It was a pleasure to work with her, and I'm sorry to see her go."

Busy with the convention coverage in Atlantic City, he said he would start looking for a replacement the following week.

To add insult to injury, the termination of O'Sullivan

was announced at the next morning's production meeting—at which Maureen was present. The night before, Morgan telephoned production assistant Anne Perkins, telling her, "Maureen might not be feeling well in the morning; go over first thing and pick her up," Perkins said. "I didn't know until the next day that she'd been fired."

Pat Pepin, who had joined the show a month earlier as a secretary and receptionist, happened to be sitting next to O'Sullivan in a conference room at the hotel when the news of her separation was announced to the staff by Morgan. "I remember Maureen looking down at the table, not looking at anyone, looking a little weepy. It was cruel and so awful that she was there."

Someone gave Maureen a little pat on the head. Standing next to her was Bob Cunniff, who knew that she was going to be fired, but hadn't been told when. Before Maureen even had a chance to dry her eyes, an excited Barbara Walters, unnoticed by O'Sullivan, came up to Cunniff, asking quietly whether he thought she should talk to Morgan about the job. "I said, 'Well, I think that your asking me indicates you obviously plan to and you want someone to be your ally. Absolutely, I'd be happy to.'"

Barbara's life was about to change as dramatically as that of another person in Atlantic City that day—a New Dealer from Minnesota named Hubert Horatio Humphrey, who would be Lyndon Johnson's choice for the vice presidency.

Shortly after the meeting ended, Barbara talked to Morgan, pleading for a chance. A few days later, as speculation on the set about Barbara's future mounted, a knowledgeable player in the backstage intrigue telephoned New York *Post* TV columnist Bob Thomas with a hot tip. He duly wrote, "Reporter Barbara Walters is being groomed for a more prominent role on the 'Today' show when Maureen O'Sullivan departs late next month." Guesses were that Barbara herself had placed the call; who else would have benefited from such an item?

However, Morgan was still more than a little hesitant

about promoting her to be the new Today Girl. His inclination was to begin a talent search for another winsome actress to fill O'Sullivan's shoes. Like a white knight, Hugh Downs came to the rescue, suggesting to Morgan and NBC executive Bill McAndrew that they give Barbara a chance. " 'She's a writer,' they said. I argued that she was not just a writer, but a producer, and very bright. And good-looking. Besides, she had been on the air several times," Downs said.

From the day he joined the show, Downs had been impressed with Barbara's work. He was especially fond of a highly complimentary feature story she wrote and produced about him—childhood photos and all—that was aired to welcome him as the Today show host.

With no spectacular talent finds on the horizon, Morgan finally made the decision to bring Barbara on slowly, a few days a week at first—with no fanfare or publicity. Nobody knew who she was except viewers of the Today show, so they'd just start seeing more of the pert brunette reporter with the funny way of talking. If she bombed, no one would be the wiser and Morgan could go back to looking for a "real" personality, and Hugh would eat crow. "There was no big buildup, so there [was] nothing I had to live up to," Barbara said not long after she got the tryout.

"They didn't have anybody else they could pull in making a big hoo-ha," said Jane Schulberg, "so they just sort of threw her into the breach—and Barbara is terrific in that sort of crunch."

By October 1964, Barbara finally had the job.

Now Morgan was saying, "We want intelligent, creative women with expertise on this show. The day of the Today Girl who simply sits on the panel, looks charming, and passes tea is over. [Barbara's] promotion is due to the recognition of her growing ability."

Victoriously, Hugh Downs observed that Barbara's "whole image is perfect for that first cup of coffee."

At age thirty-five, after some three and a half years as

a writer, after running and working harder than anyone else, she had become a member of the on-camera team of America's most successful early-morning television program.

While NBC brass hoped to ease Barbara into the job without any fanfare, her pal, columnist Jack O'Brian, blared the trumpets in a two-page bit of promotional puffery—"Dawn Greets Barbara, a Girl of 'Today'"—in the October 11, 1964, New York *Journal-American*'s TV section. "She wants to remain as she is," he wrote, "the prettiest reporter in television."

Barbara had made the first big step. The outdated, fluffy Today Girl sobriquet was dropped and she was billed as *"Today* reporter Barbara Walters."

She was on her way.

In the few months after her promotion came the first of the perks: a shiny, chauffeur-driven NBC car began picking up Barbara in the predawn hours outside the Gubers' doorman building on West Fifty-seventh Street, taking her to the studio, where she was coifed and pampered by hairdressers and makeup artists. Her closets started filling with a borrowed wardrobe of size-eight designer outfits that she was wearing on the show, with a credit for the manufacturer. She also moved out of the cubbyhole she shared with Cunniff and into the office Maureen O'Sullivan had just vacated. And she was assigned her first secretary, Pat Pepin.

While those amenities were nice, they didn't impress Barbara, who'd grown up in show business, and knew the realities so well.

Her main priority was to make certain that the NBC brass knew they weren't dealing with a rube. Barbara wasted no time putting together a crack management team to handle her business affairs with the network, and her publicity with the news media; she was one of the first in the business to protect her interests in that way.

Through Lee, Barbara had become close friends with personal managers George (Bullets) Durgom and his partner, Ray Katz, whose company at the time handled talent such as Jackie Gleason, opera singer Marguerite Piazza, Merv Griffin, Kate Smith—and later superstars like Cher, Lily Tomlin, and Dolly Parton. When Barbara got the job, she and Lee asked Katz, who was based in New York, to negotiate her first talent contract with NBC.

When the legendary Durgom, a diminutive heavy-hitter who got his nickname because his bald pate was as smooth and shiny as a bullet, showed up at NBC to check on the negotiations, his presence there, which was strictly for psychological reasons, had the planned effect. It sent shivers up and down the spines of Morgan and the people in business affairs who were shocked to see the muscle Barbara had at her command. She'd gotten her message across, which was, "Don't play games with me!"

After the contract was negotiated, Barbara's salary jumped from several hundred dollars a week as a writer to around eight hundred a week plus various fees as a reporter. Within a short time it escalated to more than a hundred thousand dollars annually. Requests for interviews, speaking engagements, and other outside activities that came with her growing celebrity were funneled through the Durgom-Katz office. Katz became her liaison with the network, ironing out problems if they arose. "Basically," he said years later, "it was uncomplicated because her career took on a very aggressive position by virtue of her talent. It probably was the simplest job I ever had.

"From the time I first got to know Barbara, anybody could tell that she was going someplace. She was very impressive. She was a very attractive girl, who handled herself magnificently. [The television networks] were starting to realize that women were very valuable assets if they had journalistic talent. Because of her experience [at NBC] they realized they had a big winner."

Long before O'Sullivan left the show, even before Lee

and Barbara were married, while they were still double-dating with Ray Katz, Barbara had spelled out her career goals and ambitions to him.

"She loved the potential of being an on-the-air performer," he said. "They became aware of it at NBC and that's why they jumped on it together. Barbara was someone who everyone knew could become one of the foremost [TV personalities]—there was no question about it."

As Lou Walters' daughter Barbara was "savvy" about all aspects of the industry, Katz observed. "The show business of her father and what she heard all of her life rubbed off on her so that she had a better knowledge of the basics about the [television and entertainment] business. She saw how her father operated; she saw how he produced shows and handled stars. It absolutely rubbed off. That's how she became socially involved with people in the business like Lee Guber. It's through all those kind of associations that your life emerges."

Katz handled Barbara through most of her first contract with NBC. But when he was forced to relocate to the West Coast to work more closely with Durgom, it was decided that Barbara would be placed in the hands of another mutual friend, Lee Stevens, at the William Morris Agency.

"Lee Stevens was a friend of Lee Guber's, too," said Katz. "He was a talent agent, but because of the personal relationship he developed with her, he became everything for Barbara—her personal manager *and* agent. She had respect for him and he certainly had a high regard for her, and realized where she was going and that it was pretty nice to get a client like that on the rise." Stevens would do an amazing job for Barbara. He would become the first agent to get a television journalist into the big-money league.

One of the keys to Barbara's success was her instinctive ability to know from a public relations point of view how to handle herself. Prior to Stevens taking over Barbara's management, Ray Katz, at Barbara's request, hired her first personal publicist, the New York firm of Arthur Jacobs and John Springer.

"Barbara wasn't the first girl at *Today*, but she was the first who got that kind of media attention," said Springer. "People like Maureen O'Sullivan and Estelle Parsons never got the attention that Barbara got."

Barbara had been a flack herself, learning the game from masters such as Bill Safire, Tex McCrary, Ted Cott, and her father. Moreover, she had powerful columnist friends like Jack O'Brian and George Sokolsky in her corner. When Springer's firm got Barbara's account, "She knew the ropes," he said.

However, Barbara downplayed her knowledge, remembered Peter Levinson, who worked on the Walters publicity campaign for Springer at various times in the mid-Sixties. "She acted like, 'You'll have to explain this whole show biz thing to me. My father had the Latin Quarter but I was never really involved with show business and you'll have to tell me who all these people are and so forth.'" At the time, Levinson said, he didn't know Barbara and felt she was sincere in "the way she handled it."

What Barbara wanted from Springer for the cost of his services—for which she was personally paying a retainer of eighteen hundred dollars a month—"was everything that publicity could get her. She wanted items in columns. She wanted feature stories. She wanted attention in the press—and the right kind of attention. She wanted class stuff. We got a lot of attention for her."

In one of Levinson's first meetings with Barbara, she told him, "I know you guys know what to do—so do it. I hope I've got something you can sell. I guess I'm the first woman promoted from a writer to a personality."

While the publicity would get her name known among a wider audience than *Today* viewers, Barbara's main goal was to have the NBC brass see it as often and in as many places as possible.

During 1965, her first full year as an on-camera personality, Springer's office generated major features about Barbara, most of them based on her Algeresque rise from writer to on-air reporter-personality—in *TV Guide*, the Sunday Boston *Herald-Advertiser*, the Newark *Evening News*, the Boston *Record*, the New York *Post*, and New York *Herald-Tribune*, among others.

Typical of the hype was a feature in the New York *Daily News* Sunday magazine—the *News* had the largest circulation of any daily newspaper in the country. Under the headline "Guess Star, Can you identify this personality?" was a six-inch, single-column bio of Barbara: "This young lady's assignments range far and wide . . . A native of Boston, Mass. . . . She lived in Florida . . . Today's mystery Miss began her TV career on graduation from Sarah Lawrence . . . The performer is married to theatrical producer Lee Guber . . ."

For anyone interested to know the answer to the celebrity quiz, readers were advised to turn to page twenty of the magazine where there was a headshot of an attractive woman with more of a smirk than a smile; her Audrey Hepburnish brunette hairstyle glossily sprayed, her eyes emphasized with dark liner and false lashes: "TODAY'S GUESS STAR, Barbara Walters ('Today')."

Like a politician running for office, Barbara had a knack for coming up with quotes that caught the fancy of reporters doing interviews with her; she'd repeat the successful phrase over and over again, changing the wording here and there, and they'd pop up in story after story. One of her favorites was in response to questions about how she liked her new job. "I love my work. I'd pay them if they didn't pay me," she'd tell *TV Guide*. "The money is wonderful, but sometimes I think I'd work at this job for nothing, I'm so crazy about it," she'd say to the *Herald-Trib*. "I'd do my job for no pay at all, I love it so much," she'd gush to a Boston paper. Another favorite was, "It's the only job like it on TV," which sometimes became, "If I didn't have the best job of any woman in TV, I probably wouldn't work."

Barbara's face, declared a feature in the Miami *Herald*'s Sunday magazine, "is becoming as familiar to the viewers as the pattern of their breakfast coffee cups."

Barbara exulted in all of the mostly canned attention. "I'm having a love affair with the red light on the TV camera," she enthused with a blush of modesty. "I also plead guilty to euphoria when someone on the street recognizes me."

The initial campaign to make the Barbara Walters name part of the American psyche reached its peak in late 1965 when an editor at *Life* magazine, having seen all the publicity generated by Springer, telephoned Barbara directly at NBC to arrange to do a feature on her. Getting in *Life* was a dream come true for any up-and-coming celebrity in those days; it was like being on the combined covers of *Rolling Stone*, *People*, *Spy*, and *Vanity Fair* in the Eighties.

The day after *Life* called Barbara, Ray Katz telephoned Springer. "He said, 'Well, you people have done exactly what we wanted.' It was like thanks, you did the job— you're fired," said Levinson. "And that's exactly what happened. Katz said, 'John, thanks a lot, we don't need you anymore.' She fired Springer, saying *Life* magazine had called."

The *Life* layout was phenomenal. The big, bold headline read, "BARBARA WALTERS OF 'TODAY' SHOW LOOKS SHARP— and is Early to Rise, Wealthy and Wise." The lead photo, one of many of her at work and at home, showed her wearing a little black dress and four strands of pearls, with her legs tucked girlishly under her. Barbara was in the center of the photo. Off to the left, almost squeezed out, and in profile, was Hugh Downs, looking more like Barbara's second banana than the star. The caption said, "Downs and the staff listen carefully to what she has to say." The article made it seem that Barbara was running things.

At first Downs had noted Barbara's groundswell of publicity with curiosity, then growing concern, and finally,
with the *Life* piece, absolute fury. This neophyte—whom
he had proposed for the job in the first place—was upstag-
ing him.

NBC sources later disclosed to Springer that the real reason Barbara dropped his firm's services was because of the
dissension all her publicity had generated on the *Today* set,
with most of the anger coming from Hugh Downs's corner.
Downs was said to have had a fit over the *Life* piece; he
would later downplay any possible feud with Barbara, saying he had his own publicist. But NBC brass stepped in
and told Barbara to turn off her publicity machine, post-
haste.

"There was great resentment from an area in the *Today*
show," Springer acknowledged. "My understanding was
it was Downs, but I never bothered to pin it down. I was
just told that NBC had decided that she should not have
her own personal public relations person at that time."

Others at NBC News also became aware that Barbara
had her own publicist and therefore was violating some un-
written code of the journalism profession.

"One of the things that I thought was odd and different
about Barbara and related to her ambition and to the business of being something a little bit different from a journalist is that she had a person who was assigned solely to the
promotion of Barbara Walters," said Bill Monroe, who had
served as NBC News Washington Bureau chief, and the
Today show's Washington interviewer, between 1961 and
1969, and later as executive producer and moderator of
Meet the Press.

Monroe, later editor of the Washington *Journalism Review*, observed that Barbara's use of a publicist "[was] a
more clearcut indication that she looked on herself as a
personality as opposed to a journalist. I didn't know other
journalists who did that, and this set her apart a little bit

in my mind as somebody who had something else on her agenda beyond strict journalism. This was a show biz kind of thing. Her show-business background and her awareness of the need for promotion in show business probably had a lot to do with her approach."

Peter Levinson ran into Barbara several times after Springer's firm was axed—at the Princess Hotel in Acapulco, in an elevator at Saks Fifth Avenue, at a party at the Waldorf—and each time she treated him as if he were a stranger. "She was ten feet away from me and she acted like she didn't know who I was," he said.

Meanwhile, Barbara abided by the ban against having a personal publicist, at least for a few years. But when her power base expanded at NBC, she hired another press agent—and no one at the network even considered trying to stop her.

Despite the publicity and the perks, Barbara worked even harder than she did before the promotion, refusing to allow her growing fame to go to her head.

"She was doing more of what she always did, which was to work her tail off," observed Gail Rock.

> She just really plunged in and did it. There wasn't any jumping around, opening champagne and celebrating. Barbara was the daughter of a show-business person who'd been around this all of her life and knew what it did or didn't mean to be a celebrity. It was mostly crap basically, and she knew that. Her experience as a kid being around a lot of celebrities prepared her for it. She may never have expected it to happen to her, but she knew what to do when it did.
>
> She knew how to be charming and gracious. I never saw her do any big ego trip. She certainly didn't do that with the staff because we all knew her when—and she had a lot of support from us. She got more polished and more chic and more fashionable fairly quickly. Suddenly we were seeing the Dior this and the Chanel that.

Because of the briskness, control, and intensity she saw in Barbara, Pat Pepin felt trepidation when she was asked by a *Today* executive to become Barbara's first secretary in the winter of 1964. In the beginning, Pepin said, Barbara treated her "like something you put on a powder puff. She was so wonderful to me." But by the time Pepin left the job some two years later, the two were not on friendly terms.

Barbara was trying to do everything herself, including answering all of her own fan mail that was starting to dribble in, when Pepin, a history major who had completed two years of law school at Boston University, joined her.

"But then they did something with Barbara's hair [it was lightened] and it caused such an uproar. The mail just literally poured in. It was mostly, 'We don't like your hair.' We were inundated," Pepin recalled. "There was no way she was going to start dictating letters to every one of those silly people who were worried about her. Things were done to correct the problem with Barbara's hair, but the mail kept pouring in. Finally, she told me to take care of it."

After about six months—with increasing demands on her time, such as speaking engagements and the commentaries she was doing for the popular NBC Radio Network program "Emphasis" in addition to her *Today* show duties—Barbara seemed suddenly "insecure and [she] needed the support of a little network of women," Pepin observed. Besides Pepin, the group included Rock, Anne Perkins, Jane Schulberg, and Barbara Gordon, who later became a successful author.

"She was like one of the girls all of a sudden," Pepin said.

The insecurity simply was, "I'm out on a plank. There's a lot of things riding on this." On the line was Barbara's career, of course. She was not being treated as a *Today* show "girl," but rather a female personality regarded with some respect. She felt it was important to make it because

of that fact. It was delightful to be with her at that point.
Having seen her in the past as being very controlled and
very intense as a writer, suddenly her hair, her makeup,
her clothes all became horrendously important—girlie
things that she rarely worried about before.

Despite the fact that Barbara sought support from those
young women, she never socialized with them outside the
office and never took her secretary to lunch during the year
and a half Pepin worked for her. "Barbara was not the easiest person to get to know," said Pepin. "She was not very
outgoing."

Barbara was once assigned to go to historic Williams-
burg, Virginia, to do a story. During a lunch break, Jane
Schulberg, who was on the shoot, was chatting with the
cameraman about nothing in particular, and in the background they noticed Barbara silently pacing back and
forth. When they got into the car later, Barbara suddenly
spoke up. "What do you guys talk about?" she asked. "I
don't ever have anything to say once we stop working."

"And it was true," observed Schulberg. "She didn't,
and it made her very uncomfortable. She didn't care about
hearing stories about the cameraman's wife or his grand-
children, so she just felt like a sore thumb sitting there.
But in a working situation she had plenty to talk about.
Barbara's *real* different."

Once several of the young women on the staff ran into
Barbara, her parents, and her sister coming out of the
Walterses' apartment building. It was the first time they'd
learned that her sister was retarded. Barbara seemed extremely nervous and embarrassed.

Al Morgan's secretary, Nancy Fields, said that "a lot of
people thought she was aloof. I think Barbara knew that,
too—that she could have been friendlier than she was. She
was friendly at the friendly times, but there were times
when people thought she was too cold."

"I don't think she really gave a hang about what any

of us thought," reasoned Gail Rock. "She was really upwardly mobile. She was more concerned with trying to get attention from the people at the top. She was very hip about office politics.

> Barbara is someone who has a very good sense of what is appropriate behavior—she knows how to play it. She knows when to be silly, when to be raunchy, when to be professional, when to giggle and when not to giggle. She doesn't make a whole lot of false steps. She senses the context she's operating in, and she fits herself into that. It's almost like being an actor—just fitting herself into whatever the flow is. It's a consciousness she needed to be successful. It's to know when to cut loose and when to be professional. If we were sitting around having a drink after a day's shoot in Podunk, Barbara was delightful company—funny and spontaneous. But when she's on the job you didn't see her make many false steps. She was always a tremendously alert observer of people. She knew how to gauge what was going on, what was the appropriate thing to do, how to fit in.

Within her first year on the air, NBC arranged to promote Barbara as a *Today* personality with a guest appearance on Johnny Carson's *Tonight* show, which emanated in those days from a studio next door to *Today*'s. When Barbara got the word she came wandering back in a daze to tell the girls, *"I am going to be on Johnny Carson?"* She said it almost questioningly, in awe. "For a week we were building for her appearance," said Pepin. "She had people come in with dresses. They decided she should wear a yellow dress, and she was very concerned about that. She didn't feel yellow was her best color. The night of the show she came in and said, 'Will you guys stay with me?' And we said, 'No, Barbara, you're a big girl and for God's sake you know Johnny Carson. You just go out there and do your thing.' And we went home and she did great." Whenever

Barbara sat in for Johnny, she garnered the highest ratings
of any substitute host at that point.

While Barbara may have had her insecurities and fears,
she wasn't about to stand for any slights to her growing
stature. On assignment in Los Angeles for the first time
since her promotion—she was there to do celebrity interviews for the new TV season on NBC—she hit the ceiling
when the Beverly Hills Hotel put her in a standard room
because that's apparently what was reserved for her by the
show, and no one at the front desk knew who she was. Barbara got on the telephone and screamed holy hell to New
York, and when that didn't work she called Bullets Durgom. Suddenly it was "Miss Walters, we're so sorry," and
Barbara was placed in an elaborate suite. To get around
L.A., she had a limo at her disposal.

Barbara always chose her causes carefully, weighing the
benefits to herself. When Pat Pepin had a run-in with the
powers that be over a personal scheduling matter, an issue
that would result in her leaving her job, Barbara decided
not to get involved, never offering to help mediate the
problem. The day Pepin gave Barbara her notice, "[Bar-
bara] was saying things like, 'You're letting me down. Why
didn't you come to me?' That was the end of it. She rushed
off. It was the only time I ever felt other than super things
for Barbara. There were no goodbyes, no balloons or
luncheons," said Pepin.

But Barbara also showed a compassionate side for colleagues with problems. When one young woman had an
abortion, which was not legal at the time, Barbara took
her in and helped her get back on her feet. Another time,
she canceled a trip to help arrange for a physician friend
to take the case of a woman staffer who had suspected
breast cancer. There were numerous such episodes. Barbara would always send flowers and cards on special occasions and take time to visit colleagues who were sick at
home or in the hospital.

*   *   *

On the job, Barbara was driven, compulsive, a perfectionist.

On one early assignment, after she'd gotten her new job, she'd gone to New Jersey with a crew to interview the poet LeRoi Jones. Barbara had done her usual competent job. On the drive back to Manhattan the crew was happy and relaxed—except Barbara. Most reporters would be writing their copy or editing the piece on paper at that point. But Barbara sat in the back seat like a caged tiger who hadn't been fed in a week. Tense and fretful, she was obsessing about the questions she felt she could have or should have asked but didn't, furiously writing them down in a notebook. Had they not been on a tight deadline, Barbara would have forced the crew to return and do the interview again. That kind of compulsiveness would continue throughout her entire career.

"She worked like a dog after she got the job," said Bob Cunniff. "I would sneak out of there and go home by five-thirty, six o'clock, and she'd be there working away, hacking at her typewriter, on the phone. Given her new prominence, Barbara initiated a lot of projects because that's her nature. She seized this opportunity and did a lot more film pieces and more interviews. She became more confident. She felt, given a little more power, that she could function better. There was certainly a lot more assurance in her after the promotion."

Because of her rigorous schedule, Barbara took good care of herself, without overdoing it. She never drank or used drugs. She always went to bed early, which did cause problems in her relationship with Lee. But she was not a fanatic about diet or exercise. In fact, she *never* exercised—hated it. She wasn't a swimmer or a tennis player and not a lover of the great outdoors. Often in the predawn hours, before going on camera, she'd breakfast on brownies or Mallomars.

She'd schedule luncheon engagements at least three times a week with old friends, adjusting her life to a normal routine even though the hours were horrendous. "Barbara floated through it," said John Lord. "There's something about her whole makeup, psychological and physical. It's remarkable. She always took care of herself. I remember when we took the show to New Orleans, Barbara was still in bed doing her nails when everyone else was running around. She was able to relax and made sure she did."

"I don't know how she did it," said Gail Rock, "but she had tremendous energy. It always amazed me. I never saw her come in unprepared or tired."

Barbara hit the ground running—and never stopped.

She attended a bunny school and waited on tables one night at a Playboy Club, appearing live in full tail and ears to discuss the bunny life with an enraptured Hugh Downs, who noted, "This is the first time I knew you had a figure." (The idea came from a magazine piece written by Gloria Steinem.)

She went to Paris to comment on the latest fashions, and to interview singer Yves Montand in the historic first program ever to be broadcast live from Europe via satellite— "I can hardly believe I'm here," Barbara exclaimed to housewives on Main Street, U.S.A., as the cameras carried her image on the Early Bird communications satellite from the balcony of Montand's apartment on the boulevard Saint-Michel. There was one glitch: the French technicians forgot to turn on her audio. "Ouvrez le microphone!" a *Today* director screamed from a control room in Brussels. "Ouvrez le microphone and keep the goddamn microphone open!"

Barbara did one of her first exclusive interviews with President Johnson's daughter, Luci Baines, who discussed her life in the White House. She also covered Lynda Bird and Luci Baines Johnson's weddings; interviewed Mrs. Rose Kennedy, Truman Capote, Ingrid Bergman; two First Ladies—Mrs. Johnson and Mrs. Eisenhower—and Princess Grace of Monaco. Barbara had begun laying the groundwork for the future: her trademark of conversing intimately with the world's most famous and infamous celebrities and political leaders.

Barbara pursued less glamorous assignments with the same enthusiasm, vigor, and attention to detail—a feature on the state reformatory for women in Wilmington, Delaware; a story on the life of a Marymount nun; an investigation of school dropouts in Marion, Indiana; a trend piece on Manhattan's new discotheque scene; a report on anti-Semitic housing practices in Grosse Pointe, Michigan; the mod scene in England, and the "new Bohemia" in New York's East Village.

Shad Northshield, who became the number-three man in charge of the NBC News division and later executive producer of the *Huntley-Brinkley Report*, explained her success:

> When Barbara started, NBC was just one hell of a place. It was just wonderful; much more experimental; much more loose, and it was tiny compared to CBS, which was a center of arrogance and phony tradition. There were very few producers and very few reporters and they were good and we had fun. Barbara fit in there just perfectly because she was smart.
>
> She came along when television news discovered the need for, or a desire for, a woman and she was *enough* of a journalist, and *enough* of a performer, and at the right place, and certainly at the right time, to become well known.

STARDOM, BANKRUPTCY, AND A BABY

Of the two most important men in Barbara's life at the time—outside of the powers at NBC and the *Today* show—Lou Walters was in desperate personal and financial straits, and Lee Guber was privately expressing unhappiness about the increasingly lonely life he was being forced to lead because of his wife's blossoming career.

At a time in his life when Lou should have retired to watch proudly as the Walters name became even more famous because of his daughter, he was as hyperactive as ever. He was seventy, in ill health, and he dreaded the idea of solitude. There was something in the Walters genes that demanded work, action; Lou had it and Barbara inherited it.

While Barbara was making her mark on television, Lou was trying to hit it big in Miami with another new venture called the Aqua Wonderland Revue—an extravaganza consisting of water-ski events, fireworks, dancing waters, and an "international" variety show at the city's new Marine Stadium. The city leased the facility to him after he promised a twenty-five percent return from the half-million dollars in net revenue he projected to generate from ticket sales. Lou also was producing his "Oui, Oui Paree" review in the Café Le Can Can at the Carillon Hotel.

But the two-act, twenty-two-scene water spectacular—replete with shapely baton twirlers, champion divers, and lavishly costumed girls doing water ballet acts—sank like a rock, drawing only several hundred people per performance to the 6,500-seat stadium. Just to break even, Lou needed to sell three thousand tickets per performance for what he called "the best water show in America."

The city of Miami never saw a penny of profit and, in fact, lost a little more than $2,300 on the Walters fiasco. Officials froze some seven hundred dollars due Lou to make sure all bills would be paid. In the end, Lou Walters owed the city of Miami $31.12.

Meanwhile, through the mid-Sixties, Walters continued to be a subject of interest to the Federal Bureau of Investigation, his name cropping up in criminal intelligence reports and memorandums involving various antiracketeering investigations such as the bureau's "top hoodlum program." There was never any evidence in the memos that Walters himself was a target. But the records showed that he was interviewed by agents at various times regarding other suspected mobsters.

Lou was hurting and Barbara knew she had to do something to help him—without further injuring his already damaged pride and reputation. Without his knowledge, Barbara telephoned Sonja Loew, pleading with her to talk to Elias Loew to see if he would rehire Lou at the Latin Quarter in New York. "I don't usually do this, Sonja," Barbara said. "But my father is very sick, he had a heart attack, and it would be such a wonderful thing if Mr. Loew would call him and say, 'Come on, Lou, come back to the Latin Quarter.' It would be very important to him."

Lou and Loew hadn't been on speaking terms since the

Café de Paris imbroglio some seven years earlier, and Loew—who had his pride, too—probably would have hung up on Barbara had she called him personally.

"Barbara wanted it done without Lou ever finding out that she was behind the request," said a friend. "It was very nice of her because she knew it would make Lou happy in his last years. Barbara was always a good daughter like that."

Sonja telephoned Loew immediately. Even though they had been divorced for some two decades, she still wielded considerable influence over him. Loew was a tough old guy, but he had a special place in his heart for Lou, and when he heard that his former business associate was down on his luck and in bad health, he agreed to call him and hire him back on an initial six-month contract as general manager of the club. Lou never found out how he came to be rehired. "I missed New York and the Latin Quarter," he told the New York *World-Telegram*'s Leonard Harris. "When Loew said let's start over, I said okay." Barbara's behind-the-scenes lobbying had worked.

Back on the job, Lou was in the columns again and seemed, for the time being, on top of the world. But the nightclub business had changed for the worse and Lou blamed the decline and fall on the medium that was making his daughter's name a household word. "Not because [TV] keeps people at home at night," he said, "but because it helped to inflate entertainers' salaries. . . . A little television exposure makes a star."

More problems were in store for Lou after he returned to the Latin Quarter. Twenty-eight girls were on the line at the club—the picket line. The showgirls had gone on strike over pay, hours, backstage accommodations, and a dispute over management's contributions to a pension and welfare fund for performing artists. The walkout, which never was resolved, would eventually result in the Latin Quarter's demise in 1969.

Financially, Lou was in deep trouble. In November

1965, the Internal Revenue Service placed levies for back taxes against his accounts—both of which were closed out—at the First National City bank branch at Forty-first Street and Broadway, and at the North Shore Bank of Miami, at Seventy-first Street and Harding Avenue, in Miami Beach. To help her father, Barbara lent him at least $5,000 in cash. Among his creditors, Lou owed $100,000 in taxes to the IRS and $8,300 in taxes to the state of New York. He claimed household goods and personal effects of only $400.

On December 3, 1966, Lou and his lawyer, a card-playing crony named Louis Schenfield, journeyed downtown to the U.S. District Court for the Southern District of New York, where Walters filed for bankruptcy. The bankruptcy papers were officially recorded two days later on the fifth and made the newspapers on the sixth. "Lou Walters Is Bankrupt," said the *New York Times*; "Showman Lou Walters Says He's Broke," proclaimed the Miami *Herald.*

At the *Today* show, everyone had read the *Times* story, but no one said anything; they knew Barbara was embarrassed and saddened for her father.

Virtually penniless, with the Latin Quarter closed, and his health deteriorating, Lou returned to Miami with Dena where he'd live out the rest of his life, mostly in a nursing home, financially cared for by Barbara. Her sister, Jackie, was also in Miami, at the Hope School, where she worked with other retarded people like herself. Barbara would care for all of them, just as she had sadly predicted years earlier.

So much happened so soon after Lee and Barbara tied the knot: they bought their three-bedroom apartment on West Fifty-seventh Street, furnished and decorated the place— friends scoffed at how garishly the place was done—and then suddenly Barbara got her promotion. Their lives changed virtually overnight—or at least Barbara's did— and her budding stardom would have a negative impact

A sophomore at Sarah Lawrence, Barbara, left, applies makeup for the role of Mary Boyle in Sean O'Casey's *Juno and the Paycock.*

A star of the "Today" show, Barbara applies her makeup for another early-morning stint with WNBC anchorman Chuck Scarborough. *(Harry Benson)*

Friendly smiles bely Harry Reasoner's and Barbara's feelings toward each other. Barbara was ABC's "Million Dollar Baby" anchorwoman. *(UPI/Bettmann Newsphotos)*

Barbara, standing, left, with other staffers of her high school literary magazine, *Birch Leaves*.

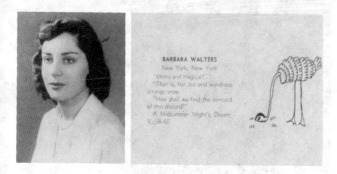

BARBARA WALTERS
New York, New York
"Merry and tragical!"
"That is, hot ice and wondrous
strange snow."
"How shall we find the concord
of this discord?"
A Midsummer Night's Dream
V, i, 58-60

Graduating from Sarah Lawrence, Barbara's depicted as an ostrich with head in the sand. She avoided campus politics and activism during the McCarthy era.

A rare photo of Barbara's sister, Jackie, who was retarded, with parents Lou and Dena at the Latin Quarter. *(Historical Association of Southern Florida/Miami News Collection)*

Barbara with a grieving Dena and relatives at Lou's funeral in Miami. *(Miami Herald)*

Barbara got an exclusive interview with Ted Kennedy after the Chappaquiddick incident.
(Miami Herald)

Fidel Castro favored Barbara with a tour of Havana in his jeep. She was his pet American TV journalist.
(AP/Wide World Photos)

Barbara shocked friends and colleagues when she described "Tricky Dick" as "sexy." She was one of the few interviewers he trusted. *(Nixon Archives) Inset, bottom:* Everyone speculated on a romance between Barbara and Henry Kissinger during the Nixon years. *(UPI/Bettmann Newsphotos) Inset, top left:* Barbara once begged President Ford for an interview, a scene that an observer said made him wish he had an airline barf bag. *(UPI/Bettmann Newsphotos) Inset, top right:* Egyptian President Anwar el-Sadat was fascinated with Barbara's million-dollar-a-year salary. His was only twelve thousand annually. *(AP/Wide World Photos)*

Barbara fell in love with the controversial, secretly gay Roy Cohn while she was in college. Their curious relationship, which infuriated and mystified her family, friends, and colleagues, lasted a lifetime. *(Harry Benson)*

Barbara's daughter, Jackie, at the White House, forged friendship with President Carter's daughter, Amy. *(AP/Wide World Photos)*

A rare photo of Barbara with adopted daughter, Jackie, who was almost six feet tall when she was thirteen. The two had a stormy relationship. *(Ann Clifford/DMI) Inset:* Jackie, pictured here at a year old, was named after Barbara's sister. Despite the cozy family scene, marriage to producer Lee Guber, Barbara's second, was already rocky. *(Historical Association of Southern Florida/Miami News Collection)*

Barbara's relationship with Bear Stearns & Co. CEO Alan (Ace) Greenberg was considered serious by friends. *(Ann Clifford/DMI) Inset top:* At home, Barbara and her poodle under Richard Avedon photo of mother and daughter. *(Andrea Alberts) Inset, bottom:* Hotelier Claude Philippe and Barbara had a discreet romance in the early 1960s. He used a code for her name in his datebook, L.Q. signifying the Latin Quarter, her father's well-known nightclub. *(AP/ Wide World Photos)*

Bicoastal bliss—that's the way friends describe Barbara's third marriage, to TV mogul Merv Adelson. *(AP/ Wide World Photos)*

Despite persistent gossip items that they were romantically involved, economist Alan Greenspan was a considerate friend who listened to Barbara's problems. Here Barbara covers daughter's face to avoid the camera. *(AP/ Wide World Photos)*

Always working, Barbara reads Spiro Agnew's book in limo before interviewing the former Vice President regarding his assertions about Zionist influence in the media. *(Harry Benson) Inset, left:* Barbara sometimes allowed little Jackie to sleep with her and sometimes they bathed together. It was in the tub that she first told her daughter she was adopted. *(Harry Benson) Inset, right:* It was a lonely "poor little rich girl" existence for Barbara in this big house on Palm Island in Florida in the 1940s. *(Miami Herald)*

Barbara autographing her 1970 bestseller, *How to talk to anybody about practically anything*—a book she didn't actually write. *(AP/ Wide World Photos)*

Throughout his life as the "Modern Day Ziegfeld," Lou Walters was surrounded by beautiful show girls, and colleagues say he did not always avoid handling the merchandise. *(Miami Herald)* Inset: A line of beautiful show girls along with the gaudy and the garish were Lou Walters' trademark. *(Historical Association of Southern Florida/Miami News Collection)*

(AP/ Wide World Photos)

(Miami Herald)

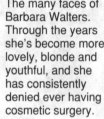

The many faces of Barbara Walters. Through the years she's become more lovely, blonde and youthful, and she has consistently denied ever having cosmetic surgery.

(AP/ Wide World Photos)

(Harry Benson)

(AP/ Wide World Photos)

on their relationship. Lee wasn't jealous of Barbara's career; it's what attracted him to her in the first place. "I find women who do things more interesting than women who don't," he said. But he was hurt by her devotion to the career above all else.

In private, he was telling friends that he was lonely. Curiously, even in those early years of their marriage, Barbara never once said—even for attribution—that she loved Lee. She's always used the word "like" rather than love.

Lee was convivial, outgoing, and a night person, but Barbara was on the other side of the international dateline as far as he was concerned. "Lee liked to sit around and drink and talk with people and I'm sure the restrictions of her life didn't sit too well with him," said Frank Ford. He recalled going to see *Man of La Mancha* with the Gubers and expected to have a full and pleasant evening with them. "But Barbara left at intermission," Ford said. "Lee had to put her in a cab and she went home. She didn't stay for the second act because she had to get up so early in the morning. We went back and saw the rest of the show. This was the kind of pressure they were under."

Because of her schedule, Barbara was usually in bed by nine or ten o'clock to be up at four, and she'd spend the early evening hours working on scripts or reading books for the next day.

Naturally, all of this was putting a strain on their social and sex lives—stress and frustration that eventually would drive Lee into the arms of at least one other woman. A female friend of Lee's recalled running into him at a party one night when Barbara was already home asleep. "There were a lot of celebrities there," said the woman, "and Lee said, 'Oh, these people are so busy impressing each other, they have no time for a love life.'" She noted the frustration in his voice. Because of Barbara's schedule, friends commented wryly that, "Lee has to make an appointment with Barbara for a conjugal visit."

"Even when I finally get to bed," Barbara acknowledged,

"I usually have some homework to do. Sometimes I ask myself, 'What am I doing getting up at four to beat my brains out while my husband and everybody else in the world is asleep?' But I get up anyway."

When Barbara first got the on-air job, Lee got up with her, they'd have breakfast together, and then he'd watch her report on the show. "After a few weeks," Barbara admitted, "he would check to see what time my spot would be on the air and stayed in bed [alone] until then. Now I must confess his interest in the show has slowly deteriorated."

As Barbara's visibility increased, so did the demands on her time. "When Barbara was really becoming a big name and in great demand for personal appearances and such," an associate recalled, "Lee said to me, 'Our apartment now is like the William Morris office. Everybody's calling—they want Barbara for this and Barbara for that.' "

Judith Crist saw Lee as "extremely understanding. There are not many husbands who would tolerate Barbara's absolute career- and ego-centeredness as long as Lee did. He was able to do it because he was a mensch and he was a grownup. There are not very many men who can deal with their wives getting up at four o'clock in the morning to go to work and having to go to bed very early. Barbara would tell me her problems; why she couldn't go here and there at night because of the crazy *Today* schedule. Their marriage lasted much longer than one would have imagined."

One evening the Peysers were invited to dinner and Barbara talked about an interview she had just conducted with Lauren Bacall and Jason Robards, who were then married to each other. After describing the awe with which Bacall referred to Humphrey Bogart, her first husband, Barbara finished her discussion asking, "I wonder how long this present marriage will last?" Later, when everyone was saying goodbye, Lee came forth with a surprisingly hostile remark. "I bet that as soon as Barbara left, Bacall or Robards

asked, 'I wonder how long *her* present marriage will last?'"
The elevator's arrival got Barbara off the hook.

"I never saw the kind of warmth between Barbara and
Lee that you might expect," said John Lord. "On the other
hand, she's not that demonstrative a person and neither
was he. I would have felt a close relationship would have
been very difficult."

Most of Lee's Philadelphia friends disliked Barbara, feeling that she was cold and unfriendly. One agent friend of
Lee's sarcastically referred to her as "Mrs. Warmth."

"Lee was a wonderful, terrific guy. He had a great joy
about himself," said Frank Ford. "I always thought he deserved someone nicer than Barbara. I thought he was too
good for her. He was such an outgoing, friendly guy, who
didn't seem to care whether you were a cabdriver or a captain of industry—he would pretty much treat everyone the
same way. She was in an industry where who you know
is very important; who you associate with is very important; who you party with is very important. Guber wasn't
that way at all. He was more egalitarian by far."

By 1968, with her fortieth birthday looming, Barbara faced
the realization that she wasn't going to have children of
her own; she'd already had several miscarriages, was on all
sorts of medical regimens, and her biological clock was
winding down.

On one occasion, when the *Today* show was doing a special evening edition, Barbara, who had gotten home from
the hospital that very day after having had a miscarriage,
appeared on the air that night. "It was so important to me
to be on . . . I didn't have a car and I remember standing
on the corner trying to get a cab. I couldn't run. I remember thinking, 'I am out of my mind.'"

Later Barbara confided to a friend, "I don't have time
to wait and go to all those gynecologists. I have to get on
with my life and I want a baby and I have to accept that
if I'm not going to have one, I have to adopt one."

"Her star was very much in the ascendancy at that time," said Frank Ford. "Instead of trying again to have a child she decided it would be easier to adopt so she would not have to give up her career by being big and fat and having to stay off the camera."

Guber's first wife, Edna Tuttleman, said she was told about the adoption plans by Lee himself when he telephoned her seeking records of their divorce which were required for the adoption proceedings. "He said Barbara did not want to go through another pregnancy," Tuttleman recalled. "He said she had a miscarriage and it took so much time and trouble in her career that they decided it was safer to adopt." Some of Barbara's friends speculated that her pregnancy problems were related to her fears of having a retarded child like her sister.

Lee and Barbara began pursuing the standard avenues for adoption, working through agencies, but were unsuccessful in finding a suitable child. At the office, Barbara told Judith Crist about her efforts to adopt, leaving her "with the impression that there were several opportunities that came to nothing."

Finally, Barbara turned to the one man in New York who she knew would do anything for her and could accomplish the impossible—Roy Cohn. If anyone could locate a child for her, or put her in touch with the proper people, it was Roy. Lee, who despised Cohn, was against the idea, but Barbara would hear no arguments.

"Roy was influential in helping get Barbara the child she adopted," confirmed Shirley Budd. "He was influential in giving her the right resources for adoption. Roy was always very wonderful to Barbara."

Cohn wasted no time putting Barbara together with a friend who would legally find her a suitable newborn. Cohn's assistance in helping Barbara at that critical point in her life is the reason for her unstinting loyalty to him through the subsequent years—an allegiance that included defending him to his many detractors, attending his parties when she had better things to do, testifying on his behalf during disbarment proceedings in 1985, and being at his side as he wasted away from AIDS.

Had it not been for Cohn, Barbara might have well remained childless. She vowed privately never to forget the favor he bestowed upon her, subjecting herself to intense criticism for being his friend, long after their curious romantic involvement had ended. She never publicly discussed the favor that Cohn had done for her, and few, if any, of her closest friends were aware of it. But in a speaking engagement in Philadelphia in January 1989, she hinted about it. "There is an incident that happened when I was relatively young when Roy did something that was very helpful and caring," Barbara said cryptically.

The child, a beautiful girl, was born on June 14, 1968, and Barbara and Lee took her home a few days later. Barbara took some time off from the show to settle into motherhood. She named the baby Jacqueline Dena Guber. For a long time, many people thought the baby was named for Jacqueline Kennedy, but in fact Barbara named the infant for her sister and her mother, which was curious for two reasons. For one, Jews don't usually name their children after living relatives. For another, Barbara seemed to be laying a heavy burden on the child by naming her after a person who had been the cause of so much emotional turbulence in her life, but Barbara maintained that she was paying homage to her sister to whom she was devoted.

The baby brought Barbara a sense of happiness that she had never experienced before. "When Barbara adopted that child," said her friend, Anne Williams Ferguson, "she was practically burbling. She came out here [San Francisco] on some assignment and we were having breakfast and I'd never seen so many baby pictures. She adored that child. It was rather touching."

Never once, though, did Barbara consider taking an extended leave of absence from the *Today* show to stay at home with her baby.

With a French nanny and a Jamaican cook to take care of Jacqueline, Barbara changed her work schedule minimally. She tried to get home a bit earlier in the afternoons to play with the child and was there at bedtime. "She was so thrilled with that baby," said Nancy Fields. "The nurse used to come into the office with it."

Barbara's travel increased with her growing importance on the show, and she was leaving Jacqueline increasingly in the care of the staff at home. It hurt Barbara to be away from her baby and once, while the show was on location in Ireland, program executives had the toddler and nurse flown over because Barbara seemed so miserable without her. But for the most part, history was repeating itself. Barbara, who had such a lonely childhood because of Lou's devotion to his work, and Dena's dedication to Jackie, was raising her daughter much the same way.

"One of the things that has echoed in my head and heart over the years," said Joan Peyser, "is Barbara saying to me, 'I'll never do that to my child,' and, of course, like so many others, she has behaved to her own daughter precisely the same way her parents treated her—traveling for business and leaving the child alone."

BARBARA'S RABBI

Because of her show-business upbringing, Barbara had taken on the role of the *Today* show's celebrity interviewer. She had the foresight to see the concept as a vein of gold left untapped since Edward R. Murrow's highly successful *Person to Person* program went off the air in 1961. Murrow, his trademark cigarette smoldering between thumb and forefinger of his left hand, had intimate and entertaining at-home visits with personalities ranging from Marilyn Monroe to then-Senator John F. Kennedy, from Zsa Zsa Gabor to Fidel Castro.

The concept was similar to the highly successful *Barbara Walters Special* programs that would begin in 1976. But back in the late sixties, while she was still on *Today*, Barbara latched on to the genre and never let go.

Barbara was also becoming more independent, assertive, and aggressive in her interviewing style, sometimes causing friction with her colleagues and bosses. For example, in 1968, Fred Astaire, who rarely granted TV interviews, decided to give the *Today* show an exclusive so he could plug his new film, *Finian's Rainbow*, in which he starred and had a financial interest.

Naturally, Morgan assigned Barbara to do the interview and Bob Cunniff to be the writer-producer of the segment. In a meeting with Cunniff at the Plaza, Astaire made it clear that he wanted no questions asked about his relationship with a pretty dancer who'd performed with him. Cunniff saw no reason not to agree to Astaire's request. "It didn't matter to me," he said. "First of all, if there had been a romance, it was dead by that time."

Cunniff told Barbara about the understanding, but she laughed in his face.

"I'm going to ask him," she said defiantly. "What kind of journalist would you call me if I didn't ask that question?"

"A journalist who's looking for more information than a dead romance," a perturbed Cunniff responded.

"Well, I don't care," said Barbara petulantly. "I'm going to ask him."

Seeing he was losing the battle, Cunniff said, "Okay, just do me one favor—wait until the interview is just about over or he's going to get up and walk out."

Barbara agreed: "Since you're going to cut the film anyway."

The interview went off without a hitch until Barbara asked the question, which she handled in a reasonably tactful way, suggesting that Astaire and the dancer had been more than friends. "Astaire immediately dried up," said Cunniff. "He tried to be diplomatic but it was all over. There was nothing more to be said. He had no answer whatsoever."

In the editing room, Cunniff cut the question because "there was nothing there." Just as he was finishing, the telephone rang. " 'Can I see the Astaire thing?' Barbara asked, a note of confrontation in her voice. I said, 'Sure. It's good stuff. Go ahead.'

"So she went up to editing and I get another call—'Where's the [dancer] question?' Barbara demanded to know.

" 'I took it out.'

" 'Well, I want it back in!'

" 'I'm not going to put it back in. If you want to go to Al Morgan and put it back in on your own, you're free to do so.' "

Barbara did just that, taking her case to the producer.

"She'd walk into Al's office and say she didn't want a certain part of her interviews deleted, or that she didn't get enough time," said Nancy Fields, who remembered numerous such incidents beyond the Astaire situation. "She'd work hard to get it back. She fought hard for it."

"I was very annoyed," said Cunniff. "She's a very persistent person. I would say that's certainly one of her major talents. She goes after what she wants to go after and usually gets it. It's in her nature.

"Al called me up and said, 'What's the problem?' "

"I told him what had happened.

" 'Fuck her!' said Morgan brusquely."

Barbara's question remained on the cutting room floor. How did Barbara react to losing?

"She shrugged," said Cunniff.

Years later, Barbara was again interviewing Astaire—this time on the ABC-TV newsmagazine 20/20, which she was cohosting with Hugh Downs. "They're out walking in the woods, as Barbara does with all those people, with their arms locked," said Cunniff, who was watching at home. "Astaire had just told Barbara that he planned to get married again. And she said to him, 'You know, I've often wondered about [that dancer].' "

Again Astaire didn't answer the question, offering only a shrug.

"But I thought to myself—'Damn it, she finally got it in!' " said Cunniff.

*   *   *

Al Morgan, who had recently signed a new three-year contract, learned of his axing as producer of the *Today* show on Yom Kippur—the Jewish day of atonement—1968.

Morgan's deteriorating relationship with Hugh Downs was the primary reason he was ousted. Some say it got so bad that the two weren't speaking on the set. Downs himself acknowledged that "the behind-camera conflict between myself and Al Morgan seemed impossible to resolve . . . something was chemically wrong . . . it had become more than a personality conflict."

One former *Today* executive described the situation between Downs and Morgan at the end as "sort of a running gun battle."

The program seemed like a banana republic where every few years a coup was initiated and a new leader put in power. Morgan, in charge for more than five years, had lasted longer than most.

The replacement of Morgan had been quietly under consideration for some time. Not only was Downs lobbying for his ouster, but NBC News executives felt the show needed an infusion of new blood and thinking at the top; Morgan was considered too show business at a time when the political and social fabric of the country was being torn apart—Vietnam, women's liberation, the sexual revolution, Nixon and Agnew, violence in the streets, yippies and hippies. NBC News brass wanted the *Today* show to deal increasingly with those issues, but as one former executive said, "Morgan would have been just as happy producing the *Tonight* show."

His replacement was Stuart Schulberg—a rarity in the world of broadcast news executives. Erudite, literate, he was a hands-on producer and director who was responsible for a number of highly acclaimed NBC documentaries.

Barbara's first hard-news political scoop—a story that caused a giant stir in Washington and put her name on the front page of the *New York Times* and in full-page NBC

promotional ads in major newspapers around the country—was handed to her on a silver platter in early 1969
by the subject of her story, an ardent admirer named Dean
Rusk.

With the election of Richard Nixon in November 1968,
Rusk resigned after eight difficult years as the controversial
Secretary of State of the Kennedy and Johnson Adminis-
trations, to make way for William P. Rogers. Rusk had always been a viewer of the *Today* show and was so impressed
with Barbara that he wrote her a fan letter, which had a
place of prominence on the wall of her seventh-floor office.
"If NBC vice presidents ever begin to bother you," Rusk
wrote, "show them this letter and others like it and tell
them to leave you alone." Rusk wrote the note because "I
appreciated the fact that she seemed to do her homework.
She knew what she was talking about. She was a very good
newswoman."

"Rusk liked her," said NBC Washington correspondent
Ray Scherer, who would have liked to have gotten the interview himself. "They had a special kind of rapport."

Every major league reporter in Washington was chasing
Rusk for the first interview in the wake of his resignation,
but he'd rejected all of them. When NBC joined the list,
Rusk perked up. "I'll do it if Barbara Walters asks me,"
he said.

Nancy Dickerson, an NBC News personality at the time,
heard a different rendition of how the interview came
about.

"At a big party at the State Department on the last night
Dean Rusk was in Washington," Dickerson recalled, "he
told me that none of the three anchors had ever asked to
interview him in the entire eight years he was in office. And
so Barbara came along and asked him and he was so glad
to be invited he said yes."

Whichever way it happened, a breathless and excited
Barbara flew to Washington, while members of the writing
and news staffs pulled together a list of questions dealing

with the Vietnam War and Johnson's surprise decision not
to seek reelection. At the Hay Adams Hotel, Barbara and
Rusk had lunch and then adjourned to an upstairs suite
where the interview was filmed.

"During a break, when we came to the end of the first
reel of tape," Rusk recalled, "we were sitting there smoking
our cigarettes and Barbara turned to a colleague from NBC
who was with her and said, 'We're not coming through
with tough, hard-hitting reporter's questions. We gotta do
something about that in the remaining twenty minutes.'
So, the first question after the break she asked me how I
and my associates in government 'could have been so stupid' about the buildup of the Vietnam War. I was amused.
I knew the background of that question, so I laughed, and
I think NBC took the laugh out!"

Rusk gave Barbara an hour with enough hard news coming out of the session for the *Today* show to go with a much
ballyhooed five-part series, and for the evening news to use
snippets, a great coup for Barbara, who was both making
and breaking news with her exclusive. Stuart Schulberg
was impressed.

As a result of the Rusk interview, noted Scherer, "Suddenly Barbara was in Washington and she was established
and she was big. Because [Washington political figures] saw
her on the *Today* show, they took her as an established
personality. That was in the days when the *Today* show
had such a lead. If you were on *Today*, you were automati-
cally somebody to talk to." Scherer liked Barbara and
enjoyed working with her. "She was an interesting combination of both entertainment and journalism," he felt.

Bill Monroe, the *Today* show's interviewer in Washington, said the initial feeling among the Washington reporters about Barbara's move into their territory "was certainly
one of wariness and doubt and a sense that glamour was
coming into vogue and taking over." However, Monroe
felt Barbara had come up through the ranks legitimately—
moving forward "because of her considerable drive and

ambition. I appreciated the fact that she got interviews
with the biggest names often as the result of persistence,"
he said.

Barbara's exclusive with Rusk brought her to the attention
of Don Meaney, the vice president in charge of TV news
programming, who was instrumental in the decision to
heavily promote the interview in newspapers and on the
air—resulting in tremendous exposure for Barbara, and
helping to establish her credentials in Washington.

A handsome, amiable, and able administrator, Meaney
became Barbara's key booster and adviser within the news
division, sparking rumors that their relationship was more
than professional. In fact, there was no romance between
the two.

"Don was a big advocate and supporter of Barbara's,"
said Doug Sinsel, the producer of the *Today* show and
Schulberg's deputy. Meaney traveled with the *Today* show,
often spending time with Barbara on the road. In New
York, they were frequently seen together at lunch, and Barbara had invited Meaney to meet her family during a visit
to Miami. Jane Schulberg recalled that once, returning
from an assignment, "Barbara went out of her way to say,
'I know that a lot of people are talking about me and Don,
but it is not an affair.'"

"Don Meaney was there at the beginning," said Ray
Scherer.

> He was always in the background handling her—her [busi-
> ness and professional] affairs and whatnot. They were very
> close. Barbara looked to him for advice and he was very
> helpful in her career at that time. She was becoming an
> important personage and [NBC brass] thought they ought
> to have a vice president along to see that everything went
> right—to act as a buffer for her; to make sure she got all
> the perks to which she was entitled. That was his role—
> just kind of looking out for her. There may have been an

element of editorial control in the thing, too—making sure she didn't go off the deep end here and there on something; that was probably one of his roles, but it was pretty well hidden.

Colleagues of Barbara during those days felt someone like Meaney was necessary to act as a governor to limit her fervor while covering news stories. They point to Barbara's aggressiveness at Richard Nixon's 1968 inaugural ball, during which she drove Secret Service agents up the wall. A reporter watching her work that night was taken aback by her pushiness:

> I had been covering Presidential stories in Washington for years so I held the Secret Service agents in great deference. My jaw dropped when I watched Barbara that night—how intrepid she was. Gutsy is the only way I can describe it. She would constantly roam beyond the Secret Service lines with a microphone to interview whoever came by. The agents would warn her, "Don't do that!" But she would go right back again when they turned their backs. She was very difficult that night in the sense that she didn't pay any attention to the normal restraints that are put on correspondents. She'd go where she wanted to go.

Another broadcast journalist remembered Barbara

> literally pacing back and forth like a caged tiger—very undone—trying to get interviews with people coming off elevators. That never happened again—she never got that kind of grunt assignment again—and I'm sure that was because of Don Meaney's help. Barbara has always said that when a man does that kind of thing he's lauded for being a tough reporter, but when a woman does it she's considered an aggressive bitch. In many instances that's true. As a woman I've felt that. But Barbara often went too far— pissing off both her male and female colleagues in the press.

Jane Schulberg saw Barbara getting "more and more leverage . . . having more and more influence [and] beginning to throw her weight around more . . . during her friendship with Meaney. So it was a very strategic friendship in that sense."

Despite their close friendship at the time, Meaney saw Barbara in retrospect as "driven . . . often difficult . . . and determined [to be] an anchorperson. She was willing to do whatever was necessary. She was the kind of person who certainly could raise her voice sharply. Barbara could take things very badly. If she decided something was wrong, her view was the only important one. She would be heard very loudly and clearly."

After the Rusk exclusive, Barbara began to get bigger and better stories to cover.

One of those assignments—a prestigious one—was to cover the investiture of Britain's Prince Charles as the Prince of Wales on July 1, 1969. "Barbara was scared to death," said a colleague, "because of how complicated the story was."

Ray Scherer, who had just been made London correspondent, was assigned to do the live coverage with Barbara from Caernarvon, Wales. The two spent several days in a little cottage boning up on the pageant—the mumbo-jumbo about heraldry and that sort of thing—so their commentary would make some semblance of sense. By the day of the big event they figured they'd wing it and let the satellite-transmitted pictures tell the story.

In the booth, moments before air time, Barbara and Scherer put on their headsets. What they heard put smiles on their faces for the first time since they got to Wales. Somehow, the lines had gotten crossed and they were listening to the expert commentary of the British Broadcasting Corporation's reporters.

Barbara and Scherer parroted the BBC play-by-play expertly. Their narration was so extensive that *Today* producer Al Smith, who was unaware that they were repeating the BBC commentary, put his finger to his lips several times, signaling them to talk less. When it was over, Stuart Schulberg was extremely impressed, sending a letter of congratulations to both of them for their expert coverage. Everyone in the news division felt they had done a wonderful, knowledgeable job—unaware of the reason why.

As the Sixties drew to a close, Barbara was intent on getting as much serious journalistic exposure as possible—beyond what the *Today* show could offer her. She had tasted credibility with her Dean Rusk scoop and liked the flavor, but she still felt insecure and not respected as a journalist.

She heard that Shad Northshield was producing a blockbuster three-hour special—a decade-ender—called *From Here to the Seventies*. The program would feature NBC news correspondents—with Paul Newman as host—celebrating and mourning the triumphs and tragedies of the past ten years, and looking toward the next ten.

At the time, Barbara and Northshield had the same business manager, Marty Bregman, who called the producer saying, "You're going to have seventeen correspondents on that show. Is there any possibility of Barbara being on it?"

Northshield was not surprised by the request. "There was a feeling," he said,

not shared by me, that there was something sacred about journalism, and that Barbara wasn't part of that—and it expressed itself openly and very often. Barbara's effort to get on my show in 1969 would have given her a certain kind of respectability.

She wanted to be in that group of correspondents because the *Today* show was never regarded as having the same kind of level of prestige as the *Huntley-Brinkley Report* or the documentaries. It wasn't boring enough to be thought of as that, so everybody sneered at it.

Northshield asked Bregman, " 'Why the hell didn't Barbara call me herself?' And Bregman responded, 'Well, she's just too shy. She asked me to do it. I'm not pressuring you.' I said, 'You better not be. Sure, she can be on it.' I always thought Barbara was damned good and that would be great."

Barbara became the eighteenth "correspondent," doing a commentary about "The new sexuality."

"She was photographed standing at the edge of a swimming pool at a beautiful place in the Hamptons, probably owned by some close friend of hers. And she looked into the camera wearing a very demure dress—high collar, long sleeves—and her opening line was 'Take the Pill on the third day of the menstrual cycle,' or whatever the directions were, and I thought I was going to faint," recalled Northshield.

"It was her idea and it was terrific and those words—menstrual cycle, etc., etc.—had never before been used on television. Her piece, which was very moral by the way, ran six or eight minutes. I had to squeeze it in."

Barbara showed her gratitude to Northshield by sending him a beautiful gift from Tiffany's: a Lucite rendition of the moon, where Neil Armstrong had just walked—"a giant leap for mankind" and another big step forward for Barbara Walters' career.

A BESTSELLER

Barbara was fast becoming the best-known and most recognizable woman on television. She was to news what Howard Cosell was to sports and Sammy Davis to entertainment; audiences either hated her or loved her, there was no middle ground. Thus, by 1970, she'd become famous and controversial enough for a major publisher to see a bestseller if her face and byline were on the cover.

How to talk with practically anybody about practically anything was the brainchild of Doubleday editor Ken McCormick, who had read a magazine article by Barbara in which she dealt with the art of conversation. Impressed, McCormick wrote Barbara a note saying her piece "would make a wonderful book because everybody is afraid that they can't talk."

At a subsequent lunch, Barbara told McCormick she'd thought about the idea and felt a book could be done, covering such subjects as talking to a celebrity, socializing at parties, dealing with difficult people, and one that surely must have seemed politically incorrect to feminists—a chapter that eventually was entitled "How to Win a New Boss or Husband: A Good Girl's Guide for When to Be Sexy and When Not."

Barbara had even roughed out a couple of chapters for McCormick, who found his future author "engaging and outgoing, and her ideas marvelous."

Barbara was all set to sign a contract, she told the overjoyed editor, except for one small problem—she didn't have time to actually *write* the book *herself*. No problem. Doubleday had a wonderful woman in Toronto—a brilliant ghostwriter named June Callwood, whom McCormick thought Barbara should meet as soon as possible.

"Ken called me and said this woman who did the morning show on NBC was going to do a book and she had submitted a partial manuscript that needed work and would I come down to see if we got along," said Callwood years later.

> She had been trying to put together her ideas about how you can be a social being. The prose wasn't working for her, but the ideas were there. During our interview it came out that Arlene Francis and Kitty Carlisle were her ideal of real style; they were somewhat role models for her. She thought they were marvelous because no matter how they felt, they behaved like ladies; they had certain social graces.

From talking extensively with Barbara, Callwood came away feeling that she had been living her life by following a similar philosophy—"that no matter how bad you felt, you came out with your party face."

The two agreed to work together; they found that the one thing they had in common was that both disliked small talk; ironic since the book was about the art of conversation. It was decided that Callwood would fly to New York once a week and interview Barbara for two hours—from two to four—in her apartment. Callwood felt she could write the ten chapters based on five such afternoons.

Barbara signed a contract with Doubleday "for a comfortable advance, nothing terrific—twenty-five thousand dollars, maybe thirty thousand," said McCormick.

As a veteran journalist and observer of people, Callwood found it fascinating to spend time with a powerhouse like Barbara. "What I saw was something that predated the women's movement—enormous determination, and a shaky woman in a lot of ways, emotionally very vulnerable."

During their conversations Barbara talked about her career and the problems she was facing in the male-dominated world of television. She also talked about her sister and Lou and her own speech impediment. "She had a lot on her back, a lot of anxiety, but she had the will to surmount the obstacles."

Callwood saw that Barbara was clearly focused on success. "She was going to ram her career through and do it—and do it to the hilt. She had thought through very carefully what it took to succeed. She had such a clear picture of how to do it—she had an iron, resolute will to succeed."

But none of that surfaced in the book.

"We were doing a very slick job, a commercial job, and maybe one of the reasons she was doing it was part of her self-promotion. It was certainly not intended to be revealing of her."

Callwood turned in the manuscript on schedule.

"June wrote a really wonderful book," Ken McCormick said. "But Barbara called me up and said, 'Listen, this is so much better than I could do; anybody would know I could not have written this book. Is there any way we can get this down to *my* level?'" Editors usually hear just the opposite—can the narrative be elevated? But McCormick said he was not shocked by Barbara's request. "She was a realist. She had a voice and she was talking to America, and June was another voice, a much more articulate one."

Callwood—"flattered that her job was *too* good"—was summoned back to New York with an eight-day deadline to do a complete rewrite. She took a room at the Plaza and every day Barbara would meet her there to make the changes. Those sessions Callwood found intriguing.

> The kinds of things she was saying to me were, "This is too intelligent for me to say; this is too big a word for me to use; people will know I don't use this kind of language." She took out all thoughts that had any complexity—saying that was *me*, not *her*. She took out interpretations and subtleties and *big* words—that's what she called them—"*big* words."
>
> I had once written a book on human emotions and had a little background in the complexity behind behavior. I found Barbara fascinating and I really was anxious to allow part of her to show through. But she didn't want that at all. So the book became what it was—a glib little handbook. There's so much more to her than that, but that's the way she wanted it.

Not only did Barbara forbid the inclusion of anything intimate about herself, she also propounded a view of reality that Callwood found quite curious.

> We had a hard time understanding one another on why someone like Arlene Francis was so enchanting. Barbara felt she was because Arlene Francis "knew how to be a good guest—she's a wonderful guest," Barbara would say. "And Kitty Carlisle is a wonderful guest." She must have said that ten times. "Kitty," Barbara said, "came prepared to be a wonderful guest." And I asked, "Is it because they feel so good about themselves?" I felt that people bubble over because they feel terrific about themselves, and communicate that they feel good. But she didn't see that at all. She said it was because "it was a social occasion and it was expected of them."

You don't have to play Freud to characterize her view. She had been doing so much performing in order to keep her privacy that she really believed when she saw someone else doing well in a social situation that they were doing what she did. She saw it as a performance.

Not a performance was Barbara's love for her daughter, Jacqueline, and compassion for her sister. "The child was just the center of her life," said Callwood, who found it odd, though, that she'd never met the toddler during her many visits to the Guber apartment. "There was a tremendous connection to that child—a real need to have something to mother. The side of Barbara that I found most appealing was that tenderness—and her real pain regarding her sister. That was what she seemed least able to deal with. One would think that she would be happy to display this human side, but she was more comfortable being brusque."

While Callwood got along well with Barbara in person, she found her telephone manner abhorrent.

"She was terribly, incredibly rude to me," Callwood said.

When I phoned her about something I'd be treated so badly I was just devastated. She was curt and dismissive. But she was the same way to her husband, too. It was getting close to five o'clock one afternoon and I was getting ready to leave. He called and they were making arrangements to meet at a movie theater. She said something like, "Awright, I said six o'clock. I meant six o'clock!"—something like that—and slammed down the phone.

When Callwood wrote the original manuscript she often invented anecdotes and stories that illustrated Barbara's points. Callwood had also "put in some of me where it was compatible with her." During the rewriting, Barbara didn't seem to care about Callwood's creations; she only wanted the names changed to those of celebrities she knew.

The rewrite of *How to talk with practically anybody about practically anything* went through smoothly—"It was the easiest book I ever wrote in my life," said Callwood. "A piece of cake."

Barbara dedicated the book, published in October 1970, "to the men I have always found it easiest to talk with—my husband, Lee Guber; my father, Lou Walters; and the enlightened males at NBC who took a chance on an unknown girl and ultimately made this book possible."

In the case of *How to talk* . . . Callwood was the most invisible ghostwriter that money could buy. Her name did not appear anywhere in the book—there was no "as told to" or "with June Callwood" credit, or even the thank-you that is so often the case when a ghostwriter works with a celebrity. And there is no evidence suggesting that Barbara ever mentioned Callwood's help during the publicity tour for the book—which became a bestseller, going through a number of printings, becoming a Literary Guild selection and a successful paperback.

During her book promotion, Barbara boasted to a *Long Island Press* reporter, "All in all it took me two years to put together. The most difficult part was putting together the table of contents. . . . Then I talked to friends and discovered what their difficulties were." And to a reporter in Boston, where Barbara was beating the drum for the book, she asserted that one of her cardinal rules was "Never fake."

In 1977, *Variety* published an item that was picked up by *People* magazine stating that Callwood, rather than Barbara, had actually written the book. Years later, Callwood revealed that after those items ran Barbara asked her to issue a denial.

"She got into a thing with *People* magazine that said I

had written the book, and she asked me to write a letter saying I hadn't," Callwood said. "It was hair-splitting, so I wrote to *People* and said that it was her book, and Barbara sent me a thank-you note."

NOT FOR
WOMEN ONLY

She is afraid of silence; she plunges and gropes; she flails about in conversations as though they were trap doors and the bottom might fall out of whatever's being discussed. She makes me nervous," commented *Life* magazine's caustic TV critic, John Leonard, who used the pseudonym Cyclops.

Describing Barbara as "energy looking for a lightning rod down which to dissipate itself," he said, "she makes the morning squeak, like a toothbrush."

Indeed, by 1970 the critics were starting to give Barbara a drubbing, looking behind the hype the publicists had been generating, carefully exploring this phenomenon of early-morning television that Barbara Walters had become.

For the most part, she ignored the gibes. As long as they spelled her name right, she was happy. Barbara made it a practice never to read unfavorable reviews or uncomplimentary fan mail, both of which were filtered by her secretary before reaching her eyes. But she was aware of what was being said about her. "There's a trend toward hostile pieces now," she told *TV Guide*, "eager young reporters with a let's-look-at-her-seams attitude, especially if it's someone who's already had a relatively good press. I'm *not* a terrible person. I'm *not* mean. Why should anyone want to attack me?" Despite the critics' bad-mouthing, the *Today* show had become hers, Hugh Downs as the official host notwithstanding. Now she wanted other worlds to conquer.

As she had made it known to Don Meaney and other colleagues and friends, her goal was a network anchor job, and if that weren't possible—at least for the moment—she wanted some kind of program of her own. That's why in 1970 Barbara's prescient agent, Lee Stevens, negotiated a nonexclusive contract that gave her the flexibility to do specials, news, and other programming aside from the *Today* show.

So it came as no surprise to anyone that Barbara jumped at the opportunity to become moderator of what had been a relatively obscure local morning talk and public affairs show called *For Women Only*, on WNBC-TV, the NBC owned and operated station, in New York, the largest and most prestigious television market in America.

Under Barbara's stewardship, the program became highly rated and widely talked about, which led to its national syndication. In the scheme of television programing, it was a precursor of the very successful women-oriented theme shows of the 1980s, such as those hosted by Phil Donahue and Oprah Winfrey. For Barbara, the show would make her even more of a household name, increasing her power base and extending her influence, particularly at the network, where she was lobbying constantly for bigger and better opportunities.

The chance to get her own show arose when the host of *For Women Only*, Aline Saarinen, who also was the *Today* show's art and culture critic, was named chief of NBC's Paris bureau, the first woman from any of the networks to head a foreign news bureau. As with Barbara, other talented women—though not many—were beginning to make significant strides in network television news.

Brilliant, cultured, prim, and proper, Aline was the widow of the noted architect Eero Saarinen when she was hired at *Today* along with Judith Crist during the Morgan era to do commentaries. One of her first, which sparked enormous viewer response, was on what she viewed as the six ugliest things in America. She chose the split-level ranch home, the Pan Am Building, the Marines' Iwo Jima Memorial, Mount Rushmore, anything by Dali, and any lamp from Bloomingdale's.

According to friends, Aline was everything Barbara aspired to, so at first their relationship was strained, but they eventually became friendly "in a guarded kind of way," said John Lord, who dated Aline. "Barbara was a bit jealous because Aline was a woman who always had good things and knew what they were and knew how to do it," said Lord, who spent considerable time with both women. The first time Saarinen walked into the *Today* offices, wearing a blue silk dress with white polka dots and white gloves, Barbara hid her envy with a look of amusement. A former writer and art critic for the *New York Times*, Saarinen was noted for her extraordinary style and circle of prominent friends; she bespoke class.

"The one thing I wasn't too fond of in Barbara was her desire to be accepted socially on the right side of town," Lord said. "One of her less attractive features was her social climbing. She'd seen a lot of people who had extraordinary style—and Aline impressed her mightily because she had that style. Barbara didn't feel inferior—I think she was somewhat in awe of her, and saw Aline as someone to emulate."

Lord witnessed Barbara's extraordinary penchant "for power and position" when the *Today* show traveled to a southern city where she introduced him to the influential family of a friend from Sarah Lawrence. It didn't take Lord long to see that under the family's gloss, which so impressed Barbara, was a manner that he found offensive.

"One evening we were sitting around after dinner and the black butler was requested to sing—and sang—'Ol' Man River,' " recalled Lord, still amazed at the incident years later. "I was pretty much shocked, but Barbara said, 'Well, it just happens.'

"She may not have liked what she saw, but that would not be the most important thing. The most important thing would be to be a part of that set. What Barbara liked was the *notion* of power and position and *apparent* respectability."

Agreeing with John Lord's assessment, a college friend said, "I had a sense of Barbara's enviousness of a certain class of people. Wasp society and that sort of implied power impressed her."

More power was what Barbara was hoping to derive with her new program, the name of which was changed to *Not for Women Only*. Barbara's energy and drive seemed infinite. Not only was she managing her *Today* show duties—budgeting time to pursue big-name interviews—but she was beginning to deal with the other demands of celebrity, such as speaking engagements, magazine and newspaper interviews, even movie offers. And wanting and needing her attention at home were Jacqueline and Lee. Now she had her own daily television program on top of everything else.

She wanted it all; she was insatiable, unstoppable.

Every Tuesday, right after *Today*, Barbara would race to the *NFWO* studio where she'd do all five half-hour shows for the week before a live audience in one marathon taping session, which usually started at ten and ended around two-thirty in the afternoon. The program aired at nine o'clock weekday mornings, right after *Today*, which was a perfect lead-in for her.

From the start, Barbara made an impact.

"What has changed—and for the better," noted *Variety*,

"has been the approach the *Today* show regular has brought to the series. Miss Saarinen had gradually evolved the show into a deadly serious (and icily cold) forum of public affairs discussions which were noticeably over-paneled with academic guests. . . . Miss Walters, who has herself been accused of being coldish in the past, is providing considerably more warmth to the proceedings."

The first show on September 13, 1971, was promoted as "the clash of the sexes," which Barbara explained as "an attempt to appraise the situation right now, to determine where we're going now that women have established themselves on an equal basis with the male."

When Barbara took over the show, and topics such as the "clash" program were announced, women's rights leaders felt that the program could become a forum for their views; after all Barbara was viewed as a trailblazer. Later, movement leaders would have mixed feelings about Barbara's role as a mover and shaker when it came to feminism; her pioneering, it occurred to some of them, seemed to be more for Barbara Walters. But Barbara rationalized that women were in her corner, otherwise she felt she would not have become so successful. "A woman could not do a television show today," she asserted, "unless other women liked her. They have approved of me, and for this I'm grateful."

On the other hand, she told another interviewer, "I've always thought a little bit of a woman goes a long way. At a press conference whose voice is the first one you hear? Nancy Dickerson's. It's easier to listen to a man's voice. A man is more authoritative. Also, he can be amusing without being coy, and pertinent without being fresh."

Once, asked whether she felt the *Today* show exploited her as a sex object, Barbara exclaimed, "I should hope so."

"Barbara did not use *Not for Women Only* as a base to bolster the women's movement," said Julie Van Vliet Rubenstein, who produced the program for almost eighteen months. "The show dealt with women's interests because of the *time of day* it was on—but that's about all. Barbara was not that interested in the women's movement."

However, she was looking to make headlines and she did, getting a number of exclusives out of her interviews on the program. As she took on the role of Mother Confessor of Television, more and more famous people were willing to open their closets and divulge their skeletons in response to her often cloying style, garnering headlines for Barbara in the process. Mrs. Dwight David Eisenhower, for instance, spoke out for the first time about rumors of a drinking problem. "I'm going to ask you something, because it's been a rumor for years, and I want to finally put it to rest," said Barbara to the former First Lady. "You know what the rumor is."

"Oh yes, that I'm a dipsomaniac," responded Mamie, noting that people had the impression she was an alcoholic because she had an unsteady gait and bumped into things. Setting the record straight, she explained that her problem was equilibrium, not booze. "I have what they call a carotid sinus and they can't operate on it—your vein presses on your inner ear. Oh, I'm black and blue from walking around my own house." Mrs. Eisenhower told Barbara she was never bothered by the rumors—"I knew it wasn't so. And my friends knew I was not [an alcoholic].''

Behind the scenes, Barbara could be a veritable virago. Querulous, impatient, anxious, Barbara would telephone Rubenstein at home, berating the producer for her selection of guests and topics—"Who are these awful people you've got?" Barbara demanded to know. "What are we going to do?!''—suggesting in her tone that the taping would be an utter disaster, and she'd be made to look a fool because of Rubenstein's ostensible blundering, all of which was absurd. "And I'd get off the phone, feeling sick, and tell my husband, 'This is crazy! I'm not going to live this way!' " said Rubenstein, who subsequently became a segment producer for Dick Cavett at PBS, and later rose to the post of executive editor of the Literary Guild. "And then I'd get in the studio the next day and she'd be wonderful and she'd come up to me afterwards and say, 'That was terrific. I'm sorry.'"

Even though they worked closely, Rubenstein found Barbara difficult to get to know—private, detached: traits seen in her by so many others. Yet defenders frequently said her standoffishness was really shyness or nearsightedness. "People think Barbara ignores them, is bitchy—but she just can't *see* them," said one partisan.

"You could have a very good time with Barbara putting your feet up and talking clothes and hair and makeup and stuff like that," said Rubenstein, "[but] she wasn't there to be a friend. I viewed her very much as a boss."

By this point in her career, Henry Kissinger had become one of Barbara's news sources and friends. One morning, just prior to a *NFWO* taping, Barbara was holed up in her dressing room with Kissinger, apparently discussing an interview for *Today*, which was still Barbara's main priority. Rubenstein saw that the time slotted for taping was beginning to run out; the crew was on overtime, and the audience was getting antsy. All Rubenstein could do was bang on the door in frustration, but Barbara refused to budge.

"Well, finally she came out—but she came out only when she was ready. She was one hell of a prima donna," Rubenstein said. "Barbara did not extend herself to the crew or do anything to make life easier for the people around her. She was a professional. She wanted to get the job done—but no one would ever refer to her as a gentle soul."

But her drive and ambition helped make the program a success. Within six months, the ratings tripled. The program, with Barbara at the helm, "has become one of the most improved and provocative shows in the entire early morning schedule," the *New York Times* concluded.

"Barbara did her homework because she was determined to be a star and she knew the only way that she could be a star was by being well prepared," said Rubenstein. "Barbara did a very good job of carving out a very nice lot for herself with a combination of doing her homework, having a skill to get good guests, and then asking the kind of questions that would keep the guests happy. Barbara did not go after the jugular. She used that [method of interviewing] very effectively."

Barbara left most of the work of conceiving program topics and booking guests to Rubenstein: "Is the Family Dying?" "Activism in the Clergy," "Sensitivity Training," "Superstition and the Occult," "TV and Children," were typical shows. One idea that Barbara originated, and for which she worked hard to get on the air—making call after call, writing letter after letter, calling in her chips, using her many contacts—was on the wives of Nixon Administration cabinet members, which aired for five days in the first week of February 1972.

Barbara rounded up five colorful and articulate spouses: the controversial Martha Mitchell, wife of Attorney General John N. Mitchell; Lenore Romney, a former actress, whose husband was Secretary of Housing and Urban Development; Mrs. William P. Rogers, wife of the Secretary of State; Mrs. Elliot L. Richardson, wife of the Secretary of Health, Education, and Welfare, and Barbara Bush, wife of the then U.S. Ambassador to the United Nations.

An ABC producer once described Barbara as "the best booker in the business," and he was right; her intuition that the cabinet members' wives show was worth all her time and effort and would be a huge success was correct. It yielded huge ratings and enormous press comment: the New York Times devoted six columns across the women's page to a feature headlined "A Talkative Day in the Life of Martha Mitchell and Friends." It also led to a decision by WNBC executives to put the show into syndication, giving Barbara another national audience, some seventy cities within the first year. Rubenstein said,

Barbara wanted to do cabinet members' wives because she knew it would give her high visibility. Because it was a local show, she really wasn't doing them a favor by having them on, but it got tremendous press and this was a case where those guests were helping her, and Barbara certainly used her influence and power to get them. That show was an example of how Barbara used *Not for Women Only* as a way to demonstrate what she could do with a program of her own, and the caliber of people that she could get together. She used it to show NBC the kind of thing she could do.

Madeline Amgott, Rubenstein's successor when the show went into syndication, agreed, describing *Not for Women Only* as Barbara's "own personal showcase; it was very important to her career."

A QUIET
SEPARATION

Barbara's enormous success—her news scoops, exclusive interviews, the book, her syndicated show, her growing influence on *Today*—could not be duplicated at home in her marriage. She would claim when she and Lee separated that her busy career had no adverse effect on their relationship: "It wasn't just because I have to get up early in the morning. . . . I can't blame the show or my career. . . . I think everything that happens in your life has an effect on your marriage," she told *TV Guide*. But her words rang hollow. Her career came first, and everyone, especially Lee, knew it.

Lee's brother-in-law, Ben Cossrow, noted years later, "Barbara traveled a lot. She once went to China with Nixon and Lee's complaint was, 'I don't want a wife one day a month.' He wanted a wife twenty-nine days out of the month. She traveled tremendously, extensively—and it got to him. She was a career woman, period. She wanted to follow her dictates in connection with her career. She wanted to follow her feelings."

Lonely by day, feeling forsaken and abandoned at night, forced to travel by himself, Guber began looking elsewhere for love, or at least affection. Friends felt Lee was either "an angel or a saint to put up with Barbara."

On the flip side, Barbara had concluded that she had far outdistanced and outperformed Lee; he was still in the back stretch while she was crossing the finishing line. He had not lived up to her expectations in terms of being the powerful and successful mate she had sought. Barbara had started confiding in certain close friends that her marriage to Lee was on the rocks. One of those confidantes was Aline Saarinen, who told another friend, "Barbara says she's outgrown Lee. I wouldn't be surprised if they get divorced. She's getting more powerful and more sure of herself. Lee was a marvelous crutch for her at first. In many ways, he was her father all over again."

To many of their friends, Jacqueline was the bond that kept Barbara and Lee together. But that was a somewhat misleading assumption. Lee felt that Barbara, who wanted the child, wasn't devoting enough time to her. Frank Ford recalled visiting the Gubers in New York and hearing Lee voice such complaints, despite Barbara's public pronouncements that she spent every available minute with the youngster when she wasn't working. "She has a nurse during the week," Barbara told the *Christian Science Monitor*, "but Saturday and Sunday she's mine completely."

Ford heard and saw a different scenario:

Lee would put the baby in a carriage on a Saturday or Sunday, and walk her over to Central Park and say, "Here I am at my age and I'm pushing a baby carriage!" My impression was that Lee was a devoted father, but that he felt walking the baby was something that either the mother did or the mother and father did together. But she was upstairs catching up on her beauty rest. That's what Guber told me—"She needs the weekend to catch up on her sleep and rest." What I saw of Barbara was that she was wrapped up in Barbara Walters.

In June 1972, after celebrating Jacqueline's fourth birthday, Lee quietly moved out of the Gubers' apartment and into a hotel a few blocks away. "Lee and I share an enormous love for our child," Barbara said after the breakup. "We have simply told her that there are times when mommies and daddies are happier not living together, but that we love her very much and that we still like each other."

Barbara and Lee, both very private, kept their separation so quiet that many of their closest friends were unaware of it until the story broke in the gossip columns a month later. Lee didn't even tell his pal Frank Ford right away. A neighbor and friend, the writer Jacqueline Susann (*Valley of the Dolls*) and her husband, Irving Mansfield, learned about the split by happenstance. They were to have dinner with the Gubers and Mansfield ran into Lee on the street, mentioning their imminent get-together. "I think you'd better make other plans, Irv," Lee told Mansfield. "Barbara and I have separated."

Columnists Earl Wilson in the New York *Post* and Suzy—Aileen Mehle—in the *Daily News* simultaneously broke the story on July 19, 1972. "We had problems we couldn't solve," Barbara told Wilson—problems she described as "too painful" to discuss. Lee characterized them as "personality and professional problems. . . . A lot is happening for her and a lot is happening for me. We both have to look after ourselves."

The real reason for the separation may have been that Barbara discovered Lee had a mistress. The "other woman" was a divorcée seven years younger than Barbara; she sometimes worked as a costume designer, but usually was taken care of by well-to-do men. Dark-haired, brown-eyed, Jewish, with a fantastic figure, a sweet but sultry manner, and the reputation for "being dynamite in bed," she had been involved with Guber to the extent that he paid for the decoration and furnishing of her bedroom, which was done all in pink, according to a friend in whom she confided about the relationship.

"She did in fact have a long, in-depth, very discreet, very private affair with Lee while he was married to Barbara," said the friend, a writer who also became involved with the woman. "They had used her apartment for their assignations, and Guber had furnished her bedroom; it was very feminine, very richly done." Like Guber, the woman was a native of Philadelphia, where her father owned a delicatessen. According to the friend, Guber broke up with her when she became ill with Hodgkin's disease in the year before Lee and Barbara separated. The woman died in 1976, the year the Gubers' divorce became final.

Edna Shanis Tuttleman, Guber's first wife, said she had heard that Barbara "had thrown Lee out—and I said to myself, 'Good for her.' I felt he finally got what he deserved."

In the end, Guber said he respected Barbara tremendously, "but I just don't think she is the greatest woman since Clara Barton."

"At the divorce settlement, Barbara really got all she could out of him," Tuttleman said. "She had gotten as much money as he possibly could have given up. I was hearing that from my own children who became close to Barbara." However, in press reports Barbara stated that she never asked for alimony.

A longtime woman friend of Guber's said he seemed so much happier after he and Barbara separated. "Lee was very sociable. He always liked to have parties. I can't remember going to a party when he was married to her, but the minute they split he had these constant Sunday night bachelor dinner parties at his new apartment. Lee was very domestic, a wonderful cook. He put out a big buffet and invited a lot of the old gang from Philly."

Guber also started squiring beautiful socialite Lynn Revson, whom he introduced to his Philadelphia friends, sparking talk for a time that they'd get married. But in May 1982, he took as his third wife the advertising executive and writer Lois Wyse.

On March 27, 1988, Guber died of brain cancer at the age of sixty-seven. In the weeks preceding his death, Barbara visited him on a regular basis. "It was very nice of her," said Frank Ford, who delivered the eulogy at Guber's funeral. "It surprised me in a very nice way."

"THIS IS
BARBARA WALTERS—
WE'RE JUST
BREAKING HER IN"

Barbara had become a "friend" of the Nixon White House, which thought of her as an interviewer who could be trusted—a "standup girl," as Roy Cohn, a Nixon crony, called her. This was the same paranoid administration that had a secret "enemies list" that included among its suspected adversaries a number of America's most respected journalists; it was one of the few "A" lists that Barbara didn't make during her career. She was a favorite of Nixon's—the "I am not a crook" President; earner of the sobriquet "Tricky Dick."

Barbara's effort to gain an insider's foothold began when Nixon was still President-elect and she was aggressively pursuing every opportunity to get his attention. The Nixons were in New York attending a church service conducted by Dr. Norman Vincent Peale. Knowing the press would turn out in force for the event, Dan Rather of CBS arrived early to get a spot close to where Nixon would be passing. The crowd of reporters and photographers grew quickly and Rather was having a difficult time holding his ground.

Suddenly he became aware that "someone was torpedoing toward the front at about knee height," but he promised himself that whoever the "miserable thudpucker" was he'd "get crowned" if he tried to take his spot.

"Just as I figured," recalled Rather, "this intruder wriggled through the crowd, straightened up out of a kind of Vietnamese crouch, and stepped on my new shoes."

Rather was shocked to see Barbara Walters. And he was furious because he could tell that she was going to try to move in on his position. He told her in no uncertain terms, " 'If you think you are going to stand there, and do anything . . . it ain't going to happen.' She proceeded to con me a little, which she does beautifully. For all her toughness and ability to be aggressive when she has to— sometimes when there is no call to do so—Barbara knows how to use her femininity."

Barbara sweet-talked and cajoled—and refused to budge, in spite of how angry Rather had become. She listened to none of his arguments about moving, and when he vehemently complained that she'd ruined his new shoes, her immediate response was "NBC will pay for them." Barbara stayed. Rather was never reimbursed for his shoes.

What he got was a lesson in the kind of tough, aggressive competitor he and other hard-news reporters like him were up against when Barbara was on the scene.

And when it came to Nixon, no other reporter could beat her in getting scoops.

Barbara once declared she would "kill myself" to get an interview with Nixon. "It built my reputation, both good and bad. I was called very aggressive—tough. It was the only way."

Barbara had pals on the inside at 1600 Pennsylvania Avenue who vouched for her.

For example, Bill Safire had become a leading Nixon

speechwriter. Safire acknowledged that if anybody at the White House asked whether Barbara would be a good choice to interview Nixon or other administration officials, "I would say great things about her, but I was not the one who would decide who would interview President Nixon. That was [H. R.] Haldeman and [Ron] Ziegler and Herb Klein and people like that." However, Safire confirmed as "consistent" reports that he favored Barbara as an interviewer of the President because she could be trusted. "I would say good things whenever asked."

Barbara also did a competent job on her own of ingratiating herself with Nixon. In *How to talk with practically anybody* . . . Barbara said of Nixon, "I find that he has sex appeal—he's slim and suntanned . . . well, he's just sexy, that's all."

It was a line that melted Nixon's heart, and caused many of Barbara's friends and colleagues to gag. Nixon had been called a lot of things in his day, but never sexy. Barbara knew how to push the right buttons; even Richard Nixon could be turned on.

"When she wrote that about him," said a close woman friend of Barbara's,

> any number of people asked me, "What kind of an incredible hypocrite is she? Nixon sexy? Come on!" But she meant it because in my experience Barbara always found extremely powerful, dark men—and I don't mean men with dark brown hair, but dark in temperament, dark in negotiation and maneuvering, dark in manipulation—she found those types attractive and sexy: the Roy Cohn type and probably the Lou Walters type. So she meant it. And she was running around doing promotion for that book on television and, of course, everyone asked her how she could say Nixon was sexy, and I felt sorry for her because I knew she had told the truth. Everybody thought she was using a journalistic trick, but she meant it.

Whether she did or she didn't, the payoff for Barbara was enormous.

Barbara first met Nixon while she was at the White House interviewing his daughter, Tricia, for the *Today* show. The President walked in unexpectedly and Barbara beguilingly asked him whether she could have her picture taken with him. Dazzled, Nixon invited her into his office for a private chat. Out of it came an exclusive interview for Barbara with Prince Philip; she'd been trying to get Philip to accept her invitation to appear on *Today*. Nixon promised to help—and the prince instantly agreed. Barbara later boasted that it was an interview "most other people couldn't get." Walters was the first reporter ever to ask the prince whether Queen Elizabeth might abdicate in favor of her son Charles; he answered affirmatively, and the British press and public went bonkers.

When Barbara covered his daughter's wedding, Nixon sent a handwritten note to her apartment:

> Dear Barbara,
>   Last night we saw a replay of NBC's coverage of Tricia's wedding.
>   I want to tell you again how much I enjoyed and appreciated your very thoughtful and gracious commentary during the program. I hope your listening audience continues to grow!
>
>   RN

Nixon suggested to his foreign policy adviser, Henry Kissinger, that he give his first television interview to Barbara, which he did. Later, at a state dinner at the White House, after she'd interviewed Prince Philip, Barbara thanked the President, telling him, "I'd be happy to give [you] ten percent as my agent."

"Whom would you like me to get next?" he asked. "How about you, Mr. President," she responded.

In March 1971, Barbara was preparing to go to Palm Springs for a short vacation with Lee when Nixon's press secretary, Ron Ziegler, telephoned. Could she come to Washington? *Could she!* Lee was left once again to go on vacation without his wife. Nixon had decided he'd be the first President to single out one television interviewer for an exclusive filmed conversation, but he wasn't doing it out of the goodness of his heart: Nixon's standing in public opinion polls had declined and his advisers were concerned that the electorate wasn't getting the desired image of him.

At the White House, several interview options had been under consideration. Finally, "It is our feeling," wrote White House appointments secretary Dwight Chapin in a March 5, 1971, memorandum to Nixon's austere chief of staff H. R. Haldeman, "that the best situation is to have a One on One done by Barbara Walters. Needless to say, the Sunday night slot on NBC would give us by far our greatest impact."

Another option was for Barbara to do the interview for the *Today* show, which is what happened.

With its enormous audience—Middle America personified—the *Today* show was the perfect vehicle to carry Nixon's message. And with Barbara asking the questions—the woman who thought him sexy—Nixon felt safe. His only stipulation was that the interview be presented in its entirety. NBC News and *Today* show executives readily agreed. What a coup for Barbara and the network, they thought; Richard Nixon all theirs from seven to nine, minus time out for commercials and station breaks. Nixon's people were also smiling; the President couldn't buy air time like that, even with the proceeds from a secret slush fund.

Preparations for Barbara's arrival were underway at the White House in the days preceding the interview. Aide Mark Goode sent a memo stamped "Confidential" to Haldeman suggesting that "the President undergo a wardrobe change before his interview with Barbara. . . . His shirt and tie should be chosen . . . as for a live appearance. I also recommend that he wear makeup. I am sure Miss Walters will be made up, and the contrast would be evident if the President were not. . . ."

In an ACTION MEMO, Haldeman posed some questions regarding the upcoming interview: "What has the best effect on the audience, the hard fast antagonistic approach, or the low-key calm approach? Is it better to give long answers or short clipped ones? Is it better to limit to one subject or to prove that the President can handle anything?"

In a "Memorandum Re the Barbara Walters Interview," staffer Richard Moore submitted "Suggested Talking Points." Concerning possible questions regarding the First Lady, Pat Nixon—whose birthday would be the day after the interview ran on *Today*—Moore wrote, "Mrs. Nixon's concern for other people and their own right of privacy was vividly illustrated by the recent visit of Jackie Kennedy and the Kennedy children. I think the country would be fascinated by this story and perhaps there would be a tactful way of encouraging Barbara to bring up the subject."

Another aide, Constance Stuart, put together a list of possible questions that Barbara might ask along with suggested answers for the President. One was "How old is Mrs. Nixon going to be?" The answer was "She will be fifty-nine but most people don't believe it." Another question was "Have you bought Mrs. Nixon's present yet?" Nixon's suggested response was "I've got a few surprises planned."

Chapin sent a confidential memo to Goode noting they didn't have "demographic information" on the *Today* show. "It would be helpful if the speech writers and those working on thoughts to shoot in to the President were aware of the audience characteristics of that particular show. . . . Perhaps if we had audience demographics we would have wanted the President to couch his remarks in a certain way."

The day of the interview Goode sent the President a memo saying, "No 'hot news' will be covered."

The session was filmed at 8:00 P.M. on Thursday, March 11, in the White House Blue Room, which Nixon's aides felt was a flattering color for him, and aired the following Monday, March 15.

Nothing of any great substance came out of the interview. Nixon attributed youth unrest to the loss of old-fashioned values. He joked about his profile, which many compared to a ski slope, and Barbara asked one of her signature questions:

"There has been a lot of talk, Mr. President, about your image and the fact that the American public—forgive me, Mr. President—sees you as a rather stuffy man and not a human man. Are you—oh, dear—are you worried about your image, Mr. President?"

It was the money question that Nixon had been waiting to answer; the reason he sought to appear on the *Today* show in the first place. The whole idea was to show the people the "real" Richard Nixon, to increase his popularity rating. He told Barbara that he had "very, very strong" feelings that it did not become a President to be "constantly preening in front of a mirror, wondering whether or not he is getting across as this kind of an individual or that. . . . I am not going to change my image. I am just going to do a good job for this country." (It was fourteen months before the Watergate break-in; three and a half years before Nixon, faced with impeachment, resigned in disgrace.)

Barbara later told *TV Guide*, "I died all weekend long as I was editing that film. How could I have called him stuffy? Finally, I came to feel that somehow it had been all right to call him stuffy."

For Barbara, the Nixon interview ranked with her trip to India with Jackie Kennedy and her exclusive talk with Dean Rusk as another major milestone in her career.

*   *   *

Barbara was beginning to seem joined at the hip with the Nixon crowd. Her closest bond appeared to be with Henry Kissinger, who became Nixon's Secretary of State. It was gossip columnist Earl Wilson who, on October 26, 1972, first asked the burning question "What About Henry Kissinger & Barbara Walters?"

At the time, the portly former accountant and professor with the Dr. Strangelove accent was being portrayed as a ladies' man, an image on which he seemed to thrive. Actress Jill Ireland had been linked to him, as had Washington hostess Barbara Howar, among others. Now rumors were rampant that he and Barbara were romantically involved. Washington reporters, envious of Barbara's scoops, were prattling on and on that Kissinger was helping her because they had a close relationship.

Barbara first met Kissinger at a buffet at Howar's Georgetown home. Not long afterward, Barbara's friend Mollie Parnis, the fashion designer, who had powerful Washington connections and oversaw a salon of political and media heavyweights in her New York apartment, threw a small party and invited both of them. Barbara had to be in Washington the next day and flew back with Kissinger. The two formed a close and mutually beneficial friendship; Barbara got numerous exclusives, and Kissinger became a TV celebrity of sorts.

Kissinger liked to joke about his relationship with Barbara. At a diplomatic gala, he teasingly offered Israeli Ambassador Simcha Dinitz three Phantom jets for the privilege of sitting next to Barbara. "Make it six," responded Dinitz.

Rumors of a romance were fueled because Barbara was often seen on Kissinger's arm at various parties and functions in New York and Washington. A television writer friend of Barbara's recalled the two of them showing up at a soiree thrown by Clay Felker, then editor of *New York* magazine.

"Barbara, wearing a white dress and looking very pretty,

made a grand entrance with Kissinger and everybody was so impressed," said the friend. "And after about ten minutes Henry went up to her and said he had to leave. Barbara actually looked panicked. She thought she was going to spend the evening at the party with him. She expected him to take her to dinner afterwards. My heart just went out to her. Here was this great, wonderful entrance with this famous man and then he disappeared on her. She looked terribly disappointed and hurt."

Barbara once dropped in on a *Today* show cast party with Kissinger in tow. In a modest, falsetto voice, she said to everyone, "I've brought a friend. Can I bring him in?" recalled Jane Schulberg. "She knew how to use that connection—not just with the folks on *Today*, but with the network executives, who were impressed more than anyone."

When the *Today* show was on location in Washington just prior to the airing of Barbara's first exclusive conversation with Kissinger, recalled Bill Monroe,

There was an NBC party and Barbara came rushing in and swept up to Stuart [Schulberg] in my presence and talked excitedly about how good she thought the interview was. Having waxed enthusiastic about it for several minutes, she said, "Of course, I realize I wouldn't have gotten this interview had I not been a woman, but I think it's a good interview." I found it kind of ingratiating to have her say that. I don't think it was entirely because she was a woman, but I think that probably helped her, and she had the grace to admit it. Nobody had needled her about it. It came out spontaneously and she made it as sort of an admission.

When Kissinger gave Marvin Kalb of CBS an exclusive interview after the Vietnam cease-fire took effect, Barbara was furious; she had an agreement that he'd talk to her first, and he'd apparently reneged on their deal. An apologetic Nixon immediately telephoned Barbara, assuring her she'd get the first major interview with Kissinger when he returned from Hanoi; she did and it ran in two parts on *Today*.

The Walters-Kissinger relationship was strictly platonic and professional, as were most with the men to whom she was linked. Most of her relationships were working ones; Barbara's professional and social lives were almost completely integrated. For a time, there were stories that she was dating the Iranian ambassador and the head of the Organization of American States, but again they were friendly news sources, not lovers.

As Barbara once confided to a *Today* show colleague, "If you gave me a choice between the interview and the date, I would take the interview."

Today show executives had mixed feelings about Barbara's ties to the Nixon White House. Stu Schulberg and Doug Sinsel were particularly concerned that Nixon and his people were using the program for their own means as much as possible, with Barbara as the conduit.

According to Sinsel, "Stuart had to constantly remind Barbara, 'You're not just getting those interviews because you're Barbara Walters; you're getting them because you're Barbara Walters of the *Today* show—because they want something that we have—and that's air time and the right audience.'"

The Nixon people, Sinsel asserted, would arrange events to coincide with the *Today* show time slot; later, they even determined the most widely watched half-hour in the program and used that for events such as the Vietnam hostage releases, and the touchdown or takeoff of the President on Air Force One.

Schulberg ruled that no ground rules could be set by *Today* interviewees. So he was beside himself when he learned that Barbara had agreed to allow Ethel Kennedy to view a feature story for her approval before it was aired.

"It had to do with some project in Brooklyn," Sinsel recalled,

> and at one point Ethel said, "I'd like to see it before it airs," and Barbara said, "Oh, of course we'll show it to you." Stuart got wind of it and told Barbara, "There is no way in the world that Ethel Kennedy is going to see this tape before it goes on the air because if she wants it changed, I won't do it." And Barbara's comment was, "Well, I promised . . . I agreed to it." Stuart told her he didn't care. "You are never to allow anyone to approve or disapprove an interview on this program, or it won't go on."

Schulberg kept Barbara on a tight leash, lecturing her in a fatherly way on the ethics of journalism. "Stuart made it clear that we were being used and our job was to make sure as journalists that they were not allowed to get away with anything," Sinsel said. "Barbara may not admit this but Stuart would sit there talking about the dangers and she would listen."

But Barbara's ambition and drive sometimes got in the way of Schulberg's efforts to keep her under control, and he or Reuven Frank, head of the news division, had to bring her down a notch or two.

"The next morning after one of her interviews we'd be on the front page of the *New York Times* and Barbara would be all excited—'Oh, isn't this wonderful!' She enjoyed it, obviously," said Sinsel. "I remember Reuven saying, 'Of course I saw the *Times*, but I'm not so sure our job is to be worrying about whether we make or don't make the front page. Our goal shouldn't be worrying about whether an NBC News interview is or isn't going to be in the *Times*.' This is where I think the balance was kept."

But Barbara loved the publicity and was in heaven seeing her name in print. On May 6, 1974, she got one of the major accolades, a cover story in *Newsweek:* BARBARA WALTERS—STAR OF THE MORNING.

"I remember laughing because she *should* have been the happiest woman alive," Sinsel recalled. "But she said, 'Oh, Lord, *Time* is running so-and-so on the cover. . . . I wonder if they'll outsell *Newsweek?*' And Stuart shook his head and looked at her and said, 'You're insatiable.' "

Barbara was aware of the negative talk among her friends and colleagues about her apparent closeness to the Nixon White House. "Some people think I'm the Nixon girl, the White House pet," Barbara told a *New York Times* writer. "That depends on your point of view. Remember, I was the first one to get an interview with Teddy Kennedy after Chappaquiddick."

Nevertheless, the next exclusive interview was with H. R. Haldeman; the next stop, China—all courtesy of Richard Milhous Nixon.

Bob Haldeman, the straight-backed, crew-cutted former advertising executive who became one of the most powerful men in Washington during the Nixon years as a key member of Nixon's Teutonic guard, was directed by his boss to talk to Barbara on camera. The resultant sit-down—in front of the fireplace in Haldeman's office—turned into a three-parter on *Today* and again garnered front-page headlines for Barbara and a huge audience for the Nixon line. Haldeman charged that critics of Nixon's Vietnam peace plan were "consciously aiding and abetting the enemy."

Barbara received a thank-you note from Haldeman for having him on.

"I found him warm and amusing," she later said. "At one point it was hot in the office and we were perspiring. So, when we stopped to reload the cameras, I powdered myself and offered to powder him as well. He was laughing as I did it. As a joke, would you believe I playfully put the powder puff in his mouth!" (Almost three years to the day of the Walters interview, Haldeman was sentenced to prison for conspiring to obstruct justice in the Watergate scandal.)

The same week that Barbara interviewed Haldeman, she got her biggest gift yet from Nixon. She was chosen to accompany him on his historic trip to the People's Republic of China in February 1972. Barbara would be one of only three women journalists in the entourage and the only one who was not a regular White House correspondent. In all, eighty-seven journalists were chosen; the other two from NBC were John Chancellor and veteran China watcher John Rich. Don Meaney would also be along.

The mere fact that Nixon—a rabid anti-Communist— had decided to visit China was a story in itself, and Barbara was the first to break it on the *Today* show, angering many Washington reporters who felt Nixon or Henry Kissinger had leaked it to her.

Naturally, NBC and *Today* brass were overjoyed with Barbara's invitation and so was she, at least on the surface. Inside, though, she had considerable qualms about going, she confided to her friend Joan Peyser.

"We went to lunch and she told me about the invitation to China," Peyser said. "She was more worried than joyous. The effect was more anxiety than pleasure. She told me she was worried because her world was such a backstabbing place; that it was dangerous to go away for that length of time; she just felt she had to protect her holdings."

Meanwhile, Barbara began packing. She was anxious about the trip and how she would look to the *Today* audience.

"I'm taking clothes from my favorite designers—Kasper, Mollie Parnis, Adolfo, and Halston," she told *Women's Wear Daily*, sounding more as if she were headed for a week in Palm Springs than to the home of a Third World revolution. "I've been warned that it's bitter cold by the Great Wall . . . [so] I'm taking a new reversible coat—brown canvas on the outside, beige and brown lambskin on the inside—by Georges Kaplan. . . . I'm taking fur-lined boots, brown suede boots, and an Adolfo fur hood. . . . But I've definitely cut down on lingerie. I'll just wash a few things out each night. I won't have a hairdresser. I'll just take some electric curlers or wear my hair pulled back."

She was going on the perfect television story—lots of pomp and circumstance; the flags of China and the United States flying side by side; Nixon on a podium with Premier Chou En-lai, toasting each other; Nixon walking on the Great Wall of China; Nixon meeting with Chairman Mao Tse-tung; a Chinese band playing "Home on the Range," and "America the Beautiful." Great pictures; enormous exposure.

The two women journalists covering the story along with Barbara were veteran White House reporters Helen Thomas of United Press International, and Fay Wells of Storer Broadcasting. The word among the other reporters as to why Barbara was chosen was, "Nixon wanted names; he wanted celebrities like Barbara and [Walter] Cronkite," said Thomas.

"She had more visibility; she was a celebrity," agreed Wells, who was Barbara's roommate for three days during the eight-day trip. "But I didn't see much of her because she always had her producer and her soundman and her cameraman and they were out doing features. I had to refill my own tape recorder, my own batteries and all that stuff. They handed her a mike and everything was ready. The producer had the schedule. He'd say to her, 'Be downstairs at four-thirty.' The car was waiting for her to take her here and there."

Barbara and Lee were still together when she went to China—their split was still several months away. Wells recalled that one night Barbara came into their room and said, " 'Fay, I'm so lonesome. I haven't been able to talk to my husband.' And I said, 'Well, Barbara, why don't you pick up the phone? I do. I talk to my husband every night.'

But I guess she was so used to having people do things for her it just never occurred to her to pick up the phone herself."

Barbara's close ties with the Nixon Administration had sparked contempt toward her from many of the other reporters on the trip. That was one of the reasons, it was believed, that Don Meaney was sent along. Behind his back, he was referred to as "the vice president in charge of Barbara Walters," and Barbara was described as "Madame Chiang." Barbara always seemed to be at Mrs. Nixon's side; she had access that others didn't. News photographers were so outraged that they dumped a large accumulation of film scraps in her hotel room to show their dislike for her.

Following a banquet in Hangchow, Nixon introduced Barbara to Premier Chou En-lai. "This is Barbara Walters," he said, smiling. "We're just breaking her in."

Despite the heights to which she had climbed, Barbara was the object of other reporters' ridicule, the brunt of their jokes. They howled at one famous NBC newsman's recounting of Barbara covering Nixon in China. The retelling, which still occurred at parties in the late 1980s when Barbara's name would come up and the newsman was present, portrayed her—supposedly inexperienced in the ways of a working reporter—as watching and mimicking the movements of Helen Thomas. Whatever Thomas did, Barbara's colleague claimed, Barbara would do. Whenever Thomas took out her notebook, Barbara followed suit, looking as if she were taking notes.

"It was like sitting at a dinner table where there are more forks than you know what to do with, and you watch the person next to you to see which forks they use first," said a prominent journalist who, over the years, had suffered spasms of laughter listening to the story.

In fact, Barbara acknowledged that she went on the trip

feeling terribly inadequate. . . . I could often hear Walter Cronkite or John Chancellor doing their broadcasts and I felt, "How can I even consider myself on their level? They're so much crisper—so much better reporters than I." I was very depressed. I never remember feeling more inept.

I was shy and quite frightened, which resulted in a reputation for being ice cold. . . . When I got back I found that *they* had expected *me* to kind of cremate them and walk away with all the stories, and get an exclusive with Chou En-lai.

Barbara complained that she'd lost five pounds because of the stress, lack of eating and sleep on the assignment, and being unhappy with her work. "I had boned up so thoroughly before I left, but after I got there it was nothing like the actuality. So as a result I found myself constantly dissatisfied with everything I did and always feeling after a broadcast or telecast that I wished I had handled it differently."

Despite her insecurities, Barbara seemed to become an overnight China expert based on the fact that she'd been there for eight days and was a celebrity. She wrote a lengthy chronicle of the trip for the *Ladies' Home Journal*, and was invited to address the prestigious East Asian Institute of Harvard College, and the Woodrow Wilson School of Public and International Affairs at Princeton.

During the trip Barbara spent most of her time following Mrs. Nixon on visits to schools, communes, and such. In her spare time, Barbara shopped. "Show me a department store," she said, "and I'll tell you how the people live." Curiously, one of the questions she asked an interpreter was whether people in China married for love. The interpreter told her no; that they got married because they were politically compatible. "There are no love stories in China," Barbara noted on her return.

On the day the press contingent arrived in China, all of the reporters had been given what was called "the

Bible"—an elaborate briefing book containing the history of the country and its people, filled with lovely photographs and details about the President's itinerary. To the journalists, it was a beautiful memento of the trip, a historic souvenir to treasure and to put on the book shelf.

Barbara and Fay Wells had been assigned to share a hotel room in Shanghai on the last night before returning to the States. The next morning Barbara departed early for the airport. As Wells was leaving the room, she happened to look in the wastebasket and saw that Barbara had deposited her "Bible" there.

"I was utterly aghast," said Wells. "She didn't realize those things are precious. I guess it was just another story for her."

CHALLENGING THE QUEEN OF THE MORNING

In 1973, CBS mounted another assault on the *Today* show's dominance, pitting Sally Quinn, the princess of bitchy, gossipy profiles of Washington politicos and celebrities against Barbara Walters, the undisputed queen of early-morning television. The press went wild: Sexy Blond Bombshell vs. Iron Maiden.

Quinn, thirty-two, a writer for the *Washington Post*'s trendy Style section, was the choice of CBS News senior vice president Gordon Manning; during the 1968 political conventions, the eye-catching, willowy Quinn had worked as a gofer for Manning, and they'd gotten to know each other.

But it was Quinn's appearance as a guest on Barbara's *Not for Women Only* that convinced Manning she'd be perfect for early-morning TV. Manning sent for a dub of the Quinn segment, and Barbara gladly had it sent over, not realizing it was Quinn's unofficial audition tape. Richard

Salant, the head of the CBS News division, felt that "Sally walked away with the show."

Quinn had earned quite a reputation for her slick, daring reportage. Of Rudolf Nureyev, she wrote: "He has a fabulous behind. Women follow him around and stare at his fanny as blatantly as some men would stare at a woman's bosom." Henry Kissinger, describing tough women journalists in Washington, said, "Sally Quinn makes you want to commit suicide."

In many ways, Barbara and Sally were very much alike. Quinn got her job at the *Post* without any news experience whatsoever; like Barbara, Quinn could be brassy and acerbic, but she also knew how to use her feminine wiles to get a story. Quinn's friend Warren Beatty warned her during the height of the Walters-Quinn hoopla, "You've been made out to be a smug, tough, competitive little cockteaser, and people aren't going to like you for it."

The daughter of a retired three-star Army general, she was a graduate of Smith College and had worked in secretarial and clerical jobs. She moved easily in Washington social circles and had been a debutante and a member of the Junior League. In 1969, Benjamin Bradlee, the *Post*'s executive editor, hired her to cover Washington parties and eventually married her.

In early June 1973, Manning flew to Washington to meet with Quinn, telling her, "We're going to revamp the CBS *Morning News*, and we're looking for a woman who can knock Barbara Walters off the air. We think you're the one who can do it."

Flattered, excited by the prospects of the glamorous world of television, the celebrity stature, and big salary, Quinn gave an enthusiastic yes; it would be the worst career move she'd ever make.

"Sisterhood may end on August 6 at 7 A.M. sharp. That morning Sally Quinn will go on the air opposite Barbara Walters," said a headline in *New York* magazine over a profile of Quinn; a hatchet job written by a *Washington Post* colleague, Aaron Latham. The story ran with sexy photos of Quinn and dealt with her romances and her less than feminist reporting style. "Powerful people say things to women they would never say to men, especially over a martini," Latham quoted Quinn. "When somebody calls me 'sweetheart' at a party, I know I've got it made. . . . If a Senator is putting his hand on my fanny and telling me how he is going to vote on impeaching President Nixon . . . I'm not so sure I'm going to remove his hand."

It was not the kind of publicity for which CBS was looking, and it set the tone for the dismal failure that the mating of Quinn and anchorman Hughes Rudd became.

Then Rudd ignited the flames a bit more. In calling Quinn a "super reporter," he took a swat at Barbara, saying, "That's where [she's] weak," eliciting an angry retort from Barbara: "Frank McGee [the *Today* host] never worked on a newspaper, either. He's done very well as a reporter."

Naturally, the press tried to turn the story into a brawl between Barbara and Sally.

"There is no feud . . . and there will not be!" Barbara insisted. "I like and respect her. I am pleased that my success on *Today* seems to have convinced another network that it is important to have a woman on a national news program."

Quinn later acknowledged in a 1976 article in *Family Circle*, "From the beginning Barbara and I made a pact that we wouldn't be provoked into saying bad things about each other."

Usually insecure, Barbara for once felt no angst about the competition; Barbara was riding high and felt in complete control. A couple of days after Quinn made her debut, Barbara went on a three-week vacation to Israel (where she interviewed Prime Minister Golda Meir and Defense Minister Moshe Dayan) and smugly told a reporter, "[The Walters-Quinn brouhaha] couldn't have been better timed. I was in the midst of negotiations on a new contract. All the talk about me being queen of TV certainly didn't hurt." (Barbara's new three-year contract called for four hundred thousand dollars annually, covering her work on *Today*, *Not for Women Only*, and special reports.)

Before she left for Tel Aviv, Barbara wished Sally well in a brief note.

As any executive producer worth his six-figure salary, Stuart Schulberg had prepared for the worst—that Sally Quinn would be a success. On the first day, Schulberg changed *Today*'s normal routine, producing a two-hour special from the Plaza Hotel, featuring a fashion show, music from Duke Ellington, a tennis clinic, and other summertime features. Over at CBS, Quinn was apologizing to viewers for her sore throat and fever.

Schulberg had other special programs already formatted but they weren't necessary.

The coanchor team of Quinn and Rudd never got off the launching pad. From day one, it was clear that CBS had blundered badly; the new star of the CBS *Morning News* bombed. Quinn had never received any formal training for the job; she knew nothing about performing and was lucky to have been told that the little red light on the camera meant she was on the air.

At the *Today* show, Barbara, Schulberg, and the others were dumbfounded at what they were seeing on the other network. The highly touted Quinn appeared to be suffering from mike fright, showing her nervousness by biting her lip as she read the news. *Time* magazine called her reading voice "an arid monotone."

"The thing I remember the most is how astonished we were at the lack of care CBS took with Sally," said Jane Schulberg.

According to Schulberg, Barbara never once flinched. "She did things that Sally either didn't do or wasn't prepared to do. Barbara worked on everything. She paid attention to every detail of how she looked—what she looked like when she moved on camera—her voice, her lighting, her makeup, her hair; she worried everything to death—and she knew that Sally Quinn wasn't going to do that."

In January 1974, Quinn and CBS parted company; she got her old job back at the *Washington Post*, wrote a book about her sad affair with television entitled *We're Going to Make You a Star*, in which she blamed CBS for her problems, and married Ben Bradlee.

All of the publicity for Quinn actually had the result of strengthening Barbara's position. "In the past," she said a few months after Quinn's departure, "I'd sometimes worried that I dressed too sophisticatedly, or was too sharp on the air. Now here I was half Jane Wyman, half Shirley Temple, and people began to stop me on the street and say, 'Don't worry, Barbara, it's all right, you won't lose your job.' It was really very touching."

"READ BARBARA'S CONTRACT!"

W hile Sally Quinn posed no problem for Barbara, the man with whom she now worked on a daily basis, *Today* host Frank McGee, was making her life a living hell. If Barbara ever had a colleague who loathed her and held her in utter contempt, it was McGee.

The McGee regime began in October 1971 when Hugh Downs decided to retire. The Downs era had been a prosperous one for *Today*, and an extremely successful period for Barbara. "Probably the happiest time on the show," she said, "was with Hugh. . . . The chemistry worked. [We] liked each other enormously. We made each other look good . . . played up to each other's strengths. We were kind to each other."

It wasn't quite the fairy tale Barbara made it appear, but the relationship with Downs was certainly nirvana compared to the one with McGee. In his mild-mannered, affable way, Downs made it quite clear that he was number one, not Barbara—despite the fame she was gaining and the publicity she was generating for herself.

"Hugh had confidence that he was the star," said Doug Sinsel.

> Barbara could have as much as she wanted to a certain point, but Hugh ruled the ship. He had no qualms about saying in Barbara's presence, "Let's not forget *I* am the host. . . . You are *not* the cohost." He did not view her as an equal in that sense.
>
> Hugh had a very serious side to him, a way of letting Barbara know when he was unhappy. And when he was, we knew it and she knew it. If there was a situation where Hugh felt the show was unbalanced—meaning too much Barbara—he would make that known to both Stuart and me. He'd say, "I want this changed. I should lead this off; I'm going to interview Senator so-and-so in Washington, and I don't need Barbara to join this one."

For the most part, though, Downs was supportive of Barbara.

Not so with McGee, an abrasive, stubborn, able, and talented NBC reporter and anchorman, who had substituted for the vacationing Downs on several occasions, impressing the brass with his grace and style and convincing them he'd make a fine replacement when Downs eventually left the show.

Just prior to joining *Today*, McGee had been part of a rotating team of NBC anchormen that consisted of John Chancellor and David Brinkley; the three had been assigned to take over the *Huntley-Brinkley Report* in the wake of Chet Huntley's retirement in July 1970. The new arrangement confused viewers and the ratings plummeted. Chancellor was made sole anchor—and McGee became Barbara's nemesis.

McGee was a self-described "mean son-of-a-bitch; I'm like a collie puppy," he once said. "I come bounding into a room all fat and grinning and I expect everybody to like me. If they don't, I bite them."

He was a rare bird in the sophisticated world of network television. Outwardly suave, handsome, with a hypnotically smooth-as-syrup voice, he grew up poor in Norman, Oklahoma—the son of an oil field worker. In those days Frank was a hot-tempered shitkicker without the conservative bent of a redneck. A liberal, Frank defended the underdog, and it often got him into hot water. When a friend was scolded in high school because he argued with the history teacher about the Civil War, Frank came to his defense, put up his version of a First Amendment argument, and was flunked by the teacher; he lacked a half-point to graduate and never received a high school diploma.

During a stint in the Army, he got busted from sergeant to private because he spoke up to a young officer. At Berkeley, his GI Bill subsidy was cut off because he had angry words with an instructor. In television, McGee finally found a niche where he could express his views and get paid well, too. He was hired at a station in Tulsa, where he quickly earned a reputation as an effective, intelligent reporter with an extraordinary on-air presence.

Frank came to the attention of NBC and the network hired him to help cover the beginnings of the civil rights movement; he scored a number of firsts—including the earliest coverage of Dr. Martin Luther King, Jr., and of Rosa Parks, who defied the "Colored in the back of the bus" law in Montgomery, Alabama. Later, he was assigned to all the big stories—from assassinations to space shots.

By the time he got to *Today*, McGee was one of the brightest stars in the NBC news galaxy. And Barbara was fast becoming another—via a much different route—and when they collided between seven and nine each morning, the sparks flew.

Not long after he became host, McGee slyly hinted at the friction when he told an interviewer, "Friends have been asking me, 'When are you going to *get* Barbara Wal-

ters?' My answer is 'Never.' There's room for both of us."
But he really didn't feel that way.

McGee did all he could—other than to put his hand
over Barbara's mouth—to minimize her time on air with
him. He did the sign-on and sign-off each day, asked the
first question of every guest on the show, and often interrupted when Barbara was doing an interview. He rarely
talked to her off camera, and never socialized with her.
Every so often he'd pay her a compliment that felt more
like a slap in the face: "We'll make a journalist out of you
yet, Barbara," he'd say, and she would do all in her power
to keep herself from kicking him.

During station breaks, Barbara would grate on McGee
like chalk on a blackboard—rambling on about a chic
party she'd been to the night before or the important person she'd gone to dinner with—and he'd refuse to even
look at her, his eyes rolling, his jaw clenched. When the
local stations took over during longer breaks, she'd drive
him batty by singing tuneless lyrics to herself, reciting
grade school rhymes she'd memorized, scribbling thank-
you notes to friends while reading the words aloud to herself, or intoning "I'm going to be a wonderful person
today . . . wonderful people smile a lot . . . wonderful people
never gossip."

McGee even tried his best to keep Barbara from getting
her face on camera when he was away, determining who
would sit in for him (it was usually Edwin Newman), and
that made her even more furious.

"It was a very unhappy time," Barbara acknowledged
years later. "While Frank was there I was not allowed to
participate in any of the Washington interviews. He
wanted to do them alone. There was a big meeting with
the president of NBC, and we finally compromised. I could
come in and participate in an interview after [Frank] had
asked three questions."

To get around the absurd rule, Barbara went out and
got her own interviews so McGee could not be a partici-

pant. That aggravated the situation even more—and the hate emanating from McGee toward Barbara was palpable.

"McGee thought Barbara was stupid and dismissed her as not worthy of his attention," said Jane Schulberg,

> and that drove Barbara crazy. McGee had utter contempt for her. He was a real chauvinist—utterly opposed to women in the marketplace.
>
> He would keep her out of an interview if he could; he actually wanted her off the show; he wanted her out; he didn't want to have to talk to her, to look at her. If he was in a grumpy mood, he would try to humiliate her, and if he was in a good mood, he would ignore her. Stuart was the lion tamer, the negotiator. He was trying to make the show work and he had these two monsters in there.

Frank Blair, who was on the set every morning delivering the news, recalled years later, "When McGee took over, boy! . . . One way to put it is that he kept Barbara in her place. I don't think she liked that very much. She couldn't lord it over Frank. He was the boss, the head man, and that was the way it was gonna be, and Barbara resented it. He kept a tight rein on her."

Blair himself shared some of McGee's contempt for Barbara. "Sometimes," he said, "she asked the questions one would expect from a cheap, tabloid reporter. . . . If she was pointed and perhaps unduly personal with some interviewees, it seemed to me she was sugary with others, especially those in positions of power. She sometimes held back, refusing to put the hard questions."

Judith Crist, who was still doing the movie and theater reviews on the show, also witnessed the Walters-McGee feud, and felt most of the problems "came from Barbara." In Crist's opinion, McGee felt that one day Barbara would be promoted to cohost, and that's what angered him.

"Frank clearly hated her," said Sinsel. "He did not think she belonged there. His attitude toward her was total hostility, jealousy. He was a hard-line Oklahoman who brought himself up from the sticks; a typical midwestern, self-educated, hard-working television newsman who cut through all the stuff and had no patience for fluff or flamboyancy. Barbara was everything Frank McGee grew up to hate—New York, Lou Walters' daughter, that sort of thing. He looked on her more as glitz and show business and limelight—a celebrity."

(Barbara was contradictory on the issue of whether she did or didn't consider herself a celebrity. She told the *Ladies Home Journal*, "I *love* being a celebrity. I *love* knowing that people want to meet me . . . the security that it gives." Three months later she noted to a reporter for the Sarasota *Herald-Tribune*, "I don't think of myself as a celebrity at all.")

While Stuart Schulberg was furious with McGee's sexist attitude toward Barbara, he more or less agreed privately with McGee's assessment that Barbara was not the brightest journalist he'd ever encountered. True, she was tough, aggressive, obsessive about doing her homework, dedicated to the pursuit of netting the blockbuster interviews and the headline-grabbing stories. Barbara certainly was doing her job better than almost anyone in the business, and Schulberg knew that he shouldn't be complaining, looking for flaws, defects.

Still, he felt she had little or no intellectual depth. Snaring the interview, grabbing the headline, getting the reputation were her primary goals, he felt. And those underlying feelings, that hidden resentment, caused problems between them.

Her personality also grated on him. "She could be awfully damned tough and self-centered when crossed or frustrated or, in her opinion, not supported on the air or otherwise," he once said. "I don't mind her outbursts in private, but I resented them in front of the production crew and in front of guests."

Staffers recalled how Barbara would come to Schulberg's

editorial meetings and infuriate both him and McGee with her haughty attitude and demands. "She'd sashay in and make a big production about nothing," said a member of the staff. "She would brag about whatever spot she had filmed and then she would say how much time she needed. But the fact was Stuart gave her only what he wanted to. She never won those battles. But she was always pushing herself around, showing how important she was."

"The big problem," as Jane Schulberg saw it,

was that Stu was producing a show and Barbara was producing a career.

Stuart truly was a journalist; Stuart cared about the oppressed, if you will, and loved politics, loved news, and was wonderfully educated. He found Barbara, in a very real sense, quite provincial. She had her career and that circle of people she considered to be the *right people*, and it was really a very narrow little circle.

Stuart didn't think of her as being particularly well educated, or a particularly knowledgeable person, and he found her very incurious. She had no interest in the history of a subject, or the state of society, or the state of the world. If you were famous at the moment, then she would want to know how you got to be that way, where you came from, who you slept with, who you didn't sleep with. Stuart felt she was essentially a gossip columnist.

When she came back from one of her early trips to Israel [the one she took a few days after Sally Quinn debuted; in fact, it was Barbara's first trip to Israel], Stuart felt she had been clearly snowed by [Defense Minister Moshe] Dayan and all those guys. They just dazzled her. McGee had her on the air and was asking her about the Palestinians and Barbara clearly didn't have the background, she didn't know the history—and she was furious because McGee had embarrassed her on the air. Stuart was just appalled [at Barbara], and reminded once again, that she was not, certainly in his terms, a journalist.

In a back-handed compliment to Barbara, Stuart once told

a *Newsweek* reporter: "Barbara has a very strong respect for power and position. She will not ask the ultimate jugular question. But she gets people who won't sit down with a scowling Dan Rather or a very persistent John Chancellor. I'd rather have seven-tenths of an interview than none."

Another producer who worked with Barbara also saw a lack of intellectual depth in her. Barbara's interests, the producer observed, "were show business because of her father" and "clothes."

"I don't think Barbara would go home and curl up with a good novel because she had a fascination with a certain author outside of professional reasons. Barbara's interest in politics was simply doing her homework for a particular guest," the producer added.

Jane Schulberg said her husband was often amazed at the things Barbara didn't know, and showed no interest in learning about.

"He was stunned once because she didn't know anything about the Rosetta stone. Barbara said, 'Why do we have to put that crap on about whatever the Rosetta stone is?' And there was Stuart sputtering like Donald Duck, 'The Rosetta stone, for God's sake . . .'

" 'Well, who cares about that stuff?' Barbara would say. 'I know what people want.' "

But Stuart Schulberg also felt that if there was a catastrophe, he would want Barbara in front of the camera because she could do the job; if there was a newsmaker whom he wanted to have interviewed, he could depend on Barbara to ferret him or her out.

"Despite wanting to swing her out a window, he had full confidence in Barbara," Jane Schulberg said. "He thought of her as being very shrewd, very good at what she did.

"She amazed Stuart. He always used to ask, 'What drives this woman? What does Barbara want?' "

The answer, it appeared, was that Barbara wanted it all. She wanted the respect and credibility of a hard-news reporter and the glitz, glamour, publicity, lifestyle, and riches of a celebrity; all of it was what she wanted, and she would get it, too.

Frank McGee, who was fifty-two years old, was hospitalized with bone cancer that had been diagnosed before he came to the *Today* show. He had tried to keep his illness a secret from the staff and NBC as long as he could. In the early hours of April 17, 1974, he died in his sleep.

A few days after McGee's death, NBC executives announced that they were going to start a search for a new *Today* host to replace the late Frank McGee. When Barbara heard that she immediately telephoned Lee Stevens, her agent at William Morris, who got on the phone with the powers at NBC.

Stevens said, "You mean cohost."

The NBC executives seemed dumbfounded. "Cohost? Cohost? What do you mean, cohost?"

He told them, "Read Barbara's contract!"

When NBC renewed Barbara's contract, the network's negotiators didn't argue against a seemingly innocent clause Stevens added that called for Barbara's promotion to cohost if McGee left, voluntarily or otherwise.

Thus, five days after McGee died, Don Meaney announced, "Barbara Walters will be cohost of *Today*. This is the first time the program has had a cohost, and *Today* is now the only TV network news or public affairs program to have a female cohost."

Barbara got the job, she would later say, "quite literally over Frank McGee's dead body."

ROYAL LOVERS

I can work with whomever they choose," Barbara said three months after Frank McGee's death. "I don't want to have too much say in the final decision—although if they picked someone I absolutely hated, I'm sure they would not try to shove him down my throat."

If Frank McGee had been the pit bull in Barbara's professional life, Jim Hartz became the basset hound. Amiable, easygoing, almost cherubic in looks and demeanor, his selection in July 1974 as *her* cohost brought a calm to the stormy set of *Today*. The tension that was constant between McGee and Barbara had vanished and so, too, would the ratings. The tranquillity of the new team of Walters and Hartz seemed to have a tranquilizing effect on viewers, who eventually started bailing out in measurable numbers, some jumping to ABC where a *Today* clone called *Good Morning America* would be unveiled.

Hartz, a thirty-four-year-old Oklahoman, had been McGee's protégé; he respected and was in awe of his mentor. Like McGee, Hartz had learned the basics of broadcast news at a local station back home—they called him the "Tulsa Tiger"—and quickly earned a reputation as a bright, able, and effective reporter. As with McGee, he came to the attention of NBC executives and was soon working in the rarefied world of network news. He followed in McGee's footsteps, covering some of the same beats, such as space and aviation. At McGee's urging, he'd also done several stints on *Today* as a substitute for Frank Blair.

But unlike McGee, Hartz was a gentle man who liked Barbara.

"Jim was sweet and Barbara had no objections," said Jane Schulberg.

"Regarding the competition that Frank and Barbara might have had," said Hartz,

> Barbara and I were thrown together in such a way that we didn't have a lot of competing interests. A lot of stuff I wanted to do [on the show] she didn't give a damn about and vice versa. I liked to get out and do things. I did a story on the killing of the seals by Norwegian fishermen on the ice floes in Newfoundland—and Barbara couldn't have cared less about getting dressed up and going out in thirty-degrees-below-zero weather to do a story like that.
>
> During the Bicentennial I loved going out to the states and doing those stories. She didn't care particularly about the Bicentennial. She never wanted to make the trips. The Bicentennial shows were Americana, which has always been a favorite subject of mine. Barbara was more interested in that period of her career in Kissinger and more glamorous figures.

The glamorous interview had become Barbara's forte. In May 1975, she added Fidel Castro to the growing lineup of world leaders who were willing to sit down with her as a way to gain access to a large American television audience. "Where's Barbara?" Castro asked when a contingent

of fourteen reporters accompanied Senator George Mc-
Govern to Cuba. Barbara scored another beat, riding
through the countryside as a passenger in the bearded dic-
tator's Jeep. It made for great television pictures, but there
was little depth to the interview.

With Barbara now the cohost, she felt a bit less anxious
and stressful and decided to take a brief vacation, an activity that she usually found abhorrent. John Lord had observed that she had difficulty enjoying *any* form of pleasure,
and that vacationing was just one of them. "It was an inhibition," he said, "that certainly was there." Not one for
introspection, Barbara herself admitted that, "One of the
problems with my life, probably the only problem, is that
I feel guilty doing *anything* just for *pleasure*. I have to learn
sometimes how *just* to have *pleasure*."

Barbara tried to have it in Haiti, of all places, and it was
a scene that few who observed her stay will ever forget.

Barbara decided on the land of Baby Doc because it was
the favorite getaway spot for Stuart and Jane Schulberg,
and Barbara's publicist and friend, Nancy Love. They
stayed at the Grand Hotel Oloffson, an ornate Victorian
hideaway in Port-au-Prince that had become the "in" gathering spot in the mid-Seventies for celebrities and other
interesting characters. The hotel, owned by the Schulbergs' friends Al and Sue Seitz, was once described as a
"primitive bivouac." The place had loads of charm, but
few if any luxuries; people stayed there for the ambience,
not for special treatment. It was a place where the towels
didn't match and the hot water sometimes worked. Seitz's
motto was "The guest is always wrong."

So it came as no surprise to anyone that Barbara hated
both the country and the hotel. As Jane Schulberg said,
"It was poor. It was black. It was difficult. A tough country.
Not Barbara's kind of place."

From the moment she arrived at the Oloffson, Barbara
started complaining about the lack of amenities: no room

service, no telephones, no beauty shop, no massage, no full-length mirror. When she discovered that there were no other big-name celebrities staying at the hotel that week, she virtually had a fit in the lobby, saying loudly, "Okay, where is everybody? How come nobody's here?"

Al Seitz couldn't believe what he was seeing: "She was such a pain in the ass it's unbelievable. She hated the best room and she hated Haiti. Every place we took her to dinner was lousy, and these are great restaurants. And afterward not one goddamn thank-you."

Sue Seitz had a confrontation with Barbara on one of her first nights in Haiti when the Seitzes, the Schulbergs, and Love took Barbara to the grand opening of a new luxury hotel, Habitation Le Clerc.

"This is really my kind of place," Barbara told Sue enthusiastically. Then, referring to the Seitzes' famed Oloffson, Barbara said, "Now you understand, *that* is a place where I *wouldn't* send people. I hope you don't mind."

Sue was shocked at Barbara's comments. "I said, 'Indeed I do mind; you're a guest of ours and I think that's kind of rude.'"

All but ignoring Seitz, Barbara went on. "But *this* is *really* what I like."

"It wasn't a very kind thing to say, but she just does it," Seitz said. "She has a very lofty idea of herself and it doesn't occur to her that she may be insulting people because she is that way."

The one activity Barbara did find to her liking in Haiti was shopping. Port-au-Prince is a bargain-hunter's paradise, where colorful and inexpensive Haitian art and clothing are plentiful. Seitz operated a small boutique called Bagaille, near the hotel, where she and a partner sold lovely, handmade cotton things.

Even though the shop's prices were extremely low, "Barbara bargained us down to the end, down to the core," Seitz said. "I saw it first-hand with my clothing; getting me down in prices to nothing. She's like a little Jewish lady in the garment center. In some ways, though, that sort of makes her real. She is what she is."

Frugality is a trait that Barbara doesn't deny—has even boasted about—saying she sometimes rode the bus home from the studio rather than take a cab. "I'm kind of frugal," she once said. "I'm always afraid it will be over." When she complained to a friend about getting around New York, it was suggested she get a limo, but Barbara told her it was too expensive, she couldn't afford it. Although her father was a gambler and spent it when he had it, thriftiness is a trait that runs in her family.

At *Today*, Jane Schulberg said, Barbara often used a secretary to "take coats at her parties. The secretary would come not as a guest but as a servant. Barbara always did that sort of thing. She was always using NBC cars to do shopping and messengers to bring personal stuff back and forth. It was all the same to her."

It was easy for people to gloat over Barbara's penny-pinching, but the sad fact was that she never was able to conquer the crushing insecurity she had felt as a child and young woman over Lou's financial ups and downs as a businessman and as a gambler. Not surprisingly, Barbara took few if any risks with her own hard-earned money. Once, though, she was almost taken to the cleaners when she invested in an oil venture that offered huge profits and big tax savings. Barbara was among a number of celebrities who had been wooed—and she lost $28,500—in what became one of the most complex, protracted securities and tax-fraud cases in history.

Under Barbara's current contract with NBC—the one that gave her the cohost job on *Today*—she had the option to branch out into other forms of programming. In order to do so, though, she decided to reduce her role on *Not for Women Only*. Some stations had started dropping the show, and Barbara felt her career had benefited as much as it could from it. She now wanted bigger and better forums for her talents. In June 1975, Barbara convinced her friend Hugh Downs to return to television, becoming the alternate host of the show, freeing her for other assignments and specials. Eventually, she would leave it altogether.

That year, Barbara and Tom Snyder cohosted a three-hour prime-time program called *Of Women and Men*, which dealt with the women's liberation movement. Looking glamorous and changing gowns for the third hour of the show—from simple red to ruffled black—Barbara commented on sexism in television, on the scarcity of female news executives, and pointed out that the show was the first documentary in which she'd been involved. (She apparently forgot about her appearance on Shad Northshield's decade-ender, which was considered a documentary-special.) The *New York Times* critic John J. O'Connor called the broadcast "a touch too superficial. . . . It is limited despite three full hours."

Later in the year, Barbara accepted Howard Cosell's invitation to be a guest on his Saturday evening program on ABC, *Saturday Night Live With—Howard Cosell*. Her appearance sparked snide comments, since many inside and outside of the business viewed her as the female equivalent of the aggressive.

But her biggest endeavor, one on which she worked for months, was the pilot for what she hoped would be a series of Barbara Walters specials. The program received such bad reviews it would be her last, at least at NBC.

The special, which aired at one-thirty on the afternoon of September 25, 1975, was called *Barbara Walters Visits the Royal Lovers*. At best, it was a model for the very successful *Barbara Walters Special* shows that she would do at ABC; at worst, it was a harbinger for the infernal but popular *Lifestyles of the Rich and Famous*, hosted by former supermarket tabloid reporter Robin Leach.

Barbara's ninety-minute production was a big gamble on NBC's part. Not only was it an expensive venture—shot on location in Europe at a cost of a quarter of a million dollars—but the network preempted two of its most popular daytime soaps and moneymakers—an hour of *Days of Our Lives* and a half-hour of *The Doctors*.

The idea for the special—which focused on the ostentatious and grandiose lifestyles of the Duke and Duchess of Orléans, pretenders to the throne of France, and Queen Margrethe of Denmark and her husband, Prince Henrik—grew out of the high ratings the *Today* show received from Barbara's coverage of Princess Anne's wedding, Prince Charles's investiture, and the spectacular party given by the Shah of Iran to celebrate the 2,500th anniversary of the palace of Persepolis.

When Barbara saw the viewer numbers for those programs, she felt she was onto something. She hoped to develop the new program into a series of *Barbara Walters Visits* specials that combined entertainment and news.

"I realized," she said, "that people want glamour and tradition, but also with some reality. So whenever I had lunch with an executive and he would ask me the kind of thing I want to do, I would talk about it."

Finally, daytime programming vice president Lin Bolen and NBC president Bob Howard listened to Barbara's pitch and "agreed to go for broke."

Chosen to produce the show was the Emmy Award–winning NBC documentary producer Lucy Jarvis. From the beginning, according to a key member of the small production team, there was constant tension and petty jealousies between the two women. Their problems would have a major impact on the program's content.

Yves Saint Laurent was shown designing a blue chiffon dress for Barbara; she was filmed borrowing ruby and diamond jewelry from Cartier, spinning in front of mirrors, hugging a duchess, and using phrases like "frightfully amazing, my dear." At Maxim's, with a violinist serenading them, the camera focused on Barbara dining with her friend Alexis Lichine and the duke and duchess; at a gala ball at Versailles, French President Valéry Giscard d'Estaing gave her dull quotes about the royal lifestyle; Barbara showed viewers Marie Antoinette's *"actual"* bedroom—"the money! the gold! the brocade!" she gushed. "Boy, wait 'til my mother sees me back home."

Dena may have loved it, but the critics didn't.

John O'Connor in the *Times* said the program "may well be the most ridiculous curiosity of the season . . . a rambling essay on the glamour and wealth of what Miss Walters calls 'the high life,' for which she discovers that 'it's not too hard a taste.' "

In one segment, observed Los Angeles *Times* TV critic Mary Murphy,

> the film-makers have Walters running from window to window in Versailles in a take-off on a French farce. It's at this point when you pray the program will be lost or preempted so we will be spared the embarrassment of watching Barbara at play. The problem is that the film-makers are so busy enthroning Walters that we learn little, and nothing of consequence, about the life-style of contemporary European royalty. Walters is the most powerful newswoman in America, yet send her to Europe to interview royalty and she becomes a cooing school girl. It's Barbara in Wonderland.

Even the more congenial Kay Gardella of the *Daily News* was taken aback, calling the program "pretentious," and observing that viewers "might easily wind up with a royal pain in the neck."

The question Gardella asked readers was whether Barbara could return to the day-to-day routine of the *Today* show after wearing Saint Laurent gowns and Cartier jewels and dining with royalty. Gardella didn't realize at the time how prescient her query was.

*   *   *

Stuart Schulberg felt that Hartz had brought a "warm, sane, stable quietude to *Today*." But the new team was losing viewers daily. Hartz was too laid back; there was no electricity between him and Barbara. At one point, Richard Wald, the NBC News president, approached Hartz and "told him to sit up and show more drive [and] stop sitting there in front of the cameras with [your] chin in [your] hand," said Frank Blair.

Moreover, *Good Morning America* at ABC was coming on strong with more flash and glitz than *Today*, which looked staid in comparison. As a result, the ratings were dropping, a slippage that had started even before McGee's death, but was increasing at an alarming rate. Eventually the ratings plummeted by as much as thirty percent.

"We were going through a real hectic period," said Hartz. "I don't know what happened to the ratings, and no one really gave a shit. NBC itself was in turmoil. Stuart was tired. He'd sit in his office and say, in effect, that he was burned out, that he wanted to do something else."

In March of 1975, Frank Blair left the show, later admitting that he had become a "compulsive" drinker. Most mornings, he wrote in his memoirs, "the thought of food was repulsive to me and I'd drink instead of eat."

On the air, Barbara—while officially Hartz's cohost—was the one in command. She was now often asking the first question in interviews, and alternating in the opening and closing of program segments. She was also reading the news headlines for the first time. Prior to McGee's death, Schulberg did not permit her to do that, saying she lacked authority and her slight speech impediment did not sound appropriate.

While Barbara was growing concerned over the drop in ratings and the apparent lethargy of the show, her star continued to rise. She won an Emmy in the service and talk show category, was named Broadcaster of the Year by the International Radio and Television Society, and lauded by

Time magazine as one of the one hundred most influential leaders in the country.

The only dark cloud during that period of elation was a personal attack on her by Frank Sinatra, who had begun verbalizing in public his animosity toward the press. He called Barbara "the ugliest broad in television." She was shocked and hurt by the outburst, telling TV critic Dan Lewis of the Bergen (New Jersey) *Record*, "I always thought we had a nice relationship. My father was always good to Frank. I just don't understand it." Some years later, Barbara again was the target of verbal abuse from Old Blue Eyes. He called her "a real bow-wow . . . a pain in the ass who has a lisp and should take diction lessons."

Before Christmas 1975, with her contract about to expire in less than a year, Barbara began having very private, informal talks with NBC executives about her future at the network. The vagueness and friendliness of those chats took on a harder tone within weeks when Lee Stevens delivered to an NBC vice president a list of contractual demands fit for a movie queen that left those in the executive suite in a state of shock.

Barbara asked for an unprecedented salary of one million dollars a year for seven years; approval of all major changes on *Today*; the right to endorse any products without NBC approval, except for those on *Today*; reimbursement for home entertainment expenses and for a personal publicist, and a hairdresser and chauffeured limousine paid for by the network. The salary, while mind-boggling, was something the network could deal with, but some of Barbara's other demands infringed on the autonomy of the news division and the producer of the *Today* show and were considered inviolable. During none of these preliminary negotiations did Barbara ever once say what job she wanted in exchange for the increased salary, power, and perks she was demanding. Everyone just took it for granted that she would be happy to remain as the cohost of *Today*. In fact, she wanted to coanchor the NBC *Nightly News*.

The NBC people felt they had plenty of time to negotiate and declined to make any early concessions. Lee Stevens said fine, letting it be known that he intended to "test the marketplace and see what people at the other networks might think of Barbara."

PART IV

MILLION-DOLLAR BABY

On one of the first pleasant Saturday mornings in what had been a cold and blustery March in 1976, Frederick J. Pierce, the president of the ABC Television Network, played tennis at the Westchester home of his friend and neighbor Lou Weiss, who headed the television department at the William Morris Talent Agency.

During a break in the game, Weiss, who, along with Lee Stevens, handled Barbara and often did business with Pierce, dropped a piece of news that caused Pierce's ears to prick up. "You know, Fred," Weiss said, casually spinning his racket, "Barbara Walters is looking for some additional challenges. She's not too thrilled with staying on the *Today* show. She wants to move into a different level in her career. I think you might have a shot at attracting her if the conditions are right and the money is right because NBC is not handling her well. She's looking for broader exposure."

What sort of exposure and for how much, Pierce wanted

to know, appearing as nonchalant about the prospect of buying Barbara as Weiss was about selling her.

"For example, coanchoring the evening news and doing some prime-time specials," said Weiss. "Say a million a year."

Of course, Weiss added quickly, Barbara would have to feel confident that ABC—then in last place in the network news race—was committed to the development of a first-rate news organization and that management would give her full and complete support with continuity.

As he listened to Weiss, Pierce thought that this was a once-in-a-lifetime opportunity, coming at a time when ABC was making a name for itself in entertainment and sports, and was looking to strengthen its mediocre news division.

Pierce had been named president of ABC Television in October 1974, when the network was in the basement in every area of programming. Not long after his appointment, he lured CBS programming "wunderkind" Fred Silverman as president of ABC Entertainment. By the time Pierce and Weiss had their first talk about Barbara, ABC had become *the* hot network and Pierce was the man responsible.

While Pierce had pulled a few white rabbits out of the hat for ABC, he was not the most loved man by ABC News executives. To them Pierce didn't care about news: Entertainment? News? It was all the same to him, they felt. That's one of the reasons why Pierce wasn't shocked when Weiss mentioned the million-dollar figure. It was the contention of Barbara's agents that a newsperson with high visibility should be paid as well as a singer or a comedian or an actor. They all were performers. Both sides—Pierce and Barbara's people—were in accord on that issue.

"Fred Pierce was a man of no taste and no sensitivity, but he was very, very smart," said one former high-ranking ABC executive of the time. "ABC News president Bill Sheehan used to run on the small track at the Y on West

Sixty-third Street across the street from the ABC broadcast center. You had to go twenty-four laps for a mile and
after each lap Sheehan would say, 'Fuck Freddy Pierce.'
That's how strong the feelings were about him. Getting
Barbara Walters, and paying her a million dollars a year,
was a Fred Pierce special."

As Weiss talked about Barbara's potential availability,
Pierce pictured her as a "star personality with a lot of journalistic credentials" who would give ABC News an instant
boost because of her reputation. Also, the news operation
would get enormous publicity and credit for hiring the first
female anchorperson on any network. Moreover, signing
her would cause major problems for *Today* and give an
added edge to ABC's *Good Morning America.* And he saw
the specials that Weiss mentioned as a "Lucky Strike
Extra"—a way of reviving Edward R. Murrow's successful
Person to Person formula. In all, Pierce concluded, a million
dollars, though unprecedented at the time, seemed a bar-
gain.

First thing Monday Pierce called Bill Sheehan and scheduled a meeting for later in the day.

Sheehan, in his early fifties, was considered a controversial news executive because of themes instituted at ABC
News during his watch that critics felt reeked of local news
superficiality. The Chicago *Sun-Times*'s Ron Powers was
the recipient of a leaked memo written by Sheehan in
which he urged the evening news staff to give more emphasis to stories involving celebrities, pop culture, fashionable
trends—emphasizing that "people are interested in many
things that are not intrinsically important." In a few years,
most of the ideas proposed by Sheehan would be imple-
mented at all the networks, but at the time they seemed
blasphemous.

"What would you think if you could get Barbara Walters?" a gloating Pierce asked Sheehan.

The prospect excited Sheehan, who saw ABC "buying

a ready-made name" in Barbara, a quick transfusion for his long-anemic news operation. But when Pierce mentioned the price tag, Sheehan was dubious. But Pierce told him a deal could probably be structured whereby Barbara's salary could be shared equally with the entertainment side, which would foot the bill for her specials. With that, Sheehan gave Pierce an unequivocal yes. That day Pierce also briefed ABC president Elton Rule and chairman Leonard Goldenson, who gave him the "go sign" to get Barbara.

After Pierce left his office, Sheehan leaned back with a smile of satisfaction on his face. He was under pressure to improve the ratings and Barbara could be the answer, the savior of his job. What a coup, he thought, to steal her away from NBC. But the anticipatory glow he felt faded as he gazed at one of the monitors in his office and saw the image of Harry Reasoner, his anchorman, delivering the news. Sheehan knew that Reasoner would be the biggest obstacle they'd have in making the Barbara Walters project viable.

"Harry is the most important element," Sheehan thought. "Harry and Barbara have to get along or it will not work."

On camera, Reasoner had a folksy, affable, farmer-in-the-dell quality about him. But off camera, he was a man with a large ego, a big salary, and, like Barbara, a heavy-hitting management team—Marvin Josephson and Ralph Mann of International Creative Management (ICM)—who had helped negotiate his career to the top.

A former newspaper reporter, novelist, government information officer, and father of seven, Reasoner started in 1956 at CBS where his star rose quickly. He covered Vietnam; was a correspondent on *60 Minutes*; sat in for Walter Cronkite. For a time he was considered by some to be the heir apparent to Cronkite's throne. In surveys, the viewing public said they liked him and found him credible—almost as much as Chet Huntley and Cronkite himself. But some executives did not support him; they saw Reasoner as quite talented, a fine writer, but often lazy. Because one news executive was unhappy with Reasoner's performance during the 1966 off-year election, he didn't get a campaign assignment in 1968, which infuriated him. With two years left on his contract and suddenly not feeling loved at CBS, he quietly began contemplating a change.

In November 1970, Reasoner shocked his colleagues and CBS brass by jumping ship, leaving the home of Murrow to go to third-rate ABC, where he was teamed with the knowledgeable and aristocratic Howard K. Smith, coanchoring the *Evening News*—raising the ratings, and thereby boosting ad revenues. By 1975, however, the program had reached its peak and the inevitable ratings slide began. Reasoner disliked the idea of sharing equal billing with anyone. To protect his position he even talked Roger Mudd out of seeking the coanchor post when Smith left the program.

In early spring of 1976, despite the low ratings, Harry Reasoner was complacent as ABC's sole anchor. He was like a fisherman in a rowboat—unaware that a Great White Shark was slowly circling him, moving in for the kill.

Reasoner was rudely awakened from his reverie when Sheehan invited him to lunch a few days after the Pierce meeting and told him that serious talks were underway with Barbara Walters who, if all went well, would become his partner in October 1976.

"His reaction," said Sheehan, "was not good. He made it clear in the beginning that this was not a great idea. He didn't want to have his presence [as anchorman] diluted. Harry told me, 'I need more time to do it myself.' At that point, he was not reacting to Barbara Walters, but to Harry Reasoner being divided by a factor of two. His attitude was, 'If this is successful, she'll get all the credit and if it's a failure, I'll get all the blame.' I think it was a self-fulfilling prophecy on his part."

A few days after their conversation Reasoner came

across a short news story datelined Columbus, Ohio. "*Hustler* magazine publisher Larry Flynt," said the Associated Press dispatch, "has offered Barbara Walters and nine other prominent women one million each to pose nude for photographs in the monthly publication." Flynt said he chose Barbara because she represented a "desirable" woman about whom the average man had "erotic dreams." Reasoner felt sick.

ABC executives worried not only about Reasoner's reaction to working with Barbara, but also about Barbara's personality and the impact it would have on Reasoner and the news operation as a whole. "Barbara had a reputation as being difficult to get along with," said a former ABC News vice president who was involved in the decision to hire her. "We all knew that she wasn't the easiest person to work with, and that she could be bitchy at times. Barbara and Harry were a volatile mixture."

On a typical news day, what with commercials and the commentary and other regular features, Reasoner had under ten minutes of air time, most of it spent reading the introductions and closings to reports by the correspondents. A coanchor would reduce that to about five minutes per show.

The time element was one of Reasoner's early complaints, so somewhere along the line Pierce decreed that, with the consent of the affiliate stations, ABC would be the first network to do a nightly hour of news, allowing the coanchors more time to do their own reports—exclusive interviews by Barbara, essays by Reasoner. It was, said Sheehan, "part of the bait to make Harry interested, to make ABC News interested. [An hour newscast] had been a dream of every news president of every network since the programs went to a half-hour."

When Sheehan met with Reasoner and told him about Barbara, he mentioned the expanded news possibility.

The hour newscast, Sheehan observed, "was more of an incentive to Harry and to ABC News than it was to Barbara. It made Harry much more comfortable with this deal than he would have been otherwise. For Barbara that was just frosting."

The affiliate stations refused to go along with the hour-long concept, which was still a dream of network news division chiefs in 1990.

Barbara quickly began hearing stories that Reasoner hated the idea of her joining him. Reasoner said he wasn't sure what to expect of Barbara. "I was with her on Nixon's China trip, but I never actually saw her work. All I know about her from that trip is that she rides the bus well." Reasoner had a reputation among women in the business as being something of a chauvinist. Having had her problems with Frank McGee, Barbara made it clear to ABC executives that she wouldn't make the move if Reasoner didn't change his attitude.

"She was candid about that," said Sheehan. "She said she'd been through that once in her life and did not want to go through it again. She wanted to have Harry comfortable. That was definitely a bridge that had to be crossed by us on behalf of Harry and by Barbara on behalf of herself."

Like old-fashioned parents, the ABC executives and Barbara's people arranged for her and Reasoner to court each other as if a marriage were being arranged—a shotgun marriage. The two would meet at a suite ABC maintained at the Essex House, or at Barbara's apartment on West Fifty-seventh Street. Sometimes they would be alone, at other times they'd be chaperoned by Lee Stevens, Pierce or Sheehan, or all three. The goal was conciliation before any final deal was cut; Barbara and Reasoner had to be comfortable with one another; they had to reach an accord.

For everyone, though, the bottom line was power and money. Barbara wanted to be the first woman news anchor; she wanted to be the first newsperson, male or fe-

male, to get a seven-figure salary. She wanted the prestige
and security. ABC wanted the eminence that Barbara
would offer and the revenue she could generate—a rise of
only one Nielsen ratings point in the evening news meant
an added two million dollars. At the minimum Reasoner
wanted equal pay and to maintain his dignity; the idea of
public castration, which is the way friends felt he saw it,
did not appeal to him.

As Nick Archer, then vice president of ABC Television
News Services, put it, "In the end, it had to do with Harry's
ego—the fact that we were telling the public and everybody
else that Harry couldn't hack it himself; that he needed
help, and not only did he need help, but he was getting
a woman to help him."

"They each had their own interests at heart and they
were protective and zealous about their reputations, which
were at stake," Sheehan said.

After a number of secret meetings in March and early
April between Barbara and Reasoner, everyone involved
in the negotiations believed that he'd finally become comfortable with the idea of working with her. At least that's
what Harry said, after making some noises about quitting.
A promised raise of about one hundred thousand dollars
a year that gave him parity with the half million dollars
that Barbara would get for doing the evening news was certainly an incentive. But inside Harry was seething.

Meanwhile, Sheehan was holding meetings with the vice
presidents of the news division to get their input.

The only woman in the group was Marlene Sanders,
who was appointed vice president and director of television documentaries little more than a month before Pierce
and Weiss had their tennis court discussion about Barbara.
She was the first woman to hold such an executive position
at any of the networks.

Like Barbara, Sanders started in television in the 1950s
in a low-level production job in New York. Unlike Barbara,
Sanders moved into hard news. She became ABC's second

woman news correspondent in September 1964. Sanders learned for the first time in 1988 that Barbara—apparently without the knowledge of her colleagues at *Today*—had quietly auditioned for the same job, which was during the period of Barbara's uncertainty over whether she'd succeed Maureen O'Sullivan.

Before Barbara joined Reasoner, Sanders had been the first woman to anchor a network evening news program: it happened when ABC's Ron Cochran lost his voice one night and Sanders sat in for him. She also pulled a three-month anchoring stint in 1971, substituting for Sam Donaldson on ABC's *Saturday Evening News* while he was in Vietnam.

"I told Bill Sheehan, 'It's time for a woman. I support the concept of a woman,' " said Sanders.

> But I personally didn't think [hiring Barbara] was such a great idea because she didn't have the news credentials. But I did nothing but support it. Everybody [the other vice presidents] groaned and moaned about it because everybody knew that she really wasn't an anchor type, with her speech and her credentials. Everybody knew there was going to be a lot of trouble over it, which there was.
>
> I was very rueful. I had been the first woman anchor and I thought if I had kept my nose to the grindstone and stayed on the air maybe it could have been me. I had mixed feelings.

After Barbara was hired, she sent Sanders a note thanking her for her support, but no bond developed between them.

During the meetings with the vice presidents, Sheehan never mentioned the salary that ABC was considering paying Barbara, and those involved in the talks came away feeling that her hiring was a fait accompli. If they all screamed and hollered and said no, she'd still be hired. They also felt that all the talk about expanding the news was just that. While they believed Sheehan was sincere, they felt

Pierce knew from the beginning that the affiliates would never buy his proposal.

In early April, news of the negotiations leaked out. Barbara told the *New York Times*, in a story suggesting that ABC had come to her, that she'd had a "preliminary meeting" with the other network. "Miss Walters," noted the *Times*, "said she gave no answer to its query nor would she for a while." Sheehan was quoted as saying that there had been "early" discussions.

On the *Today* set, Jim Hartz, who was aware that Barbara was renegotiating her contract with NBC, read the *Times* story and smiled to himself, thinking she'd leaked it as a negotiating tactic. "She's good at that," he said.

Barbara told the *Christian Science Monitor* that while she had "great respect" for Reasoner, "It's just too early to say if anything will develop . . . too premature even to say that I am seriously considering it." NBC News president Richard Wald said he "would not be happy" if Barbara left, but he refused to discuss whether she would make a good anchor. In fact, he'd already ruled out such a possibility for her at NBC, which he didn't tell the paper. "I guess in some formats she might," was all he said.

As the days progressed, Barbara was seesawing on the move and a series of urgent hand-holding meetings was held with her, Goldenson, Pierce, Rule, and Sheehan—none of whom wanted to see Barbara slip away after such a massive effort was made to court her. Barbara had qualms, which she didn't voice to the ABC brass, about whether she could handle news anchoring, which was a far different job from interviewing. Barbara began asking friends and colleagues for advice.

One of those she turned to was Hartz. "She had bantered about it but I didn't think she was serious. Then one day we were sitting in her office and she asked me whether I thought she should make the move. I said, 'I think you'd be dumb to go over there.' She asked me why and I said,

'It's a two-bit news operation.' Her response was, 'It might not always be.' "

In Miami, Dena confirmed that Barbara had made her aware of the ABC negotiations from the beginning. "She calls me practically every other day," her mother said. "I admire her much more for that than all she's accomplished in her profession."

On April 22, 1976, Barbara Walters officially became television's "million-dollar baby"—a sobriquet bestowed upon her by the press. She was now the highest-paid journalist in the world, the first network anchorwoman. All of the hard work, the battles she had fought, the personal life she had tabled for her career, all of it had paid off. Lou Walters' insecure little girl was, seemingly, on top of the world.

The contract with ABC called for her to coanchor the *Evening News* five days a week; appear on a dozen *Issues and Answers* programs, and do four specials a year under the aegis of her own production company, Barwall Productions, Inc. ABC agreed to pick up all the expenses for those programs. Five hundred thousand dollars would be paid by the news division for working with Reasoner; the remaining half-million would be her salary for doing the specials, paid by the entertainment division.

Some of Barbara's demands, however, were rejected during a marathon weekend bargaining session at the Essex House. ABC refused to pay for baby-sitters for her daughter when Barbara was away on assignment; refused to reimburse her for the cost of entertaining ABC officials in her apartment, and declined to include in the *Evening News* a regular feature segment by Barbara because it meant giving up editorial control. However, the company tacked on four thousand dollars to the million as pocket money for the baby-sitting and entertaining costs, and gave her a side letter agreeing to include an occasional Barbara Walters segment in the news. Barbara also would get a researcher, an additional secretary, a makeup consultant, a wardrobe person, a private office, and first-class hotel accommodations "acceptable to Artist," as the contract language read.

Naturally, Barbara was overjoyed.

"When ABC made me the offer to be the first evening news anchorwoman, it was a very great challenge," she said.

> The challenge was so exciting and so demanding that I felt I simply couldn't turn it down. It is true that ABC offered me a great deal of money, but NBC matched the money. I never negotiated; that is, I never demanded a particular amount of money from either ABC or NBC. NBC matched the money because they wanted to keep me at NBC. ABC's offer was the same from the first day to the last day. They were always aboveboard. I left NBC because I felt that this was an opportunity I simply couldn't turn down.

She liked the anchor job, Barbara told another reporter, "because you are the automatic head."

That night, on the ABC *Evening News*, Harry Reasoner, belying his inner feelings, said, "Some of you may have seen speculation about this in the papers. It's had more attention than Catfish Hunter, and Barbara can't even throw left-handed. Many of the stories said that I had some reservations when the idea came up. If I did, they've been taken care of, and I welcome Barbara with no reservation." He said that a woman coanchor "may well be an idea whose time has come."

At her own network, John Chancellor, with whom Barbara had wanted to coanchor, told viewers of the *Nightly News*, "NBC valued Barbara's service highly, but the negotiations for a renewal of her contract involved a million dollars and other privileges, and this afternoon NBC pulled out of the negotiations, leaving her a clear path to ABC. We wish her luck in her new job."

NBC executives left the bargaining table, contending that her contractual demands were more like those of "a movie queen" than a network journalist, which Barbara quietly branded as a lie. But even more important, the NBC brass had come to the surprising conclusion that Barbara was expendable, according to David Adams, who was vice chairman of NBC, and was involved in the decision to let her go.

She'd been promised an anchor job at ABC and we were not prepared to match that part of the offer because the judgment was that she wasn't all that good; that she wasn't that necessary or that important to be able to dictate terms such as she dictated. Thirdly, we felt she would not be very effective as the anchor of NBC's principal national news program and that it was out of place for her to demand that. We perceived Barbara as effective in a talk show format such as the *Today* show, which was only in part a news program.

Dick Wald, as head of news at that time, was very strong about not accepting her demand to be an anchor. He stated that very clearly and very strongly. Julian Goodman, who had been the number-two man in the news division before he became president of NBC, felt much the same. The general feeling among the people who were directly involved was that the company was being pushed around by somebody who was too big for her britches.

We felt she wouldn't be effective on the news and, if ABC wanted to give her a million dollars to do it, let them go ahead. Barbara was a popular figure, but she was not suitable in our judgment to be the center of a news program. Our people felt that the NBC *Nightly News* was the jewel in our journalistic crown and had to be treated seriously, and had to be anchored by a professional with journalistic background—and she was not that person. There was an executive meeting at which I was present and we decided to take our offer off the table. It was Julian Goodman who first said, "We should take the offer off the table and terminate this because it's been going on for weeks and weeks." I didn't convey the message but she was effectively told, "We're terminating this negotiation. We're withdrawing our offer. Do what you want."

After she left we just went on with our business. The Barbara Walters chapter at NBC was finished.

On the night of the announcement that Barbara was leaving the network, and despite the apparent acrimony between her and NBC brass, she made a surprise appearance at NBC president Herb Schlosser's fiftieth birthday party.

"Everyone from Julian Goodman to Dick Wald was there," recalled Jim Hartz. "It was a very strained situation. It wasn't Herb Schlosser's favorite party." David Adams, who also was there, added, "It was rather awkward and a little embarrassing for everybody. The feeling was that her coming to that party said something about her lack of taste and judgment."

But Barbara, who arrived with her date, Alan Greenspan, wanted to get something off her chest. She cornered Wald, complaining about the NBC announcement earlier in the day that decried her contract demands and said the network was ending its negotiation with her. Barbara told Wald she wanted the opportunity to give her side on *Today* the next morning; Wald agreed. Barbara also told him she would have stayed at NBC had she been offered the coanchor job, but Wald claimed that neither she nor her agents formally made that demand; that it had only been discussed abstractly. Had they asked, though, the answer would have been an emphatic no.

The next day, Barbara told the *Today* audience that she couldn't "resist" the ABC offer and that the decision to leave was "very difficult . . . very emotional."

After the show, Barbara took the shuttle to Washington where she had lunch with Joan Braden at Sans Souci, a French restaurant in Georgetown. For the first time with Braden, Barbara spoke in detail about the tough times she had while growing up, the financial insecurities she faced because of Lou's fast and loose ways with money. "She told me she had a tough life and I told her she deserved the money," Braden recalled. "She said one of the reasons she wanted to make that kind of money was to help her family." Later, Barbara told *People* magazine, "Now I can put some [money] away for the future."

Despite those hard times, Barbara's big-money deal with ABC was viewed grudgingly by many of her friends and colleagues. Nancy Dickerson, for one, admitted, "I felt a bit of envy. They chose a personality rather than a newsperson."

The weekend following the announcement, the look, sound, and feel of Barbara Walters—her entire persona—was immortalized in a character portrayed by a young comedian, Gilda Radner, one of the Not Ready For Prime Time Players, on NBC's *Saturday Night Live*. Sounding more like Elmer Fudd than Barbara Walters, Radner introduced "Baba Wawa" in a sketch about a television anchorwoman being interviewed about her new million-dollar-a-year job. Radner's imitation of Barbara became a highlight of the show and was done every so often thereafter, usually pegged to a story in which Barbara was involved, such as a visit she made to Iran.

Radner said she ran into Barbara once at a party at the Canadian consulate "and she couldn't have been nicer. I introduced myself as the woman who does the Baba skits, and she seemed fascinated. Obviously, she'd never seen me do them." Barbara asked Radner to do the bit for her and "she cracked up. She kept asking me how I did it." Gilda told her it was simple. She explained that she just changed the letters *l* and *r* to *w*. "You know, I'm working on those *r*'s myself," Barbara told Radner. Later Radner said she heard from friends at ABC that Barbara had begun pointedly calling Reasoner "Hawwy Weasonah."

The name and image of Baba Wawa stuck, making it difficult for many viewers thereafter to take the real Barbara Walters seriously. A few months later, as the hoopla over

Barbara's job continued unabated, the *Village Voice* head-lined a story: IN DEFENSE OF BABA WAWA, running photos of both Radner, mimicking Walters, alongside the real Barbara. By the late 1980s, people still referred to Barbara as Baba Wawa. Barbara once jokingly told the New York *Post*, "It's a good thing I'm not teamed with Tom Brokaw. He can't pronounce *l*'s."

On June 3, 1976, Barbara made her last live appearance on the *Today* show, jokingly stage whispering to viewers: "Shhh—sleep late. Tomorrow I'm not on." At the end of the program, when the audio man in the control room played "Auld Lang Syne," Barbara said, "I can't take this," but she didn't shed a tear. On the screen the words "Bon Voyage, Barbara" were superimposed.

Afterward, there was a going away party for her in Studio 3-K.

In a farewell speech, Barbara mentioned the criticism of her drive over the years. "I get very defensive about stories that say I am an aggressive woman who wants to take over the world," but she never denied those assertions. And in an apparent slap at NBC, she said she looked forward to "goodwill" in her new job at ABC without "nitpicking and hypocrisy."

As the party drew to a close, Barbara, a tear glinting for the first time, embraced teleprompter operator Charley Kirnard, who had known her since the 1950s, when both of them worked for Tex McCrary and Jinx Falkenburg.

"Sometimes," Kirnard said, "people say to me, 'What a snob Barbara Walters is.' I tell them that they are wrong and that she is a very deep person. It doesn't come across on the air, but she really is."

Watching the proceedings with a jaundiced eye and a drink in hand, Stuart Schulberg said, "I've been asked many times what Barbara Walters is really like. I always replied that if I tried to answer we wouldn't be able to get the show on next Monday. She's a private person and a public phenomenon."

NBC stubbornly refused to allow Barbara to make an immediate move to ABC, claiming that she still had contractual obligations to sponsors, even though she wouldn't be seen again on *Today*. She would be held to her contract until it expired in September.

It was the Bicentennial summer, a busy news time that included not only the national birthday party, but the national political conventions in New York and Kansas City as well. For the first time in years, Barbara wouldn't be there to cover them, but she was there as a guest of ABC: Martin Rubenstein, the ABC attorney who negotiated her contract for the network, was assigned to be her escort.

But for Barbara—for whom any idle time is anathema—it was the summer of her discontent: "the worst summer I can remember," she said. She suffered from more than her usual anxiety, and was plagued by fatigue and sleepless nights. She spent five days in France; ten days with Jacqueline poolside at the Beverly Hills Hotel, where her daughter learned to dive and where Barbara unsuccessfully tried her hand at tennis. She also did some work on a segment of her first special scheduled to debut in December, and worked on a couple of magazine pieces regarding her new job. Mostly, though, she fretted.

As she said, "It was hardly a glorious vacation."

"IS BARBARA
A JOURNALIST OR
IS SHE CHER?"

If Walter Cronkite or John Chancellor rather than Barbara Walters had been the first broadcast journalist to receive a million-dollar annual salary, one wonders whether there would have been the same national furor. The reaction to her new paycheck could not have been more contentious had she personally walked into the Bank of America with a machine gun, ordered the tellers to empty the vault, and mowed them down in cold blood. Fellow journalists fumed, news executives sputtered, pundits seethed, and editorial cartoonists depicted her reading the news in décolletage.

"What Makes Barbara Walters Worth a Million?" asked a headline in the *New York Times,* summing up the tempest that had been unleashed. An outcry of anger was raised, some of it likely sparked by sexism, among the best and brightest in the news business.

"When I first heard the offer," said *60 Minutes* correspondent Morley Safer to a Miami University audience, "a wave of nausea was my first reaction—with my second reaction being a spasm of nausea." Commenting on the fact that Barbara never seemed to mind doing dog food commercials on *Today*, he added, "She may be one hell of a reporter for all I know, if Alpo salesmen are reporters."

When Cronkite heard the news, he experienced "the sickening sensation that we were all going under, that all of our efforts to hold television news aloof from show business had failed."

Chancellor privately told colleagues that he was thankful NBC had decided to let Barbara go rather than give in and allow her to be his coanchor. David Brinkley, who was now working with Chancellor, said, "Being an anchor is not just a matter of sitting in front of a camera and looking pretty."

Former CBS News president Fred W. Friendly ridiculed the deal, saying, "It's sort of a throwback to the days of Walter Winchell when news was done by name people who got a lot of money—but there wasn't much journalism in it. People are not interested in getting news from people making a million dollars a year. I don't think people will accept news from millionaires. . . . Giving money to Barbara Walters is not going to give ABC parity [in news]."

Friendly's successor as head of CBS News, Richard Salant, declared, "I'm really depressed as hell. This isn't journalism—this is a minstrel show. Is Barbara a journalist or is she Cher? In fact, maybe ABC will hire Cher next. If this kind of circus atmosphere continues, and I have to join in it, I'll quit first. If Barbara Walters is a five-million-dollar woman, then Walter Cronkite is a sixteen-million-dollar man."

Connie Chung, then a Washington correspondent for CBS, dismissed Barbara as "an interviewer, a talk-show hostess; she does specials, not reporting, but *we* actually cover stories and then go back and report them." (In the spring of 1989, CBS, anxious to acquire a female heavy-hitter for its magazine program, *West 57th*, hired Chung away from NBC for a reported $1.5 million. Not one eye-brow was raised over the salary; seven-figure paychecks had become commonplace.)

ABC-TV sportscaster Chris Schenkel questioned the network's sense of values. Contending that sports was the only major profit center for the network, he asked, "If Bar-bara Walters is worth one million dollars, what are we worth?" And tossing a dart at her during a speech before the Executive Club in Phoenix, he proclaimed, "Barbara is the kind of girl who would vote a town dry, then move."

Bill Stout, a reporter at KNX-TV in Los Angeles, said the offer "proves how absurd the values are in the televi-sion industry" and predicted that other nationally known reporters would begin demanding higher salaries.

Russell Baker, in a *Times* column headlined GREENING OF THE PRESS, imagined that one day all reporters would be earning Barbara's kind of money. "In anticipation of the great day," he wrote, "I have already begun to practice thinking like a Republican."

Newsweek questioned Barbara's on-air style, contending that "her aggressively eager persona may not sit well with an audience accustomed to low-keyed avuncular anchor-men."

A headline over an Art Buchwald column in the *Wash-ington Post* asked, "A Million-Dollar Baby Handling 5-and-10 Cent News?"

Washington columnist Charles Seib observed, "The line between the news business and show business has been erased forever. [She's] up there with the likes of Johnny Carson and the rock star of your choice."

Even on Capitol Hill, Barbara's raise caused a fury. Senate Communications Subcommittee Chairman John Pastore called the salary "ridiculous." During an appropri-ations hearing, he declared, "The networks come before my committee and shed crocodile tears and complain about their profits. Then they pay this little girl a million dollars. That's five times better than the President of the United States makes!"

One of the regular features on *60 Minutes* at the time was "Point Counterpoint" with writer Shana Alexander verbally squaring off with conservative columnist James J. Kilpatrick. Alexander, who'd been mentioned as a possible successor to Barbara, felt her deal with ABC was "bad for news . . . not because the news biz and show biz are getting mixed up. They got mixed up a long time ago [but because this] whole country seems to be turning into a game show with game show standards and game show payoffs. But if we're all in this media circus," she emphasized, "I want to see Barbara in the center ring and if you think this is a sexist remark, you're damn right." Kilpatrick observed that Barbara's salary "is a quantitative measure of her worth today to ABC. If she bombs, she won't be worth six bits tomorrow and that isn't news biz or show biz. That's economics."

Over the years Barbara had developed the ability to isolate herself from criticism. But the deluge she now faced was hard to ignore. Even her mother tried to get Barbara to pay heed. During a visit to Miami, Dena asked Barbara to look at some stories. Barbara kept saying, "Mother, don't tell me. It hurts me; it spoils my day. I forget all the good things and remember only the bad."

Barbara tried as best she could to respond to the general clamor that her career move had aroused.

"I know there are many people who believe news people should be more pure than show business people," she told Les Brown of the *New York Times*. "They seem to feel that if you get a million bucks, you're a superstar. And if you're a superstar, you're show biz. And if you're show biz, you can't be pure and can't do justice to the news."

But the the attacks continued thick and fast. The ABC executives were thrilled. It was the most publicity their news operation had ever enjoyed. As one vice president said jubilantly, "How much would it cost to buy that amount of space and attention? It was worth a million right there."

But Barbara wasn't pleased, to say the least.

She decided to retaliate personally when former *Today* colleague Frank Blair commented publicly that during all the years he worked with her she was "aloof, very cold, very aggressive . . . rude and inhospitable." He told an advertising association gathering in Jacksonville, Florida, that while Barbara would be doing an interview on *Today* members of the crew and staff would often make remarks like "Oh, shut up, Barbara, and let him speak." Blair asserted that NBC officials were "delighted" to see her leave.

One of the articles Dena had given Barbara to read carried Blair's remarks. Barbara angrily tracked him down and telephoned him, demanding to know why he had gone after her, all of which she later reported in detail to the New York *Post.*

"Frank, why did you do it? For twelve years we were on the air together. We walked down the hall together with our arms around each other. When you left, we had a big party for you which I hosted," Barbara said she told Blair.

"Well, you're fair game," she claimed he responded. "They wanted something provocative."

"I don't want to get into a name-calling contest with Frank Blair," Barbara maintained. "We had a good relationship. He's a decent man. I'm sorry his own bitterness has been directed against me."

Barbara's comments concerning her purported camaraderie with Blair brought snickers from *Today* staffers. As Jane Schulberg noted, "Barbara treated Frank Blair much the way Frank McGee treated her—with complete contempt."

But Barbara wasn't through with Blair. She claimed to *Post* reporter Helen Dudar that Blair had not left the show voluntarily in 1975, and that his last months with *Today* were unhappy because he wanted a crack at being cohost.

Gloating over her own success, Barbara added, "I think

it must be very difficult for him and a lot of others who see what's happening to me, someone who started as a writer twelve years ago."

Barbara even called the *Today* show offices to garner support against Blair's blast. She said the stagehands and cue-card holders to whom she spoke didn't think she was anything like the way Blair had described her, and she noted that the staffers were going to put it in writing.

In fact, such a declaration was issued, signed by a dozen *Today* employees—wardrobe ladies, a director, a hair stylist, and a talent coordinator, among others. The letter lauded Barbara for her accomplishments and professionalism and noted that there were those who were trying to undermine her. She was praised by the signatories as a warm, thoughtful, and friendly person.

The missive, Barbara told Tom Snyder on his talk show, was sent to United Press International, which did a story and moved it on the wire, but she complained that few newspapers seemed interested in running it.

All of the sniping had upset and depressed Barbara. She felt hurt and violated, and was already beginning to wonder whether she'd made a terrible error by taking the job. The criticism would go on unabated for months. But that was nothing compared to what she'd face when she actually started working with Reasoner.

As a female TV colleague and friend of Barbara's put it so aptly, "Every time Harry went on the air with Barbara he looked like he smelled something bad."

NIGHTMARE AT ABC NEWS

In preparation for the first show and as a means of demonstrating to Barbara, Harry, the competition, the critics, and the public that they meant business, ABC News executives performed major surgery on the *Evening News*: the old newswriters were replaced by new newswriters; the old set was replaced by a new one; almost a dozen new correspondents, three of them women, were hired; the news budget was expanded by twenty-five percent; a new producer, Robert Siegenthaler—described variously as the "lion tamer" and the "hand holder"—was brought in to shape up the show and try to keep the peace between Barbara and Harry. There were several weeks of rehearsals and dry runs, including tests of Barbara's reaction speed to breaking news items. Barbara's biggest problem was reading the Teleprompter, and the set and cameras had to be rearranged several times. On the first day she reported to work, Barbara told Harry, "You're in a no-win situation," and he responded, "*You're* in a no-win situation." Then the two of them shook hands reluctantly and agreed to swim or sink together.

It seemed the whole world was watching at 7:00 P.M. on Monday, October 4, 1976, when the ABC *Evening News* with Harry Reasoner and Barbara Walters premiered. ABC executives were aware that the ratings for the first week or so would be enormous—and exaggerated—because most of the new viewers would be curiosity seekers, like those who show up at the scene of an automobile accident. The feud between the two had been given such a huge buildup that viewers expected—were hoping?—to see Barbara make a major gaffe, to watch Reasoner pummel her to the ground. It was the biggest television event since Jack Ruby shot Lee Harvey Oswald on camera. The hope at ABC, of course, was that Walters and Reasoner would be able to keep some of those new viewers without resorting to violence.

"About two seconds before we went on the air I thought, 'Please, God . . .' but that was all the time I had to think about it," Barbara recalled. Reasoner, looking dapper in a suit and checked blue shirt, opened the program with a teaser about the latest from deposed Agriculture Secretary Earl Butz, who had been accused of making racist remarks, and then he introduced Barbara, who looked radiant. Her hair shining with blond highlights, Barbara was wearing a red silk dress, topped by a blue velvet vest with a small jeweled pin on her left lapel. The two were sitting at a sleek, silvery gray gull-wing desk with two monitors for interviews.

At first Barbara seemed tense and stilted, but appeared to relax when she did her big item of the evening—the first of a two-part pretaped satellite interview about events in the Middle East with her friend President Anwar el-Sadat of Egypt. Sadat seemed as excited about the premiere of the new show as anyone. Revealing that he had been asked to send troops into Lebanon, he noted gallantly, "I must tell you quite frankly, Barbara, this is for you for the first time." (In the second part of the interview, on Tuesday night, Sadat, whose annual salary was twelve thousand dollars a year, couldn't help mentioning Barbara's extraordinary paycheck. She smiled, claiming she worked "not for money, but for love," causing Sadat to chortle.)

Broadcasting magazine, in an editorial about the debut, noted, "If the Sadat remark was not cued by an ABC press agent, it sounded that way. That sort of thing will be edited out of future interviews unless Miss Walters is to be a million-dollar baby in a five-and-ten-cent show."

One of Barbara's biggest fears before the first program was that she'd flub a word, giving credence to all the naysayers who contended that she wasn't a newsreader—that her speech impediment would, in fact, impede the newscast. "I'm being tested again," she said, "and it will be my luck to flub the first four words." In the first show, though, she had a bit of trouble with only one word—administration—but recovered quickly. (Barbara later reacted to such problems in good humor. On a subsequent broadcast, she had trouble during rehearsal pronouncing the letter *r* in Mount Ararat—it came out sounding like "Mount Awawat." Jokingly, she handed the script back to the writer asking why it couldn't be Mount Kisco.)

Near the end of the first half-hour, Barbara said how happy she was to be working again, telling her NBC fans who had switched over to watch her, "I missed you." She also noted that many of those watching the program were there because of "curiosity brought on by . . . my hourly wage," and expressed hope they would tune in again out of conviction, promising that "Harry and I will try to bring you the best darn news program on the air. I'd like to pause from time to time as we shower news items on you and say, 'Wait a minute. What does this mean to my life and yours?' "

At the close, Reasoner joked—or at least it seemed that way—that he'd "kept time" on Barbara's stories and told her, "You owe me four minutes." In fact, as time would tell, he wasn't kidding.

Bob Williams of the New York *Post* felt Barbara's "decibels climbed to those of someone who can't quite make herself heard over a bad long-distance phone connection" during her interview with Sadat. "She, of course, will bear further watching and adjustment. One could hardly accuse her of being anything less than calm, if not collected, in her first outing, but she certainly was not as suave or skilled as Reasoner."

Time magazine observed acidly, "The format ABC has fashioned around its new evening star may not be the best, but it is as personalized as Walters' weadily wecognizable delivewy (W-R substitution, speech therapists call it)."

John J. O'Connor of the *Times* saw a "not entirely tenuous" connection between the debut of the Reasoner-Walters show and the season opener that same night of *Mary Hartman, Mary Hartman,* an offbeat soap opera parody. In one scene, a mental patient assures Mary that her recent breakdown on a TV program had made breakdowns respectable. "I wouldn't be surprised," she said, "if Harry Reasoner did it next."

A major irony in Barbara's move to ABC is that while *she* was the first woman to be made an anchor and to get the largest salary ever paid a newsperson, everyone seemed to be bending over backward to make sure *Harry* felt equal—because if he was not kept happy, if he blew his stack, the whole show could go down the tube.

Besides getting equal pay, he got equal time, and equal space. Harry *did* make up for the four minutes he lost to Barbara on the first show, and would continue to do so. Once, an interview by Barbara ran more than five minutes. Reasoner was furious and went out and did a report on football that ran the same length of time. In the newsroom and Studio 7, from where the program originated, there was an undeclared war between supporters of Barbara and of Reasoner, each side keeping a count of the number of minutes each had on air, reporting the number to their respective leader.

The executives placated Reasoner in every way possible, even making sure his new office was as big as Barbara's new office—to the inch; Reasoner's chambers were decorated in subdued manly beiges and rusts, while Barbara's looked more Latin Quarter than news department: a French Provincial ambience with pink velvet pillows, pink velvet chairs, and a pink-sprayed typewriter. The room was decorated by a set designer brought in from NBC. No one had ever been given such royal treatment at ABC News and a lot of staffers besides Reasoner felt resentful.

Even when it came to something seemingly as minor as makeup, Harry demanded and received equal treatment. Well-known makeup artist Way Bandy claimed that when Reasoner learned that Bandy was doing Barbara's face for a photo layout in a national magazine, Reasoner insisted Bandy do *his*, too. "I hear he made a big scene about it," Bandy said.

As feared—despite all the equity and parity in the world—Harry wasn't happy and it showed, first off camera, then on.

One producer recalled getting on an elevator with Barbara during the early days of the program and stopping at an intermediate floor where Harry stood waiting to go up. Never saying hello, not even offering a curt nod of recognition, he got in the car, turned his back to Barbara, pressed the button, and ascended in deadly silence.

"It was terrible for Barbara," recalled a woman colleague who was involved in the show. "Half the job of a friend of mine was to keep Harry from striking Barbara at the end of each show because she'd reach out to touch him and he'd draw back as though she had come down with the plague. He'd turn around to the guys on the set and say, 'Okay, I need a drink. Who's going to come drinking with me?' This all was in earshot of Barbara." Most of the crew on the show were old buddies of Reasoner's and would gab with him, all but ignoring Barbara.

Veteran ABC news executive Av Westin, who would eventually have the assignment of breaking up the team of Walters and Reasoner, said Harry viewed Barbara as an interloper on the air, and that it clearly showed: "Conversations had overtones of sarcasm [and] facial expressions conveyed a patronizing tolerance of Barbara."

Barbara's early *Today* colleague Anita Colby recalled watching one night and being appalled at Harry's treatment of her. "He made a remark that had some sexual connotation and I felt it was very rude. I don't know how she could keep a stiff upper lip. It would have dissolved me into tears—but she's tough. I was so angry I wrote a letter of complaint to the president of ABC."

Barbara had done a story about Henry Kissinger. As an aside, she said to Reasoner, "You know, Harry, Kissinger didn't do too badly as a sex symbol in Washington." Reasoner, glowering, responded, "Well, you'd know more about that than I would."

While Colby wrote complaining about Reasoner, a good bit of the mail was unfavorable toward Barbara, too. Viewers who wrote in received an unprecedented form letter from ABC asking them to "keep an open mind and tune in for a reasonable period before making your decision."

One of the executives at ABC from whom Barbara sought advice and solace was Marty Rubenstein. "Barbara very much wanted it to succeed—to the point of asking me, 'What do I have to do to make it succeed?' I don't recall whether she cried or not, but she was very concerned, emotionally concerned. She has a great deal of professional pride. She doesn't like the thought of failure, and the program obviously was not succeeding and that disturbed her tremendously."

At first, the Walters-Reasoner program's ratings and audience share jumped, but the viewers apparently didn't come from CBS or NBC. Analysts determined that more than a million and a half persons who didn't normally watch any evening news program tuned in to see her and Harry go at it. By the end of the first month, however, the ratings had slipped to slightly above what they were before Barbara came aboard.

Before long the worst-case scenario had become a reality: the tension between Reasoner and Walters had become so apparent that they rarely were shown together on camera. It was as if there were two separate shows, one anchored by Reasoner, the other by Barbara. There were times, Barbara later told the *Ladies Home Journal,* "when [Harry] would come down and barely say good evening. It was as if we were in two separate studios and we didn't know how to find our way back to each other."

As Roger Rosenblatt pointed out in the *New Republic,* "Harry Reasoner . . . seems as comfortable on camera with Walters as a governor under indictment."

By the time Barbara and Harry began rehearsing for the November 1976 election night coverage, "they weren't talking to each other except on absolutely necessary things," said Walter Pfister, who was ABC's vice president and executive producer in charge of special events coverage from 1973 to 1978. Pfister, who had the difficult task of whipping the two of them into shape for election night, mostly met with Barbara and Reasoner separately, "because I knew what the chemistry was. Barbara was going through a tremendous amount of pressure at the time. She resented Harry's attitude. Her ego was bruised."

Election night coverage involves an ability to deal with huge amounts of new information and an easygoing give and take between the anchors—both of which were lacking as the race between President Gerald Ford and former Georgia governor Jimmy Carter got down to the November 2 wire.

"Barbara was at a great disadvantage," Pfister said, "[because] she'd never done an election night as far as I knew, and Harry had a reputation of not working very hard. So we had a strange combination of kind of a natural athlete like Harry not going into training and not doing much homework, and Barbara who'd never been on the playing field before, but [who was] working like the devil to try to make it work."

By election night, everyone from the copy boys to directors knew that Barbara and Reasoner were at war, and some were even savoring the situation. "Barbara was nervous and uptight and everybody was very concerned about her condition because she's a high-strung person," said Pfister. "There were times when I felt really sorry for her. When the pressure built up she'd get bitchy; she'd become demanding but underneath was this layer of tension, but there was nothing anyone could do. At the end of the night Barbara just wanted to get out of there."

After the election coverage and the criticism of her work, Barbara told *TV Guide*'s Frank Swertlow, "I could have died. I wanted to call ABC and say, 'Let me out of the contract. I can't take it anymore.'"

By Thanksgiving, the *New York Times* reported "friction" between Barbara and Reasoner, and indications that their personalities "have not been meshing." Siegenthaler said the two had "a correct professional relationship on television, and that is what counts." He predicted it would take a year for the program to become a contender.

The situation was even worse in January 1977 when ABC covered the Carter inaugural festivities. "Neither one of them wanted to sit in with the other," recalled Pfister, "so I held two separate meetings. I went over the format with Harry and his writer and his people in his office, and then I had the same meeting with Barbara and her writer. I had no choice; we couldn't say, 'We're not going on because they're not talking to each other.'"

For Barbara, the adverse publicity about her salary combined with the unbearable problems of working with Reasoner had made her life a nightmare. Had she been able to predict what was going to happen, she would have taken the job for less money, or not taken it at all, she confided to friends.

DOYENNE
OF DISH

For months Barbara was the target of sorties by journalists and critics from print and television. Despite the onslaught, she was able to forge at least one close, mutually beneficial, and enduring relationship with a journalist who refrained from joining the lynch mob: a promising "doyenne of dish" named Liz Smith.

The daughter of a cotton broker from Fort Worth, Smith came to New York in the late 1940s with a degree in journalism from the University of Texas and a failed marriage to an Air Force man. After stints at a movie magazine and low-level radio and TV jobs, she went to work for Hearst's flamboyantly conservative *Journal-American*, where she helped put together items for a venerable gossip column that ran under the Cholly Knickerbocker pseudonym. The column actually was the long-time domain of fashion designer Oleg Cassini's brother, Igor. When Cassini left, Smith, who'd actually been writing the column for five years, hoped to fill his shoes, but the job went instead to a New York socialite because Smith was considered an unknown by the *Journal-American*'s publisher.

Subsequently another Texan, Aileen Mehle, better known as Suzy, took over the column, which ran under the byline of Suzy Knickerbocker. Finally, in February 1976—a couple of months before Barbara made her move to ABC—Smith was hired by the New York *Daily News* and her column caught on.

During the height of the brouhaha over Barbara's big-bucks deal, Smith saw her as a phenomenon and powerhouse worth cultivating, so she telephoned and invited her to lunch, and Barbara readily accepted.

Barbara always loved gossip and maintained friends in the business, dating back to her nightclub-hopping days with Hearstians Jack O'Brian and George Sokolsky. Now, more than ever, feeling alone and isolated, with the press attacking her from all sides, Barbara felt the need for a journalist in her corner, especially a woman; Liz Smith happened to come along at the right time.

Smith and Barbara had their first get-together at the Café des Artistes near ABC and felt an immediate rapport. "Instead of it being a professional lunch, we were very friendly and dishy and had a lot of fun," Smith recalled. "Afterwards, she invited me to her parties and introduced me to people like the Kissingers. She didn't act like she was doing it deliberately. She just did it. She liked me. I think she really loves me. She was important to my career. She's just been such a good friend to me. If you're writing a column, people are afraid of you and wary and everybody doesn't run up and lick your hand," Smith observed. "There's a difference between writing a column and having any kind of social acceptance. While I wasn't really looking for social acceptance, because of Barbara I got a lot of it."

Smith began writing positive items about Barbara in her column, and staunchly defended her against detractors. "People like to take shots at her because she's so omnipresent. Privately, she's just an extremely nice, generous, loving person."

John Springer, who worked as Barbara's personal publicist on two different occasions, said he found it all but impossible during his tenure to place items about Barbara with Suzy because of the Walters-Smith relationship. "Aileen and Liz are bitter rivals," noted Springer, "and because Liz is so friendly with, and fond of, Barbara, and always prints material and information on Barbara, Aileen wouldn't. I could never break Suzy's column with an item about Barbara. If I called her, she'd say, 'Give it to Liz. She does the stories on Barbara Walters.'"

While Suzy and Barbara are friendly—except for a time during the mid-1980s—they are not on an intimate footing as are Liz and Barbara, nor has Aileen ever sought to be close to her. Suzy once told a colleague that Barbara "is not my kind of woman. She's an operator of the first order, seeking as much publicity as she possibly can get for social purposes, for her career, for 'Isn't Barbara great?'"

Suzy always had disdain for the kind of items Smith wrote about Barbara, which the columnist has described as "puff pieces—the most incredible sort of fawning and flattery. It's sort of a quid pro quo. Liz goes out to lunch with Barbara, and Barbara gets a great big wonderful story written about her. There's never been one derogatory line."

Susan Mulcahy, editor of the gossip column in New York *Newsday*, noted that Smith "writes about Barbara more than any of the other columnists."

"Liz is like Barbara's personal publicist," maintained publicist Peter Levinson, a former colleague of Springer's.

By the late 1980s, *Spy*, a New York–based, antiestablishment satirical magazine, began running a popular feature called the "Liz Smith Tote Board," which contained a monthly tally of the names most often mentioned by the columnist; Barbara was usually at or near the top of the list.

"I do mention her a lot because I have access to her and just through knowing her personally, and being friends with her, pick up a lot of little things to say about her," said Smith. "I'm not kidding myself that [celebrities] all love me for myself. But as a matter of fact, I think Barbara does. So many wonderful things happened to me as a result of knowing her. I don't make any bones about it when I write about her. She's my friend and everybody knows that and if they want to discount what I write they will."

The countless mentions of Barbara in the columns of Liz Smith and others documented nothing more than her glamorous life in the social whirl of New York City. Barbara had come a long way from the shy and withdrawn Kappa Pi reject of years gone by. She had compensated for that snub to some extent with her group in college. But in the Seventies and Eighties, Barbara had become the queen of the ball, the fairest of the fair; she'd been invited into, had pledged for, and was one of the most adored members of the most exclusive and fabulous sorority of all; she was at the top of the A list of the Women Who Count. Virtually every morning Liz Smith, or the other chroniclers of the rich and famous—William Norwich, Cindy Adams, Jim Revson, Richard Johnson, and sometimes even Suzy—told readers of their columns what Barbara had done the night before: cohosting a party for media baron Rupert Murdoch's wife Anna's new novel; being an attendant at Arianna Stassinopoulos Huffington's wedding; dining with other swells in one of the venerable salons—Alice Mason's, or Mollie Parnis's, or Mildred Hilson's; attending a charity gala where Barbara and other society and celebrity guests—Malcolm Forbes, the Calvin Kleins, the Donald Trumps—routinely paid $2,500 each for a tax-deductible seat.

SOLVING THE
BARBARA PROBLEM

Within six months after the Barbara and Harry show debuted, everyone in the executive suite at ABC News knew it was an utter, complete, and embarrassing disaster, but no one was willing to pull the plug. Too many careers and reputations were at stake; one major blunder had been made; no one wanted to be responsible for a second. They thought if they kept quiet long enough, the problem might go away and Harry and Barbara would settle into a relationship as harmonious as June and Ward Cleaver's. Besides, Barbara's coanchor contract was tighter than a Harry Reasoner smile in response to a Barbara Walters quip. Among the cognoscenti, Barbara and Harry had become known as "Price and Pride."

In the first half of 1977, Barbara was beset by rumors that she was on her way out. *TV Guide,* in an unprecedented editorial, suggested that she should quit. "The problem is she is miscast in the anchor spot," the magazine said, advising her to return to interviewing.

"Dumping on Baba Wawa has become the chicest occupation around town these days," noted a *Village Voice* writer. The Palm Beach *Post-Times* agreed: "Men bluster she's a bomb. . . . Women swear her slurry speech is worse, her upper lip more frozen, and they don't like her eye shadow or her earrings. . . . [There are] Baba Wawa and Hawee Weasonuh jokes."

Besides being embattled during this period, Barbara faced the loss of the most important man in her life. After a long illness, Lou Walters died in Miami on August 15, 1977. Her sister, Jackie, would die in November 1985, and her mother, in June 1988.

One of the most vicious stories about Barbara appeared in a women's magazine called *Viva*. The lead paragraph described Barbara as talking "in her lisping, upper-class-cum-Jewish-Bronx accent, her improbably lacquered hair looking as if it were placed in one piece on the top of her head, her bottom lip protruding like a rubber flap. On TV, at least, her clothes come off looking like early Sears, Roebuck catalog specials." The writer of the piece later asserted that he never wrote those and other negative descriptions about Barbara but that they were put in during the editing process.

Barbara seemed to become the bull's-eye for every rabid male chauvinist and jealous female in America. She'd also unfairly become *the* scapegoat for everything that was perceived as wrong with television in general and broadcast news in particular. So fearful was she of actual retribution that early on she'd hired bodyguards to protect her daughter.

Reports circulated that ABC was thinking of sending her to Washington, where she would continue to coanchor, with Reasoner remaining in New York. Two hundred and fifty miles seemed distance enough to keep the two from tearing each other apart. "We get along very well," Barbara responded to talk about the shift. "But that's like saying you've stopped beating your wife." Reasoner told another reporter, "We're not great drinking buddies."

A few hours after Bill Sheehan told a reporter he would not be adverse to Barbara working out of Washington, she telephoned and gave him a piece of her mind. He then issued a public statement saying she would remain in New York.

Meanwhile, Reasoner had made plans to bail out that were kept secret from Barbara.

"I made a deal with Harry that if this didn't work out in the first year and a half," Sheehan acknowledged, "he'd be free to leave. It was something that he wanted and the feeling was at the time, 'Well, if it isn't working by that time, then we'll be trying to do something else anyway.' "

Amidst all of the sturm und drang Barbara continued working as hard as ever. She did her first special; she interviewed Fidel Castro in a program that received excellent reviews; she moderated one of the Ford-Carter Presidential debates; and she covered Queen Elizabeth's Silver Jubilee, among other high-visibility assignments.

The beginning of the end came in January 1978.

Seven months earlier, veteran ABC Sports boss Roone Arledge took over the presidency of the news department as well, replacing Sheehan, who resigned shortly thereafter. Reasoner would later say that Arledge was brought in "to salvage the wreckage of Fred Pierce's judgment." Around the same time that Sheehan left, Marlene Sanders departed for CBS. Others who had been in power when Barbara was hired would follow suit. As Reasoner put it, "The debacle of the two of us as a team led to a general shakeup."

Arledge's mission was to reverse the performance of the *Evening News*. He quickened the pace of the show, hired more staffers, and made greater use of electronic gizmos. Barbara was assigned to do stories and interviews outside of the studio on a more frequent basis—thus separating her from Harry.

In early January, Arledge learned from Reasoner about the verbal agreement he had with Sheehan. Feeling he had no other alternative, Reasoner decided to exercise his option and return to CBS, leaving ABC effective June 1. He'd been the anchor there for almost eight years. His resignation settled fifty percent of the dilemma.

To deal with what was referred to as "the Barbara problem," Arledge conceived a newscast *without* an actual anchor, thus avoiding embarrassing Barbara and circumventing her contract without violating it. Instead, the new show, called *World News Tonight*, would have three desks—one for foreign news, with Peter Jennings in London; one for national stories, with Max Robinson in Chicago; and the other desk in Washington staffed by Frank Reynolds, who would act as the ringmaster.

Barbara was headquartered in New York, where she'd be the new team's star reporter, chasing big-name interviews, but not reading or introducing stories. In effect, she'd been demoted from being the highest paid newsreader in the world to the highest-paid legwoman. Reasoner called the new format "the Arledge shell game," adding, "He more or less successfully concealed from the watching public the fact that Barbara was no longer any kind of an anchor."

But Barbara, who immediately bonded with the flashy Arledge, claimed she was delighted. "This is what I've been wanting to do since I came here. From the day I was hired, I asked them not to put me on the air *just* to read."

"Barbara's own initiative kept her going," said Bill Sheehan. "Roone liked her and kept her involved, kept her active in major stories. There was never any feeling regarding Barbara that we'd thrown away a million dollars. It's not amazing that she stayed on top because she worked at it very hard. She didn't coast. She has this drive that just won't stop. She's an ambitious woman."

Within a year, the amount of time Barbara spent on the nightly news was reduced from three times a week to once a week, and eventually to occasional major interviews. Her specials and her eventual coanchor role on *20/20* would bring her even greater fame and power.

In his 1981 autobiography, *Before the Colors Fade*, Reasoner maintained that the hiring of Barbara was a "bad idea—not because a woman coanchor is a bad idea, not because Barbara Walters was a bad idea as an individual. It was a bad idea because, whether it was a stunt or not, it was going to be perceived as a stunt."

SPECIAL LADY

Amidst the tumult of 1976, the announcement that Barbara's contract called for her to do four prime-time specials was all but lost. There were sporadic mentions that her *Royal Lovers* special at NBC was a bust, so none of the critics or TV columnists had any great expectations for the scheduled shows, ignoring what would become an overnight cash cow for ABC and a major success for Barbara. The premiere of the first special in December would change all that.

From the very beginning, Fred Pierce had a gut feeling that the *Barbara Walters Special* programs would be the tail that wagged the dog.

"Everyone underplayed the value that the specials had," observed Pierce, who left ABC in 1986. "They saw them as being a sop, so to speak, to Barbara. But from my point of view, I knew they were going to have a lot of value—not only financially, but imagewise. Over the years, those programs gave ABC a tremendous amount of visibility.

What those specials did financially was hedge any down-side risk in hiring Barbara."

In fact, Barbara's bounty was virtually covered before the ink on her contract was dry.

"The four specials were fully sold to General Electric be-fore she came on board—the profit paid for her salary and the shows and everything else," revealed Marty Ruben-stein. "So from a business point of view it was a stroke of genius on the part of Pierce."

When Barbara learned that the commercial time had sold out "she was terribly excited," recalled Rubenstein. "She was absolutely delighted that somebody wanted to buy prime-time specials with her appearing on them."

Work on the first special began during the late summer before Barbara started her coanchor duties. Despite some of the personality problems that surfaced during produc-tion of the *Royal Lovers* show, Barbara named Lucy Jarvis as the producer of the first four specials because there was still "an underlying respect and affection for each other," said a member of the production team. That would change—there would be serious friction between Walters and Jarvis during the shooting and editing.

The first special, as determined mostly by Barbara, would feature a profile of one of her idols, singer Barbra Streisand and her ex-hairdresser lover, Jon Peters (Barbara was known to do an excellent imitation of Streisand); a visit with President-elect Jimmy Carter and his wife, Rosa-lyn, in their home in Plains, Georgia; and a tour of Barba-ra's own Manhattan apartment.

Problems surfaced immediately in Los Angeles during the Streisand shoot.

"It was not a pleasant situation," said John J. Desmond, the director. He said that "contractually Barbra Streisand had the approval of the final edit" and, as a result, Strei-sand, a perfectionist like Barbara, was extremely concerned about every aspect of the production and postproduction process. Streisand's powerful agent, Sue Mengers, policed the proceedings to make certain her client was protected.

During the taping, Barbara asked Streisand some questions of a personal nature that apparently were not part of the ground rules the two had agreed upon and Streisand became worried they'd become part of the final cut. "Sue Mengers got violently angry and kept after Barbara Walters, but she never ruffled a feather," said the director. "Barbara said to Sue, 'No, of course, I told Barbra that we won't use this.' Mengers was absolutely baiting Barbara, and Streisand was getting very nervous over all the commotion."

Barbara was under intense pressure to complete the program on a tight schedule, so she kept her focus on getting the job done, ignoring—but not forgetting—the personality conflicts that were erupting. General Electric, she was aware, had bought the show with designated time slots and the first special was scheduled to run in the lucrative advertising window just before Christmas. She also wanted the show finished without any adverse publicity surfacing about production problems; Barbara was getting enough guff over her salary and coanchor role.

In Plains, the Carters were unprepared for the onslaught of a Hollywood-style crew descending upon them—sound and lighting technicians, cameramen, director, producer, assistant producer, makeup artist, and what seemed like miles of electrical cables strewn about their home. Outside, the crew set up a generator and parked a trailer packed with video gear that was used as a control room. The Carters were used to the quick and dirty television of two-men news crews, but nothing like the arrival of Barbara Walters. "We descended," said associate producer JoAnn Goldberg, "like Genghis Khan."

Flying in and out of Plains was difficult and dangerous, with Barbara and the crew using single-engine planes during a period of terrible weather. The night before the actual interview, Barbara flew in after doing a late night newscast in New York, arriving at the ungodly hour of four in the morning because area airports were fogged in. "I went into makeup," said Desmond, "to see how she was. She said, 'Don't ask. Don't ask. I'm just fine, just fine.' She always kept her physical dilemma out of it."

During the time Barbara's production team was overrunning the Carter household, the president-elect was involved in the important task of putting his administration together. "There was actually one point while we were setting up around the house where he was on the phone and being backed into the bathroom for privacy so he could discuss potential cabinet appointments," Goldberg recalled. "He couldn't get away from us. He was always trying to find a corner to conduct business."

Back in New York, the last segment shot was the one in Barbara's apartment. It was a decision of Barbara's that would have made Machiavelli proud. Barbara realized at the outset that it would be difficult getting celebrities to invite her into their homes for future specials. So she decided it would be good public relations to open her own apartment to the cameras. That way, she felt, she wouldn't be asking other celebrities to do something she wouldn't do herself.

The problems started again during editing, which was done in the ASCAP Building where Barbara's production company had its office. Streisand had one of her people present to monitor the process.

"What we were doing was taking editing notes from Streisand's group," said the director, "and it was sometimes very difficult to accommodate her" because several cameras had been used, making editing more complex. "It seemed to me the interview lost a lot of spontaneity in order to conform to Barbra Streisand's notes."

One staffer recalled getting a telephone call at home one night while the editing of the Streisand segment was still underway. "It was Barbra Streisand telling me that it was imperative that we use the exterior shot of the front of her house that showed a pot of begonias," the staffer said. "I thought it was a joke, but I was afraid not to go along with it so I said I would pass the information on and I did, and it [really] was her."

Years later, Barbara stated publicly that Streisand "worried about everything—every question I'd asked, every word she uttered."

During the editing, Barbara and Jarvis started to go at it.

One of the issues was Barbara's unhappiness with the opening montage that Jarvis had ordered, said Desmond, who was caught in the crossfire. Twelve years after that first show, Barbara still felt the opening was "terrible," and emphasized the fact at the beginning of her fiftieth special in 1988.

"They had words. There was a lot of friction; voices were raised and tempers were short," said Desmond. "At one point I stepped in and said, 'Stop it!' And the ladies obeyed me. Barbara left and I scolded Lucy. They were protecting their own territory. Barbara was enormously concerned since it was her first special, and Lucy was feeling that it was her show."

The first *Barbara Walters Special* aired at 10:00 P.M. on December 14, 1976. Millions of Americans watched the program. One who didn't was coanchor Reasoner, who said he was "out drinking." The critics generally panned the show. *Variety*, for one, said, "The banality was equally dispensed. . . . If this is a preview of future Walters specials . . . she may be doing irremediable damage to the reputation she's trying to cultivate as a journalist. . . . It's one thing to go easy on a fellow media star like Streisand, but one might expect tougher questions than were aimed at the new President."

But what do critics know? Barbara garnered a thirty-six percent share of the TV viewing audience—a record rating for such a program in prime time. The show was a hit.

Meanwhile, a furor almost as big as the one over her salary and coanchor job exploded because of a loaded question she posed to the Carters and a plea she made to the President-elect. Viewers were shocked and critics flabbergasted when Barbara said, "I don't know how to ask you this, so I'll just ask it . . . Do you sleep in a double bed or twin beds?" The President-elect, looking at his wife, smiled, giggled, and said, "Double bed. Always have. Sometimes we sleep in a single bed. But it's much more comfortable in a double bed." But causing the most outrage was Barbara's closing line to the President-elect. In her most effusive manner, she asked Carter to "be wise with us, Governor, be good to us."

In private, ABC News executives who watched the show were horrified. "You could have thrown up," Marlene Sanders recalled as her reaction.

Raising the loudest outcry publicly was CBS's Morley Safer who, on his *Morley Safer's Journal*, aired on 270 radio stations around the country, reported, "There she was, the first female American pope blessing a new cardinal."

Safer stated that Barbara had "effectively withdrawn herself from the profession of journalism" and become "fair game" for criticism by her peers.

> The interview with Governor Carter is really what ended Ms. Walters' brief career as a journalist and placed her firmly in the ranks of . . . what? The Merv Griffins and Johnny Carsons? Well, sort of. What right does any reporter have to issue such a benediction? And why indeed 'Be wise with us, be good to us?' Why not be firm with us, be kinky with us, or even be funny with us? . . . It is as if Mr. Carter had just become Louis XIV and, without Pope Barbara's admonition, he might be dumb with us and mean to us.

In a blast at Barbara's tour of her apartment, Safer stated, "Perhaps it was a sense of financial superiority that made Barbara's benediction irresistible. Sandwiched between the white bread of the Carters and the pumpernickel of Streisand, we were treated to the pastrami of Ms. Walters herself."

At the time, Barbara declined to respond. "He is entitled to his opinions," she said, adding that she was pleased with the Carter interview because it "conveyed a certain sense of the new President that people before were not familiar with." A dozen years later, Barbara said, "I'll never hear the end of that."

Less than two months after the special aired, the press learned that Barbara and Lucy Jarvis had severed their ties, but no reason was ever given as to why.

Richard Turley, a New York lawyer, claimed Jarvis told him that she had spirited the master videotape of the special out of the country so that she could reedit it to her liking.

Turley said he first met Jarvis at the twenty-fifth wedding anniversary party for gossip columnist Cindy Adams and her husband, Joey, at Roy Cohn's house, not long after Barbara's special aired. Turley had approached Jarvis about producing a TV special featuring his friend Aileen (Suzy) Mehle.

During the course of their association, Turley said, "Lucy told me that things were so out of control that she took the master tapes to Paris and holed up in the Ritz Hotel for two weeks reediting the show to her satisfaction. It was a big power play between these two television egomaniacs."

In the beginning, despite her reputation, Barbara didn't have the kind of carte blanche entree into the homes of celebrities that she would possess in later years. In fact, for the first few years, booking guests was an uphill battle because many celebrities were fearful that Barbara would be tough on them, and that they'd be put in a position where they couldn't handle themselves.

Barbara and her staff developed a sales pitch, telling potential guests that the special was a safe vehicle to show their good side, to respond to a controversy, or to react to criticism. In other words, to generate positive publicity. While no one was ever again given the right of final edit, or control over content, guests were allowed to delineate areas that they *didn't* want Barbara asking them about.

But once the cameras were rolling, Barbara found to her delight that invariably the celebrities themselves would bring up the subjects they least wanted to discuss. For the most part, Barbara was able to gain their confidence because of her appearances on the news. Being interviewed by the woman who was trusted by Richard Nixon and Middle Eastern leaders carried considerable weight with a sit-com star, a rock musician, or an actor.

As it turned out, the news nourished the specials and vice versa. Barbara was finding that important news figures were more agreeable to being interviewed by her because they saw the enormous audiences she was able to generate with her quarterly specials.

By the spring of 1982, despite incredible popularity and consistently strong ratings, no major magazine or newspaper had ever done an in-depth profile of the specials, something that Barbara quietly craved. The only press comments were in the form of reviews, which for the most part continued to be negative.

"The press never really paid attention to the specials," said JoAnn Goldberg. "There was never a major article. Nobody ever came on location. No one ever even *asked* to come on location."

While Barbara sought a story, she was wary of the press, and feared allowing access to a writer in sheep's clothing who might do a hatchet job. In Barbara's mind, all reporters she didn't know were suspect, so she had to be careful whom she selected.

The opportunity for the kind of piece Barbara desired was offered to her in the salon of Richard and Shirley Clurman. The Clurmans' apartment, a few blocks from Barbara's 555 Park Avenue digs, was often the setting for elegant dinner parties, studded with members of New York's media, political, and business aristocracies: the William Buckleys, the David Halberstams, the Henry Kissingers, the Edgar Bronfmans, the Henry Grunwalds, Barbara Walters and various escorts, to name but a few.

Richard Clurman was a respected and longtime news executive at Time Inc. Shirley Clurman, who had been close to Clare Boothe Luce, the ambassador, congresswoman, writer, and widow of *Time* magazine's cofounder Henry R. Luce, was working as an assistant editor at *People* magazine. The title, however, was a misnomer. Clurman was actually a *People* operative and evangelist—using her substantial influence and contacts to promote the magazine's image and help it to gain access to people who ordinarily wouldn't deal with the publication. She received a retainer for providing ideas, access, and occasional story files.

Knowing that Barbara was seeking a story on the specials, Clurman gave a small dinner party to which she invited Barbara and Patricia Ryan, the new managing editor of *People*. "I said to Barbara, 'You know, we could do something on you.' I found Barbara a very interesting and engaging kind of person," said Ryan. "I liked her and thought she would be an excellent story for us."

Ryan didn't get an immediate okay because Barbara was angry at *People* for negative comments made about her in a story published two years earlier. She had vehemently complained to *People* editor Richard Stolley, who stood by his reporter, Cheryl McCall.

Another sticking point for Barbara in dealing with *People* was Stolley himself. Barbara had a crush of sorts on him. Shirley Clurman once arranged for Stolley to accompany Barbara to a dinner party at the Clurman apartment, but the evening disintegrated when Barbara squared off verbally with another guest, Pulitzer Prize–winning journalist and author David Halberstam.

At the Clurmans' that evening, Barbara worked the room, resourcefully seeking questions from each guest for a forthcoming interview with President Reagan. Before conducting interviews, Barbara routinely picked the brains of people around her, claiming that in this way she'd ask the kind of questions to which people wanted answers.

When she got to Halberstam, he told her bluntly that he had no questions for her. Halberstam was one of those journalists who saw Barbara as a symbol of the incursion of entertainment into the field of news, and therefore refused to play her question game.

At the dinner table, Barbara and Halberstam got into a heated debate over the subject of Israel. Acting offended and hurt, Barbara excused herself at the first opportune moment, asking Stolley to take her home. Any chance for a relationship between them, at least in Barbara's mind, had fizzled.

But Shirley Clurman assured her that *People* would give her fair treatment, and Barbara consented.

Unaware of the past problems that *People* had had with Barbara, Pat Ryan assigned the *Barbara Walters Special* story to Cheryl McCall.

The itinerary called for McCall and a photographer to accompany Barbara and her entourage to Austin, Texas, where Barbara would interview country singer Willie Nelson. McCall would then follow Barbara to Los Angeles to watch the segment being edited. The *People* cover story would coincide with the broadcast of Barbara's twentieth special, which also featured Carol Burnett and Clint Eastwood.

Problems between Barbara and McCall began virtually the moment they stepped into the first-class section of the plane to Austin. Barbara was traveling with her secretary and JoAnn Goldberg. Intently studying the briefing book, containing detailed biographical material on Nelson that was put together by an associate producer, Barbara noticed that some of the best stories carried McCall's byline. As a result of doing those stories, McCall, Willie, and his wife, Connie, had become close friends, which didn't sit well with Barbara.

In Austin, Barbara ordered McCall to stay in the background when she greeted Nelson for the first time. Barbara went forward and shook Nelson's hand. But when Willie spotted McCall standing off to the side as instructed, his face brightened and he made a beeline for her, giving McCall a big hug and a kiss. It was an awkward moment for Barbara, the star of the show, and she was livid because Willie appeared happier to see McCall than to meet his famous interviewer.

In Los Angeles, Barbara and the group checked into the Beverly Hills Hotel.

McCall was sitting by the pool reviewing her notes when Barbara paged her demanding to know why she wasn't with her to watch her do a paper edit of the Nelson transcript. When McCall explained that she had plans to accompany Nelson and his wife to the premiere of his new movie, Barbara threw a fit. "*Young lady!*" Barbara screamed. "If you get one thing wrong, if there are any inaccuracies in your story, I will be calling your editor because you are not being professional. You are not spending enough time with me. You're supposed to be doing the story on ME, NOT WILLIE!"

McCall explained that watching Barbara edit a transcript would wind up as one line in her finished story. And furthermore, "I'll make my own judgments! I am not your daughter! I am not your employee! I don't work for you!"

McCall, in her early thirties, felt that Barbara was not treating her with the respect she deserved as an experienced journalist.

It was like a whole mother-daughter thing of trying to make me feel guilty about how hurt her feelings were for leaving her home and going out.

She's incredibly manipulative; she's a control freak. She uses everything in her arsenal from yelling at you, to guilt. She doesn't use that on her staff because they are her subordinates and she just orders them. Direct orders. She issues rapid-fire orders and expects them to be done.

She's imperious. She treats people as though they are servants, not as though they are equal contributors when, in fact, she couldn't do what she does without them. She doesn't recognize that. She feels the world revolves around her. She perceives everything from a very egocentric perspective.

The next morning McCall was scheduled to watch Barbara oversee the final cut of the Willie Nelson segment. Just as she was about to leave, McCall got a message that Barbara had banned her because of the argument the previous evening.

"Come off it!" demanded McCall when she got Walters on the hotel's house phone. "You know this is really childish. It's really unprofessional." Barbara listened, not saying a word. Finally, McCall said, "Let's just call off the whole story right now. I'm supposed to do this from beginning to end. If you don't want to finish then I'll just go back to New York now."

Barbara relented and McCall was permitted to go along. When the session was over, McCall flew back to New York to write her story.

While the piece was being edited, Pat Ryan received a call from Henry Grunwald, Time Inc.'s editor-in-chief. Barbara had telephoned him complaining that the story being readied for publication was mean-spirited. Grunwald was "alarmed by whatever was alarming Barbara" and he wanted the matter fixed pronto, said Ryan.

"I don't remember the piece as being particularly scathing," said Ross Drake, the senior editor responsible for the story. "There were some things in it that I suppose Barbara could have objected to. I wasn't shocked that she was trying to get something done about it, and I wasn't surprised that she had a little muscle."

"People on the staff were basically outraged because Barbara, who claims to be a journalist, broke all the rules of journalism," asserted McCall. As an analogy, she explained, "If I had stolen a tape from ABC and showed it to the source first, and that subject tried to keep it from going on ABC, there would have been hell raised. What she did by complaining had a chilling effect. She does not see other journalists in the same light as herself. She thinks the rules don't apply to her."

An internal investigation by Ryan and other *People* editors determined that Shirley Clurman had leaked the story to Barbara.

"After reading Cheryl's story, Shirley said she knew Barbara would have a fit, so she called her right away," a Clurman confidante said. "Then Barbara got on the horn to Grunwald. Shirley was caught because Barbara complained."

Ryan immediately met with Grunwald, telling him, "This is intolerable. We're just going to have to get rid of [Clurman]." Grunwald said, "All right, if that's the way you feel and you know it happened."

Ryan then met with Clurman. "I went through why I felt so strongly [about what she had done]," said Ryan. "She was the one and only person that I ever remembered doing this. I wasn't after getting remorse. Nobody shouted. It was a calm conversation. I was rather forthright and determined that this would be the end of it. She didn't quit. I probably did not use the word 'fired'—you tend not to say, in the Hollywood tradition, 'You're fired'—but I said, 'I can't have somebody on the staff doing this, so I'm sorry [but] we have to end this agreement.'"

That night Clurman attended the ballet with Grunwald. Out of friendship, he asked her whether she'd like him "to stick his head in and fix things up for her," but she said no, Clurman later confided to a friend.

Not long after she left *People*, Clurman was hired as a "talent coordinator" on the staff of *20/20*, the television newsmagazine that Barbara was cohosting with Hugh Downs.

"I only agreed [to give *People* the story] out of my trust for Shirley," Barbara later explained.

> She told me it was a wonderful staff over there, and that the article would be very fair. She never read me the article. I was speaking to her—we speak almost every day of our lives—and she said, "I have to tell you this is the most vicious piece I've ever seen," and she was sure it would be heavily edited. But I never heard one line of that article. I don't want to be dramatic, but I have a daughter I love dearly, and I swear on my child's life, I never saw one line. I never called Henry Grunwald who is a close personal friend. I called *People* only once to say, "I hear this story is very tough," and suggested [Ryan] call Willie Nelson, or his manager, or anyone else to research it. But that was it.

Clurman said she regretted mentioning the "viciousness" of the article to Walters. "It's like living a Kafka story. I would rather take a bottle of pills than ever divulge a story," Clurman asserted.

The June 21, 1982 issue of *People* carried the story: "Behind the scenes as Barbara tapes Willie Nelson." It sparked outrage from hundreds of readers who wrote in protesting a comment from Barbara saying that if there were such a thing as reincarnation, "I'd like to come back dumb, blonde, and Catholic." Barbara's dream story had turned into a disaster for all concerned.

Over the succeeding years even the critics had come to accept Barbara and her specials. By the night of November 29, 1988, when *The 50th Barbara Walters Special* was aired—a two-hour prime-time celebration of twelve years of programs in which Barbara had interviewed 120 celebrity guests—she and the show were lauded.

"A veteran of more than thirty years in television," wrote critic John O'Connor, "Ms. Walters has carved a secure niche for herself in the charmed circle of electronic royalty. She is, in her own way, right up there with Johnny Carson and Carol Burnett."

BARBARA, BEGIN, AND SADAT

Barbara's biggest exclusive, the one of which her colleagues and competitors were the most envious, and the one she was the proudest of, was getting the first joint interview with Egypt's President Anwar el-Sadat and Israeli Prime Minister Menachem Begin.

The interview, on Sunday, November 20, 1977, gave "Bar-Ba-Ra," as Sadat pronounced it, more respectability and credibility as a journalist than anything she had done before or after—at least that was the public's perception. More than a decade later, at speaking engagements, where her fees ranged as high as twenty thousand dollars per appearance, her audiences invariably asked whether she believed peace would ever come to the Middle East. Her fans saw Barbara as an expert on Arab-Israeli relations, a master diplomat, the memory of that now historic TV interview having taken on mythic proportions.

For Barbara, the Begin-Sadat interview was an important turning point. Because her role as anchorwoman had been such a fiasco, she felt she had fallen back to ground zero—that she was starting over again; that she had to prove herself once more. Barbara needed a blockbuster story to restore her own, and ABC's, faith in her abilities. Some years later Barbara pointed to her coup, saying, "It gave me confidence that it hadn't just been luck before."

Competition on the Middle East story was intense. A week before Barbara's exclusive, Cronkite talked to Begin and Sadat, in separate filmed interviews, on the CBS *Evening News.* Earlier, ABC broke the story that Sadat was willing to visit Begin in Israel. But Arledge wanted the big one—the joint interview—and personally gave Barbara that assignment. If anyone could get it, he felt, she could.

Barbara had been trying to get a joint interview, even on a split screen from Cairo and Jerusalem, for months.

Barbara, Cronkite, and Chancellor were on the same historic flight with Sadat from Cairo to Tel Aviv. On the plane, Barbara handed Sadat a note saying, "Will you allow me to interview you in Jerusalem?" So that he could answer quickly without alerting the other anchormen she wrote "yes," "no," "alone" . . . "with the Prime Minister." For the entire flight, Barbara was tense, wondering whether her competitors had the same assignment and if one of them had secretly wangled it. When they got off the plane, an aide to Sadat handed back the note to Barbara. It said "yes," "alone."

Barbara managed to corner Begin and Sadat after they'd finished addressing the Israeli Parliament. While reminding the world of the deep differences between the two nations, Sadat delivered an eloquent plea for peace. A jubilant Begin told Barbara he had good news. He'd talked to Sadat and asked him what they could do for "our good friend Barbara," and the Egyptian leader agreed to allow her to interview them together. Begin told Barbara it would be the only such interview. All she could do was cross her fingers and hope nothing would happen to change their decision.

Finally, when the three of them were together a short while later in a conference room in the Knesset, Begin said to Sadat, "Mr. President, don't you think she's the prettiest reporter you've ever seen?" Responded Sadat, "Oh, Mr. Prime Minister, I can't say that. I have to go back to my country where we also have pretty reporters." But then Sadat reached over and gave Barbara a kiss. Both leaders allowed Barbara a half-hour to question them.

During the interview, Sadat told Barbara that the Israeli and Egyptian Ambassadors in the United States would be able to meet and talk together for the first time. In an apparent allusion to Israel's feelings about dealing with leaders of the Palestine Liberation Organization, Begin told Barbara that the Palestinian Arabs should be represented by "proper spokesmen." The picture of the two leaders sitting together for a joint interview with Barbara was more symbolic than what they actually said.

ABC interrupted programming to put five minutes of the interview on the air shortly after 5:00 P.M. that Sunday afternoon, feeding their radio stations also. Because of the off-and-on coverage of the historic visit by Sadat to Israel, ABC preempted early portions of the Ohio State–Michigan football game, where a trip to the Rose Bowl was at stake; thousands of viewers called the network to complain.

When Cronkite heard that Barbara had gotten the interview, he asked for and got equal treatment, coming in second. After the interview was finished, and off camera, Cronkite asked them, "Did Barbara get anything that I didn't?" Chancellor didn't get his interview until the following morning.

One of Barbara's prized mementos of her career is a photograph of Begin and Sadat taken the day of the interview. On one side is mounted a sheet of paper listing Barbara's questions and on the other the autographs of the two leaders.

"That was the most personally thrilling interview I've ever done," Barbara told the *Christian Science Monitor*.

A year after the historic scoop, Barbara, Cronkite, and Chancellor shared the ten-thousand-dollar Hubert H. Humphrey Freedom Prize of the B'nai B'rith Anti-Defamation League for their "public diplomacy" in the Arab-Israeli bid for peace. "I have a terrible feeling we're here today under false pretenses," Cronkite commented candidly at the awards luncheon. "The intent of none of us was to further the cause of peace. It was to get the story."

Barbara beat Cronkite and Chancellor on another major Middle East story in March 1979. The three, along with dozens of other reporters, were in Israel covering President Carter's trip, which everyone hoped would result in a peace treaty between Israel and Egypt, but very little news surfaced during the first six days. The Carter people had put the lid on. At one point Barbara tried to interview Foreign Minister Moshe Dayan, but was told no. When she attempted to coax Ezer Weizman, the defense minister, into talking for the camera, he told her jokingly, "You damn seducer." Then he pulled her close to him passionately, saying, "Put *that* on the air."

By chance, on the seventh day, Barbara and her producer were sitting in Begin's living room sipping orange drinks and eating chocolates put out by Mrs. Begin when the telephone rang. Begin went to the kitchen to answer it. It was Carter calling from Cairo International Airport to inform him that there was a very good chance for peace in the Middle East. "I can tell you," Begin told Barbara, "that the President gave me good news." Barbara was the first to break the story.

Barbara always seemed to be in the right place at the right time with the right people, whom she worked hard to cultivate and befriend. As *TV Guide* pointed out in a story on how Barbara had scooped her rivals on the Carter peace initiative, "If Vietnam had been the world's first TV war, the Israeli-Egyptian agreement was the world's first television peace."

The desire to be a major player in international stories has gotten Barbara in hot water with the media, which questioned her methods on several occasions.

In October 1979, Barbara was roundly criticized in the press for helping the Cuban Mission in New York give a dinner party for President Fidel Castro. Barbara's job was to put together the guest list of prominent journalists, which she did willingly. She also briefed Castro on the social graces, and acted as his cohost.

The New York *Post* called Barbara's role in the event "bizarre." The Soho *Weekly News* said, "Barbara Walters, whose formal job description is correspondent for ABC News and Entertainment, picked up on the second half of her title when she acted as hostess for Fidel Castro."

Barbara said she was telephoned by a Cuban official who invited her to dinner, and *she* asked, "May I bring some friends of mine in the communications business?" "Any friends you want," Barbara said the official told her.

Barbara's guest list included a number of newspaper executives, but absent were representatives of competing networks NBC and CBS. "I thought of the other network heads," Barbara said, "and thought, 'Macy's doesn't tell Gimbels.' "

Barbara arrived early for a private interview and then went over the guest list with Castro, asking him to rescind his directive that the party be off the record. "Let me meet the guests first," Castro replied, later relenting. When the guests arrived, Barbara acknowledged, "I found myself in a position of not just a guest but cohostess." Barbara's report on her talk with Castro, televised in a special five-minute appearance on *Issues and Answers*, and as a two-minute item on *World News Tonight*, wasn't especially newsworthy, saying merely that Castro was unhappy to see Ronald Reagan as President.

Her response to her part in the soiree? "As a journalist
[I was] a little uncomfortable in the role, but I couldn't
imagine having turned it down."

Barbara became embroiled in a more serious controversy
in early 1987—one in which the journalistic ethical standards of ABC were stretched—when she acted as a go-
between for President Reagan in the Iran-Contra scandal.

On December 11, 1986, Barbara scored the first interview with Manucher Ghorbanifar, an Iranian businessman
who negotiated the Reagan administration's secret arms
dealings with Iran. Ghorbanifar was interviewed by Barbara in the Monte Carlo apartment of Saudi billionaire
arms merchant Adnan Khashoggi, who helped arrange the
deal between Washington and Teheran. Ghorbanifar said
he had gone to Lebanon to negotiate the release of three
hostages from terrorist groups with links to Iran.

Since the arms-for-hostages scandal had broken just a
few weeks earlier, and reporters were scrambling to get on
the story, the interview was initially viewed as another of
Barbara's major exclusives. The print media picked up her
story, and *TV Guide*, in its "Cheers 'N' Jeers" column,
complimented her for an interview "that broke new
ground in the case."

But on March 16, 1987, *Wall Street Journal* reporters Edward Pound and Andy Paztor reported that Ghorbanifar
had used Barbara "as a conduit to secretly pass on to President Reagan his views about U.S. arms sales to Iran."

After the interview, Barbara prepared a lengthy memo
outlining statements made by the Iranian that she had not
reported on the air and sent it to the White House.

ABC subsequently released a statement saying that Barbara's "transmission of her information to the President
was in violation of a literal interpretation of news policy.
ABC policy expressly limits journalists cooperating with
Government agencies unless threats to human life are in-

volved. Ms. Walters believed that to be the case." The network said that Barbara would not be disciplined.

Barbara said she "felt terrible" acting as Ghorbanifar's intermediary, but she did it because she felt it was important for the President to get the information. "I made sure it was delivered," Barbara stated. The *Journal* story said that Barbara might have passed the information to Nancy Reagan, but Barbara said that was not exactly how it happened. "It is very unimportant whether I delivered it or somebody else did," she said.

The outcry in the media was swift and angry.

"Who does Barbara Walters think she is? Mata Hari?" asked Kay Gardella of the *Daily News.* "Her role as courier between [Ghorbanifar and Reagan] is a perfect example of what can happen with TV journalists who think their power extends beyond the parameters of their job. . . . She may have thought she was ingratiating herself with the President, and cementing her White House contact, but she sent out a signal that she's naive and foolish enough to be used."

Roger Simon, in a commentary distributed by the Los Angeles *Times* Syndicate, observed, "If you cover the circus, you can't sleep with the elephants. Not even if you're Barbara Walters."

20/20

On July 12, 1979, Carmine Galante, reputed head of one of New York's Mafia families, was gunned down in Brooklyn. It was a major story and the producers at ABC's *World News Tonight* were looking for an angle beyond the normal blood and guts coverage. One of the top investigative producers at 20/20 at the time was Lowell Bergman, who had a reputation as an expert in the area of organized crime. Bergman, who was often on the road for the newsmagazine, happened to be in New York that day and was assigned by the evening news people to come up with a new slant on the Galante rubout.

Bergman decided that an interesting peg would be to interview Galante's mouthpiece, Roy Cohn, who had a number of underworld clients.

Bergman wanted to have the tough-guy lawyer talk about the "hit" and speculate as to who might succeed Galante in the hierarchy of New York mobsterdom. The producers liked the idea and set Bergman free to get the attorney. As it turned out, every other reporter in town had the same idea, and the phones were ringing off the hook in Cohn's office. His secretary told everyone he wasn't available. Bergman was desperate to reach him, but didn't have his private number. Someone suddenly realized that one of Cohn's best friends was right in their midst; Barbara certainly would know how to reach him.

Bergman raced up to her sixth-floor office. "Do you have Roy Cohn's number?" he asked Barbara.

"Yes," she answered.

"One of his mob clients has just been murdered and we want to interview him. Can I have it?"

"No," said Barbara.

"Why not?" asked Bergman.

"Because it's personal," said Barbara dismissively.

Bergman went back to the newsroom and complained to Jeff Gralnick, the executive producer, who shrugged resignedly. "There's nothing I can do."

The story is remembered because it demonstrated to many reporters, producers, and writers at ABC News that Barbara was not, in their minds, a journalist but rather a celebrity who was treading a fine line between news and entertainment, operating in a far different stratum than everyone else, including the anchors.

But when Barbara needed help, it was a different story. ABC Capitol Hill reporter Don Farmer recalled how he had been ordered to cancel an interview with a senator because Barbara wanted to interview him.

Barbara used every ploy in the book to get a story, which often sickened her colleagues and competitors. During the 1980 Republican National Convention, Barbara was furious when she saw Cronkite do an exclusive interview with President Ford. She rushed over to the CBS booth and grabbed Ford when he came out. Photographer David Kennerly, who watched the incident, recalled, "She literally pleaded with him to come and do another interview with her. 'Oh, Mr. President, you've got to do it . . . for old times' sake . . . for Alan's [Greenspan's] sake.' That quote is imbedded in my mind. Begging is the only way I could put it. I wished I'd had one of those little airline barf bags, because I just about lost it. It was the single most disgusting display by a newsperson that I've ever seen in my life."

But Ford gave Barbara the interview.

During the Iran-Contra scandal, Barbara was aboard the Pan American shuttle from Washington to New York when she spotted attorney Leonard Garment, who represented Robert McFarlane, the former national security adviser, who figured in the probe. Barbara zipped down the aisle with a barrage of questions for the lawyer about McFarlane's role in the case. Her voice reached a crescendo that caught the attention of other passengers who turned to watch the proceedings. "You think this is Barbara Walters?" Garment said to the audience, hoping Barbara would catch the hint to leave. "It's really just a woman wearing a mask." Barbara ignored a flight attendant who told her to take her seat. "Tell the pilot he'll have to circle three times," said Garment. "Barbara Walters is working."

On a trip to India, other journalists watched aghast as Barbara shouted, "In America, I'm Number One! I'm Number One!" during an altercation with a prime minister's aide over a schedule change she wanted in an interview.

Barbara had become a power to be reckoned with at ABC, and a prima donna of the first order, according to those with whom she worked.

By the spring of 1981, Barbara's five-year, five-million-dollar supercontract was only months from expiring, and she had passed the word that she was displeased with her treatment at ABC News—despite all of her perks, money, acclaim, and power.

A major confrontation had occurred between Barbara and the news executives over her involvement and cover-

age of the March 31st assassination attempt on President
Reagan. Producers and editors thought she was on vaca-
tion so no one bothered to call her to help in the reportage.
Late in the afternoon, she called in and was assigned to
track down Gerald Ford for an interview, which she did.
But Barbara was incensed over how her piece was played.
Lee Stevens told Arledge he wanted his client's contract
terminated.

When things cooled, Barbara let it be known that she
was looking around at what the competition had to offer.
One of Barbara's major complaints was that since she was
removed as coanchor of the evening news she didn't have
a "home" where she could appear on a regular basis. She
also felt that many of her interviews with heads of state—
interviews only she could secure—were getting short shrift
on the news.

By September, Barbara had decided to remain at ABC,
even though her request to host her own celebrity interview show on the network had been rejected. She'd gotten
what Stevens described as a "comfortable raise"—more
than one million dollars a year for each of five years; the
number of her specials was reduced from four to three annually; she'd do an occasional major story for the news department; and she was reunited with Hugh Downs as a
regular contributor on 20/20—a decision that Downs had
some serious qualms about. But Barbara expressed pleasure with her new pact. "20/20 reaches a mass audience
and is enormously competitive," she told Cosmopolitan.
"I'll have a chance to do show business and news figures."

Barbara was given a plush new office at 20/20. A producer who had a meeting with her shortly after she arrived
was taken aback. "All the other offices were relatively
plain, white-walled," he said. "Her office had a small, not
very functional desk, and it was all mirrors and velour
couches. I didn't know any newsperson at ABC who had
mirrors on their walls. It was like walking into a Las Vegas
hotel room."

The producer had been asked to talk to Barbara about working with her on hard-news pieces, which she had expressed interest in doing. "Once I saw the mirrored office I said to myself, 'This ain't my cup of tea. This woman is not a journalist—I don't care whether she has access to people or not.' She traveled with a hairdresser, too. I gotta be honest, anybody who travels with a hairdresser ain't in my business."

Initially, Downs had been approached about Barbara being a regular on the show, but with no defined role, which Downs had found acceptable. But when he learned of plans to make her the cohost, he strenuously objected.

"This was not acceptable to me," he said. "I had no objection to Barbara's increased presence—we're friends. . . . This was more of a philosophical problem. Coanchoring is inherently awkward."

Downs immediately went to Barbara and told her that he wanted to remain as the solo anchor; he also forcefully made his feelings known to the program's executives. A compromise was worked out whereby Downs remained the anchor, handling the opening and closing of the show and the intros, outros, and bridges of the various segments. Barbara's job was to discuss various pieces with the correspondents, make some observations, and converse with Downs at the end of the show.

As a result of this division of roles, the program had a choppy look and feel, and Barbara was far from happy playing second fiddle to Downs.

"Finally, I had to ask myself if sharing the anchor work might not be the lesser of two evils," said Downs. "Particularly since there was a danger of losing Barbara if we couldn't come up with something that worked."

In late 1985, 20/20 was given a new format and set, and Barbara was officially promoted to cohost.

*   *   *

At 20/20 Barbara's nemesis seemed to be the flamboyant Geraldo Rivera. Rivera thought of Barbara as "a sexy and benevolent despot."

"I like Barbara," he said. "She can be very intimidating, but I always viewed her as a sexy dame. My only regret about Barbara is that we never got it on. She had her sights set a lot higher." He claimed he asked but she shot him down.

On 20/20, as elsewhere, Barbara inevitably seemed to be in the middle of one controversy or another involving her exclusive interviews with major news figures.

In April 1982, for example, she scored the first on-camera talk with Danish aristocrat Claus von Bülow, who a month earlier was convicted of trying to murder his wealthy socialite wife, Sunny, with insulin injections, leaving her in a coma. (He was subsequently acquitted.) Von Bülow was accused of trying to kill her to inherit millions of dollars and marry his mistress. He told Barbara that he was innocent and hoped his wife would come out of the coma so she could prove he did not commit the crime.

The story infuriated Stephen Famiglietta, the prosecutor who won von Bülow's conviction. An assistant state attorney general in Rhode Island, Famiglietta alleged that ABC and von Bülow had made "a deal" whereby "they would allow Claus to testify in return for some exclusive privilege in the future.

"She asked what I thought were ridiculous questions," he asserted. "One that comes to mind as being most absurd was the last one: 'Mr. von Bülow, did you ever do anything to harm your wife?' I don't know what she expected him to say at that stage. I saw the whole thing as a setup, and I saw the whole thing as an attempt to portray Claus as an innocent man."

But Barbara earned the respect of some of 20/20's top producers as an excellent reporter and writer—and as a producer in her own right. Stanhope Gould, who was Barbara's producer on what many consider 20/20's biggest

scoop—the 1980 "surrender" of Sixties radical fugitive
Abbie Hoffman to Barbara herself—said, "She had the
compulsion that was necessary to make a good journalist.
She understands what it is to do a piece; she does the right
things; she works hard; she knows what works and what
doesn't."

Hoffman, who had been sought since 1974 on drug and
bail jumping charges, telephoned Barbara and agreed to
give her an exclusive interview just prior to his finally sur-
rendering to authorities.

"Barbara's a movie star journalist," observed Gould, "so
Abbie called up and said he would surrender *only* if Barbara did the interview and I was the producer. Abbie was
a media manipulator and an event producer. He wanted
Barbara because she's *Barbara*. I had known him for many
years from covering the radical movement."

Gould and Barbara chartered a private jet and flew from
Teterboro Airport in New Jersey to upstate New York
where they met with a Hoffman emissary who drove them
to a powerboat moored in the Thousand Islands area.

"It was a great story," recalled Gould.

We're cruising across this lake, me and Barbara and a camera crew, and here comes this other boat with Abbie on
it. It's three o'clock in the afternoon on a Tuesday and we
have to shoot the whole segment and be on the air Thursday night [20/20 later moved to a Friday night slot]. So
this is a project that's going to require fast and accurate
moves.

We finished doing the interview at three in the morning,
Barbara did a standup, and we slept for three hours. At
some point our presence had become known and the Associated Press had gotten on to the story. So we had to race
back to New York and get a story on the evening news that
Wednesday night. Then we had to turn around and edit
the piece for 20/20 the following night.

Barbara was really incredible for somebody like her. She
could have gone to sleep and slept all night and I could

have put in a rough audio sound track. She could have replaced it all the following morning in time for the show Thursday night. But she stayed there and wrote and helped edit. She was thoroughly involved.

The Hoffman story generated an enormous amount of publicity for Barbara and 20/20. The New York Post ran a banner headline: "Barbara Walters' Secret Date with Abbie." But again the critics questioned Barbara's role.

"Walters," commented Kay Gardella, "is both blessed and cursed. Her celebrity, high visibility, and the fact that she is a woman gives con men reason to believe she's a pushover and makes her the most sought TV reporter. . . . Abbie told her just what he wanted her to know and nothing more." Gardella noted that Hoffman was also seeking publicity for a new book he'd just written called *Soon to Be a Major Motion Picture*.

Every so often, Barbara took a personal interest in an interview subject, one of them being former private girl's school headmistress Jean Harris, convicted of the March 1980 murder of her lover, Scarsdale Diet doctor Herman Tarnower. Shortly after her conviction and imprisonment, and against the advice of her attorney, Harris agreed to give Barbara an exclusive interview. "I had been pictured as though I were some kind of a monster," Harris said. "I wanted an opportunity to talk to someone publicly so that people would have a better idea of the person I am instead of the person they made up in the papers. I always admired Barbara. I trusted her."

During the first of two interviews for 20/20, Harris became hysterical when Barbara suddenly asked her whether she loved Tarnower. "Don't ask me that," begged Harris, tears suddenly streaming from her eyes. "I shan't," said Barbara quietly, "I shan't." But the camera stayed on the broken woman. After the tape stopped rolling, Harris said she asked Barbara to cut the amount of her crying. "I asked her, 'Please, I don't want to sit here and look pathetic.' She was good about not making me look like a complete idiot. I was a zombie and she was very kind to a zombie. She tried to make me feel comfortable by saying in so many words that there's nothing wrong about crying and that there had been moments in her life when she cried, too."

Sometime after the interview aired, Harris received a gracious thank-you note from Barbara, followed shortly by a personal visit. Barbara had become fascinated with Harris's plight. Friends said that some years later Barbara was equally intrigued with the tribulations of two other women who had gotten into trouble—former Miss America Bess Myerson, who was acquitted in 1988 in an influence-peddling case involving her boyfriend, and hotel queen Leona Helmsley, who was convicted on tax evasion charges in 1989.

During her visit, Barbara "did a lot to amuse me," said Harris. "We kidded about what the jet set was doing; what all of the fancy names were doing; who was getting a divorce and who wasn't. She'd kid about what was going on on the outside."

Beyond the good humor offered by Barbara, Harris felt that the real reason for her visit was that Barbara felt compassion for her because of the adversity Barbara had faced in her own life. "I don't think there's any question about that," said Harris, who recalled that Barbara talked about the bad reviews she'd received over the years, and about the problems of her sister and her mother. She also talked about her daughter, but never once mentioned Lou.

"I asked her about her drive and the incredible pace she keeps," said Harris. "She told me it's a job she loves and I guess she's proving something to herself. She told me she did a lot of taking care of her sister and that cost money. It was quite a talk; she didn't sound like the glamorous lady you see on TV. This is a woman who has had enough bad things said about her and enough rough reviews so that she's a very compassionate person. She said to me, 'I've had hundreds and hundreds of reviews but it's the bad ones that I never forget.' "

After the visit, Harris received occasional letters and Christmas cards from Barbara, who also arranged to have Revlon and Estée Lauder send boxes of cosmetics to Harris and other inmates.

In the summer of 1986, Barbara signed her third five-year contract with ABC, with her salary reported to be close to two million dollars a year.

By the late 1980s, Barbara's heavily promoted stories were generating huge ratings for 20/20 and, as with her specials, she veered toward the tabloid side of broadcast news. She was chasing the same kind of tawdry stories as the editors of the National Enquirer, the Star, and People. In his posthumously published diaries, Andy Warhol noted: "Barbara Walters is just goo-goo with the searching look and asking the same old questions: 'How old were you when you realized you had sex?' " On what seemed like a weekly basis, Barbara was coaxing exclusive interviews from the likes of party-girl Donna Rice, whose relationship with Gary Hart destroyed his chances for a Presidential candidacy; from Oliver North's secretary, Fawn Hall, the femme fatale in the Iran-Contra scandal; and from Kitty Dukakis, the addicted wife of Democratic Presidential candidate Michael Dukakis. Barbara even played referee–marriage counselor in the beauty-and-the-beast bout between world heavyweight champion Mike Tyson and his wife, Robin Givens.

On one of her stories Barbara reportedly offered a ten-thousand-dollar "research" fee to Judith Campbell Exner, paramour of President Kennedy and Mafia chieftain Sam Giancana, in exchange for an interview to be aired on 20/20. ABC News policy forbids payments for news stories. Barbara hoped to be the first television reporter to interview Exner after a cover piece on her, written by celebrity biographer Kitty Kelley, ran in People magazine in

February 1988. In the story, Exner claimed she arranged for a number of meetings between President Kennedy and the Chicago gangland boss. Exner and Kelley, who were brought together by Liz Smith, were each paid about fifty thousand dollars by *People*. The *20/20* interview never came off but Barbara, hoping to stay on friendly terms with Exner, had her to lunch and advised her to renegotiate her collaboration agreement with Kelley.

"There had been some discussion with Exner about possibly doing an interview," Barbara said. "Executive producer Victor Neufeld and I decided against doing it. There was no discussion of ever paying her for an interview."

Whichever way it happened, the story Barbara was pursuing with Exner was another in the genre of supermarket tabloid journalism. The mistress of the titillating television tell-all: that's the way many perceived Barbara in the late 1980s.

In 1988—the year *20/20* celebrated its tenth anniversary—reports began surfacing of serious problems on the show: a number of producers were quietly looking for jobs elsewhere; several had already resigned; correspondents such as Rivera and Sylvia Chase had left; morale was low; there was some staff dissatisfaction with the executive producer, Victor Neufeld, who had replaced the respected Av Westin; and staffers felt that Barbara had been given—or had taken—carte blanche in many of the decision-making processes on the show, particularly in choosing which stories to pursue. (Arledge suspended Westin from his *20/20* job in February 1987 after he wrote a memo criticizing Arledge's management; Westin eventually was reinstated but in another job; he left ABC in mid-1989.)

"What Barbara says goes," said one of the producers who left the program. "Barbara runs the place since Westin's gone. Av had some clout and he could disagree with her or argue with her. But there's nobody there now who can change what she wants to do. It's an experience I saved myself from by leaving."

Another 20/20 insider said, "It's a subtle kind of power. It's not as if she's saying, 'This is what we *will* cover.' It's that producers get the message from her of what will and won't *get on*. What's most damaging to the show is that she's not a journalist and never has been a journalist; what she has become is a socialite. ABC doesn't care. They love her. We live in a corporate era and what she does is what they want."

Stanhope Gould, who left the show after Arledge killed an investigative segment he produced involving Marilyn Monroe and the Kennedys, said, "Av made the show successful and viable. He had a depth of experience. [But] when it came down to something that had to go to Roone, Barbara would win."

Other present and former 20/20 staffers who were approached to be interviewed for this book demanded anonymity, expressing fear that if they were named or identified in some way, they would lose their jobs because of the considerable clout Barbara wielded at ABC and throughout the industry. Still others flatly refused to talk. "She'll find out some way it was me," said one producer. "Don't even call me here. It's too dangerous. If she found out I talked, I might have trouble getting a job in this business again."

Another said, "If I tell you an anecdote, she'll track it to me. She'd remember I was involved. She never forgets anything."

On July 21, 1988, Jeremy Gerard, who covered media for the *New York Times*, reported on the problems at 20/20, quoting named and unnamed sources. The story upset Barbara, Arledge, Downs, Neufeld, and other powers at the network.

A week later Liz Smith denounced the story in her column, asserting that the coanchors "work harmoniously with Neufeld, and many of the producers are up in arms, wanting to sign a letter backing him up."

Hugh Downs wrote a letter to the editor denouncing Gerard's story. Barbara and Arledge were said to have made calls to top *Times* executives.

Less than two weeks later, in a rare Editor's Note, the *Times* said Gerard's article "violated the paper's standards of fairness. . . . [It] should not have quoted criticisms of the program and its executive producer . . . from sources who refused to allow the use of their names. It should have let Mr. Neufeld and others respond to the specific complaints."

Reporters at the *Times* were outraged. Gerard's piece had been lauded by editors who read it before and after it ran and the use of unnamed sources in stories in the *Times* and elsewhere is a common journalistic practice.

Three months after Gerard's story ran, *Spy* magazine reported that Arledge "dispatched" Barbara to Liz Smith's "doorstep" and "inspired by Walters's empty dictation [Smith] followed the ABC line." The magazine speculated in its usual tongue-in-cheek manner that one of the reasons the editor's note was printed was because of Barbara's friendship with Abe Rosenthal, former *Times* executive editor, who had become a Times Op-Ed page columnist.

However it came about, said a 20/20 insider, "Barbara and Roone were completely freaked out about the *Times* story."

MOTHERHOOD VS. CAREER

On the evening of March 19, 1988, on the occasion of her being honored by the Museum of Broadcasting for her extraordinary career in television, Barbara proudly told an audience of media glitterati: "My daughter Jackie—who is not here tonight—is about to become an intern at a TV station." To those paying homage to Barbara that night, her announcement concerning her daughter's career plans was met with murmurs of happiness. There were visions of a second-generation Barbara Walters coming up through the ranks: Jacqueline Guber, a chip off the old block.

The picture, however, was not as bright as it seemed, nor as those in the audience may have perceived it. Almost twenty years old, Jackie—a pretty, loquacious young woman who stood almost six feet tall when she was just thirteen—had gone through a turbulent childhood and adolescence. While Barbara's early problems had stemmed from her father's career and her sister's retardation, Jackie's resulted from her mother's career, and the fact that she was a child of adoption and divorce.

Like Barbara, Jackie had bounced from school to school. She started at exclusive Dalton, on New York's Upper East Side, where she was a student until the eighth grade. The first time Barbara and Lee Guber tried to get Jackie into Dalton's highly selective nursery program, she was turned down, according to a friend of Barbara's. "What they did was put a bunch of three-year-olds in a room and look at how they poured their apple juice and how they placed cotton on a piece of paper. Using that kind of criteria, they determined who would be admitted." The second time around, though, Jackie was admitted after Barbara and Lee had several private conferences with school administrators, the friend recalled.

Years later, Barbara expressed her feeling that her daughter was "not competitive enough"—something she noticed about Jackie when they played Monopoly and Barbara always won. "She's a very different child from me," noted Barbara.

Throughout her childhood, while Barbara's career was soaring, Jackie was left in the care of a French governess, Thérèse de la Chapelle, known affectionately as "Zelle," which was short for Mademoiselle. Zelle lived in the Gubers' apartment on West Fifty-seventh Street. There was also a cook, Ichodel Richards.

The mother of one of Jackie's Dalton playmates said, "I knew Zelle better than I knew Barbara. Zelle basically ran the household. She was the one I would speak to. When there were play dates for the children, I made my arrangements with Zelle. Rarely did any of us Dalton mothers come in contact with Barbara. We'd only see her at school functions. It was not like a governess to a mother when I dealt with Zelle. It was really like mother to mother; like she was Jackie's mother."

During visits to Barbara's apartment, the woman said, Jackie and her friends would play in her bedroom, and the mother or mothers would sit in the den and chat with Zelle, a cultured and warm woman, who spoke perfect English with a heavy French accent.

Jackie was so fond of Zelle that she spent at least one summer with her and her family in France, the woman recalled.

"Having Zelle . . . means I can go to China and not worry," Barbara said. "Zelle is part of the family."

Lou and Dena had sent Barbara to summer camp when she was a child and Barbara followed suit with Jackie. She also once sent Jackie to England for a summer enrichment program, picking up the tab for a friend of Jackie's who otherwise couldn't afford to go.

It was easier for Barbara to send Jackie away for summers because Barbara rarely took a vacation. As a result, Jackie could never look forward to an extended period of time alone with her mother, something Barbara faced with Lou and Dena when she was growing up.

By the time Jackie was five, she was telling her mother when she saw her on TV, "That's not you, Mommy. I like you better here at home." When she was old enough to realize that the reason she saw so little of her mother was because Barbara was a famous television star with a hectic schedule, one of the ways she showed her anger was by refusing to watch Barbara's programs.

When Barbara did her interview with Begin and Sadat, scheduled programming was preempted. Barbara called home and Jackie answered. "It's unfair, Mommy," she said. "I was watching my program about cats and just before it ended they took it off and put *you* on."

Like Barbara, who had felt shame as a youngster that her father owned a nightclub, Jackie, by the time she was eight, had a similar feeling about her mother. "She's a bit embarrassed by what I do," Barbara admitted. "She knows now that Mommy's a little bit of a celebrity." On another occasion, she said, "She likes having Barbara Walters for a mother, as she knows it may bring her special attention;

on the other hand, she worries about it and has sometimes said that people pay attention to her because she *is* Barbara Walters' daughter. I tell her that it happens to me, too, that people pay attention to me because I'm famous, but that I know which people really care."

Jackie, it seemed, suffered from the same syndrome Barbara had faced with her father, asking friends and even her mother, "How do I know why people like me? I don't know if they like me because I'm me or because I'm Barbara Walters' daughter."

Barbara tried as hard as she could to give Jackie all the love and affection she could. She was constantly torn between her career and her daughter. She'd rush home when she was still at the *Today* show and mother and daughter would take baths and sleep together. "I know people often feel children shouldn't sleep with their parents," Barbara explained at the time. "But this is special."

While taking a bath with her mother, Jackie first learned she'd been adopted.

"We were in the bathtub and she asked me about parts of my body," Barbara revealed. "I said that breasts were used by mommies to feed their babies. And she asked about her vagina. I said, 'This is where a baby comes from. There are two ways that mommies who want babies have them—through this way and through adoption.'"

Barbara felt Jackie had accepted the fact of her adoption, even telling her mother she wished she had her green eyes. But Jackie was unhappy that Barbara was essentially an absentee mother.

On her desk at the office, Barbara kept two little framed notes that Jackie had written her: "I love you. I hope you had a wonduful time in Frans. Makesoower that you biy me a present. I wil see you agen. Goodby, from Jackie." The other read: "Send me a postcard that ses wen I can sleep with you I miss you, I love you mommy, Love, Jackie."

While it was difficult, Barbara tried to bring Jackie with her when she traveled. One of the first trips, when she was still just a baby, was to Ireland with the *Today* show. When Jackie was ten, in 1978, Barbara was assigned to interview Prime Minister Begin for *Issues and Answers*. Because it was Washington's Birthday, Jackie had four days off from school and Barbara decided to take her to Jerusalem. When they arrived at Ben Gurion Airport, Barbara was informed that a bomb had gone off near the city and several persons had been injured, terrifying Jackie, who lived in fear during their entire stay. After Barbara conducted her interview, she mentioned Jackie's dread to Begin, who spent time alone with the child, calming her by telling her wonderful stories about Jerusalem as the two ate pound cake and sipped orange juice together.

Begin wasn't the only renowned person whom Jackie met. When Jimmy Carter became President, Barbara privately visited the White House with Jackie, promoting a friendship between her daughter and the President's little girl, Amy. The two children, then about ten, had dinner together at the White House, exchanged gifts, and carried on a correspondence. In February 1979, Jackie sent Amy a combination Christmas and Valentine's Day gift and a brief note, drawing a heart with an arrow through it. In May of that year, Amy wrote Jackie thanking her for a letter she'd written describing a trip Jackie had taken to Seneca Falls. Amy went on to tell Jackie how excited she was about a forthcoming trip to Vienna and Japan with her father and mother.

On another occasion, Jackie wrote to Carter himself, regarding the dangers of cigarette smoking and the President responded with a personal note on July 20, 1978.

To Jackie Guber
  Thank you for suggesting a way that the Federal government can discourage cigarette smoking—in 1975, 670 billion cigarettes.
  It was nice to hear from you.

Sincerely,
Jimmy Carter

During the height of the 1976–77 controversy over her million-dollar salary, Barbara feared that kidnappers might try to snatch her daughter. She hired security guards to protect her, had her travel under assumed names, and made certain she was never photographed. Barbara had been worried about the effect of that anxious and emotional period on Jackie. As things were settling down, she noted with a sense of relief, "My child and I are healthy. Physically and emotionally, Jackie's in good shape. She doesn't bite her nails, she doesn't twitch."

By the time Jackie reached the junior high school level at Dalton she began having problems with her studies. "Jackie was not that bright," said the mother of one of Jackie's schoolmates. "That's why she left Dalton. She was having difficulty keeping up. I don't think she was asked to leave, they don't really do that. But if your child can't keep up, it might be suggested. Barbara and Lee [they were divorced by that time] were having meetings at the school about Jackie and what to do."

Between the ages of eleven and thirteen, Jackie had become interested in boys, fascinated by video pornography, and aware of drugs. She was a child of television and was constantly besieged with the images of sex, drugs, and rock and roll that spewed forth in living color. Particularly because of who her mother was, Jackie seemed the ultimate victim of television.

Jackie grew up during the height of the sexual and drug revolutions, which made Barbara frantic with worry, like any parent of her generation. Because she had adopted Jackie quite late in life, Barbara was already in her early fifties when Jackie hit puberty and adolescence "with a bang," as Barbara once put it, which made their relationship all the more difficult.

When she was eleven, Jackie had her first boy-girl party.

Barbara was in Washington on an assignment, but flew home as soon as she could to help chaperone the event. When she got to the apartment, Jackie told her, "Don't come in this room. Close the door. Go away."

Barbara began bringing sex education books home and having frank talks with Jackie, telling her "about the difference between loving someone and not loving someone when you have any kind of sex with him."

One midnight, Barbara caught Jackie watching one of New York's X-rated cable TV shows, which Barbara found "quite filthy." After seeing that Jackie was intrigued, Barbara decided to watch one of the programs with her, because "I knew if I didn't allow her to, she was going to watch anyway after I left the room." Barbara found the program "boring" and thought Jackie had, too, thus ending what Barbara perceived as a problem. But she caught her watching again. "Jacqueline," Barbara yelled, "this is really filth and I can't condone your watching it. I mean, if you're going to sneak around and watch it without me, this is really terrible."

Mother and daughter were also at odds over sexually explicit films that Jackie wanted to see, popular movies that all of her friends' parents were allowing them to go to. For example, Barbara banned Jackie from seeing the John Travolta film *Saturday Night Fever*, because it had fairly explicit sex scenes and teenage drug use. "She said all of her friends had gone. I said, 'Fine, let them go, but you're not going.'"

When Barbara took Jackie to see the film *Private Benjamin* she was shocked to see a scene in which several characters smoked marijuana, something that Barbara had never done. "I don't even recognize when somebody uses it," Barbara said. "I've been in theaters occasionally when Jacqueline [said], 'Mommy, can you smell it?' I [didn't] know what she was talking about." The day after seeing the Goldie Hawn film, a nervous Barbara asked Jackie how she felt about the marijuna-smoking scene. "Oh, Mommy," said Jackie, "it's only a movie. What kind of dope are you?"

"I'm not particularly worried about Jacqueline," Barbara said. "It can happen with any child, I guess. I hope I don't eat my words."

(In the late Eighties, when Jackie was nearing twenty, like many parents Barbara's concern focused on the devastating and sometimes fatal diseases of the sexually active. "I talk about AIDS with her, cut out magazine and newspaper articles, show them to her, leave them around the house for her to read," Barbara said. "I did the same with herpes a few years ago, but all one can do is hope it will sink in and trust a person's good sense.")

By the time Jackie was thirteen, Barbara began noticing that the youngster wasn't as concerned when she couldn't be at home with her. Once, after an assignment, Barbara rushed to the apartment so they could have dinner together. As Barbara recalled the incident, "She wouldn't talk to me, because she wanted to have dinner with a friend. I said, 'Your friend can have dinner here,' and she answered, 'No, her mommy wants her home.' So I said, 'Well, *your* mommy wants *you* home.' And she just looked at me and said, 'You're a regular Mommie Dearest!'"

Jackie started baiting Barbara—accusing her of being a bad cook, of being afraid to drive a car, of not being able to play games. "The only thing my mommy *can* do is *television.*"

Finally, a worried Barbara—busy with her career and at a loss as to how to deal with Jackie's academic problems and the constant mother-daughter conflicts at home—enrolled her in a series of boarding schools, hoping her difficulties could be resolved by experts. The schools catered to the troubled children of well-to-do parents who could afford to pay annual tuitions ranging from fourteen thousand to thirty thousand dollars.

Jackie told an acquaintance after she graduated that all three boarding schools were "like reform schools for emotionally disturbed kids. I was a messed-up kid. I was going through my growing-up stage."

The first school, in Maine, which Jackie attended during the 1983–84 academic year, had a philosophy centered on families—getting parents involved in the lives of their children. Parents were required to attend monthly support-group meetings in New York, along with occasional weekend family-group sessions on the campus. The faculty tried to help the students understand who they were, where they were going in their lives, and what they needed to get there.

During the time Jackie was at that school, Barbara was interviewed for a cover story in *Ladies Home Journal* by the son of another famous person, Ron Reagan, Jr. Barbara said she'd never thought that Jackie would have to go away to school, "but in New York, there isn't anything for kids to do. They start going to discotheques at fourteen."

After a year, Barbara transferred Jackie to a small, all-girls school in Connecticut catering to students with average academic ability. The school offered students individual attention in subjects like English and math, along with counseling support from a psychologist and a psychiatrist. She stayed there for a year also.

In August 1985, Barbara enrolled Jackie in yet a third school—a very expensive and very structured alternative institution located in rural Idaho where she stayed from August 1985 until she got her high school diploma in August 1987.

The philosophy of the school involved having the students go back to the basics—hard physical labor such as chopping wood to instill the work ethic, and developing a healthy lifestyle.

"Most of the kids are here to be out of the environment they were in. For some reason or another the kids weren't allowed to stand up and be who they were; [they were] trying to meet certain expectations, trying to be as good as their parents," explained a member of the school's faculty.

Students were required to abide by strict agreements—
"no drugs, no sex, and no violence," said the faculty member. "We are a drug-free campus. We check baggage, go
through luggage, do personal clothing checks. Students
who are here are really making a commitment to be here
and are very conscientious about drugs. Ninety-five percent of the kids don't want to be here at first."

After Jackie graduated from the Idaho school her relationship with Barbara improved. With her mother's per-
mission, Jackie moved to Portland, Oregon, where she
shared a garden apartment with a school friend, with
thoughts of studying art, especially drawing, a subject in
which she had interest and talent. "Jackie had what I call
flair," said a friend. "She had a certain creative instinct.
She dresses sometimes absolutely outrageously, but there's
that spark that says this is somebody who sees color and
texture and has a feeling for style. You'll never get Jackie
in a Peter Pan collar or a blazer with a circle pin."

In January 1988, Jackie enrolled in the industrial video
production course at Portland Community College.

On one of her visits with Jackie, Barbara was introduced
to Joella Werlin, the director of public affairs and community relations at KATU-TV, the ABC affiliate in Portland.
The introduction was made by Barbara's friend Arlene
Schnitzer, who had worked as a producer at the station
and owned a prestigious art gallery in Portland. While Jackie was living in the city, Schnitzer became "sort of a surrogate mother" to her, said Werlin, who also became a friend
and confidante of Jackie's.

Werlin told Barbara and Jackie about the intern program at her station. "Jackie had struck me as somebody
who could perhaps really get excited about the technical
side of television and it wouldn't be competitive with her
mother," said Werlin. "Barbara was very anxious—*very
anxious*—for Jackie to be happy, for her to feel good about
herself. Barbara was just hoping that Jackie would be

spurred by some interest, and the program sounded appealing to Jackie."

Jackie became an intern at KATU-TV in the spring of 1988—just after Barbara had told the Museum of Broadcasting audience in Los Angeles about her daughter's plans. "Barbara was very attentive," said Werlin. "If Jackie failed to show up for a meeting or something, Barbara wanted to know why."

But after several months, Jackie dropped out, finding no interest in TV production, although she did become a skilled videotape editor. When she left the program, Werlin called Barbara, who naturally was disappointed. "We both agreed that it really wasn't working out for Jackie; that it was not the right time, the right place for her. I had to reassure Barbara that the purpose of our internship is career exploration. We don't expect everybody to like what they think they're going to like."

Jackie completed the video course at Portland Community in June 1988 and left the school, telling friends she wanted to pursue a career in modeling. "She's not a terribly motivated student," said Werlin. "She is not at all academically inclined."

Modeling was something Jackie had always wanted to do, and something that Barbara had been adamant against, sparking arguments between mother and daughter. In 1982, when Jackie was almost fourteen, Barbara said, "[She] talks of being a model. I say, 'Over my dead body.' " Barbara and Jackie had a "terrible struggle," as Barbara put it, when Jackie was thirteen and wanted to have her ears pierced, which Barbara also was against.

By the time Jackie had dropped out of the TV internship, Barbara had come to accept Jackie's desire to work toward a modeling career. "She doesn't want to have anything to do with television, that's for sure," she acknowledged.

While she worked at the TV station, Jackie confided in Werlin the problems she had with her mother.

"Jackie's very close to Barbara," emphasized Werlin. "She really adores her.

> But as any daughter would, growing up with that kind of mother, she has a feeling that she hasn't been able to meet her mother's expectations for her. When I met them for the first time I went to particular lengths, having been the daughter of a journalist myself, to make sure that I protected Jackie as much as I could from [the reputation] of her famous mother. When I made reservations at restaurants I didn't use Barbara Walters' name. But when we walked down the street people recognized Barbara—and that's something that Jackie has had to live with.
> Jackie's accommodated to it fairly well, but at the same time she's tried to assert herself in somewhat destructive ways.
> Jackie's had a different set of experiences than Barbara. Barbara had to work her way up in the world and Jackie has had a lot of privilege. She was also alone a lot when she was growing up and so she rebelled in a way kids of this generation do.
> Barbara experienced something that is not at all uncommon for those of us who raised strong-willed daughters, and especially when you have a mother who is accomplished like Barbara Walters.

At that event in Los Angeles where Barbara spoke of Jackie's internship, she told the assemblage that the turmoil during Jackie's adolescence "was because I wasn't home all the time. What I regret is I missed certain things. . . . But all that stuff in the Middle East was happening while Jackie was growing up. I could have done it differently but then there wouldn't have been this," Barbara said, referring to her career.

39

BICOASTAL BLISS

From the mid-Seventies to the early Eighties, Barbara had several male companions whom her friends thought might be "Mr. Right." After years of being single, she had begun thinking seriously about getting married for a third time. During that period, she and Jackie began to talk about whether the youngster would like a new daddy, but Barbara had the impression her daughter was against the idea because she wouldn't be able to sleep in her mother's bed anymore.

Barbara was always captivated by older men—businessmen mostly, powerful in their fields. "I'm attracted to them," she said, "because they give me a feeling of solidarity and security that I don't have in my own life."

One of those who fit the bill, friends thought, was erudite and cosmopolitan international wine merchant Alexis Lichine, whom Barbara met in London in November 1973 while covering the royal wedding of Princess Anne and Lieutenant Mark Phillips.

Fifteen years her senior, Lichine was Barbara's kind of
man: he possessed power, wealth, and influence. By the
time he met her, he had been married three times and was
the father of a son and daughter. His most recent wife was
actress Arlene Dahl, who started out as a Latin Quarter
showgirl. Also coincidentally, Lichine had been a friend
and associate of Barbara's beau from the early Sixties,
Claude Philippe.

Back in New York, Lichine became the man in Barbara's
life for a time. From the start, he realized that he'd become
involved with the most complex woman he'd ever known.
"Contrary to what the outside image of Barbara may have
been," Lichine said six months before his death in June
1989, "I found her soft and quite feminine—soft in terms
of not being assertive in private; feminine in terms of not
being forceful."

Lichine also found her to be moody and depressed.

Very often she would implicate herself, find fault with her
conduct; she had this tendency to accuse herself of things
falsely. For instance, she felt guilty because perhaps she was
responsible for the failure of her marriage to Lee Guber.
She expressed guilt and insecurities insofar as Jacqueline,
her daughter, was concerned. She was always trying to
compensate for the fact that she was not giving enough
time to Jacqueline. As a result she'd give in to the girl constantly, which perhaps overspoiled the child.

To the public and to her colleagues, Barbara appeared confident, self-assured, in complete control. But with Lichine
she constantly sought reassurance and advice. He often felt
that what she was searching for "was a father to pat her
on the head and say, 'You're a good girl, Barbara.' " Barbara thought of herself in that way—a good girl. It struck
Lichine as curious because here was a woman who seemed
so strong, so mature—a national personality—thinking of
herself as a little girl. "When something would happen that

made her unhappy," he said, "she'd look puzzled and say to me, 'Why did that happen? I'm a good girl . . . a good girl.' "

Despite the fact that Barbara and Lichine exchanged expensive gifts—he gave her Baccarat crystal and expensive wines, and she gave him gold cufflinks (like the kind her father wore); despite the fact that they were seen together at chic parties and White House functions, and on romantic get-togethers from Port-au-Prince to Monte Carlo; despite the fact that their names were linked as a twosome in the press, "Our relationship, I'm sad to say, was strictly platonic," Lichine acknowledged. "Barbara never viewed sex as a priority and it didn't exist in our relationship. It was apparent that it was not important to her. Power and success were the ultimate aphrodisiac for Barbara."

For a time, speculation of possible matrimony for Barbara centered on Alan Greenspan, then chairman of the Council of Economic Advisers under President Ford. Barbara had met him at a reception given by Vice President Rockefeller, and found him to be a gracious man, a good dancer, and single; he had been married in his twenties for less than a year. The two were seen together often, but he was just a good friend who was kind and considerate, and who listened to Barbara when she needed a sympathetic ear during that horrific period at ABC. "I don't know what I would have done without Alan during that NBC/ABC year," Barbara said. "I didn't go to a psychiatrist because I knew no one could help me. Every time I saw Alan, which was often, I would go through, 'Why did I leave NBC, why didn't I stay?' and Alan would listen to me, just listen. He's been there no matter who else I've been seeing. . . . We trust each other."

The reality of Barbara's relationship with men such as Lichine and Greenspan was completely at odds with the positive philosophy of winning a man that she had espoused in her 1970 book. "Nothing is more beguiling in this age of kooks and neurotics than the sunniness of a good mood," Barbara wrote. "A look of wholeness is a distinct joy. . . . So don't tell him what your psychiatrist said, and what happened when you ran into your first husband last week, or about the office bitch who is after your job."

According to a friend of Barbara's, "There was nothing romantic going on between Alan and Barbara. In fact, I remember parties at various homes like the Henry Grunwalds where she brought Alan and treated him rather rudely. He'd be in the middle of telling a story and she'd go off and talk to someone else. He seemed cowed by her, but he was a nice, safe escort."

During the middle to late 1970s, every man with whom Barbara was seen in public became her latest romantic interest—at least in the eyes of the press. It had become evident that editors had started viewing Barbara as a flashy celebrity whose social life was fodder for tabloid and gossip column chatter. In the fall of 1975, for instance, Barbara characterized as "ridiculous" reports that she was dating Senator Edward Brooke, a black Republican from Massachusetts. "I am seeing someone quite seriously at the moment and it is not Senator Brooke," she protested.

While the two had been seen lunching together in the Senate dining room and at a French restaurant in Washington, and were also spotted at parties at the Iranian embassy and elsewhere, Brooke, who was married but separated at the time, as was Barbara, termed speculation of any romance "incredible."

The issue even surfaced on the *Today* show. Barbara was interviewing White House photographer David Kennerly and asked him whether he was seeing President Ford's daughter, Susan. Kennerly shot back a question of his own, asking Barbara about her and Brooke. Barbara quickly moved on to another subject.

Stuart Schulberg told his wife, Jane, that he'd seen Barbara and Brooke together while the show was on location in Washington. And Lichine said that he had heard that Barbara and Brooke were seeing each other.

Less than a year after the flurry of publicity about them, Brooke filed for divorce from his wife of twenty-nine years, ending a lengthy separation. The Boston *Globe* noted that Barbara and Brooke had been "linked" but quoted Brooke as saying she was only a "good friend."

In late 1979, friends were discussing the possibility that Barbara would wed Sy Weintraub, an executive at Columbia Pictures. Liz Smith, who was the best source of such information since she was usually getting it from Barbara herself, reported that the two, "seem to be more in love than ever—he can't take his eyes off her—and surely wedding bells will ring in 1980."

But the bells never rang for Barbara and Sy.

By 1982, two men were competing for Barbara's affections—and bets were on again that she'd marry one of them. The suitors were a pair of powerhouses—former Controller of the Currency John Heymann, and Alan (Ace) Greenberg, the balding, muscular, poker-faced chief executive officer of the multibillion-dollar securities firm of Bear, Stearns.

Greenberg, who had been divorced for years, was a man of many interests—from hunting antelope in Africa with a bow and arrow, to playing in bridge tournaments and performing professional magic tricks. Asked by the *Wall Street Journal* in 1982 how he could run a major business and pursue a variety of hobbies, he said, "If a man doesn't play golf, watch TV, or chase girls, he has time to do a lot with his life. I don't do two out of the three." He didn't say which two.

Barbara's relationship with Greenberg became so serious that they'd gone apartment shopping together with marriage in mind, according to Liz Smith. "Barbara dallied with the idea of marrying him," the gossip columnist said. "I certainly know that Ace was just crushed when Barbara broke off with him."

After their relationship ended, Greenberg was seen

around New York with sexy, blond Monique Van Vooren, suggesting that he was neither a couch potato nor a duffer.

Barbara spent the Christmas 1982 holidays with Heymann in Mexico. "He wanted to marry her," said Smith. "The thing with John didn't last that long," said a society friend of Barbara's, "but she was very taken with him; she was stuck on him."

The big question within Barbara's circle of friends was why; why after all those years as an independent woman at the top of her profession, with so many powerful men at her beck and call, was she interested again in marriage? After all, she had failed twice in the past.

" 'Sadie, Sadie, married lady'—that's really the way Barb thinks," said a friend.

> She really wanted to be part of a couple again. Sure, there was always someone with pants on to take her out—but she felt she was at a stage in life where she wanted something permanent.
>
> Jackie Onassis is totally secure with her femininity and wouldn't have to get married again. Barbara needs a man to put quotes around her femininity. She gossips about romance all the time. "Do you have a beau?" she'll say. "Who are you going out with? Do you like anybody now? Who's asking you out?" That kind of thing. Phone calls, phone calls, phone calls with a lot of people and gossipy talk about men. In that respect, she hasn't changed much since Sarah Lawrence.

Barbara, who swore to herself she'd never again get involved with a man in show business, was about to fall in love with another.

Enter Mervyn Lee Adelson, television and movie impresario extraordinaire.

Born in October 1929, a month after Barbara, Merv was the son of Nathan and Pearl Schwarzman Adelson. Nate Adelson was a Russian immigrant who settled in a predominantly Jewish section of Los Angeles where he went into the grocery business. As a teenager in the late 1940s, Merv worked as a delivery boy for his father, and then as a liquor wholesaler. During that time he had dreams of becoming a professional baseball player. He tried college, but dropped out.

In the early Fifties the tanned, handsome young man with dark curly hair, a strong physique, a quiet and gentlemanly demeanor, and a penchant for expensive jewelry and clothes, moved to Las Vegas to make his way in the world. Merv investigated the retail grocery business in the gambling mecca and spotted a niche: while almost everything in town was open around the clock, he discovered there were no twenty-four-hour markets for those high-rollers who needed a loaf of bread or a quart of milk at four A.M.

Merv called Nate. With a ten-thousand-dollar loan from his father, he went into business. By the mid-Fifties, Merv was the owner of a successful chain of all-night Market Town supermarkets in Las Vegas, North Las Vegas, and Henderson. He also established a transportation division, using a fleet of trucks to bring fresh food products to the area. The food stores soon became the centerpiece for small shopping centers. In announcing the opening of one of his stores in 1957, Merv expressed "complete confidence in the future of southern Nevada."

In Las Vegas, Merv became friends and partners with Irwin Molasky, a home-improvement contractor from St. Louis; Allard Roen, a graduate of Duke University, and the manager of the Desert Inn; and Morris B. (Moe) Dalitz, whose name surfaced during the Kefauver crime committee hearings in Washington during the early 1950s.

In 1962, Merv, Dalitz, Roen, and Molasky founded Rancho La Costa, a multimillion-dollar resort and health spa near San Diego. Virtually overnight, it became a fashionable vacation spot for the rich and famous. It drew the superstar crowd: Carson, Streisand, Burnett, and Minnelli, among others.

During his years in Las Vegas, and after having rubbed shoulders with Hollywood stars at La Costa, Merv became attracted to the glitter and riches of the entertainment industry.

In 1969, he and Molasky put up $450,000 for a half interest in a new television and film company called Lorimar, which was named after Merv's first wife, Lori. The other cofounder was Lee Rich, an advertising executive. They started with a one-room office on Rodeo Drive in Beverly Hills, a secretary, and a fifty-thousand-dollar option on a book called *The Sporting Club*, which they made into a movie that bombed. The principals then focused their efforts on television programming. Rich was the creative genius behind the company; Merv was the businessman who made it all work.

Lorimar's first hit was *The Waltons*, and the rest was TV entertainment history. Lorimar, which later merged with Telepictures, Inc., went on to produce such blockbuster programs as *Eight Is Enough*, which coincidentally was based on the family of Barbara's friend, Joan Braden; *Dallas*, *Knots Landing*, and *Falcon Crest*—at one time 20/20's stiffest competition. By the mid-Eighties, Lorimar was producing more TV entertainment than any other company. Under Adelson's stewardship, the company made a series of lucrative acquisitions: Bozell Jacobs Kenyon & Eckhardt, one of the ten largest American advertising agencies; a home video distribution company that sold the popular Jane Fonda fitness tapes; and a magazine publishing group that included *Us*.

Just when everything was going smoothly for Merv, *Penthouse* magazine, in March 1975, published an exposé of La Costa headlined "The Hundred-Million-Dollar Resort with Criminal Clientele," which the principals of the resort charged was libelous.

The article alleged that La Costa was a hangout for underworld figures. It was also alleged that the Watergate scandal was planned at the resort, located a short distance from President Nixon's "western White House" at San Clemente.

After *Penthouse* publisher Bob Guccione refused to print a retraction, Adelson, Molasky, Dalitz, and Roen filed a libel suit against the magazine and the writers—seeking a record $522 million in damages.

The writers of the *Penthouse* story, Jeff Gerth, who subsequently became a reporter at the *New York Times*, and Lowell Bergman, who later worked for *20/20*, were dropped as defendants after they wrote a letter to the plaintiffs saying in part: "We feel it right to acknowledge the positive information we have received about you in recent years and, accordingly, to express regret for any negative implication or unwarranted harm that you believe may have befallen you, your family or businesses as a result of the *Penthouse* article."

Both sides—the La Costa group and *Penthouse*—spent millions of dollars in legal fees in what became the longest libel trial in legal history.

During the proceedings, Merv testified that the article was "ruinous." He stated that for years "people were turning their heads . . . saying, 'Hey, there is the guy from the Mafia.' . . . People don't talk to me." He testified that he was so "shattered" by the story that he became "reclusive," selling his Beverly Hills home to move to "a place not in the center of things"—the exclusive, celebrity beach community of Malibu.

During the trial Dalitz acknowledged knowing Meyer Lansky, the reputed patriarch of organized crime, and Sam Giancana, who had been chief of Chicago's crime syndicate. But Dalitz denied having had any business dealings with them. He also described himself as a friend of Teamsters' president Jimmy Hoffa, who disappeared in July 1975 under mysterious circumstances. Giancana was murdered that same year, one day before he was to testify before a

Congressional subcommittee investigating U.S. assassination plots against Fidel Castro.

In May 1982, after deliberating for two weeks, the jury found that the magazine had not libeled either the resort and four associated corporations or Adelson and Molasky. By that point, Roen and Dalitz's case had previously been severed from the others.

Two months later, in July 1982, Adelson and Molasky were granted a new trial in their case against *Penthouse*.

The matter would not reach its climax until November 1985—some six months before Barbara and Merv were married.

The first time Barbara and Merv were together was on a blind date in 1984—dinner at an Italian restaurant in Manhattan. Roy Cohn, who had handled legal work for one of the Las Vegas ventures, told friends he was responsible for introducing them. Barbara said a "mutual friend" had made reservations for them. Whoever played Cupid was right on the mark. Barbara was immediately attracted to Merv and knew the moment she met him that "he was someone special."

The restaurant was mobbed that night and the reservation was in Merv's name, which wielded more influence in Los Angeles than New York. Finally, Barbara got tired of waiting and suggested to Merv that she talk to the maître d'. He agreed, but it did no good—and they waited another half-hour until they were seated.

"It was a great equalizer," said Barbara. "It sort of broke the ice, and we were laughing at each other."

Merv met all of Barbara's criteria for a man. In addition, he had a Southern California mellowness about him that she found appealing. She had grown bored of the New York-Washington–axis man who seemed always to be "on." While Merv was an aggressive businessman, he had a laid-back style. At small gatherings, he'd charm friends by picking up a microphone and crooning "My Kind of

Girl." In Hollywood, he shied away from the glitter set. He liked to pal around on weekends with two of his best friends, actors Richard Crenna and Mike Connors, who often played tough-guy roles.

With Barbara, though, Merv's circle of friends expanded; he began rubbing shoulders with Henry Kissinger and dining with Ron and Nancy Reagan, among other high-profile political and society types.

Adelson was athletic and skied in Aspen, where he had a beautiful home. (His second wife, Gail, an interior decorator, from whom he separated in February 1984 after more than eight years of marriage, sued him in August 1988 for breach of contract over the use of the house.) He enjoyed walking on the beach in Malibu with his German Shepherd, Zack, or horseback riding. It was a lifestyle that Barbara felt she could become accustomed to, even though she was neither athletic nor outdoorsy, and favored Manhattan's polluted air over L.A.'s.

Several months after their first date, Merv proposed and Barbara joyfully accepted. The two became engaged in June 1985. Barbara told the *New York Times* they'd wed in the late fall. Ten days later, at Roy Cohn's birthday party celebration at the Palladium, a popular Manhattan club, Barbara was seen huddled with famed divorce and palimony attorney Marvin Mitchelson, asking him questions about prenuptial agreements. Mitchelson said he told her: "I never heard of a couple making a prenuptial agreement in which they didn't eventually get a divorce. It takes the romance out of marriage, signing an agreement." Based on his conversation with her, Mitchelson gave odds that Barbara wouldn't ask Merv for such an agreement, or vice versa. But no one knew for certain.

Even though Barbara said that she and Merv would marry in the fall, when the leaves changed, her marital status hadn't. Friends wondered why. They speculated that Barbara had gotten cold feet. The same indecisiveness had occurred before she married Bob Katz in the mid-Fifties and Lee Guber in the early Sixties.

"It's true that she went through periods of 'yes, no; yes, no' about Merv," said her cousin, Shirley Budd.

One friend said, "Barbara was very uncertain. She didn't know whether she wanted to be married to a man who lived in California because her life was in New York."

When Barbara sought advice from a friend and 20/20 colleague, the confidante told her, "You're not going to do any better."

Barbara's friend Wendy Goldberg, the wife of television producer Leonard Goldberg, in whose home the ceremony eventually took place, said,

> Barbara and Merv are two mature people and they don't take marriage lightly. They've both been married and they knew that the next time they made a commitment it was going to be forever. They're not the kind who say, "Okay, if it doesn't work, we'll get a divorce." They're past that stage. The marriage was on and off because it was such an enormous decision. She was single for many years. She's the kind of person who really weighs these kinds of decisions. She just doesn't say "Okay, let's try it."

But there may have been another reason for Barbara's reluctance to set a firm date. Before she took the vows of matrimony, Barbara wanted the still pending libel suit with *Penthouse* resolved in a satisfactory manner—one that would finally remove the cloud that had hung over Merv since the magazine story was published a decade earlier.

New York attorney Norman Roy Grutman, who represented *Penthouse* in the libel case, said that for months he and attorneys for the Adelson group had been trying without success to conclude the lengthy proceedings. "Each side saw that the litigation was not going to accomplish for them what their objectives were," said Grutman. "The Adelson people wanted vindication and also money, and

Penthouse wanted to be rid of this incubus. They were in an Indian arm wrestle that wasn't getting resolved."

Grutman began negotiations with the Adelson group's attorney, Irwin Buchalter of Los Angeles, to determine whether some sort of "letter of regret" could be drafted that would satisfactorily meet each side's needs, resulting in the discontinuance of the bitter case. But neither party could find the language that would offer mutual satisfaction.

Cupid changed all that.

"When Ms. Walters and Mr. Adelson were contemplating matrimony," revealed Grutman,

> I learned that one of the things that was on her mind was the public relations value of getting what I would call a deodorizing letter. It would be a letter in which things were going to be said about Mr. Adelson that would remove from him the stench which was the whole subject of the litigation.
>
> Obviously, Barbara Walters, being who she was, would not want it said that she was going to marry a man who could conceivably be deemed to have had [certain] connections. Barbara Walters or her advisers thought it would be well to remove that.
>
> When I sensed the increased interest on my adversary's part to accomplish an agreement that had previously not been possible to come by, I asked Bucky [Buchalter], "Does this have anything to do with Merv's desire to marry Barbara Walters?" And I was satisfied that that was the case. In many years of Bucky-watching, I had learned to be able to read the signs and portents without words.

In November 1985, after prolonged negotiations, the Adelson group and the publisher of *Penthouse* reached a settlement.

The final agreement, spelled out in a letter that Grutman and Buchalter had labored over, called for each side to pay its own legal costs, more than an estimated twenty million dollars.

The letter explained that the settlement was reached because "continued litigation will only be further torture and cause more expense to all parties. Accordingly, we have now reached a point where it appears that if the case were to continue through yet additional court proceedings, whoever would ultimately win would enjoy a Pyrrhic victory at best."

The two sides went on to take a conciliatory stance.

> *Penthouse* in the article . . . did not mean to imply nor did it intend for its readers to believe that Messrs. Adelson and Molasky are or were members of organized crime or criminals. In addition, *Penthouse* acknowledges that all of the individual plaintiffs, including Messrs. Dalitz and Roen, have been extremely active in commendable civic and philanthropic activities which have earned them recognition from many estimable people. Furthermore, *Penthouse* acknowledges that among plaintiffs' successful business activities is the La Costa resort itself, one of the outstanding resort complexes of the world.

For their part, the La Costa owners said in the letter that they had learned "of the many personal and professional awards and distinctions that have been conferred upon *Penthouse* and . . . Guccione."

Wendy Goldberg was watching her husband being fitted for a suit at Giorgio's in Beverly Hills when she was summoned to the telephone. Barbara had tracked her down to tell her that she and Merv had decided to go ahead with their oft-postponed nuptials. The call was on a Thursday afternoon and Barbara informed Wendy that she wanted to have the ceremony two days hence at the Goldbergs' home.

Barbara's close friend Beverly Sills was in San Francisco on business when she called home to tell her husband that she'd be taking the red-eye back to New York. Instead, he told her to head south to L.A. because Barbara had decided to go ahead with the wedding and she wanted both of them as guests.

Barbara's daughter, Jackie, "precipitated the wedding," according to Wendy Goldberg. "Jackie said to her, 'Mom, this is the most wonderful man. I don't know what's going to happen but I will always be, like, Merv's daughter.' Barbara wants Jackie to be happy, so whatever makes Jackie happy, makes Barbara happy."

On Saturday, May 10, 1986, in the Goldbergs' art- and antique-filled mansion in Beverly Hills, Barbara Walters became Mrs. Merv Adelson.

With orchids in her hair and wearing an ivory lace ankle-length gown, Barbara looked beautiful. The dress was given to her by Shelby Saltzman, of Beverly Hills, a friend and confidante, with whom Barbara had gone to Birch Wathen. Years earlier Barbara had introduced her to Barney Goodman, a British businessman, whom Saltzman married. Shelby's dress was the "something borrowed," a garter that Barbara wore was the "something blue," and a lace handkerchief from Merv's daughter-in-law was the "something new."

In the Goldbergs' projection room, Rabbi Jacob Pressman officiated. Lee Stevens gave Barbara away. Barbara's daughter, Jackie, was maid of honor and Merv's daughter, Ellie, was matron of honor. Merv's sons, Gary and Andy, were the best men. The Goldbergs' daughter, Amanda, was the flower girl, who dropped rose petals along the aisle. At Barbara's request, Beverly Sills read Elizabeth Barrett Browning's sonnet "How do I love thee? Let me count the ways." Jackie and her friend Tracy Langsom serenaded Barbara and Merv, singing "That's What Friends Are For." More than eighty guests, including some of the biggest names in the entertainment industry, were present.

*   *   *

Despite the fact that Barbara was based in New York and Merv in L.A., they had what Wendy Goldberg described as "bicoastal marital bliss. It's a wonderful marriage, a fabulous marriage. They are truly happy. They've arranged the bicoastal thing so well. They'll be one of the few bicoastal couples who will be successful. She comes here; he goes there. They do it; they work it out. But sometimes Barbara gets cranky. She's tired. *The woman is tired!* I've never known anybody to keep this kind of schedule. Ever, ever, ever! I mean, she's amazing."

In New York, Barbara put her 555 Park Avenue apartment on the market, asking three million dollars.

"The only reason Barbara decided to sell her place, which was gorgeous, was because Merv said that it really wasn't *his*," said Shirley Budd. "When he married Barbara, he wanted the feeling that he was coming to *his* home. So he prevailed on Barbara to sell." Merv had his own pied à terre at the Pierre, which he also sold. After a lengthy search, the newlyweds found the perfect abode—the entire seventh floor of the building at 944 Fifth Avenue. The twelve-room apartment, which cost them $5.75 million, was "absolutely exquisite," said Budd.

Barbara and Merv's apartment hunting—and the astronomical sums in which they were dealing—caught the fancy of New York's gossip columnists. Around the time they were buying and selling, writer Dominick Dunne, who'd just published *People Like Us*, a scathing, controversial novel about New York society in the Eighties, told an interviewer that the city's "nouvelle types" constantly talked about money. "How much the apartment cost, you know, somebody's apartment sold for six point eight and the guy who bought it just sold his to the so-and-so's for five point two and they're talking *millions* here." The New York rich, he observed, had become "like movie stars."

The new Walters-Adelson apartment had five bedrooms—the master bedroom, which was painted the color of what Liz Smith termed "expensive lingerie," had a fireplace and a red dressing room. There were three maids' rooms, a huge living room overlooking Fifth Avenue, a large library, and a dining room facing a courtyard. Barbara's New York *Post* columnist friend Cindy Adams said the couple "probably went Dutch" on the cost of the place.

"Everything is authentically antique," said Budd. "Most of her important pieces were brought over from London; she went there and chose authentic pieces with [documentation] papers. Every piece of wood in her house is an authentic piece."

Barbara retained New York's "in" decorator, the "Prince of Chintz," Mario Buatta. "The apartment is very glamorous like she is," he said. "But I wasn't allowed to do a lot of chintz."

On the other coast, Merv bought the beautiful home he once owned during a previous marriage—a sprawling, countrylike house in Bel Air with a pool, where Barbara learned to swim, a tennis court, and an indoor gym. "The vibes seemed right for both of us. . . . Merv was immediately at home, and we could arrange it together from scratch to suit ourselves," said Barbara. Because of their professions, Merv added a projection room to screen movies for guests, and Barbara added a professional dressing room "so I can save time at the studio by arriving dressed, made up, coifed, and ready for the camera."

Despite her busy schedule, Barbara, now a dutiful corporate wife, helped Merv as much as she could with his career. For instance, she was instrumental in convincing comedian Jackie Mason to choose Lorimar over another studio to produce his first film in the wake of his hit one-man Broadway show *The World According to Me*. Merv and Barbara had gone to see Mason on stage and afterward came to his dressing room "and hugged and kissed me and jumped all over me. I thought I was passing away or something." Mason told them about the project—a story about five Jewish housewives who get caught running a whorehouse—and then "Lorimar began chasing me, calling me every other day, willing to pay any price to get the screenplay."

After Barbara and Merv met with Mason, 20/20 did a feature on the comedian. The profile was introduced by Hugh Downs and afterward Barbara and correspondent Lynn Sherr, who did the piece, had a little chitchat on camera about the comic.

Barbara also did an interview for 20/20 with another Lorimar-related personality, Jane Fonda, whose popular fitness videotapes were distributed by a division of the company. That issue never was raised, but some 20/20 staffers were upset because Barbara did the interview at the request of Fonda, who was meeting with opposition at the time from people in a town where she was shooting a film. They were irate over her support of the Vietcong during the Vietnam War.

"I didn't think it was going to be a big deal," Barbara told the New York Times. "I can't question Jane's motives. I'm responsible for the piece on the air. Was it tough, was it responsible? If Jane Fonda apologizes, it's a big story." Barbara was supported by Roone Arledge.

Merv helped Barbara when he could, too. For a time gossip columnist Aileen (Suzy) Mehle had stopped talking to Barbara for personal reasons. Acting as a mediator, Merv approached Mehle at a party and asked her if she would please talk to his wife, that it would make Barbara so happy. When Mehle agreed, Barbara hugged her and their wrangle ended.

In May 1987, Suzy was among some four hundred high-profile pals of Barbara's and Merv's invited to La Costa for several days of pampering and partying. Donald and Ivana Trump flew a group of prominent New Yorkers to the spa on their new 727 jetliner. Barbara, who had just returned from a trip to China, was the emcee of the event.

Subsequently, La Costa was purchased by a Japanese investment group. When Lorimar-Telepictures merged with

Warner Communications in 1988, Merv became a vice chairman. In 1989, Warner and Time Inc. merged, becoming one of the biggest media-entertainment conglomerates in the world.

On Monday, September 15, 1986, Barbara saw the front page of the *Wall Street Journal* and felt sick. Merv had told her that the paper was working on a story about him, Lorimar, and a major acquisition in which the company was involved, but Barbara had no idea that the piece would be of such blockbuster proportions.

Everything she hoped had been buried almost a year earlier with the settlement of the *Penthouse* suit was there for all the world to see in a story that took up almost thirteen column *feet* of newsprint in America's most prestigious business daily.

The story, which took award-winning investigative reporter Jonathan Kwitny several months to pull together, was headlined "Seeds of Success; Two Lorimar Officials Have Had Ties to Men of Underworld Repute; Merv Adelson, Irwin Molasky Relied on Teamster Loans to Build Many Businesses; Entertaining at La Costa." Above the fold was a head-shot drawing of Merv, smiling, wearing a dinner jacket. The second paragraph noted that Barbara was his wife.

The *Journal* story said that Merv and Molasky were named in a May 13, 1966, internal FBI document. "Neither are known to have arrest records," wrote FBI special agent H. Edgar Strahl, "but there is no question as to their close association with the hoodlum element."

During the *Penthouse* case, and to the *Journal*, Adelson, who had never been charged with a crime, denied any criminal ties. In discussing La Costa and his friendships, Merv said, "My practice is not to associate with mobsters. If somebody says he's a mobster, I won't associate with him. You can only go by the feeling you have from the meeting you have with them."

Molasky had never been charged with any crimes either, and he also steadfastly denied any mob connections.

The *Journal* asserted that Merv's other two partners, Moe Dalitz and Allard Roen, had been linked to criminal activity. Roen, "a lifelong Dalitz protégé," the story said, had pleaded guilty to securities violations in a stock-fraud case in the early Sixties.

The *Journal* said that "a steady stream of Mafia men and racketeers" were guests, sometimes free, at La Costa, at the time Merv was president of the resort. They included labor racketeer Anthony (Tony Pro) Provenzano and Meyer Lansky, among others.

Merv, Molasky, Roen, and Dalitz became partners in ventures that received more than one hundred million dollars in loans during the Sixties and Seventies from the Teamsters Union's Central States pension fund, which at the time was reputed to be run by mobsters, according to the newspaper. Merv testified at the *Penthouse* trial that he had several discussions about the loans with Jimmy Hoffa, but asserted he was unaware of the union leader's alleged criminal ties.

The reason for the *Journal*'s story was Lorimar's agreement to buy nine television stations, six of them network affiliates, and to borrow as much as two billion dollars to finance the purchase. If the deal was approved by the Federal Communications Commission and investors, the *Journal* said, "Merv Adelson will soon become a first-rank power in American communications." In detailing Adelson's and his business partners' past, the *Journal* noted that the FCC was reviewing the pending purchase under a statute that called for an examination of the "character" of buyers of federally licensed broadcast stations.

While Kwitny was doing his reporting, which included an interview with Adelson in the *Journal* offices, Merv tried to get his former adversary, attorney Roy Grutman, to see if he could convince the paper not to go with the story.

"Merv Adelson called me," said Grutman,

and urged me to plead with the *Wall Street Journal* not to publish its story. I said, "When you were married to somebody before Barbara, on the occasion of seeing the *Penthouse* story, and to prove your machismo, and your wholesomeness to your then wife, you embarked on a legal adventure that I think cost you over ten million bucks. That was foolishness. Don't do it again." And Merv said to me, "No, I'm not going to do it. But, Jesus, I've had enough of this." I said, "Perhaps you have. I think the article is a legitimate journalistic piece." He said, "Thanks. So long."

That conversation was a far cry from the one I had with Merv when I left the courtroom after the completion of the La Costa case. He came over to me and said, "Mr. Grutman"—and that was the first time he had ever spoken to me outside of a legal setting—and I said, "Yes." And he said to me, "Someday Lorimar may want to do a movie about a fat, corrupt, scumbag lawyer. Would you like to take the part?" And I said, "I couldn't do it justice." That was the next to the last time that we ever spoke. Merv is an interesting person. He's a great American business success.

Two weeks after the *Journal* story ran, New York *Newsday* columnist Susan Mulcahy, in an item headlined "Stands by Her Man," reported that Barbara was "absolutely ill" after reading the piece on Merv. Quoting "sources close to Walters," Mulcahy reported that Barbara "actually took to her bed for a couple of days." It also was noted that Barbara had recovered to host a dinner party the previous weekend "for friends not intimidated by the furor over the [*Journal*] story."

That party, at the Pierre, was the East Coast celebration for all of Barbara's friends—three hundred in number— who weren't able to attend her wedding in Los Angeles. The biggest names in media, entertainment, and society were there. At one point, in addressing the power gathering, Barbara said wryly, "I would like to thank the *Wall Street Journal* for underwriting tonight's party. My wish for the *Wall Street Journal* is that they had to arrange tonight's seating."

The day after the Mulcahy column, Liz Smith reported that she "happened to be out on the town with Barbara" the night after the *Journal* story ran. "I think I can say there was no evidence that she was ill or had taken to her bed."

Eighteen months after the *Journal* story, Barbara's marriage to Merv was the subject of a feature story in the March 1988 issue of *Ladies Home Journal.*

In the article, writer Christine Sutherland, describing Barbara as "fiercely protective" of Merv, asked her about the *Journal* story. "It was unpleasant at the time, and it hurt, but it seems light-years ago. And you know, the man who wrote it is not with the *Wall Street Journal* any longer!" In saying that, Sutherland described Barbara's face as "suddenly becoming hard."

After learning of Barbara's comment, Paul Steiger, deputy managing editor of the *Wall Street Journal,* wrote a letter to the editor of *Ladies Home Journal:* "In your March issue you quote Barbara Walters as saying that the author of a *Wall Street Journal* article about her husband no longer works for us. In fact, Jonathan Kwitny remains a staff reporter here and we stand by his story."

"Barbara," observed a friend, "plays hardball."

On a warm evening in September 1988, seven days before her fifty-ninth birthday, Barbara Walters, looking at least a decade younger, appeared before a standing-room-only crowd of her fans in the large auditorium of the Ninety-second Street Y, on New York's Upper East Side. Those in the audience—mostly upper-middle-class Jewish women —had paid as much as twenty dollars each to hear Barbara reminisce about her favorite celebrity interviews, and to get an opportunity to ask *her* questions, something they'd watched Barbara do for close to three full decades. Barbara was a marvelous speaker that night, enthralling those who had come to see her in person.

During the question session, a woman stood up and asked Barbara how she would like to be remembered. There was a flurry of nervous laughter in the audience— as if some expected her to fire off a glib response, and move on to another question. But Barbara was quite serious and sincere in her reply.

"How would I like to be remembered?" She repeated the question thoughtfully. "I think, professionally, as a good journalist. It means a lot to become a journalist, and we're conscious of our peers. But, much more, privately, as a loving wife and mother and friend. I try—I have to *try* to be a good journalist."

Barbara said she hoped her obituary would say that.

Among those sitting in the first few rows, which were reserved for Barbara's friends, family, and other VIPs, was her husband, Merv. It was one of the few times he'd seen Barbara work before a live audience and he was mesmerized by her poise and confidence.

After the lecture, Merv and Barbara had time for a quick kiss goodbye before a limo took her to the airport; she had an exclusive interview the next day in Boston with Kitty Dukakis.

Merv was left alone to have dinner with Barbara's cousin and her husband, and they talked about her successful lecture that evening.

"You know, Shirley," Merv said over salad, "Barbara could just as easily have been an actress. She's just so *good* at it."

40

UPDATE: 1991

I had no plans to add new material to this book after its hardcover publication in March 1990.

At the point I finished writing, everything appeared on track in Barbara's life; she seemed happier and more content than friends could ever recall. Rarely, they observed, was she melancholy. The dark clouds of depression that had sporadically cast a shadow over her had vanished, they felt, forever.

Barbara's career, as usual, continued to blossom like a perennial. More exclusive interviews came her way. Her power base at *20/20*—and within the news and entertainment divisions at ABC—was impregnable. Jane Pauleys and Deborah Norvilles seemed to come and go on the networks, but Barbara remained singular in her staying power, a fact that still, after all these years, left many of her colleagues, critics and viewers baffled. *The Barbara Walters Special* continued to garner glowing ratings and respectable revenues at a time when the networks were coming on hard times, vis-a-vis competition from cable television, a time-shifting viewership, and a down-shifting economy.

As a society creature in New York, Barbara was out and about virtually every evening. She'd become THE doyenne of the night, still courting the rich and famous, and being courted by them. Her friend, gossip columnist Liz Smith, was documenting Barbara's comings and goings more than ever.

Barbara and Jackie had, at least for the time being, resolved many of the differences that had arisen during Jackie's adolescence. Jackie still hoped to become a model—finally with Barbara's blessings. They even appeared together publically at an awards ceremony, and a warm photograph of mother and daughter—the first in years—celebrated their apparent harmony in a national magazine. As a friend asserted: "Jackie's now a happy kid who's in good shape."

Much of the exhilaration and joy that friends and colleagues saw in Barbara—"the glow," as one put it—was attributed to her marriage to Merv Adelson. It seemed that Wendy Goldberg's prediction would come true: Barbara and Merv WOULD survive their bicoastal lifestyle.

At the time Barbara gave that poignant talk in New York—the one that held Merv in such awe—their love was beyond question, friends felt. Mr. and Mrs. Adelson, confidantes were happy to reveal, were walking on air. This book, then, seemed to have a happy ending, requiring no epilogue.

But that soon changed. The Adelsons' bicoastal bliss subtly shifted to discontent and disharmony. By the fall of 1990, talk of divorce was in the air. It seemed apparent that the old pressures that impacted on Barbara's two previous marriages—her career, her reserve, some would say her indifference—had surfaced once again, friends observed.

BARBARA WALTERS' MARRIAGE HITS ROCK BOTTOM was the headline that greeted readers at supermarket checkout counters around the country in the late summer of 1990. PALS FEAR IT'S ALL OVER AS HUBBY TELLS HER: IT'S YOUR CAREER OR ME. For almost six weeks this tabloid story—claiming that Barbara and Merv were headed for a divorce unless she chose between him or her career—was ignored by the mainstream media.

It wasn't until Barbara telephoned Liz Smith some weeks later that the essence of the story was confirmed. The next morning the New York *Daily News* carried a front-page story that Barbara and Adelson had split. Barbara had told Smith that it was a trial separation. The gossip columnist reported that Adelson's business interests—which had shifted from entertainment to investments and real estate development—now required him to spend most of his time in Los Angeles, while Barbara needed to be in New York. Smith expressed the belief that the couple would "remain the closest friends . . . I personally hope they will find that their separation isn't worth the separation."

The explanation—that distance did not make the Adelsons' hearts grow fonder—was full of holes. It's quite clear that both sides knew what their marital game plan would be when they stepped under the Chupah four years earlier.

What really caused the split? Was it Barbara's career? Her detachment? Her aloofness? Had Barbara failed again as a wife . . . Merv as a husband?

The answers are not easy to come by, because Barbara is a very private person—loath to reveal her inner feelings, even to her closest confidantes. Merv, too, masks his emotions; he is, as one close observer put it, "pretty much a loner. He doesn't confide in a lot of people."

What's clear, however, is that Adelson worked harder than Barbara to make the marriage work, according to insiders.

"Merv basically tried very hard to share his life," said a Los Angeles society matron and friend. "Merv tried very hard to get Barbara to share her life. But basically she would never do anything he wanted to do. He's a big sports

fan. He loves going to the Lakers games. He likes skiing.
Merv is at his best on his horse in the Rockies. That's
where he's the happiest—with the cowboys. But Barbara
just couldn't come through. Merv was really in love with
Barbara. He really had to stretch to keep the marriage
going.

"We were together at dinner one night. Barbara looked
beautiful. Merv was at her side and he held his hand
against the small of her back—a sweet, intimate, very supportive gesture. But she just didn't get it. To her, marriage
was having the same man take you to the same tired black-
tie dinners—and Merv grew to hate that. I mean, how
many times can you have dinner with Henry Kissinger?"

Actually, in the early months of their marriage, Merv
had been mesmerized by the world Barbara opened for
him—the mighty people in the high places. As an intimate
of Adelson's revealed: "Around the time Merv met Barbara he had difficulty finding a balance between power,
business and a more rounded life. Everything went to the
power—all of his energies. There's no question that Merv
was seduced by Barbara's power. Merv takes great pride
in what people do, and Barbara's accomplishments are as-
tounding. We're talking about a one-time grocery-store delivery kid who ended up dining at the White House.
Barbara's power was very, very seductive to him.

"Merv wanted Barbara's power. He wanted the house
in Bel Air, the apartment on Fifth Avenue. But then he
looked around at his life and said, 'Is this all there is?' Merv
got sick and tired of Barbara's salons and fancy dinner parties. He hates—*hates*—cocktail parties. In fact, he *always*
hated the social aspect. In many ways, Merv's an old-
fashioned guy. He cannot abide women who argue or fight,
he abhors that . . . but Barbara's a powerful, tough lady.
In the end, what Merv really wanted in a wife was someone
who would always be there for him. This is a guy who really
wants a woman who will bring him his slippers, a woman

who orients her life to taking care of him. Can you even imagine Barbara doing that?"

"I married Merv for my old age," a friend quoted Barbara as saying shortly after the wedding. But several years later, on the verge of their split, Barbara had an addendum for her friend. Now she was saying, "I married Merv for my old age, but now I realize I'm not going to have an old age." Said the friend: "Being alone is not fun. Barbara thought that because the rest of the world wants love and companionship that maybe she did, too. But it's very difficult for someone like Barbara to be there for someone—not only because of her personality, but because of her career and her travelling. Barbara feels her life is so exciting, interesting, marvelous and glamorous that she doesn't need to share it with anyone."

Another friend of Barbara's, who was shocked and saddened by the Adelsons' separation, expressed the feeling that love and marriage are not important to Barbara. "Barbara's not in love with Merv now," the friend observed. "Obviously, if she was, she wouldn't have split with him. I'm really very, very sorry that this happened because I thought that Barbara had finally married a man she loved, and that the marriage would last."

In the late summer of 1990, while they were still together, Barbara and Merv, vacationing at their home in Aspen, threw an impromptu, informal party for some friends and family—actually an old-fashioned barbeque. The guest of honor, who happened to be in Aspen at the time, was British Prime Minister Margaret Thatcher. Wearing an apron and wielding a fork, Merv cooked the steaks while Barbara and her friend, Mrs. Thatcher, chatted privately. Barbara expressed to Mrs. Thatcher her reservations about the marriage, and it was said that the prime minister advised Barbara to end it if it was not working out. Not long after, Barbara revealed the separation to Liz Smith.

Barbara Brogliatti, who had worked for Adelson at Lorimar and who also acts as a spokesperson for Barbara and Merv, asserted in mid-October of 1990 that, despite the separation, Barbara and Merv are "extremely close friends . . . they are people who love each other. They have dinner together when Barbara's in L.A. I don't know if they are cohabitating."

Brogliatti contended that the separation resulted because "Merv's circumstances changed since they got married. He sold his companies. He had less reason, if any, to come to New York. His new business keeps him in Los Angeles. Merv is someone whose lifestyle is one of athletics and beach and that type of thing. It's two different lifestyles and neither of them would think of asking the other one to change."

Asked if there was any chance of a reconciliation, Brogliatti observed, "What tomorrow may bring, I have no guess."

But another friend saw a denouement to the Adelson marriage. "Eventually they'll divorce. The prenuptial agreement should be quite an interesting document!"

                                                              J.O.

NOTES AND SOURCES

During the writing of this book, I relied primarily on my interviews, and public and private documents. Two books that were extremely helpful in terms of giving me an initial grounding in the history and chronology of my subject were *The Today Show* by Robert Metz (Chicago: Playboy Press, 1977) and *Barbara Walters: TV's SuperLady* by Barbara and Dan Lewis (Pinnacle Books, Inc., 1976). Barbara Matusow's *The Evening Stars: The Making of the Network News Anchor* (Houghton Mifflin Company, 1983) also deserves special mention, as does *Chronicle of the 20th Century* (Chronicle Publications Inc., 1987).

I'm grateful to the librarians and other staffers at a number of news organizations for their assistance, especially John Cronin, *Boston Herald*; Liz Donovan, *Miami Herald*; Peggy Rosenthal, New York *Daily News*; Bee Maxwell, *Los Angeles Times*; Glenda Harris, *Las Vegas Review-Journal*; and Ken Craven and John Chalmers at the Harry Ransom Humanities Research Center, University of Texas, Austin.

I'd also like to thank those who gave me their help at the *New York Post, Broadcasting* magazine, *TV Guide, Saturday Evening Post, Philadelphia* magazine, *Boston* magazine, the Lincoln Center Library for the Performing Arts, the staff at the Museum of Broadcasting, and the staffers at the Presidential libraries of John F. Kennedy, Lyndon B. Johnson, Richard Nixon, Gerald Ford, and Jimmy Carter.

Numerous other news and publishing entities were invaluable resources, and are credited in the following notes. I have a particularly warm place in my heart for Telephone Reference of the Montgomery County, Maryland Department of Public Libraries.

In the following notes, I primarily cite dates of author interviews and the placement and dates of sources quoted in the public domain, or in other documents.

EPIGRAPH

xv I DON'T THINK THERE IS ANYTHING. *Parade* magazine, November 27, 1988.

CHAPTER ONE

3 BARBARA WALTERS WAS NOT BORN. Numerous articles about Barbara and reference sources such as *Who's Who in America, Almanac of Famous People, World Almanac* directly or indirectly gave her date of birth as September 25, 1931. Barbara Walters' birth certificate on file at the Office of Human Services, Massachusetts Department of Public Health, Registry of Vital Records and Statistics, Boston, showed she was born on September 25, 1929.

6 IT IS ONLY RECENTLY. *How to talk with practically anybody about practically anything*, Barbara Walters (New York: Doubleday & Company, Inc, 1970), p. 84.

6 DENA DEVOTED HER ENTIRE LIFE. Interviews, Shirley Budd, December 5–6, 1988; March 30–31, 1989.

7 EXPANDING ON HER PUBLISHED RESEARCH. Interview, Dr. Francis Kaplan Grossman, May 3, 1989.

8 HE LOST A BLOODY FORTUNE. Budd interview.

CHAPTER TWO

9   IF BARBARA'S PATERNAL GRANDPARENTS. Interview, Lorraine Walters Katz, November 28, 1988.
10 DESCRIBED THEMSELVES AS "LITVAKS." Ibid.
11 JUST BEFORE THE FAMILY. Budd interview.
12 IT MADE ME THE MOST DESPERATELY LONELY. "Only Human" column, Sidney Fields, New York Mirror, November 9, 1951.
13 ALL OF WHOM DEVELOPED CANCER. Budd interview.
13 HARRY WAS A SUCCESSFUL MERCHANT. Interview, Lorraine Walters Katz, Asbury Park Press news stories.
13 BARNEY OPERATED A SMALL HOTEL. Atlantic City Press news stories. Budd interview.
13 BELLE WAS AN ARTIST. Budd interview. Interview, Harmon Ashley, friend and associate of Belle's husband, Sidney Schrieber, secretary and general attorney, Motion Picture Association of America.
13 FLORENCE DIRECTED A PRESTIGIOUS. Interview, Mrs. Alexandre Rosenberg, Paul Rosenberg & Co. gallery, April 3, 1989. Budd interview.
13 REBECCA WAS MARRIED. Budd interview.
13 REBECCA'S SON, ALLAN. Interview, Ashley. Mankoff's Lusty Europe (New York: The Viking Press, 1972).
13 BARBARA'S MATERNAL GRANDPARENTS. Interviews, Daniel Seletsky, June 3, 1968; Herman Seletsky, June 5, 1988; Alvin Alkon, June 2, 1988.

CHAPTER THREE

15 JUST LET ME GET MY HANDS. Saturday Evening Post, February 20, 1943.
17 HE PUT AN EXTRA FIVE IN MY ENVELOPE. New York Mirror, November 9, 1951.
17 LOUIE STAYED WITH QUIGLEY. Interviews, Ben (Ford) Abrams, January 22, 1988, April 10, 1989.
19 HE WAS A HELL OF A GUY. Seletsky, op. cit.
19 HE LIVED UP TO THE DOLLAR. Interviews, Ed Risman, January 27, 1988, March 15, 1988, August 31, 1988.
20 FOR A FAST TWO YEARS. Saturday Evening Post, op. cit.
21 YOU'RE A HAS-BEEN. Ibid.

CHAPTER FOUR

23   THE CLUB WAS LOU'S LIFE. Risman, op. cit.

24   BARBARA WAS INTROSPECTIVE. Interview, source.

26   WE WERE ALL FAIRLY COMFORTABLE. Interview, Joan Wein-
     rib Hopner, March 14, 1988.

27   HE DIDN'T TRY TO BUILD. *Saturday Evening Post*, February 20,
     1943.

28   I WAS STUCK WITH THE LEASE. *New York Post*, July 27, 1942.

28   HIS FATHER, MY GRANDFATHER. Budd, op. cit.

28   A FRIEND AND COMPETITOR. Interviews, Eddie Davis, Septem-
     ber 22 and 27, 1988.

29   I DECIDED TO MAKE THE SWITCH. Risman, op. cit.

29   SHE'D BECOME A VERY. Ibid.

29   LOU'S GAMBLING WASN'T DENA'S ONLY CONCERN. Inter-
     views, sources.

30   IT TAKES A VERY STRONG. Interview, source.

30   LOU WOULD SAY. Interview, source.

30   IF DENA KNEW. Interview, source.

30   DENA BECAME VERY VISIBLE. Risman, op. cit.

31   SHE'S TURNED OUT TO BE MY SEVEREST CRITIC. Rube
     Dorin's "Broadway Showmen" column, 1949.

31–33   CAMP FEROSDEL. Interviews, Barbara Shiffman Altman, June
     13 and 17, 1988.

32   BARBARA STARTED SMOKING. Interviews, Judy Haskell,
     March 21 and 31, 1988.

CHAPTER FIVE

36   SHE WAS A SERIOUS LITTLE GIRL. Interview, Marilyn Franklin
     Farber, March 23, 1988.

36   I FELT LIKE THE POOR LITTLE RICH GIRL. *Miami Herald*,
     March 2, 1970.

36   I HAD A VERY DREARY ADOLESCENCE. *TV Guide*, January
     2–8, 1965.

36   IT JUST DIDN'T FIT INTO MY SCHEME OF THINGS. *Miami
     Herald*, March 23, 1965.

37   THIS PLACE PUTS ON PERHAPS. Memo dated May 11, 1944,
     from special investigator in charge of the Miami Field office of the
     FBI to Director J. Edgar Hoover, Crime Survey, Miami Field Divi-
     sion, 1944. Made available to author under U.S. Freedom of Infor-
     mation Act.

37   MR. LOEW WAS FURIOUS. Interviews, Sonja Loew, January 27,

1988, January 29, 1988, March 21, 1988.

38 GO TO THE LIDO. Ibid.

38 IN NEW YORK, LOU HAD TO DO BUSINESS. Interviews, George Gill, February 3 and 6, 1988.

40 SHE DIDN'T APPEAR TO BE AN EXCEPTIONAL STUDENT. Interview, Jean Claster Milling, April 17, 1989.

40 BARBARA FLUNKED GYM. *Vogue*, September 1978.

40 SHE WAS DETERMINED AT THAT TIME. Interview, Enid Kraeler Reiman, March 6, 1988.

41 I ALWAYS GOT THE FEELING. Interview, April 17, 1989.

41 BARBARA WOULD COME TO ME AND SAY. Gill interviews.

CHAPTER SIX

44 AN INFORMATIONAL REPORT FROM THE SPECIAL AGENT. Document made available to author under U.S. Freedom of Information Act.

44 ANOTHER FBI MEMORANDUM NOTED THAT. Ibid.

44 DADDY, WHAT IS GOING. *Barbara Walters: TV's Superlady*, Barbara and Dan Lewis (New York: Pinnacle Books, 1976).

45 SHE DIDN'T WEAR MAKEUP. Interviews, Greta Joseloff Steinberg, March 7 and 17, 1988.

46 IN A SIMILAR VEIN. Interviews, Judy Nelson Drucker, February 5 and 9, 1988.

46 I DON'T THINK THAT MANY PEOPLE KNEW. Interview, Gloria Palter, February 29, 1988.

48 HE NEVER SHOWED AND SHE LOST FACE. Interview, John Throne, February 7, 1988.

48 SHE WAS OVERWHELMED BY. Interview, Stuart Jacobs, February 9, 1988.

48 THEY WERE SO CLIQUISH. Drucker interviews.

48 SHE WAS NOT PARTICULARLY OUTGOING. Interview, Annabelle Wald D'Augustine, March 3, 1988.

49 ONE OF BARBARA'S FRIENDS. Interview, Shirley Rosenfeld Berman, March 9, 1988.

49 ON CHRISTMAS EVE OF 1944. Interview, Zelda Kaplan Silver, March 7, 1988.

50 SHE WAS REALLY A WONDERFUL GIRL. Interview, Stan Reich, March 2, 1988.

50 GUARDED ABOUT THE KIDS. Interview, Ray Jacobson, March 1, 1988.

51 SHE WASN'T THE MOST OUTGOING PERSON. Interview, Edward Klein, March 10, 1988.

52 ONE CRITIC CALLED THE SHOW. George Freedley, *New York*

Morning Telegraph, November 8, 1943.

52   HE ACTUALLY LOST THE CLUB. Abrams, op. cit.

52   I THOUGHT BY BEING IN THE SORORITY. Berman interview.

52   BARBARA WASN'T HAPPY. Throne interview.

CHAPTER SEVEN

54   BARBARA HAD A KIND OF STRENGTH AND BITTERNESS.
     Interview, source.

55   A SMALL, GENTILE-RUN, JEWISH SCHOOL. Interview, Marcia
     Elson Rodman, June 8, 1988.

55   IT WAS A REACTIONARY, CLOSED ENVIRONMENT. Inter-
     view, Helen Udell Lowenstein, August 7, 1988.

56   BIRCH WATHEN WAS REALLY SNOTTY. Interview, Jeri Rosen-
     berger Soman, June 11, 1988.

56   SHE WAS A KID WHO HAD NO HOME LIFE. Lowenstein inter-
     view.

57   AFTER WE FOUND OUT THAT HER FATHER. Interview,
     David Kane, June 8, 1988.

57   OH, HER FATHER OWNS THAT NIGHTCLUB. Interview, Nata-
     lie Lazrus Roberts, June 15, 1988.

58   WE HAVE NEVER BEEN ABLE TO GET HER. Interview, source.

58   AS FAR AS I WAS CONCERNED. Rodman interview.

58   I WOULD NEVER HAVE CHOSEN BARBARA. Interview, Pat
     Meyer Kovacs, June 15, 1988.

59   ALTHOUGH BARBARA DRESSED LIKE EVERYBODY. Inter-
     view, source.

59   WE WERE VERY DIFFERENT, DISPARATE. Interviews, Joan Gil-
     bert Peyser, June 16 and 20, 1988, August 2, 1988.

60   IT WAS QUITE A HORRID LITTLE MAGAZINE. Interview, Pat
     Fry Morrissey, June 7, 1988.

60   BARBARA LOOKED AT IT INCREDULOUSLY. Peyser inter-
     views.

61   TELL ME THE TRUTH. Ibid.

61   I WAS OVERWHELMED. Ibid.

62   I FEEL . . . THAT IT WAS THIS DARK BUSINESS. Interview,
     source.

62   RELATIONSHIPS WITH MEN AND SEXUALITY. Grossman,
     op. cit.

63   I NEVER KNEW ABOUT HER SISTER. Soman interview.

63   WE ALL WENT TO EACH OTHER'S HOUSES. Interview, Patri-
     cia Leavitt Rosenthal, June 7, 1988.

63   CAN YOU IMAGINE HOW SHE FELT. Interview, source.

64   MY HUSBAND AND I LOOKED AT EACH OTHER. Peyser in-

terviews.

64 WHEN THERE WERE NO OBVIOUS PHYSICAL STIGMATA. Grossman, op. cit.

64 JACKIE WAS NOT REALLY, REALLY, REALLY RETARDED. Budd, op. cit.

CHAPTER EIGHT

67 CAN A SCHOOL WITHOUT CLASSROOMS. *New York World,* May 12, 1929.

68 THIS WAS THE FIRST TIME. Interview, Theodore Joffe Edelman.

70 JOHN CAMERON SWAYZE. *The Evening News Stars: The Making of the Network News Anchor,* Barbara Matusow (Boston: Houghton Mifflin Company, 1983), p. 57.

71 BARBARA WASN'T VERY INTERESTED. Interview, Cathryn Mansell, May 9, 1989.

72 THE SCHOOL WAS VERY POLITICALLY ACTIVE. Interview, Edith Reveley Remoy, April 14, 1988.

72 THERE WERE PEOPLE ON CAMPUS. Ibid.

72 HAROLD TAYLOR HAD A VACANCY. Interview, Harold Taylor, May 9, 1989.

73 THE STIFF-SPINED, ANGRY ONLY. *The Groves of Academe,* Mary McCarthy (New York: Harcourt, Brace & World, Inc., 1951, 1952), p. 65.

73 SHE DIDN'T CALL ATTENTION TO HERSELF. Taylor interview.

73 I DON'T THINK BARBARA WAS INTERESTED. Interview, Bessie Schonberg, May 8, 1989.

74 ACCORDING TO COHN, LOU SAID. *New York Times Magazine,* September 10, 1972.

74 FOR CHICKIE. Ibid.

74 BARBARA AND COHN WERE DATING SERIOUSLY. Interviews, Anne Williams Ferguson, September 12 and 20, 1988.

74 I WAS THERE WHEN THEY CAME IN. Interviews, Irving Zussman, February 4 and 14, 1988, March 24, 1988, January 25, 1989, June 1, 1989.

75 BARBARA DIDN'T OFTEN GET PASSIONATE. Peyser interviews.

75 I THINK IT WAS LOVE. Ferguson interviews.

75 ROY ONCE ASKED FOR HER HAND. Budd, op. cit.

75 COHN HIMSELF SAID. *New York Times Magazine,* op. cit.

75 ROY MEANT IT. Budd, op. cit.

76 SHE AND MY MOTHER. *New York Times Magazine,* op. cit.

76 EVERYTHING BARBARA GAINED FROM ROY. Budd, op. cit.

76 ROY WAS A BASTARD. Interviews, John Lord, August 16 and 31, 1988.

76 I SAID, BARBARA. Ferguson interviews.

76 I THINK SHE'S PROBABLY BEEN VERY INNOCENT. Schonberg interview.

76 BARBARA DIDN'T ASSOCIATE. Budd, op. cit.

77 KATHARINE CORNELL. *Vogue*, September 1978.

78 BARBARA AND MARCIA WERE INSEPARABLE. Interviews, Shirley Plavin Klein, April 28, 1988, May 2, 1988.

78 THEIR ATTITUDE WAS. Interview, source.

79 I HAVE THE MEMORY. Interview, Jerry Weiss, May 11, 1989.

79 HER INTEREST IN THEATER. Klein interviews.

79 BARBARA WASN'T A VERY GOOD ACTRESS. Interview, John Blankenship, May 3, 1988.

80 I THINK RAUSHENBUSH. Schonberg interview.

80 I HAD ALL THE PULL TO BE AN ACTRESS. *Boston Sunday Advertiser*, June 11, 1967

82 BARBARA ENJOYED BEING PART OF THE GROUP. Interview, source.

83 BARBARA LOOKED MARVELOUS. Interviews, Muriel Greenhill, May 26, 1988, June 7, 1988.

83 YOU HAD TO TALK TO JACKIE. Interview, source.

84 BARBARA WAS TROUBLED ABOUT JACKIE. Interview, Joe Leff, May 24, 1989.

84 DIFFICULTY WARMING UP TO HER. Interviews, sources.

84 REASONABLE, AMELIORATIVE, EQUITABLE. Remoy interview.

85 BARBARA NEVER CAME INTO OUR ROOMS. Interview, Joan McLellan Tayler, May 24, 1988.

85 IT WAS SUCH A SUBTLE THING. Greenhill interviews.

86 SORT OF A PRIVATE CLUB. Interview, Margaret Straus, May 25, 1988.

86 WE WERE ALWAYS VERY GOOD FRIENDS. Leff interview.

87 LET'S PUT IT THIS WAY. Interview, source.

88 SHE JUST KEPT RETRACING. Klein interviews.

88 I GOT THE IMPRESSION SHE WAS AFRAID OF BOYS. Interview, Marcia Applebaum Chamovitz, April 13, 1988.

CHAPTER NINE

89 BESOTTED WITH BARBARA. Interview, source.

90 TED WAS VERY DYNAMIC. Interview, Steve Krantz, May 24, 1989.

91 BARBARA GOT INVOLVED. Interview, source.

CHAPTER TEN

CHAPTER ELEVEN

120 THAT'S BARBARA WALTERS. Ibid.
121 SHE'D HAD DIFFICULTIES. Sklar interview.
122 THE STUDIO WAS FULL. Interview, Jim Fleming, August 1, 1988, January 16, 1989.
125 UNFORTUNATELY . . . HE THOUGHT. Risman, op. cit.
127 THERE AGAIN SHE WAS MARVELOUS. Fleming interview.
127 I JUST DIDN'T SEE WHY SHE SHOULD STAY. Interview, source.
128–129 I COULD STAND IT NO LONGER. Public records, State of Alabama, County of Marion. Circuit Court Case No. 6037, Barbara Walters Katz vs. Robert H. Katz, May 19, 1958.

CHAPTER TWELVE

131 I'M REALLY GOING TO BRING BACK BROADWAY. New York World Telegram, May 17, 1958.
133 ANYTHING THAT TAKES PEOPLE AWAY FROM TV. Lee Mortimer column, New York Mirror, March 2, 1958.
133 ALL KINDS OF THINGS HAPPENED. Interview, Chickie James, November 29, 1988, December 8, 1988.
133 ONE OF LOU'S ATTORNEYS. Interview, Salvatore Alfano, March 27, 1989.
133 HE WAS THE MEANEST BASTARD. Zussman, op. cit.
133 MY NAME WAS SYNONYMOUS. James interviews.
134 I'M REALLY IN A FIX. Lou Sobol column, New York Journal American, June 3, 1958.
136 THIS GIRL CAN HAVE ANYTHING. Zussman, op. cit.
136 THE CAFE DE PARIS TRAGEDY WAS A REAL EDUCATION. New York Times Magazine, September 10, 1972.
136 LOU HAD A WONDERFUL REPUTATION. Interviews, Tex McCrary, January 22, 1988, February 3, 1988.
137 I DIDN'T HAVE THE FOGGIEST NOTION. Interview, William Safire, October 31, 1988.
138 OH, MY! THAT'S NOT FOR REAL. Interview, Carolyn DeHarak, January 22, 1988.
138 THIS IS MY ENGAGEMENT RING. Ibid.
139 I THINK SHE ENJOYED. Ibid.
139 WE BECAME BUDDIES. Safire interview.
139 EVERYONE GOT THE POINT. Ibid.
139 A MEDIA BIGGIE. Ibid.
140 SHE WAS QUICK-WITTED. Ibid.
140 BARBARA . . . THERE ARE A GREAT MANY. Ibid.
140–141 HEY . . . REMEMBER THAT LESSON. Ibid.
141 I GAVE TO BARBARA AND ALL MY KIDS. McCrary inter-

views.
141   GREAT MINDS THINK ALIKE. Safire interview.
141–142 I HAD TO PLANT NEWS ITEMS. *New York Times Magazine*,
         September 10, 1972.

CHAPTER THIRTEEN

145   WE DIDN'T WANT TO RUIN. Northshield, op. cit.
146   THE PROBLEM FOR ME. *Special: Fred Freed and the Television Doc-
       umentary*, David G. Yellin and Fred Freed (New York: The Macmil-
       lan Co., 1972, 1973). (This book was also used as source material
       for other biographical and chronological details about Freed. David
       Yellin was also interviewed.)
146   GETTING IN GOOD WITH GARROWAY. Interviews, Beryl
       Pfizer, February 1, 7, and 8, 1989.
147   IT WAS A KNIFE-IN-THE-BACK. Interviews, Charles (Chuck)
       Horner, January 30, 1989, February 7, 1989.
147   SO IT COULD BE FACTIONALIZED. Interview, Craig Fisher,
       August 9, 1988.
147   FRED NEVER WANTED TO DO THE TODAY SHOW. Inter-
       view, Judy Freed, January 19, 1989.
148   I HAD GOOD JUDGMENT. Ibid.
149   IT'S A LIVE SHOW. Northshield, op. cit.
149   BARBARA WAS OBVIOUSLY VERY VERBAL. Fisher inter-
       view.
150   I DIDN'T WANT TO SOUND LIKE A HUCKSTER. Interviews,
       Anita Colby, February 6, 23, 24, and 27, 1989.
150   SHE HAD TO IMPRESS ME. Ibid.
151   THAT MAN IS IFFY. Ibid.
151   DON'T WORRY. Ibid.
151   GOD, THAT MEANS. Ibid.
152   WE DID A GOOD JOB TOGETHER. Ibid.
152   HAD I BEEN THE SAME AGE. Ibid.
152   LONGED TO BE ON TELEVISION. Ibid.
153   OH, SHE WAS SHREWD. Ibid.
154   BARBARA WAS VERY CLEVER. Ibid.
154   IF SHE COULDN'T GET IN THROUGH THE DOOR. Ibid.
154   HELLO, I'M BARBARA WALTERS. Horner interviews.
155   SHE WAS A VERY SEXY GIRL. Ibid.
155   I NOTICED HER EYES. Ibid.
156   IT IS TRUE THAT I WAS THE FIRST. Pfizer interviews.
157   I WAS AWARE OF HER BECAUSE. Ibid.
157   WE [WOMEN] WERE TOUGHER. Ibid.
157   HE JUST LOOKED AT ME. Ibid.

158   SOMETIMES THEY COULDN'T EVEN READ. Interviews, John
      Lord, August 16 and 31, 1988.
158   BARBARA KNEW ABOUT ALL THOSE BEAUTY QUEENS.
      Pfizer interviews.
158   NOBODY EVER COULD HAVE MADE IT. Ibid.
160   BY THIS TIME AT TODAY. Northshield, op. cit.
160   JOHN LOVED HER AND SHE HIM. Ibid.
160   IT ALL JELLED. Lord interviews.
161   SHE CULTIVATED THAT. Ibid.
161   ON A DAY LIKE THE FOURTH OF JULY. Northshield, op. cit.
162   I WATCHED THE SHOW THAT DAY. Interview, Ray Scherer,
      March 2, 1989.
163   SHE DIED BUT SHE TOOK IT WELL. Northshield, op. cit.

CHAPTER FOURTEEN

166   Descriptions of Philippe's style of dress, hotel life, and work, in
      part. *The New Yorker*, February 19, 1955, p. 37.
169   TO HIDE THE FACT. Interview, Jeremyn Davern, September 26,
      1988.
169   BARBARA WAS A YOUNG, ATTRACTIVE WOMAN, Ibid.
169   BECAUSE I KNEW FRENCH. Interviews, Mira Sheerin, Septem-
      ber 26, 1988, March 8, 1989.
170   THEY WERE VERY CLOSE. Northshield, op. cit.
171   SHE JUST SORT OF FADED OUT. Interview, Jimmy McCarthy,
      September 20, 1988.
171   WHEN BARBARA HEARD. Interviews, Alexis Lichine, Novem-
      ber 28, 1988, January 16, 1989.

CHAPTER FIFTEEN

173   KEN FIRST TALKED TO JACK. *Saturday Evening Post*, May 12,
      1962.
175   IT'S A TERRIFIC STORY. Northshield, op. cit.
175   I KNOW I CAN SWING THIS. Ibid.
175   BARBARA AND I WERE LINKED IN A KIND OF. Ibid.
175   BARBARA JUST WENT OFF. Ibid.
176   THAT'S THE WAY TELEVISION WAS. Horner, op. cit.
176   IT CAME AS A SURPRISE. Ibid.
176   WE TALKED QUITE A BIT. Ibid.
176   THAT WAS PART OF HER PROFESSIONALISM. Lord, op. cit.
177   I WILL KEEP AN EYE OUT. Letter to Lester Cooper from Letitia
      Baldrige, February 19, 1962, John Fitzgerald Kennedy Library, Bos-

177 ONE OF THE FIRST THINGS MISS WALTERS DID. Barbara and Dan Lewis, op. cit., p. 171.

177 SHE DIDN'T REALIZE THEY HAD TEA IN INDIA. Lord, op. cit.

178 SHE DIDN'T HAVE A GREAT DEAL OF SELF-CONFIDENCE. Interview, Marie Ridder, March 13, 1989.

179 WAS ASKING OTHER REPORTERS. Interview, Fran Lewine, March 16, 1989.

179 I HAD THE IMPRESSION SHE WAS MIFFED. Interviews, Anne Chamberlin, August 19, 1988, March 13, 1989.

180 BARBARA HOUNDED—SHE HOUNDED TO GET ACCESS. Interview, Letitia Baldrige, March 14, 1989.

180 BARBARA WAS VERY BRIGHT. Ibid.

181 SHE'S A PRETTY DAMNED GOOD REPORTER. Interview, Walter Pfister, August 2, 1988.

181 AN AGGRESSIVE, ACTIVE, INTERESTED. Ibid.

182 I FOUND OUT WHAT IT WAS LIKE. Miami Herald, June 6, 1965.

182 IT WAS MY FIRST EXPERIENCE ON SUCH AN ASSIGNMENT. Newark Evening News, May 9, 1965.

182 NOBODY GETS CLOSE. Ibid.

182 BARBARA DID A BEAUTIFUL JOB. Northshield, op. cit.

182–183 BARBARA'S BIG BREAKTHROUGH. Lord, op. cit.

183 I THINK IT'S WONDERFUL. Interviews, Joan Braden, October 26, 1988, November 1, 1988.

183 SHE TOLD ME ABOUT HAVING BEEN POOR. Ibid.

CHAPTER SIXTEEN

185 HE WAS A SIMPATICO GUY. Interview, source.

186–187 Some biographical information on Guber from "Diana Ross Is Uptight and Liberace Has a Cold," Carol Saline, Philadelphia magazine, August 1978.

186 GUBER USED THE HOTEL AS A GUN DROP. Interviews, Frank Ford, September 30, 1988, October 1 and 2, 1988.

187 THAT'S WHAT GOT LEE IN TROUBLE WITH EDNA. Ibid.

187 AND THAT WAS ONE REASON. Interview, Edna Shanis Tuttleman, October 3, 1988.

187 SHELLY . . . GET THE FUCK OUT OF HERE. Philadelphia magazine.

188 GUBER'S GOT THE BROADS. Ibid.

188 LEE HAD NEVER RAVED. Ford interviews.

188 THIS IS TOUGH, ISN'T IT, FRANK? Ibid.

189 I THOUGHT SHE WAS A DRIVING WOMAN. Ibid.
189 SHE WOULD CALL HIM EVERY NIGHT. Ibid.
190 HE ONLY BROUGHT HER HERE ONCE. Tuttleman interview.
190 SHE WAS VERY STANDOFFISH. Ford interview.

CHAPTER SEVENTEEN

191 WE LASTED ABOUT A YEAR. Northshield, op. cit.
192 THE SHOW HAD GONE SO FAR DOWNHILL. *Let's Be Frank About It*, Frank Blair (Garden City, N.Y.: Doubleday & Company, Inc., 1979), p. 344.
192 ARE YOU NUTS? *TV Guide*, August 1, 1964.
192 WHO THE HELL WATCHES TELEVISION AT THAT HOUR? Ibid.
192 A DREAM JOB. Ibid.
193 YOU HAVE TO CAST. Ibid.
195 ESSENTIALLY THE SAME CREATURE THEN. Interviews, Jane Murphy Schulberg, September 14, 15, 21, and 26, 1988.
195 SHE REALLY LEARNED HER TRADE. Interview, Al Morgan, January 23, 1988.
196 BARBARA WAS THOROUGH. Interviews, Gail Rock, August 9, 14, and 15, 1988.
196 BARBARA WAS A PERFECTIONIST. Interview, Anne Perkins, September 1 and 5, 1988.
196–197 TAKE IT OFF! Rock interviews.
197 I REMEMBER SAYING WITH BIG WIDE EYES. Interview, source.
198 SHE DID HER PARAMEDIC BIT. Rock interviews.
198 HAVE YOU EVER THOUGHT ABOUT HAVING YOUR NOSE DONE? Ibid.
198 BARBARA CERTAINLY DID TAKE A LOOK. Ibid.
199 IF I PUSH THE BANGS OFF MY FACE. Letter to *New York Post*, May 13, 1983.
199 I WORKED VERY HARD FOR TWELVE YEARS. *Life*, July 14, 1972.
200 I NEVER DID THINK OF HER LIKE THAT. Interview, source.
200 WHEN I MET HER. Horner, op. cit.
201 I'D DROP BY HER. Lord, op. cit.
201 SEX IS NOT WHAT DROVE HER. Schulberg interviews.
201 WE KNEW EVERYTHING THAT WAS GOING ON. Rock interviews.

CHAPTER EIGHTEEN

203 I FOUND MYSELF USING HER. Morgan, op. cit.

204 WE HAD ALL BEEN IMPRESSED. *On Camera: My 10,000 Hours on Television*, Hugh Downs (New York: G.P. Putnam's Sons, 1986), p. 122.

204 BARBARA WAS GANGBUSTERS. Morgan, op. cit.

204 IT WAS A MONTH AFTER THE KENNEDY ASSASSINATION. *Washington Post*, January 30, 1972.

205 SHE HAD SO MANY UNFORTUNATE RELATIONSHIPS. Anne Williams Ferguson, op. cit.

205 GUBER WAS HAVING IT OFF. Lord, op. cit.

205 TOGETHER ON AND OFF. Interview, Ben Cossrow, September 30, 1988.

206 READY TO THROW UP. Interview, Judith Crist, July 14, 1988.

206 SUICIDE DOES NOT REMOVE. *New York Journal-American*, June 23, 1954.

207 EGGHEAD R. MURROW. *Prime Time: The Life of Edward R. Murrow*, Alexander Kendrick (Boston: Little, Brown and Company, 1969), p. 421.

207 BECAUSE WE WERE OBLIGED TO TALK TO HIM. Crist interview.

207 LEE WAS IN THE BEST SENSE. Ford, op. cit.

208 THERE I WAS AT CHEZ VITO'S. *New York Times Magazine*, September 10, 1972.

208 WE WERE OUT TOGETHER. Interview, Mrs. George Sokolsky, September 26, 1988.

209 HER ATTITUDE WAS THAT IF ROY. Ibid.

209 POWERFUL . . . BUT I DON'T THINK SHE DWELLED. Lord, op. cit.

209 DORIS LILLY, A FORMER . . . COLUMNIST. *Citizen Cohn*, Nicholas von Hoffman (New York: Doubleday & Company, 1988), p. 316.

209 COHN HAD GREAT RESPECT. Interview, Robert Blecker, September 28, 1988.

210 GOT HIM! Ford, op. cit.

CHAPTER NINETEEN

211 QUINTESSENTIAL OUT-OF-TOWN PERSONALITY. Morgan, op. cit.

211 BARBARA WAS NAGGING. Schulberg, op. cit.

211–212 I THINK HAD BEEN A SPEECH THERAPIST. Morgan, op.

cit.

212   OH, I CAN'T DO THAT. Interviews, Maureen O'Sullivan, January 22, 1988, June 12, 1989.

212   DOWNS WAS OUTRAGED. Cunniff, op. cit.

212   SHE WAS THERE EVERY MORNING. O'Sullivan interviews.

213   BARBARA MADE ABSOLUTELY NO SECRET. Schulberg, op. cit.

213   THOUGHT SHE WAS WONDERFUL. *The Today Show*, Gerry Davis (New York: William Morrow and Co., Inc., 1987) p. 49.

213   DO YOU LIKE WOMEN. O'Sullivan interviews.

213   NO. I DON'T THINK SO. Ibid.

213   I GOT VERY BAD MAIL. Ibid.

214   WHY CAN'T I BE DOING THIS? Cunniff, op. cit.

214   BARBARA WAS BRIGHT AND AMBITIOUS. Crist, op. cit.

214   ROUGH COMPETENCY . . . COULDN'T DEVELOP A DEFINITE. Downs, op. cit., p. 117.

215   MISCAST . . . SHE WAS A SWEET LADY. Interview, Frank Blair, October 11, 1988.

215   SORT OF BROKE DOWN. Crist, op. cit.

215   I NEVER HAD ANY IDEA. Downs, op. cit., p. 118.

216   IT WAS A GREAT HUNGER. Crist, op. cit.

216   SHE FELT GUILTY. Interview, source.

216   OFTEN YOU'D HEAR SOMETHING LIKE. Interview, source.

216   BARBARA BURST INTO TEARS. Rock, op. cit.

217   IT WAS CLEAR THAT HAVING A BABY. Ibid.

217   JOAN, PUT THE KID AWAY. Peyser, op. cit.

217   BARBARA HAD A LOT OF FAITH. Lord, op. cit.

218   THEY WERE TERRIBLE. Ford, op. cit.

218   BARBARA DOES SOMETHING A LITTLE. Peyser, op. cit.

CHAPTER TWENTY

221   I TOLD HER FIRST. Downs, op. cit., p. 118.

222   ASININE—IT'S NOT ENOUGH . . . LIKE AN INTRUDER . . . SIMPLY NO PLACE FOR A WOMAN . . . THEY HAVEN'T CREATED A PLACE. *New York Post*, August 26, 1964.

222   IF THERE'S ANY FAILURE IT'S MINE. *New York Herald-Tribune*, August 27, 1964.

223   MAUREEN MIGHT NOT BE FEELING WELL. Perkins, op. cit.

223   I REMEMBER MAUREEN LOOKING DOWN. Interview, Pat Pepin, September 2, 1988.

223   I SAID, WELL, I THINK. Cunniff, op. cit.

223   REPORTER BARBARA WALTERS IS BEING GROOMED. *New York Post*, August 30, 1964.

224 SHE'S A WRITER. Downs, op. cit., p. 121.

224 THERE WAS NO BIG BUILDUP. *Miami Herald,* June 6, 1965.

224 THEY DIDN'T HAVE ANYBODY ELSE. Schulberg, op. cit.

224 WE WANT INTELLIGENT, CREATIVE WOMEN. *TV Guide,* January 2–8, 1965.

224 WHOLE IMAGE IS PERFECT FOR. Ibid.

226 BASICALLY . . . IT WAS UNCOMPLICATED. Interview, Ray Katz, February 16, 1989.

227 SHE LOVED THE POTENTIAL OF BEING. Ibid.

227 THE SHOW BUSINESS OF HER FATHER. Ibid.

227 STEVENS WAS A FRIEND. Ibid.

228 BARBARA WASN'T THE FIRST GIRL. Interviews, John Springer, February 7 and 13, 1989.

228 SHE KNEW THE ROPES. Ibid.

228 SHE ACTED LIKE. Interview, Peter Levinson, February 13, 1989.

228 WAS EVERYTHING THAT PUBLICITY. Springer interviews.

228 I KNOW YOU GUYS KNOW WHAT TO DO. Levinson interview.

229 GUESS STAR, CAN YOU. *New York Daily News,* July 18, 1965.

229 I LOVE MY WORK. *TV Guide,* op. cit.

229 THE MONEY IS WONDERFUL. *New York Herald-Tribune,* August 22, 1965.

229 I'D DO MY JOB FOR NO PAY AT ALL. *Boston Sunday Advertiser,* May 16, 1965.

229 IT'S THE ONLY JOB LIKE IT ON TV. *Christian Science Monitor,* November 17, 1969.

229–230 IF I DIDN'T HAVE THE BEST JOB. *Miami Herald,* March 2, 1970.

230 IS BECOMING AS FAMILIAR. *Miami Herald,* June 6, 1965.

230 I'M HAVING A LOVE AFFAIR. *Boston Sunday Advertiser,* op. cit.

230 HE SAID, WELL, YOU PEOPLE. Levinson interview.

230 BARBARA WALTERS OF 'TODAY' SHOW LOOKS. *Life,* February 18, 1966.

231 THERE WAS GREAT RESENTMENT. Springer interviews.

231 ONE OF THE THINGS THAT I THOUGHT WAS ODD. Interview, Bill Monroe, October 24, 1988.

231 [WAS] A MORE CLEARCUT. Ibid.

232 SHE WAS TEN FEET AWAY. Levinson interview.

232 SHE WAS DOING MORE. Rock, op. cit.

233 LIKE SOMETHING YOU PUT ON. Pepin interview.

233 BUT THEN THEY DID SOMETHING. Ibid.

233 SHE WAS LIKE ONE OF THE GIRLS. Ibid.

234 BARBARA WAS NOT THE EASIEST PERSON. Ibid.

234 WHAT DO YOU GUYS. Schulberg, op. cit.

234 AND IT WAS TRUE. Ibid.

234 A LOT OF PEOPLE THOUGHT SHE WAS. Interview, Nancy Fields, February 16, 1988.
234–235 I DON'T THINK SHE REALLY GAVE A HANG. Rock, op. cit.
235 I AM GOING TO BE ON JOHNNY. Pepin interview.
235 FOR A WEEK WE WERE BUILDING. Ibid.
236 [BARBARA] WAS SAYING THINGS LIKE. Pepin interview.
237 SHE WORKED LIKE A DOG. Cunniff, op. cit.
238 BARBARA FLOATED THROUGH IT. Lord, op. cit.
238 I DON'T KNOW HOW SHE DID IT. Rock, op. cit.
238 I CAN HARDLY BELIEVE I'M HERE. Newark Evening News, May 9, 1965.
238 OUVREZ LE MICROPHONE! Blair, op. cit., p. 352.
239 WHEN BARBARA STARTED. Northshield, op. cit.

CHAPTER TWENTY-ONE

242 I DON'T USUALLY DO THIS. Sonja Loew, op. cit.
243 BARBARA WANTED IT DONE. Interview, source.
243 NOT BECAUSE [TV]. Miami Herald, March 23, 1965.
245 I FIND WOMEN WHO DO THINGS. New York magazine, 1970.
245 LEE LIKED TO SIT AROUND. Ford, op. cit.
245 THERE WERE A LOT OF CELEBRITIES THERE. Interview, source.
245 EVEN WHEN I FINALLY GET TO BED. Life, February 18, 1966.
246 AFTER A FEW WEEKS. Newark Evening News, May 9, 1965.
246 WHEN BARBARA WAS REALLY BECOMING A BIG NAME. Interview, source.
246 EXTREMELY UNDERSTANDING. Crist, op. cit.
246 I WONDER HOW LONG THIS PRESENT. Peyser, op. cit.
247 I NEVER SAW THE KIND OF WARMTH. Lord, op. cit.
247 LEE WAS A WONDERFUL. Ibid.
247 IT WAS SO IMPORTANT TO ME. Davis, op. cit., p. 123.
247 I DON'T HAVE TIME TO WAIT. Interview, source.
248 HER STAR WAS VERY MUCH. Ford, op. cit.
248 HE SAID BARBARA DID NOT WANT. Tuttleman, op. cit.
248 WITH THE IMPRESSION THAT THERE WERE. Crist, op. cit.
248 ROY WAS INFLUENTIAL. Budd, op. cit.
249 WHEN BARBARA ADOPTED THAT CHILD. Williams, op. cit.
250 SHE WAS SO THRILLED. Fields, op. cit.
250 ONE OF THE THINGS THAT HAS ECHOED. Peyser, op. cit.

CHAPTER TWENTY-TWO

252   IT DIDN'T MATTER TO ME. Cunniff, op. cit.
252   I'M GOING TO ASK HIM. Ibid.
252   ASTAIRE IMMEDIATELY DRIED UP. Ibid.
252   CAN I SEE THE ASTAIRE THING. Ibid.
253   SHE'D WALK INTO AL'S. Fields, op. cit.
253   I WAS VERY ANNOYED. Cunniff, op. cit.
253   AL CALLED ME UP. Ibid.
253   FUCK HER! Ibid.
253   THEY'RE OUT WALKING. Ibid.
254   THE BEHIND-CAMERA CONFLICT. Downs, op. cit., p. 123.
254   SORT OF A RUNNING GUN BATTLE. Interview, source.
255   IF NBC VICE PRESIDENTS. New York Times Magazine, September 10, 1972.
255   I APPRECIATED THE FACT. Interview, Dean Rusk, February 19, 1989.
255   RUSK LIKED HER, Scherer, op. cit.
255   I'LL DO IT IF BARBARA WALTERS. Rusk interview.
255   AT A BIG PARTY. Interview, Nancy Dickerson, March 10, 1989.
256   DURING A BREAK. Rusk interview.
256   SUDDENLY BARBARA WAS IN WASHINGTON. Scherer, op. cit.
256   WAS CERTAINLY ONE OF WARINESS AND DOUBT. Monroe, op. cit.
257   DON WAS A BIG ADVOCATE. Interviews, Doug Sinsel, October 17 and 19, 1988.
257   DON MEANEY WAS THERE. Scherer, op. cit.
257   I HAD BEEN COVERING. Interview, source.
258   LITERALLY PACING BACK AND FORTH. Interview, source.
259   MORE AND MORE LEVERAGE. Schulberg, op. cit.
259   DRIVEN . . . OFTEN DIFFICULT. Interview, Don Meaney, September 27, 1988.
259   BARBARA WAS SCARED TO DEATH. Interview, source.
260   YOU'RE GOING TO HAVE SEVENTEEN CORRESPONDENTS. Northshield, op. cit.
260   THERE WAS A FEELING. Ibid.
261   WHY THE HELL DIDN'T BARBARA. Ibid.
261   SHE WAS PHOTOGRAPHED. Ibid.
261   IT WAS HER IDEA. Ibid.

CHAPTER TWENTY-THREE

263 WOULD MAKE A WONDERFUL BOOK. Interview, Ken Mc-Cormick, March 1, 1988.

264 ENGAGING AND OUTGOING. Ibid.

264 KEN CALLED ME AND SAID. Interview, June Callwood, March 3, 1988.

264 THAT NO MATTER HOW BAD. Ibid.

265 FOR A COMFORTABLE ADVANCE. McCormick interview.

265 WHAT I SAW WAS SOMETHING. Ibid.

265 SHE HAD A LOT. Ibid.

265 SHE WAS GOING TO RAM. Ibid.

265 WE WERE DOING A VERY SLICK. Ibid.

265 JUNE WROTE A REALLY WONDERFUL. McCormick interview.

266 FLATTERED THAT HER JOB. Ibid.

266 THE KINDS OF THINGS SHE WAS SAYING. Callwood interview.

266 WE HAD A HARD TIME. Ibid.

267 THE CHILD WAS JUST. Ibid.

267 THERE WAS A TREMENDOUS CONNECTION. Ibid.

267 SHE WAS TERRIBLY. Ibid.

267 PUT IN SOME OF ME. Ibid.

268 IT WAS THE EASIEST. Ibid.

268 ALL IN ALL IT TOOK ME. *Long Island Press*, October 18, 1970.

268 NEVER FAKE. *Boston Herald*, October 23, 1970.

268 SHE GOT INTO A THING WITH PEOPLE. Callwood interview.

CHAPTER TWENTY-FOUR

272 THERE'S A TREND TOWARD. *TV Guide*, December 30, 1972.

273 IN A GUARDED KIND OF WAY. Lord, op. cit.

273 BARBARA WAS A BIT JEALOUS. Ibid.

273 THE ONE THING I WASN'T TOO FOND OF. Ibid.

273 FOR POWER AND POSITION. Ibid.

274 ONE EVENING WE WERE SITTING. Ibid.

274 I HAD A SENSE OF BARBARA'S. Interview, source.

274 WHAT HAS CHANGED—AND FOR THE BETTER. *Variety*, October 13, 1971.

275 AN ATTEMPT TO APPRAISE THE SITUATION. *New York Daily News*, July 18, 1971.

275 A WOMAN COULD NOT DO A TELEVISION SHOW. Ibid.

275 I'VE ALWAYS THOUGHT A LITTLE BIT. *New York Post*, Au-

gust 1, 1965.

275 BARBARA DID NOT USE NOT FOR WOMEN ONLY. Interviews, Julie Van Vliet Rubenstein, September 27, 1988, October 5 and 16, 1988.

276 I'M GOING TO ASK YOU SOMETHING. New York Times, November 3, 1973.

276 WHO ARE THESE AWFUL. Rubenstein interviews.

276–277 AND THEN I'D GET IN THE STUDIO. Ibid.

277 PEOPLE THINK BARBARA. Interview, source.

277 YOU COULD HAVE A VERY GOOD TIME. Rubenstein interviews.

277 WELL, FINALLY SHE CAME OUT. Ibid.

277 HAS BECOME ONE OF THE MOST IMPROVED. New York Times, September 19, 1973.

277 BARBARA DID HER HOMEWORK. Rubenstein interviews.

278 THE BEST BOOKER. Interview, source.

278 A TALKATIVE DAY IN THE LIFE. New York Times, January 28, 1972.

279 BARBARA WANTED TO DO CABINET MEMBERS'. Rubenstein interviews.

279 OWN PERSONAL SHOWCASE. Amgott, op. cit.

CHAPTER TWENTY-FIVE

281 IT WASN'T JUST BECAUSE I HAVE TO GET UP. TV Guide, December 30, 1972.

281 BARBARA TRAVELED A LOT. Cossrow, op. cit.

282 BARBARA SAYS SHE'S OUTGROWN LEE. Interview, source.

282 SHE HAS A NURSE DURING THE WEEK. Christian Science Monitor, November 17, 1969.

282 LEE WOULD PUT THE BABY IN A CARRIAGE. Ford, op. cit.

283 LEE AND I SHARE AN ENORMOUS LOVE. TV Guide, op. cit.

283 I THINK YOU'D BETTER MAKE OTHER PLANS. Barbara and Dan Lewis, op. cit., p. 23.

283 BEING DYNAMITE IN BED. Interview, source.

284 SHE DID IN FACT HAVE A LONG. Ibid.

284 HAD THROWN LEE OUT. Tuttleman, op. cit.

284 BUT I JUST DON'T THINK SHE IS THE GREATEST. Barbara and Dan Lewis, op. cit., p. 23.

284 AT THE DIVORCE SETTLEMENT. Tuttleman, op. cit.

284 LEE WAS VERY SOCIABLE. Interview, source.

285 IT WAS VERY NICE OF HER. Ford, op. cit.

CHAPTER TWENTY-SIX

288   SOMEONE WAS TORPEDOING. *The Camera Never Blinks: Adventures of a TV Journalist,* Dan Rather with Mickey Herskowitz (New York: William Morrow and Company, Inc., 1977), p. 266.
288   JUST AS I FIGURED. Ibid.
288   IF YOU THINK YOU ARE GOING. Ibid.
288   NBC WILL PAY FOR THEM. Ibid, p. 267.
288   KILL MYSELF. Davis, op. cit., p. 69.
288   IT BUILT MY REPUTATION. Ibid.
289   I WOULD SAY GREAT THINGS. Safire, op. cit.
289   I FIND THAT HE HAS SEX APPEAL. Walters, op. cit., p. 118.
289   WHEN SHE WROTE ABOUT HIM. Interview, source.
290   DEAR BARBARA. Note dated June 12, 1972, from Nixon Presidential Materials Project, National Archives, Washington, D.C.
290   I'D BE HAPPY TO GIVE. *Boston Herald,* October 23, 1970.
290   WHOM WOULD YOU LIKE. *Time,* February 21, 1972.
291   IT IS OUR FEELING. Nixon Presidential Materials Project.
291–292   THE PRESIDENT UNDERGO A WARDROBE. Ibid.
292   WHAT HAS THE BEST EFFECT. Ibid.
292   MEMORANDUM RE THE BARBARA WALTERS. Ibid.
292   HOW OLD IS MRS. NIXON. Ibid.
292   IT WOULD BE HELPFUL IF THE SPEECH WRITERS. Ibid.
293   NO 'HOT NEWS'. Ibid.
293   THERE HAS BEEN A LOT OF TALK. *TV Guide,* December 30, 1972.
293   VERY STRONG . . . CONSTANTLY PREENING. *New York Times,* March 16, 1971.
293   I DIED ALL WEEKEND. *TV Guide,* op. cit.
294   WHAT ABOUT HENRY KISSINGER. *New York Post,* October 26, 1972.
294   MAKE IT SIX. *Newsweek,* May 6, 1974.
294   BARBARA, WEARING A WHITE DRESS. Interview, source.
295   I'VE BROUGHT A FRIEND. Schulberg, op. cit.
295   THERE WAS AN NBC PARTY. Monroe, op. cit.
296   IF YOU GAVE ME A CHOICE. To Gene Shalit, *Ladies Home Journal,* November 1975.
296   STUART HAD TO CONSTANTLY. Sinsel, op. cit.
297   IT HAD TO DO WITH SOME PROJECT. Ibid.
297   STUART MADE IT CLEAR THAT. Ibid.
297   THE NEXT MORNING AFTER ONE OF. Ibid.
298   I REMEMBER LAUGHING. Ibid.
298   SOME PEOPLE THINK I'M THE NIXON GIRL. *New York Times Magazine,* September 10, 1972.

298 I FOUND HIM WARM AND AMUSING. *Christian Science Monitor*, August 6, 1973.

299 WE WENT TO LUNCH. Peyser, op. cit.

299 I'M TAKING CLOTHES FROM MY FAVORITE. *Women's Wear Daily*, February 16, 1972.

300 NIXON WANTED NAMES. Interview, Helen Thomas, March 17, 1989.

300 SHE HAD MORE VISIBILITY. Interview, Fay Wells, March 17, 1989.

300 FAY, I'M SO LONESOME. Ibid.

301 THE VICE PRESIDENT IN CHARGE . . . MADAME CHIANG. Dan and Barbara Lewis, op. cit., p. 106.

301 THIS IS BARBARA WALTERS . . . WE'RE JUST. *New York Times Magazine*, September 10, 1972.

301 IT WAS LIKE SITTING. Interview, source.

302 FEELING TERRIBLY INADEQUATE. *TV Guide*, op. cit.

302 I WAS SHY AND QUITE FRIGHTENED. *Ladies Home Journal*, op. cit.

302 I HAD BONED UP SO THOROUGHLY. *New York Daily News*, March 2, 1972.

303 I WAS UTTERLY AGHAST. Wells interview.

CHAPTER TWENTY-SEVEN

306 HE HAS A FABULOUS. *Drunk Before Noon: The Behind-the-Scenes Story of the Washington Press Corps*, Ken Hoyt and Francis Spatz Leighton (Englewood Cliffs, N.J.: Prentice-Hall, Inc., 1979), p. 326.

306 SALLY QUINN MAKES YOU WANT. *Air Time: The Inside Story of CBS News*, Gary Paul Gates (New York: Harper & Row, 1978), p. 348.

306 YOU'VE BEEN MADE OUT TO BE. Matusow, op. cit., p. 183.

306 WE'RE GOING TO REVAMP. Gates, op. cit.

306 SISTERHOOD MAY END. *New York* magazine, July 16, 1973.

307 THERE IS NO FEUD. *Christian Science Monitor*, August 6, 1973.

307 COULDN'T HAVE BEEN BETTER. Barbara and Dan Lewis, op. cit., p. 66.

308 THE THING I REMEMBER THE MOST. Schulberg, op. cit.

308 SHE DID THINGS THAT SALLY. Ibid.

309 IN THE PAST. *New York* magazine, March 25, 1974.

CHAPTER TWENTY-EIGHT

311   PROBABLY THE HAPPIEST TIME. Davis, op. cit., p. 54.
312   HUGH HAD CONFIDENCE. Sinsel, op. cit.
312   I'M LIKE A COLLIE. Metz, op. cit., p. 216.
313   FRIENDS HAVE BEEN ASKING ME. Ibid.
314   WE'LL MAKE A JOURNALIST. Ibid.
314   I'M GOING TO BE A WONDERFUL. Newsweek, May 6, 1974.
314   IT WAS A VERY UNHAPPY. Davis, op. cit., p. 59.
315   MCGEE THOUGHT BARBARA. Schulberg, op. cit.
315   WHEN MCGEE TOOK OVER. Blair, op. cit.
315   SOMETIMES SHE ASKED THE QUESTIONS. Blair, op. cit., p. 367.
315   CAME FROM BARBARA. Crist, op. cit.
315   FRANK CLEARLY HATED HER. Sinsel, op. cit.
316   I LOVE BEING A CELEBRITY. Ladies Home Journal, November 1975.
316   I DON'T THINK OF MYSELF AS A CELEBRITY. Sarasota Herald Tribune, February 22, 1976.
316   SHE COULD BE AWFULLY. Metz, op. cit., p. 247.
317   SHE'D SASHAY IN. Interview, source.
317   THE BIG PROBLEM. Schulberg, op. cit.
318   BARBARA HAS A VERY STRONG RESPECT. Newsweek, op. cit.
318   WERE SHOW BUSINESS BECAUSE. Interview, source.
318   HE WAS STUNNED ONCE. Schulberg, op. cit.
318   WELL, WHO CARES ABOUT THAT STUFF. Ibid.
318   DESPITE WANTING TO SWING. Ibid.
319   BARBARA WALTERS WILL BE COHOST. NBC Press Release, April 22, 1974.
319   QUITE LITERALLY OVER. Matusow, op. cit., p. 172.

CHAPTER TWENTY-NINE

321   I CAN WORK. Los Angeles Times, July 21, 1974.
322   JIM WAS SWEET. Schulberg, op. cit.
322   REGARDING THE COMPETITION. Interviews, Jim Hartz, December 9 and 21, 1988.
323   IT WAS AN INHIBITION. Lord, op. cit.
323   ONE OF THE PROBLEMS. Ladies Home Journal, November 1975.
323   IT WAS POOR. Schulberg, op. cit.
324   OKAY, WHERE IS. Interview, source.
324   SHE WAS SUCH A PAIN. People, December 1, 1980.

324 THIS IS REALLY. Interview, Sue Seitz, January 31, 1989.

324 BARBARA BARGAINED US DOWN. Ibid.

325 I'M KIND OF FRUGAL. *New York Post,* October 23, 1976.

325 TAKE COATS AT. Schulberg, op. cit.

326 A TOUCH TOO SUPERFICIAL. *New York Times,* January 9, 1975.

327 I REALIZED THAT PEOPLE WANT. *Christian Science Monitor,* September 24, 1975.

327 AGREED TO GO FOR BROKE. Ibid.

328 MAY WELL BE THE MOST. *New York Times,* September 25, 1975.

328 THE FILM-MAKERS HAVE WALTERS. *Los Angeles Times,* September 25, 1975.

328 PRETENTIOUS . . . MIGHT EASILY. *New York Daily News,* September 24, 1975.

329 WARM, SANE, STABLE. Matusow, op. cit., p. 173.

329 TOLD HIM TO SIT UP. Blair, op. cit., p. 362.

329 WE WERE GOING THROUGH. Hartz interviews.

329 COMPULSIVE . . . THE THOUGHT OF FOOD. Blair, op. cit., p. 371.

330 THE UGLIEST BROAD IN TELEVISION. *His Way: The Unauthorized Biography of Frank Sinatra,* Kitty Kelley (New York: Bantam Books, 1986), p. 461.

330 I ALWAYS THOUGHT. Barbara and Dan Lewis, op. cit., p. 74.

330 A REAL BOW-WOW. Kelley, op. cit., p. 536.

CHAPTER THIRTY

335 YOU KNOW, FRED. Interview, Frederick J. Pierce, September 14, 1988.

336 FOR EXAMPLE, COANCHORING. Ibid.

336 FRED PIERCE WAS A MAN. Interview, source.

337 STAR PERSONALITY WITH. Pierce interview.

337 PEOPLE ARE INTERESTED IN. Matusow, op. cit., pp. 166–167.

337 WHAT WOULD YOU THINK. Pierce interview.

337–338 BUYING A READY-MADE NAME. Interview, Bill Sheehan, July 28, 1988.

338 HARRY IS THE MOST IMPORTANT. Ibid.

339 HIS REACTION WAS NOT GOOD. Ibid.

340 BARBARA HAD A REPUTATION. Interview, source.

340 PART OF THE BAIT. Sheehan interview.

340 WAS MORE OF AN INCENTIVE. Ibid.

341 I WAS WITH HER ON NIXON'S. *Newsweek,* October 11, 1976.

341 SHE WAS CANDID ABOUT THAT. Sheehan interview.

342 IN THE END. Interview, Nick Archer, September 2, 1988.

342 THEY EACH HAD THEIR OWN. Sheehan interview.

343 I TOLD BILL. Interview, Marlene Sanders, July 27, 1988.

344 PRELIMINARY MEETING. *New York Times*, April 6, 1976.

344 SHE'S GOOD AT THAT. Hartz, op. cit.

344 GREAT RESPECT . . . IT'S JUST TOO EARLY. *Christian Science Monitor*, April 8, 1976.

344 WOULD NOT BE HAPPY . . . I GUESS IN SOME FORMATS. Ibid.

344 SHE HAD BANTERED ABOUT. Hartz, op. cit.

345 SHE CALLS ME PRACTICALLY EVERY OTHER DAY. *Miami Herald*, April 24, 1976.

346 WHEN ABC MADE ME THE OFFER. *Ladies Home Journal*, September 1976.

346 SOME OF YOU MAY HAVE SEEN SPECULATION. *New York Times*, April 23, 1976.

346 NBC VALUED BARBARA'S. Ibid.

347–348 SHE'D BEEN PROMISED AN ANCHOR. Interview, David Adams, February 12, 1989.

348 EVERYONE FROM JULIAN. Hartz, op. cit.

348 IT WAS RATHER AWKWARD. Adams interview.

348 RESIST . . . VERY DIFFICULT . . . VERY EMOTIONAL. *New York Post*, April 23, 1976.

349 SHE TOLD ME SHE HAD. Braden, op. cit.

349 I FELT A BIT. Dickerson, op. cit.

349 AND SHE COULDN'T HAVE BEEN NICER. *US*, May 30, 1978.

350 IT'S A GOOD THING I'M NOT TEAMED. *New York Post*, op. cit.

350 SHHH—SLEEP LATE. *Los Angeles Times*, June 4, 1976.

350 I GET VERY DEFENSIVE. Val Adams, *New York Daily News*, June 4, 1976.

350 GOODWILL . . . NITPICKING AND HYPOCRISY. Ibid.

350 SOMETIMES PEOPLE SAY TO ME. Ibid.

350 I'VE BEEN ASKED MANY TIMES. Ibid.

351 THE WORST SUMMER I CAN REMEMBER. *New York Post*, op. cit.

351 IT WAS HARDLY A GLORIOUS VACATION. Ibid.

CHAPTER THIRTY-ONE

353 WHAT MAKES BARBARA WALTERS WORTH. *New York Times*, May 2, 1976.

353 WHEN I FIRST HEARD THE OFFER. *Miami Herald*, May 13, 1976.

354 THE SICKENING SENSATION. *Newsweek,* October 11, 1976.

354 IT'S SORT OF A THROWBACK. *Newsweek,* May 3, 1976.

354 I'M REALLY DEPRESSED AS HELL. Ibid.

355 IF BARBARA WALTERS IS WORTH ONE MILLION. *Los Angeles Times,* November 18, 1976.

355 PROVES HOW ABSURD THE VALUES ARE. *New York Times,* op. cit.

355 I HAVE ALREADY BEGUN TO PRACTICE. *New York Times,* April 27, 1976.

355 HER AGGRESSIVELY EAGER PERSONA. *Newsweek,* May 3, 1976.

355 THE LINE BETWEEN THE NEWS BUSINESS. *The Progressive,* August 1976.

356 BAD FOR NEWS . . . NOT BECAUSE. *New York Post,* May 3, 1976.

356 MOTHER, DON'T TELL ME. *TV Guide,* February 12, 1977.

356 I KNOW THERE ARE MANY PEOPLE. May 2, 1976.

356 HOW MUCH WOULD IT COST. Interview, source.

357 ALOOF, VERY COLD. *Miami Herald,* June 25, 1976.

357 FRANK, WHY DID YOU DO. *New York Post,* June 25, 1976.

357 BARBARA TREATED FRANK. Schulberg, op. cit.

358 EVERY TIME HARRY WENT. Interview, source.

CHAPTER THIRTY-TWO

359 YOU'RE IN A NO-WIN SITUATION. *Newsweek,* October 11, 1976.

360 ABOUT TWO SECONDS. *Time,* October 18, 1976.

360 I MUST TELL YOU QUITE FRANKLY. Ibid.

361 IF THE SADAT REMARK. *Broadcasting,* October 11, 1976.

361 I'M BEING TESTED AGAIN. *People,* October 11, 1976.

361 I MISSED YOU . . . CURIOSITY BROUGHT ON. *New York Daily News,* October 5, 1976.

361 KEPT TIME. Ibid.

362 DECIBELS CLIMBED TO THOSE. *New York Post,* October 5, 1976.

362 THE FORMAT ABC. *Time,* op. cit.

362 NOT ENTIRELY TENUOUS. *New York Times,* October 6, 1976.

363 IT WAS TERRIBLE FOR BARBARA. Interview, source.

364 CONVERSATIONS HAD OVERTONES. *Newswatch: How TV Decides the News,* Av Westin (New York: Simon and Schuster, 1982), p. 134.

364 HE MADE A REMARK THAT HAD SOME. Colby, op. cit.

364 YOU KNOW, HARRY, KISSINGER. Matusow, op. cit., p. 184.

364 KEEP AN OPEN MIND. Ibid.
364 BARBARA VERY MUCH WANTED. Interview, Martin Ruben-
     stein, November 8, 1988.
365 WHEN [HARRY] WOULD COME DOWN. *Ladies Home Journal*,
     October 1977.
365 HARRY REASONER . . . SEEMS. *New Republic*, October 23,
     1976.
365 THEY WEREN'T TALKING TO EACH OTHER. Interview, Wal-
     ter Pfister, August 2, 1988.
365 BARBARA WAS AT A GREAT DISADVANTAGE. Ibid.
366 BARBARA WAS NERVOUS AND UPTIGHT. Ibid.
366 NEITHER ONE OF THEM. Pfister interview.

CHAPTER THIRTY-THREE

370 INSTEAD OF IT BEING PROFESSIONAL. Ibid.
370 IF YOU'RE WRITING. Interview, Liz Smith, September 28, 1988.
370 PEOPLE LIKE TO TAKE SHOTS. Ibid.
371 AILEEN AND LIZ ARE. Springer, op. cit.
371 IS NOT MY KIND. Interview, source.
371 PUFF PIECES—THE MOST INCREDIBLE. Ibid.
371 WRITES ABOUT BARBARA. Interview, Susan Mulcahy, Octo-
     ber 12, 1988.
371 LIZ IS LIKE. Levinson, op. cit.
371 I DO MENTION HER. Smith interview.

CHAPTER THIRTY-FOUR

373 THE PROBLEM IS SHE IS MISCAST. *TV Guide*, February, 19,
     1977.
374 DUMPING ON BABA. *Village Voice*, January 10, 1977.
374 MEN BLUSTER. *Palm Beach Post-Times*, January 22, 1977.
374 IN HER LISPING. *Viva*, May 1977.
374 WE GET ALONG VERY WELL. *New York Post*, January 4, 1977
375 I MADE A DEAL. Sheehan, op. cit.
375 TO SALVAGE THE WRECKAGE. *Before the Colors Fade*, Harry
     Reasoner (New York: Alfred A. Knopf, 1981), p. 188.
375 THE DEBACLE OF THE TWO OF US. Ibid., p. 187.
376 THE ARLEDGE SHELL GAME . . . HE MORE OR LESS. Ibid,
     p. 188.
376 BARBARA'S OWN INITIATIVE. Sheehan, op. cit.
377 BAD IDEA—NOT BECAUSE. Reasoner, op. cit., p. 186.

CHAPTER THIRTY-FIVE

379 EVERYONE UNDERPLAYED THE VALUE. Pierce, op. cit.
380 THE FOUR SPECIALS WERE FULLY SOLD. Rubenstein, op. cit.
380 SHE WAS TERRIBLY EXCITED. Ibid.
380 IT WAS NOT A PLEASANT. Interview, John Desmond, November 14, 1988.
381 SUE MENGERS GOT. Ibid.
381 WE DESCENDED LIKE GENGHIS KHAN. Interview, JoAnn Goldberg, December 10, 1988.
382 I WENT INTO MAKEUP. Desmond interview.
382 THERE WAS ACTUALLY ONE POINT. Goldberg interview.
382 WHAT WE WERE DOING. Desmond interview.
382 IT WAS BARBRA STREISAND. Interview, source.
383 THEY HAD WORDS. Desmond interview.
383 OUT DRINKING. *New York Times Magazine*, February 13, 1977.
383 THE BANALITY WAS EQUALLY. *Variety*, December 22, 1976.
384 YOU COULD HAVE THROWN UP. Sanders, op. cit.
384 THERE SHE WAS, THE FIRST. *New York Post*, December 20, 1976.
385 HE IS ENTITLED. Ibid.
385 LUCY TOLD ME THAT THINGS. Interview, Richard Turley, November 16, 1988.
386 THE PRESS NEVER REALLY PAID. Goldberg interview.
387 I SAID TO BARBARA, 'YOU KNOW. Interviews, Patricia Ryan, February 8 and 13, 1989.
389 YOUNG LADY! Interviews, Cheryl McCall, January 25, 27, and 30, and February 8, 1989.
389 I'LL MAKE MY OWN JUDGMENTS! Ibid.
389 IT WAS LIKE A WHOLE. Ibid.
390 COME OFF IT! Ibid.
390 ALARMED BY WHATEVER WAS. Ryan interviews.
390 I DON'T REMEMBER THE PIECE. Interview, Ross Drake, January 26, 1988.
391 PEOPLE ON THE STAFF. McCall interviews.
391 AFTER READING CHERYL'S STORY. Interview, source.
391 THIS IS INTOLERABLE. Ryan interviews.
391 I WENT THROUGH WHY. Ibid.
391 TO STICK HIS HEAD IN. Interview, source.
392 I ONLY AGREED. Neil Tesser, *Chicago Reader*, June 18, 1982.
392 VICIOUSNESS . . . IT'S LIKE LIVING. Ibid.
393 A VETERAN OF MORE THAN. *New York Times*, November 29, 1988.

CHAPTER THIRTY-SIX

396 WILL YOU ALLOW ME. *TV Guide*, December 1, 1979.
397 MR. PRESIDENT, DON'T YOU THINK. *New York Post*, November 21, 1977.
397 DID BARBARA GET ANYTHING. Ibid.
398 I HAVE A TERRIBLE FEELING. *Los Angeles Times*, November 29, 1978.
398 YOU DAMN SEDUCER. *TV Guide*, May 12, 1979.
398 I CAN TELL YOU. Ibid.
398 IF VIETNAM. Ibid.
399 BIZARRE. *New York Post*, October 16, 1979.
399 BARBARA WALTERS, WHOSE FORMAL. *Soho Weekly News*, October 18, 1979.
399 MAY I BRING SOME FRIENDS. *New York Times*, October 14, 1979.
399 I THOUGHT OF THE OTHER NETWORK. *New York Post*, op. cit.
399 I FOUND MYSELF IN A POSITION. Ibid.
400 AS A JOURNALIST. Ibid.
400 THAT BROKE NEW GROUND. *TV Guide*, January 24, 1987.
400 TRANSMISSION OF HER INFORMATION. *New York Times*, March 17, 1987.
401 FELT TERRIBLE . . . I MADE SURE IT WAS DELIVERED. *Wall Street Journal*, March 16, 1987.
401 WHO DOES BARBARA WALTERS. *New York Daily News*, March 18, 1987.
401 IF YOU COVER THE CIRCUS. *New York Daily News*, March 23, 1987.

CHAPTER THIRTY-SEVEN

404 ABC CAPITOL HILL REPORTER. Matusow, op. cit., p. 178.
404 SHE LITERALLY PLEADED WITH HIM. *Blue Smoke and Mirrors*, Jack W. Germond and Jules Witcover (New York: Viking Press, 1981), p. 184.
405 YOU THINK THIS IS BARBARA WALTERS? *Manhattan, Inc.*, October 1988.
405 IN AMERICA, I'M NUMBER ONE! Matusow, op. cit.
406 20/20 REACHES A MASS. *Cosmopolitan*, June 1982.
406 ALL THE OTHER OFFICES. Interview, source.
407 THIS AIN'T MY CUP OF TEA. Ibid.
407 THIS WAS NOT ACCEPTABLE TO ME. Downs, op. cit., p. 203.

CHAPTER THIRTY-EIGHT

        cit.
420   HOW DO I KNOW WHY PEOPLE. *Ladies Home Journal*, op. cit.
420   I KNOW PEOPLE OFTEN FEEL CHILDREN. *Harper's Bazaar*, op.
        cit.
420   WE WERE IN THE BATHTUB. *Parents*, op. cit.
421   TO JACKIE GUBER. Letter, Jimmy Carter Library.
422   MY CHILD AND I ARE HEALTHY. *Ladies Home Journal*, Octo-
        ber 1977.
422   JACKIE WAS NOT THAT BRIGHT. Interview, source.
423   DON'T COME IN THIS ROOM. *Cincinnati Enquirer*, March 3,
        1980.
423   ABOUT THE DIFFERENCE BETWEEN LOVING SOMEONE.
        Parents, op. cit.
423   QUITE FILTHY . . . I KNEW IF I DIDN'T ALLOW HER. *Ladies
        Home Journal*, June 1981.
423   SHE SAID ALL OF HER FRIENDS. *Parents*, op. cit.
423   I DON'T EVEN RECOGNIZE. *Ladies Home Journal*, op. cit.
424   I'M NOT PARTICULARLY WORRIED. Ibid.
424   I TALK ABOUT AIDS. *Ladies Home Journal*, March 1988.
424   YOU'RE A REGULAR MOMMIE DEAREST. *Ladies Home Jour-
        nal*, May 1982.
424   THE ONLY THING MY MOMMY CAN DO. Ibid.
424–425   LIKE REFORM SCHOOLS. Interview, source.
425   BUT IN NEW YORK. *Ladies Home Journal*, June 1984.
425   MOST OF THE KIDS ARE HERE. Interview, source.
426   NO DRUGS, NO SEX, AND NO VIOLENCE. Ibid.
426   JACKIE HAD WHAT I CALL FLAIR. Interview, source.
426   SORT OF A SURROGATE MOTHER. Interview, Joella Werlin,
        September 28, 1988.
426   JACKIE HAD STRUCK ME. Ibid.
427   IF JACKIE FAILED TO SHOW UP. Ibid.
427   WE BOTH AGREED. Ibid.
427   SHE'S NOT A TERRIBLY MOTIVATED. Ibid.
427   [SHE] TALKS OF BEING A MODEL. *Ladies Home Journal*, May
        1982.
427   TERRIBLE STRUGGLE. *Ladies Home Journal*, June 1981.
427   SHE DOESN'T WANT TO HAVE ANYTHING TO DO. *Ladies
        Home Journal*, March 1988.
428   JACKIE'S VERY CLOSE TO BARBARA. Werlin interview.

CHAPTER THIRTY-NINE

429   I'M ATTRACTED TO THEM. *Ladies Home Journal*, June 1984.

430 CONTRARY TO WHAT THE OUTSIDE IMAGE. Interviews, Alexis Lichine, November 28, 1988, January 16, 1989.
430 VERY OFTEN SHE WOULD IMPLICATE. Ibid.
430 WAS A FATHER TO PAT HER. Ibid.
431 OUR RELATIONSHIP, I'M SAD TO SAY. Ibid.
431 I DON'T KNOW WHAT I WOULD HAVE DONE. McCall's, January 1985.
431 NOTHING IS MORE BEGUILING. Walters, op. cit., p. 144.
432 THERE WAS NOTHING ROMANTIC GOING ON. Interview, source.
432 RIDICULOUS. Los Angeles Times, September 21, 1975.
432 INCREDIBLE. Ibid.
433 LINKED . . . GOOD FRIEND. Boston Globe, July 20, 1976.
433 SEEM TO BE MORE IN LOVE. New York Daily News, December 25, 1979.
433 IF A MAN DOESN'T PLAY GOLF. Wall Street Journal, January 18, 1982.
433 BARBARA DALLIED WITH THE IDEA. Smith, op. cit.
434 HE WANTED TO MARRY HER. Ibid.
434 THE THING WITH JOHN. Interview, source.
434 SADIE, SADIE. Interview, source.
435 COMPLETE CONFIDENCE. Las Vegas Revue-Journal, July 2, 1957.
437 WE FEEL IT RIGHT. Los Angeles Times, November 17, 1981.
437 RUINOUS . . . PEOPLE WERE TURNING THEIR HEADS. Wall Street Journal, September 15, 1986.
437 SHATTERED . . . RECLUSIVE . . . A PLACE NOT IN THE CENTER. New York Times, December 11, 1981.
438 MUTUAL FRIEND . . . HE WAS SOMEONE SPECIAL. Ladies Home Journal, March 1988.
438 IT WAS A GREAT EQUALIZER. Ibid.
439 I NEVER HEARD OF A COUPLE MAKING. New York Daily News, June 24, 1985.
440 IT'S TRUE THAT SHE WENT. Budd, op. cit.
440 BARBARA WAS VERY UNCERTAIN. Interview, source.
440 BARBARA AND MERV ARE TWO MATURE PEOPLE. Interview, October 19, 1988.
440 EACH SIDE SAW THAT THE LITIGATION. Interview, Norman Roy Grutman, October 13, 1988.
441 WHEN MS. WALTERS AND MR. ADELSON. Ibid.
442 CONTINUED LITIGATION WILL ONLY. Los Angeles Times, December 21, 1985.
442 PENTHOUSE IN THE ARTICLE. Ibid.
442 OF THE MANY PERSONAL AND PROFESSIONAL. Ibid.
443 PRECIPITATED THE WEDDING. Goldberg interview.

444 BICOASTAL MARITAL BLISS. Ibid.
444 THE ONLY REASON BARBARA. Budd, op. cit.
444 HOW MUCH THE APARTMENT COST. *Washington Post*, June
     1, 1988.
445 THE VIBES SEEMED RIGHT. *Architectural Digest*, October 1988.
445 AND HUGGED AND KISSED ME. *New York Daily News*, April
     23, 1987.
446 I DIDN'T THINK IT WAS GOING TO BE. *New York Times*, July
     21, 1988.
447 MY PRACTICE IS NOT TO ASSOCIATE. *Wall Street Journal*,
     op. cit.
448 MERV ADELSON CALLED ME. Grutman interview.
449 'STANDS BY HER MAN.' *Newsday*, September 29, 1988.
449–450 I WOULD LIKE TO THANK THE *WALL STREET*. *New
     York Post*, September 29, 1986.
450 HAPPENED TO BE OUT ON THE TOWN. *New York Daily News*,
     September 30, 1986.
450 BARBARA PLAYS HARDBALL. Interview, source.
451 YOU KNOW, SHIRLEY. Budd, op. cit.

INDEX

THE AUTOBIOGRAPHY OF
ROY COHN

by Sidney Zion

"FASCINATING!"—*New York Post*

There were no neutrals in Roy Cohn's life.

His friends saw him as a patriot, a loyal pal, a fearless attorney and a party-thrower nonpareil.

His enemies knew him as a native fascist, Joe McCarthy's brains, and the legal executioner of Ethel and Julius Rosenberg.

Renowned journalist, lawyer and author, Sid Zion was a trusted friend of Cohn's for over 20 years. During the last years of his life, Cohn worked closely with Zion to fashion this book. The results are explosive.

With 8 pages of candid photos.

THE AUTOBIOGRAPHY OF ROY COHN
by Sidney Zion
_____ 91402-4 $4.95 U.S.   _____ 91403-2 $5.95 Can.

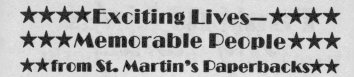

My Family

THE JACKSONS

Here it is, at last—the world's most dazzling legend, the heart-stopping, award-winning JACKSON FAMILY, as seen through the eyes of their mother, KATHERINE JACKSON. From the early days playing talent shows in Gary, Indiana, to sudden stardom as a teen phenomenon, to Michael's enormous success in the 80s and the family's unforgettable "Victory" Tour, to the arrival of Janet as a music power to be reckoned with, to what the future promises, this is the Jacksons story that no self-respecting culture lover can do without!

MY FAMILY, THE JACKSONS
by Katherine Jackson with Richard Wiseman
92350-3 _____ $3.95   U.S. _____ $4.95 Can.